PUBLISHERS
PAUL ENS AND SCOTT CHITWOOD

GRAPHIC DESIGN
SHAUN CASPER @ WWW.OPENHAUSSTUDIO.COM

MOON GIRL VOLUME ONE

THIS VOLUME COLLECTS MOON GIRL #1 THROUGH #5 OF THE COMICBOOK SERIES ORIGINALLY PUBLISHED BY RED 5 COMICS

PUBLISHED BY
RED 5 COMICS
298 TUSCANY VISTA RD NW, CALGARY, ALBERTA, CANADA, T3L 3B4

WWW.RED5COMICS.COM

TO FIND A COMICS SHOP IN YOUR AREA, CALL THE COMIC SHOP LOCATOR SERVICE TOLL FREE AT 1-888-266-4226

FIRST EDITION:
IBSN - 978-0-9868985-3-2

PRINTED IN CANADA

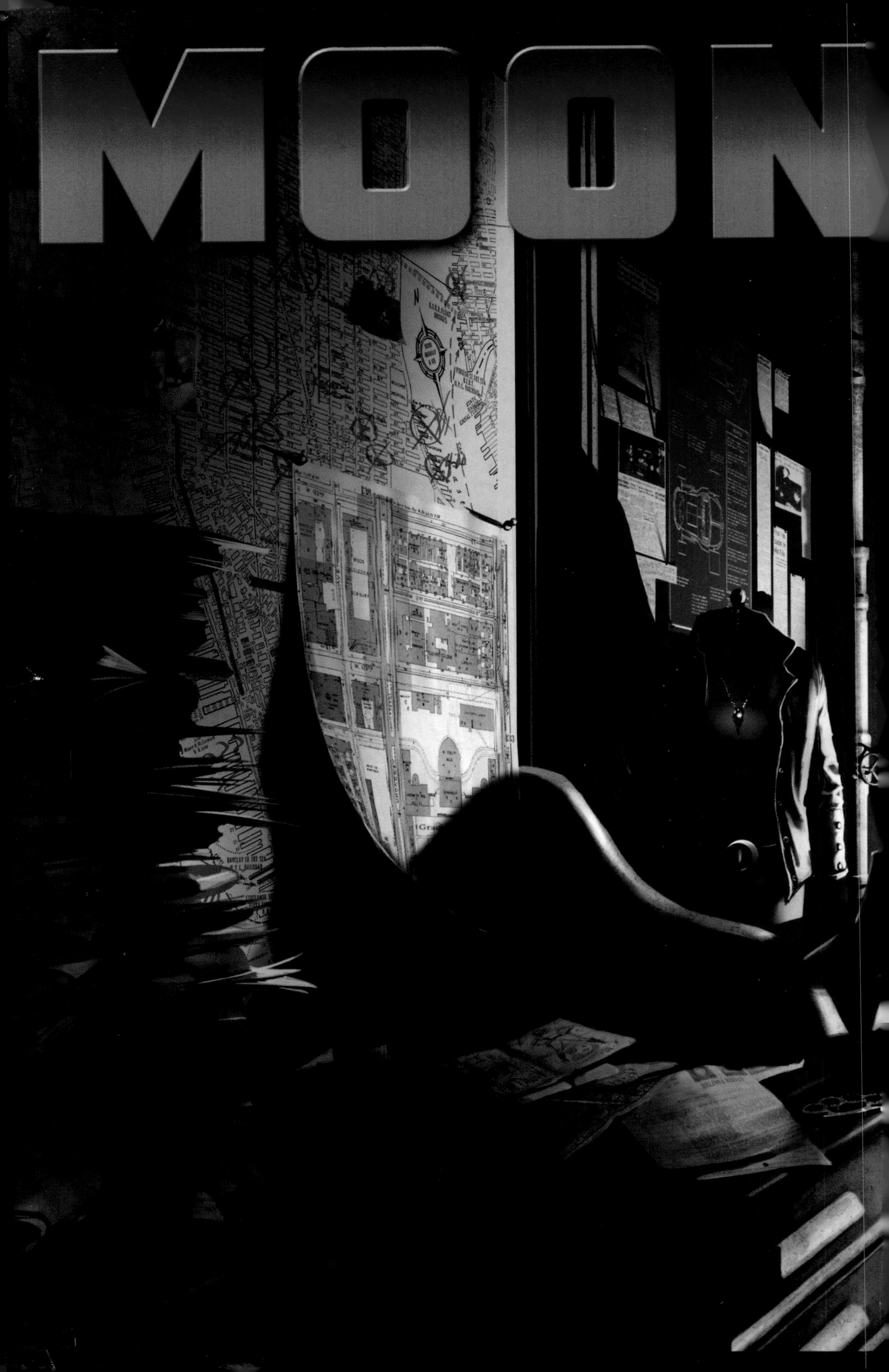
MOON

GIRL

JOHNNY ZITO & TONY TROV
STORY

RAHZZAH
ART

TROY PETERI
LETTERS

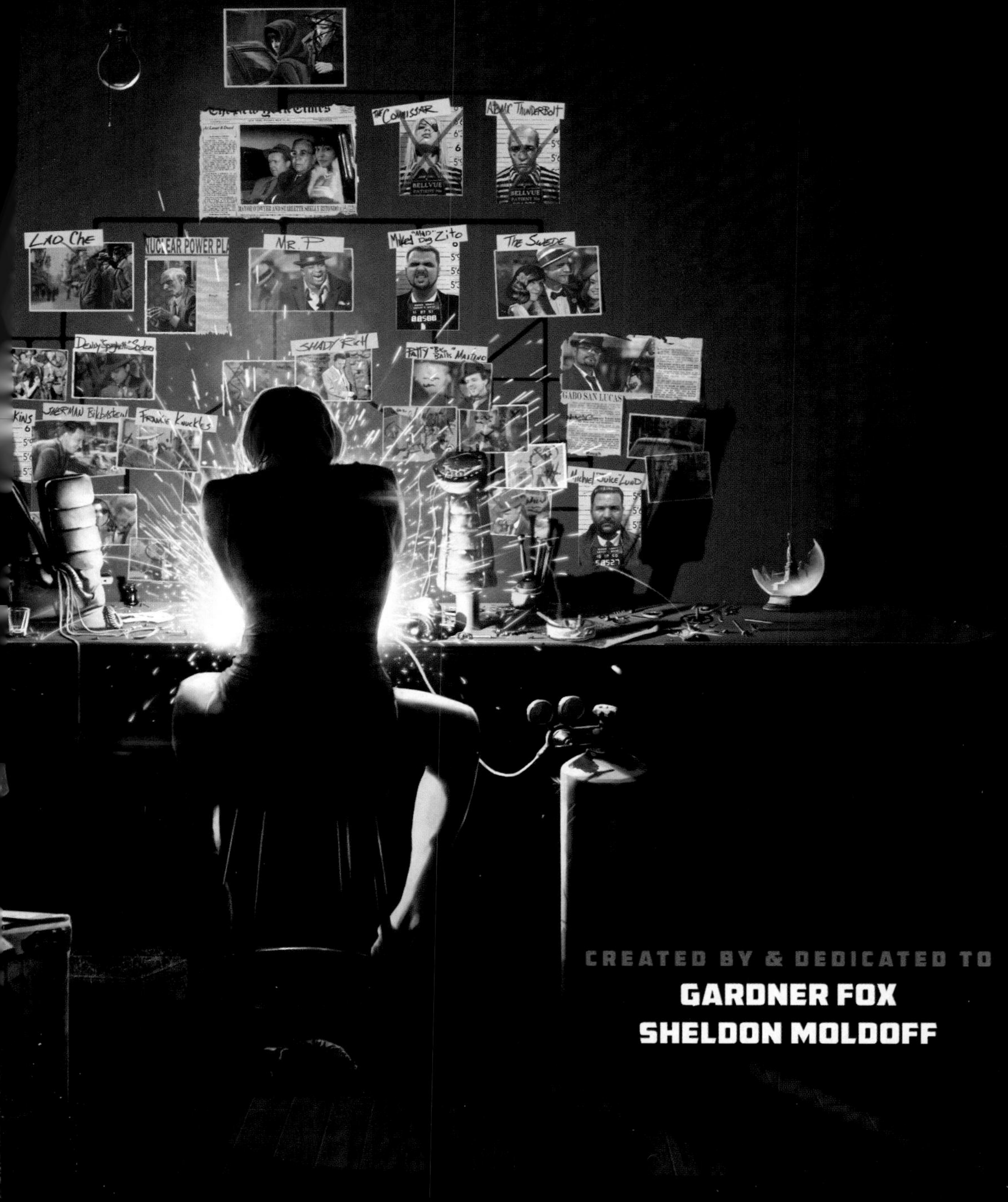

Lao Che
Mr. P
The Swede
The Commissar
Atomic Thunderbolt
Shady Rich
Frankie Knuckles
GABO SAN LUCAS

CREATED BY & DEDICATED TO
GARDNER FOX
SHELDON MOLDOFF

1

FABLES

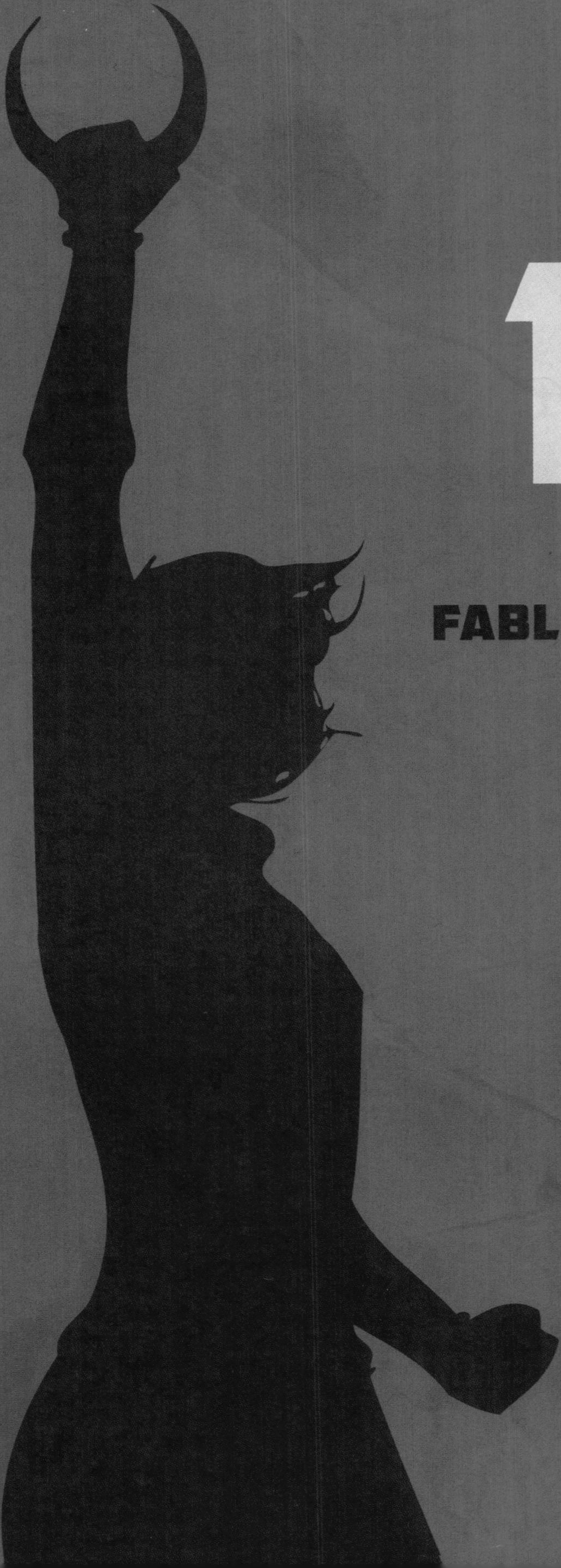

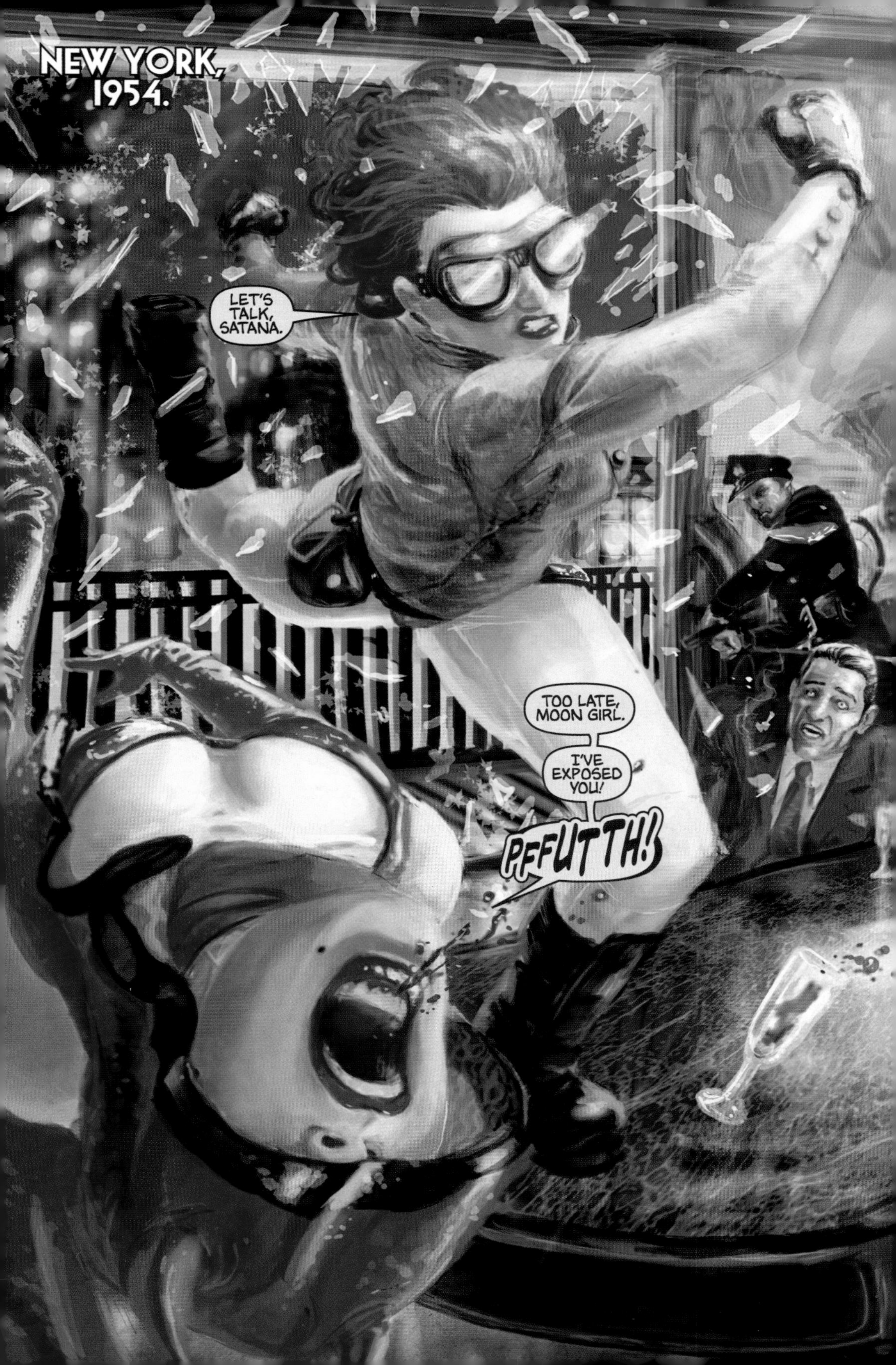
NEW YORK, 1954.
LET'S TALK, SATANA.
TOO LATE, MOON GIRL.
I'VE EXPOSED YOU!
PFFUTTH!

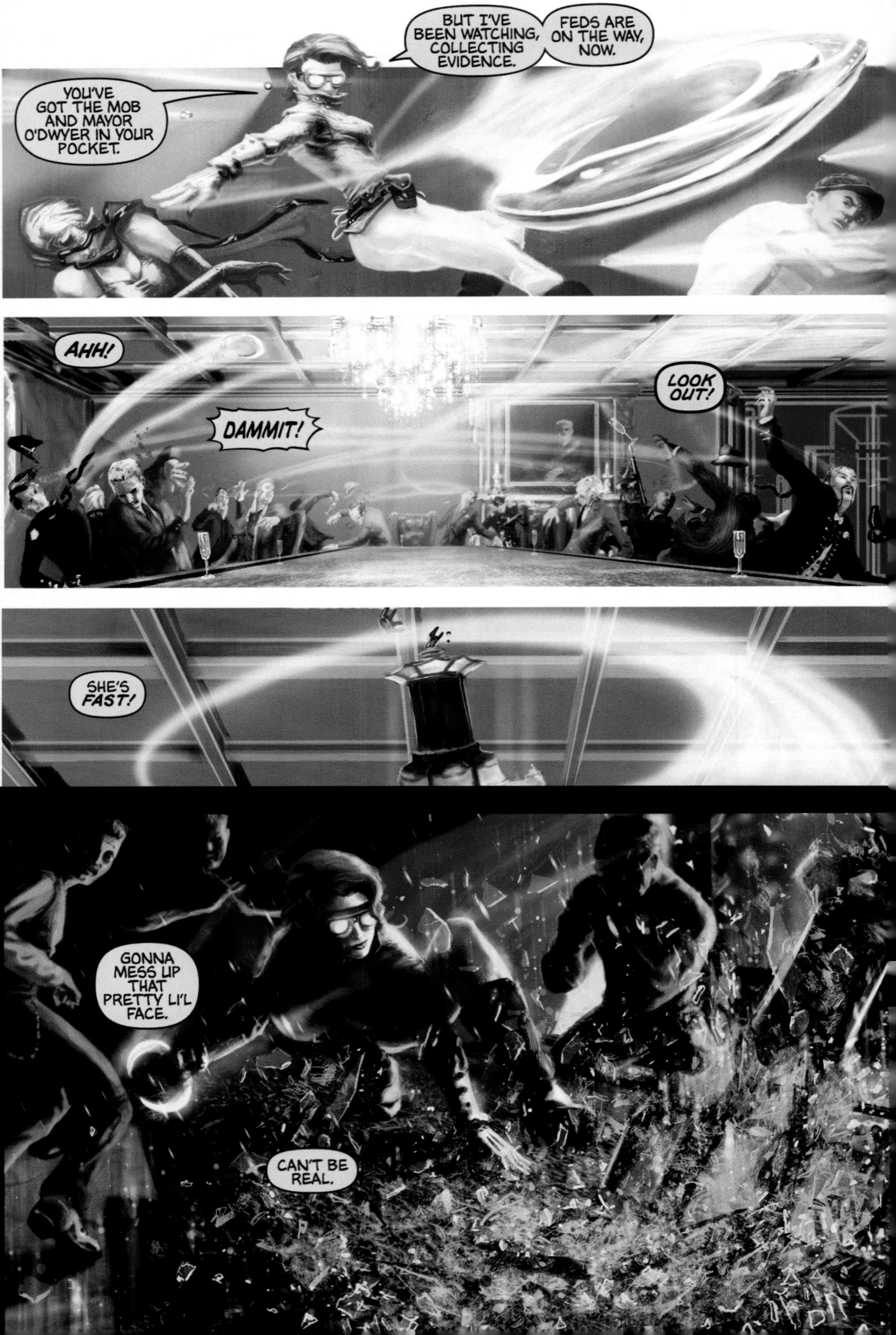
YOU'VE GOT THE MOB AND MAYOR O'DWYER IN YOUR POCKET.
BUT I'VE BEEN WATCHING, COLLECTING EVIDENCE.
FEDS ARE ON THE WAY, NOW.
AHH!
DAMMIT!
LOOK OUT!
SHE'S FAST!
GONNA MESS UP THAT PRETTY LI'L FACE.
CAN'T BE REAL.

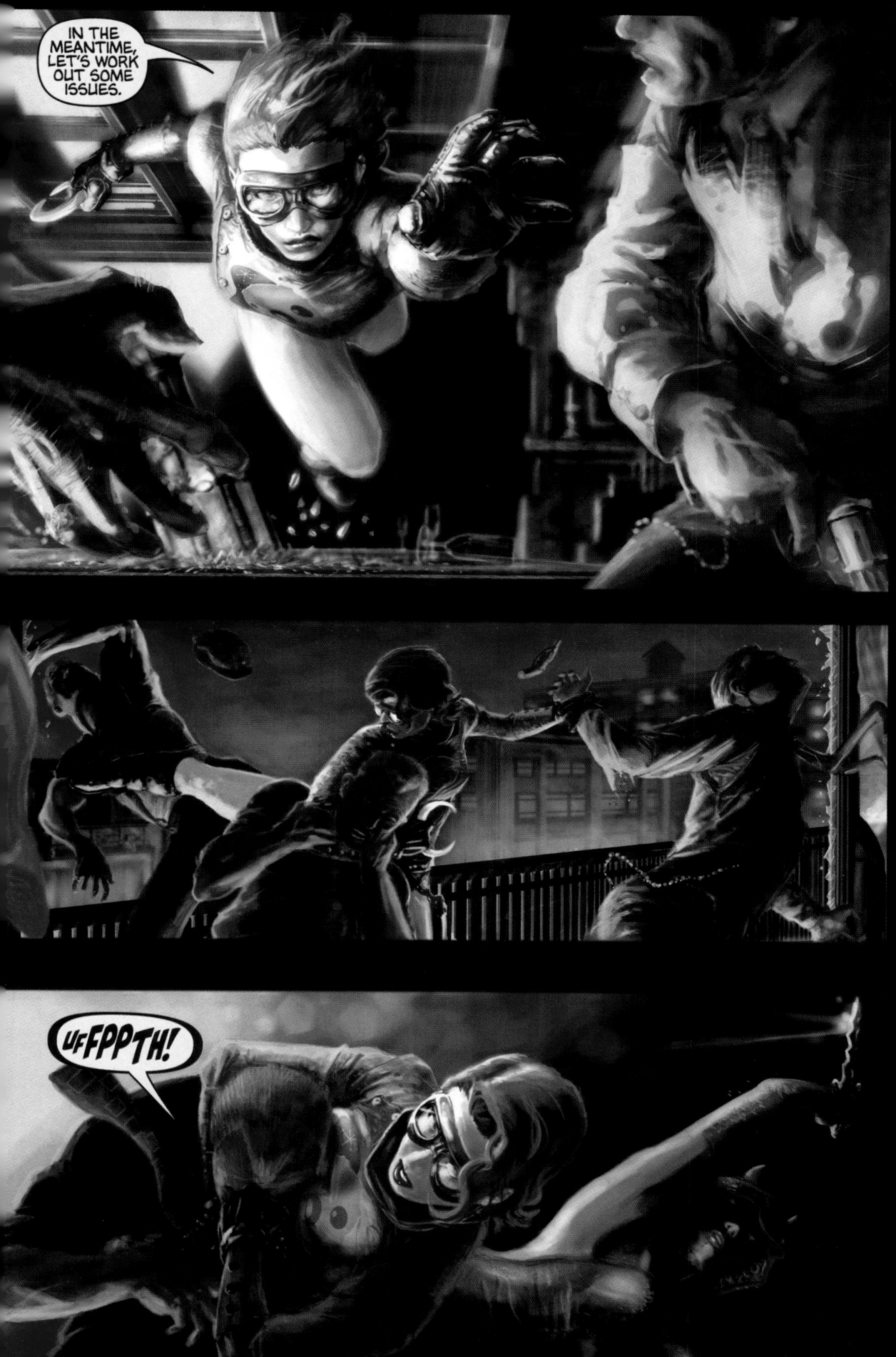
IN THE MEANTIME, LET'S WORK OUT SOME ISSUES.
UFFPPTH!

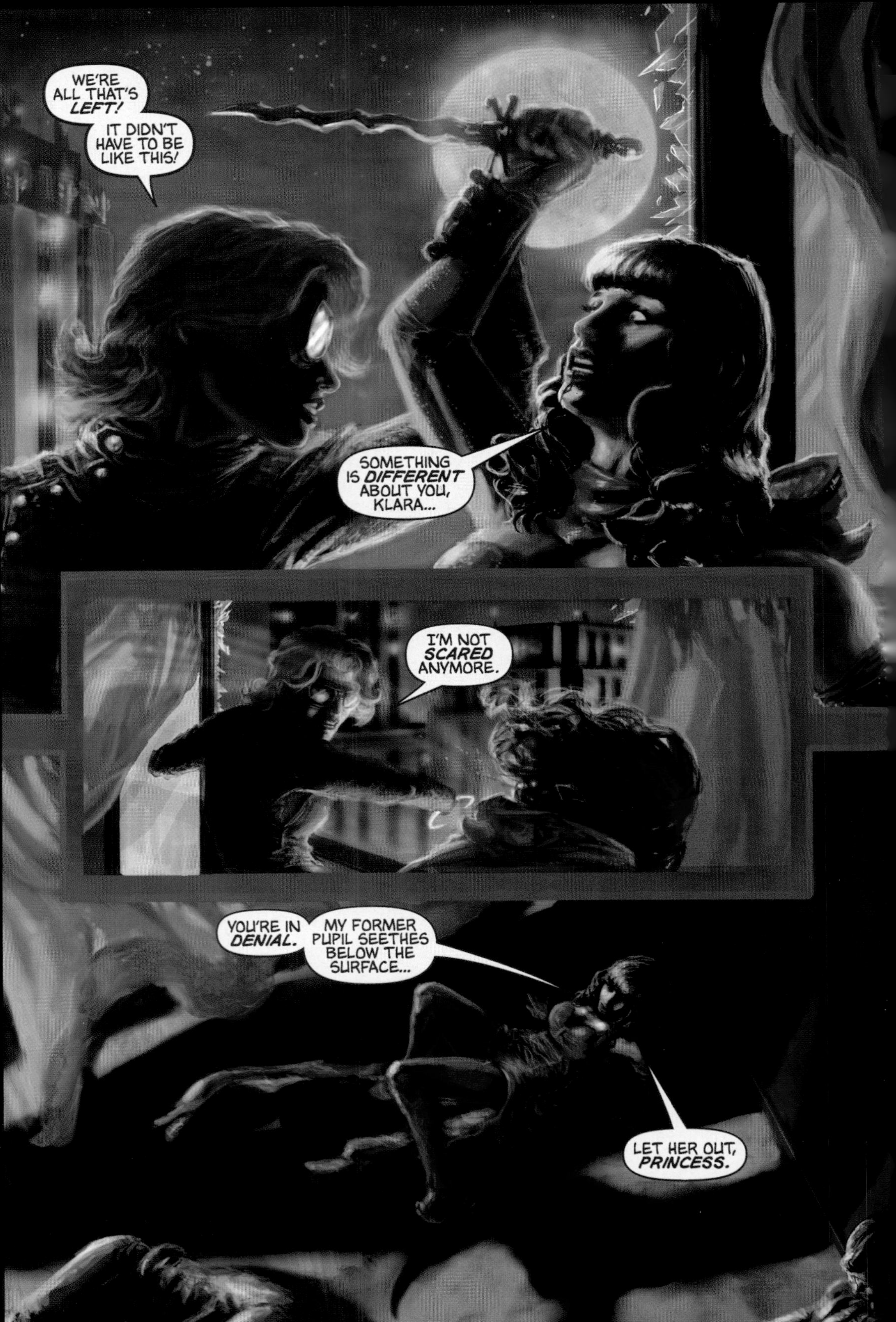
WE'RE ALL THAT'S LEFT!
IT DIDN'T HAVE TO BE LIKE THIS!
SOMETHING IS DIFFERENT ABOUT YOU, KLARA...
I'M NOT SCARED ANYMORE.
YOU'RE IN DENIAL.
MY FORMER PUPIL SEETHES BELOW THE SURFACE...
LET HER OUT, PRINCESS.

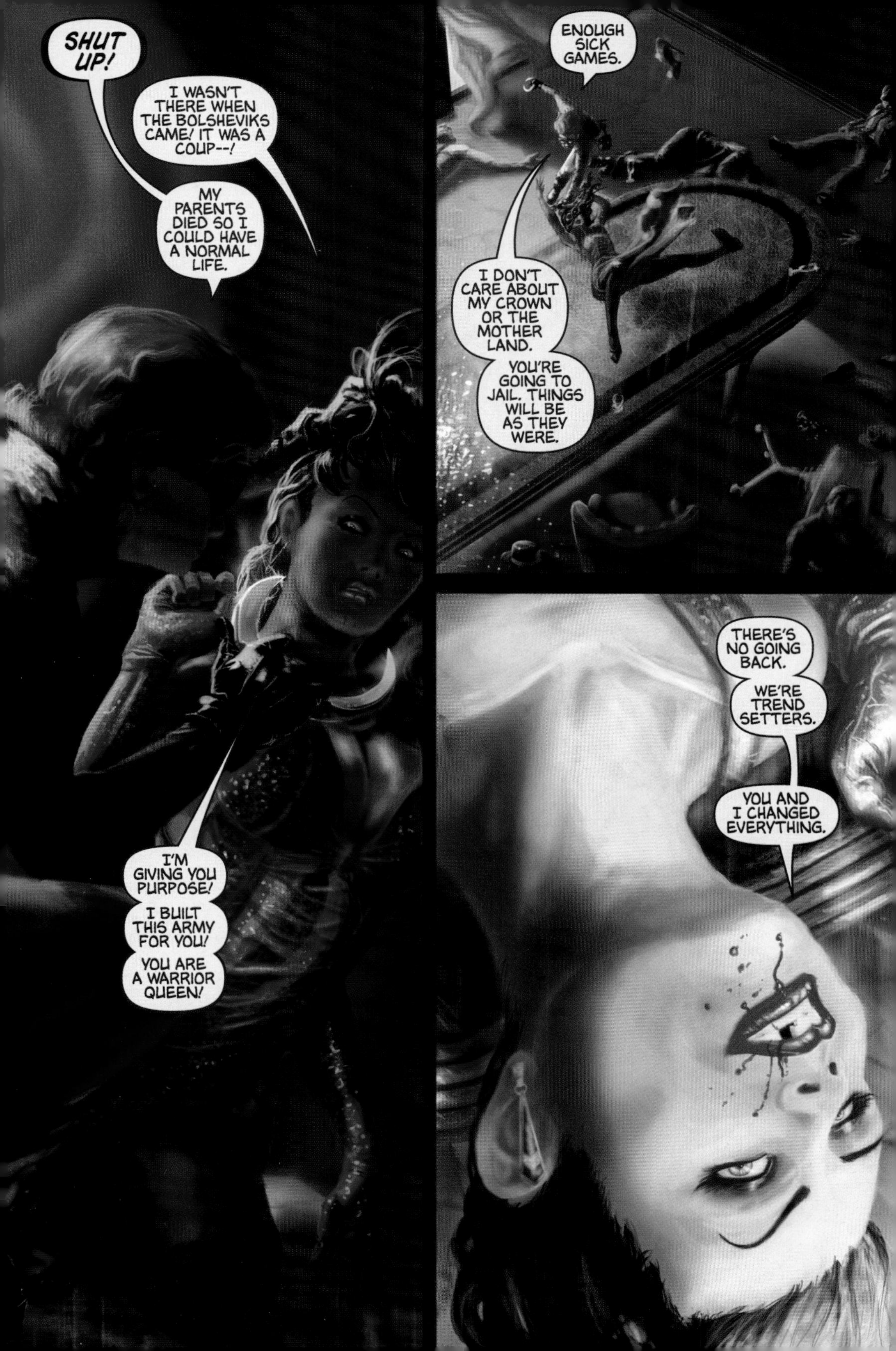
SHUT UP!
I WASN'T THERE WHEN THE BOLSHEVIKS CAME! IT WAS A COUP--!
MY PARENTS DIED SO I COULD HAVE A NORMAL LIFE.
I'M GIVING YOU PURPOSE!
I BUILT THIS ARMY FOR YOU!
YOU ARE A WARRIOR QUEEN!
ENOUGH SICK GAMES.
I DON'T CARE ABOUT MY CROWN OR THE MOTHER LAND.
YOU'RE GOING TO JAIL. THINGS WILL BE AS THEY WERE.
THERE'S NO GOING BACK.
WE'RE TREND SETTERS.
YOU AND I CHANGED EVERYTHING.

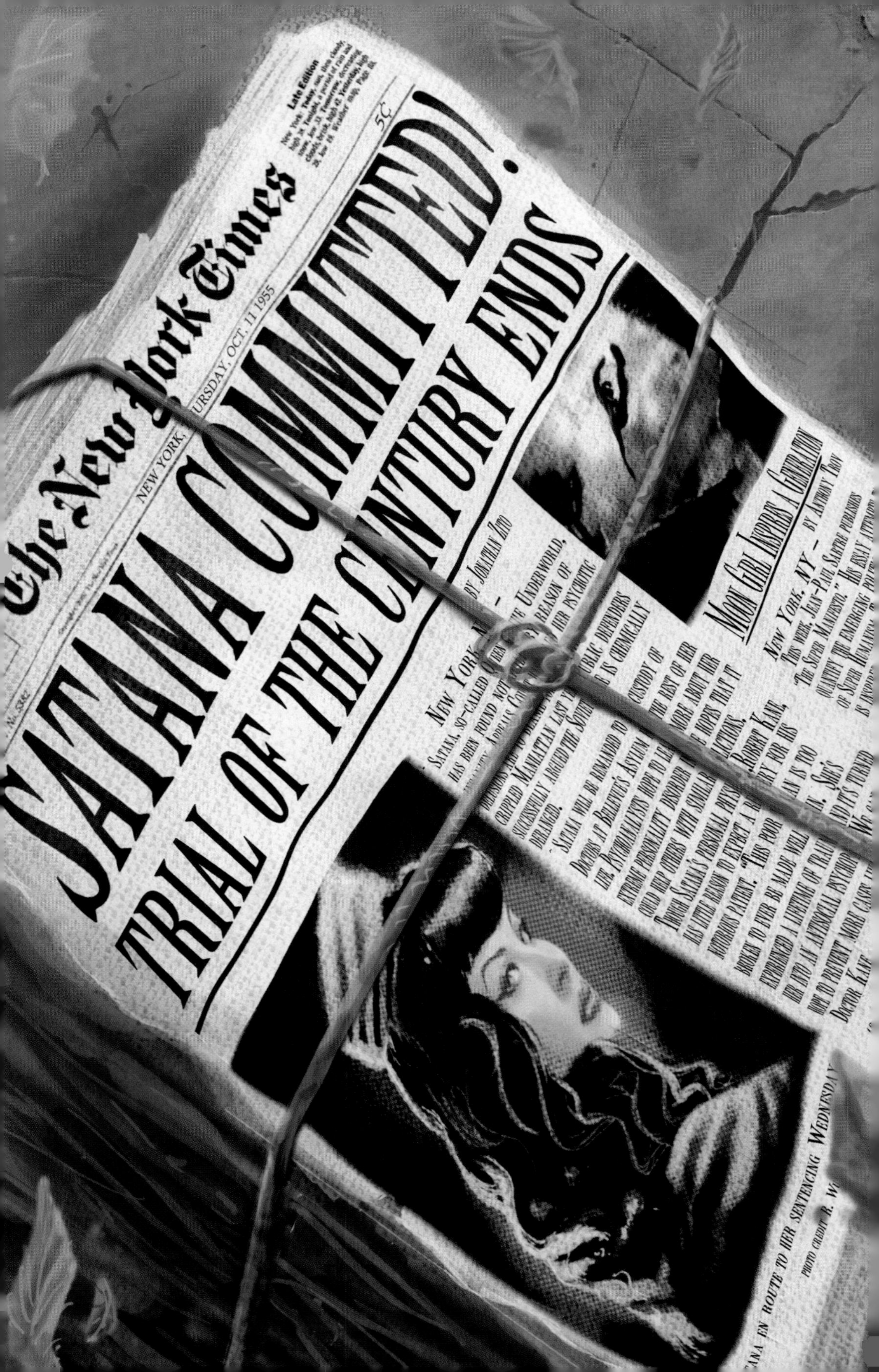
The New York Times
Late Edition
5¢
SATANA COMMITTED!
TRIAL OF THE CENTURY ENDS
MOON GIRL INSPIRES A GENERATION
BY ANTHONY TROY

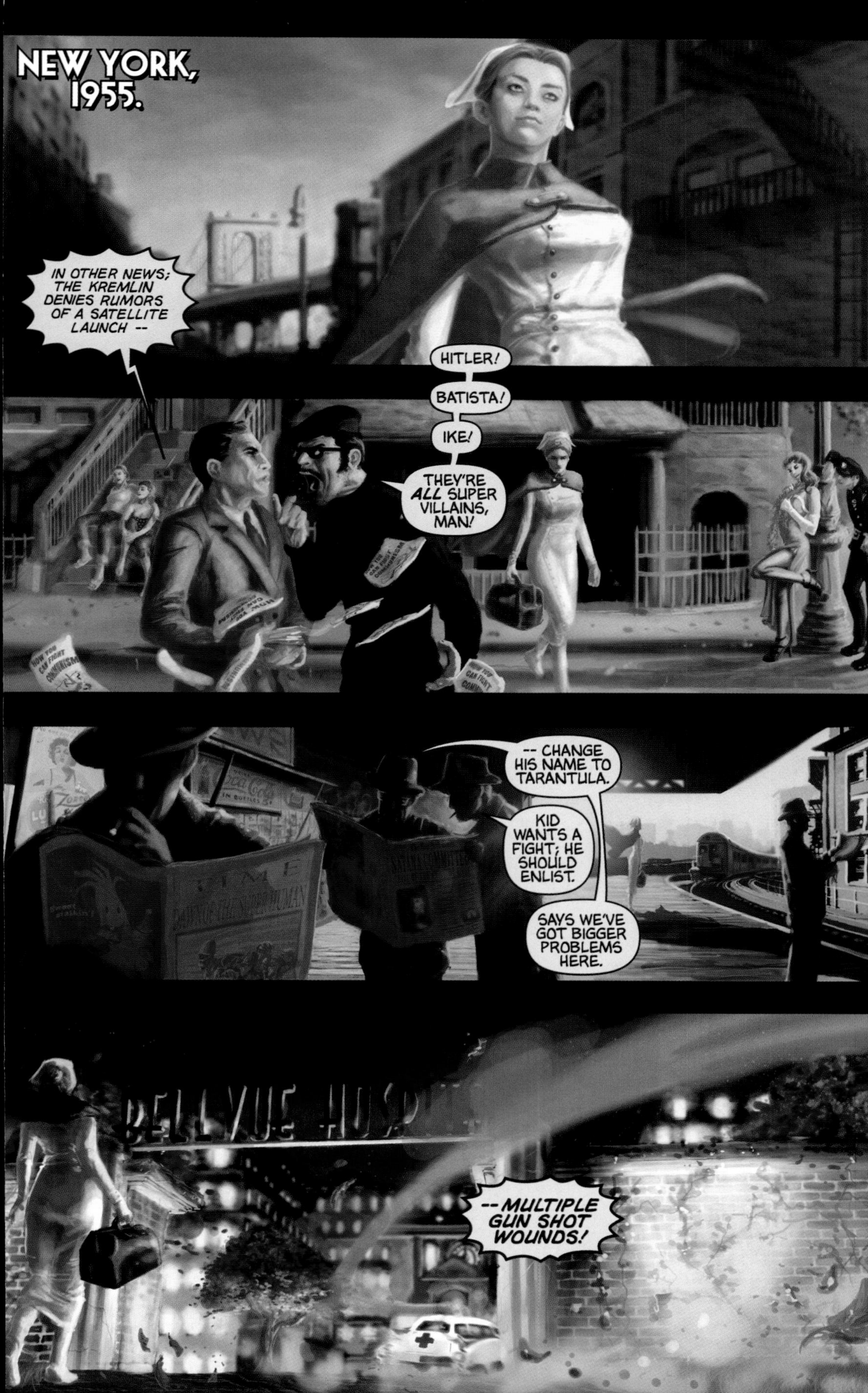
NEW YORK, 1955.
IN OTHER NEWS; THE KREMLIN DENIES RUMORS OF A SATELLITE LAUNCH --
HITLER!
BATISTA!
IKE!
THEY'RE ALL SUPER VILLAINS, MAN!
HOW YOU CAN FIGHT COMMUNISM
-- CHANGE HIS NAME TO TARANTULA.
KID WANTS A FIGHT; HE SHOULD ENLIST.
SAYS WE'VE GOT BIGGER PROBLEMS HERE.
COCA-COLA IN BOTTLES
BELLVUE HOS
--MULTIPLE GUN SHOT WOUNDS!

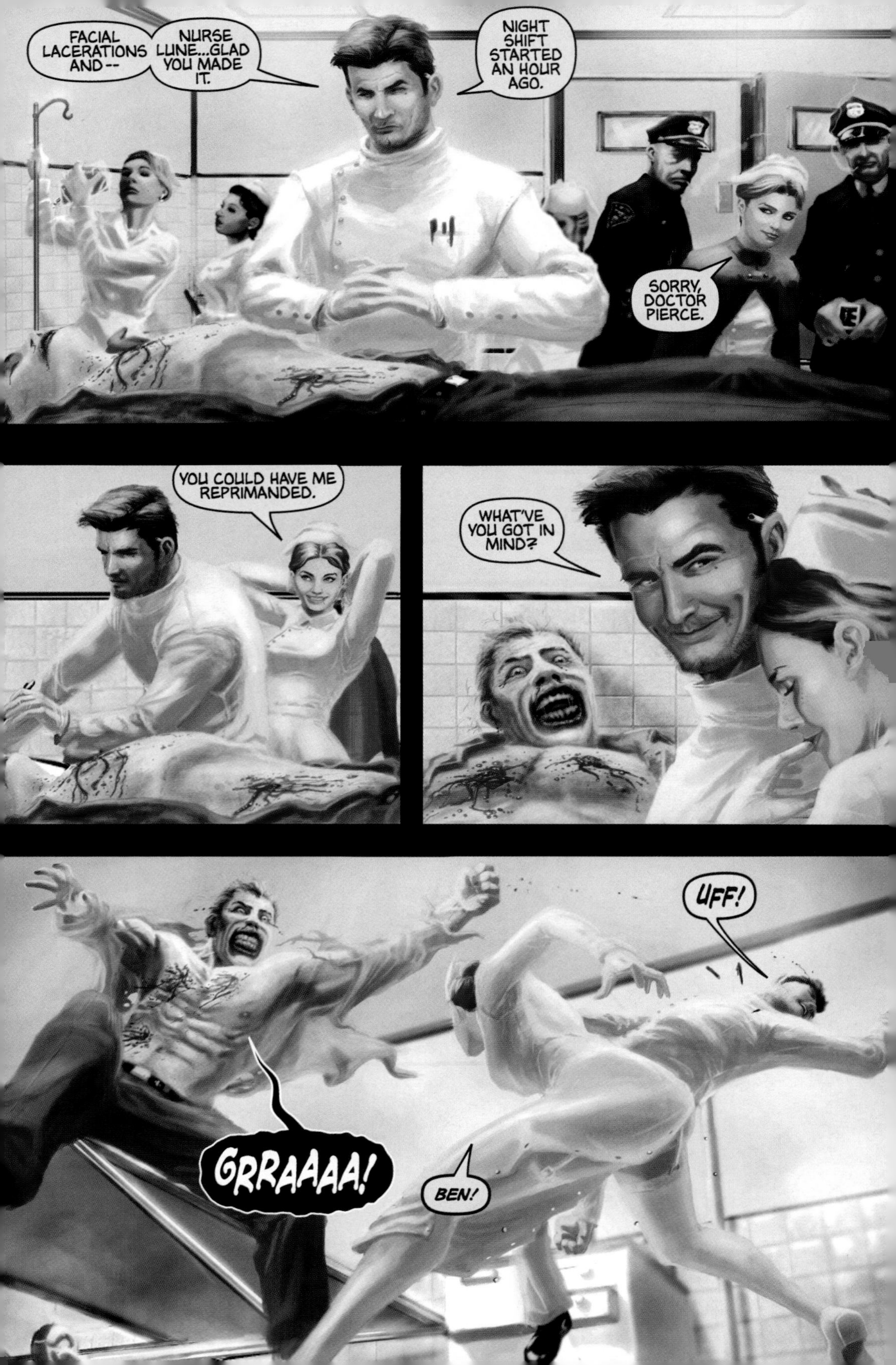
FACIAL LACERATIONS AND--
NURSE LUNE...GLAD YOU MADE IT.
NIGHT SHIFT STARTED AN HOUR AGO.
SORRY, DOCTOR PIERCE.
YOU COULD HAVE ME REPRIMANDED.
WHAT'VE YOU GOT IN MIND?
UFF!
GRRAAAA!
BEN!

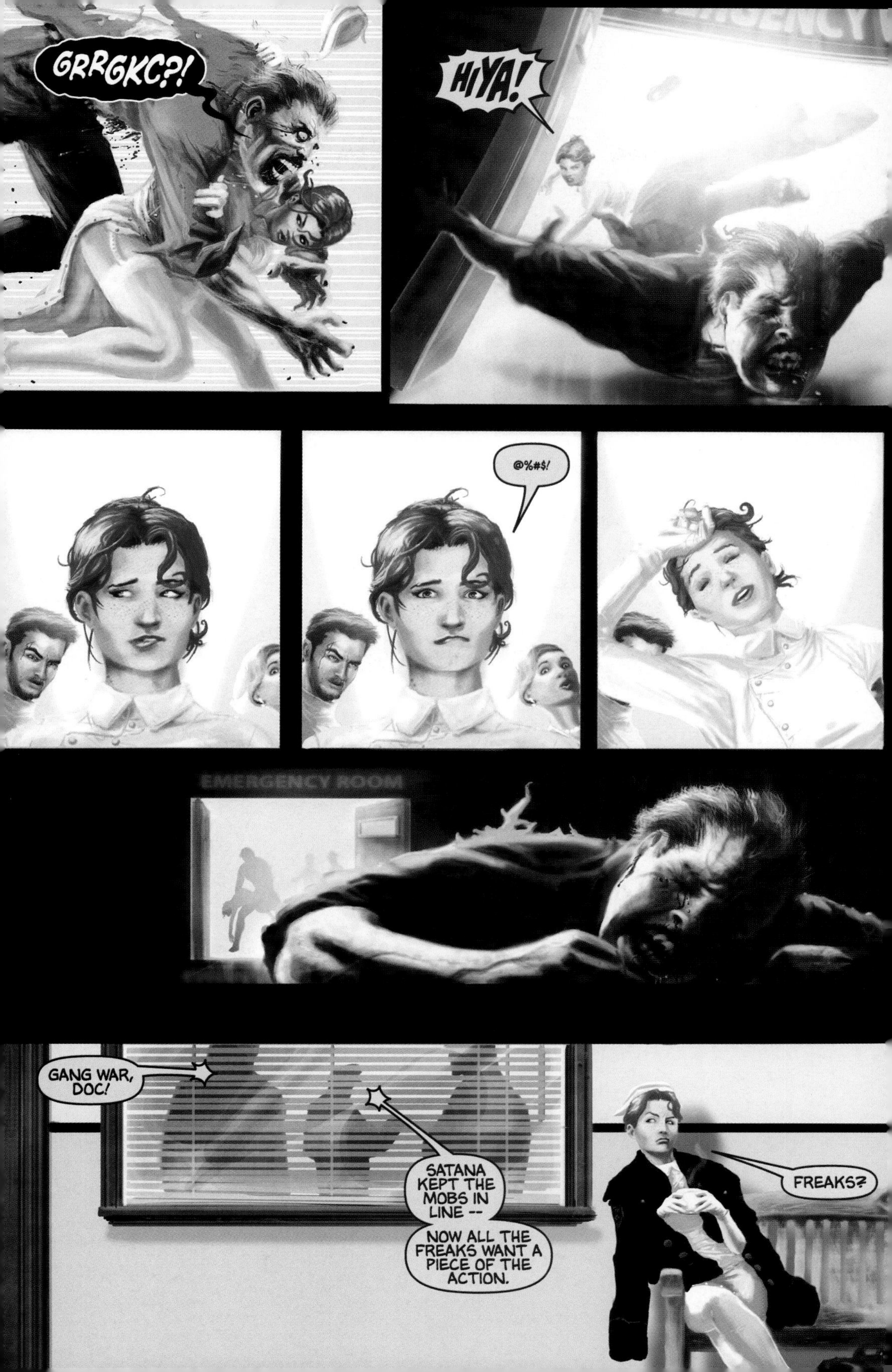
GRRGKC?!
HIYA!
@%#$!
EMERGENCY ROOM
GANG WAR, DOC!
SATANA KEPT THE MOBS IN LINE --
NOW ALL THE FREAKS WANT A PIECE OF THE ACTION.
FREAKS?

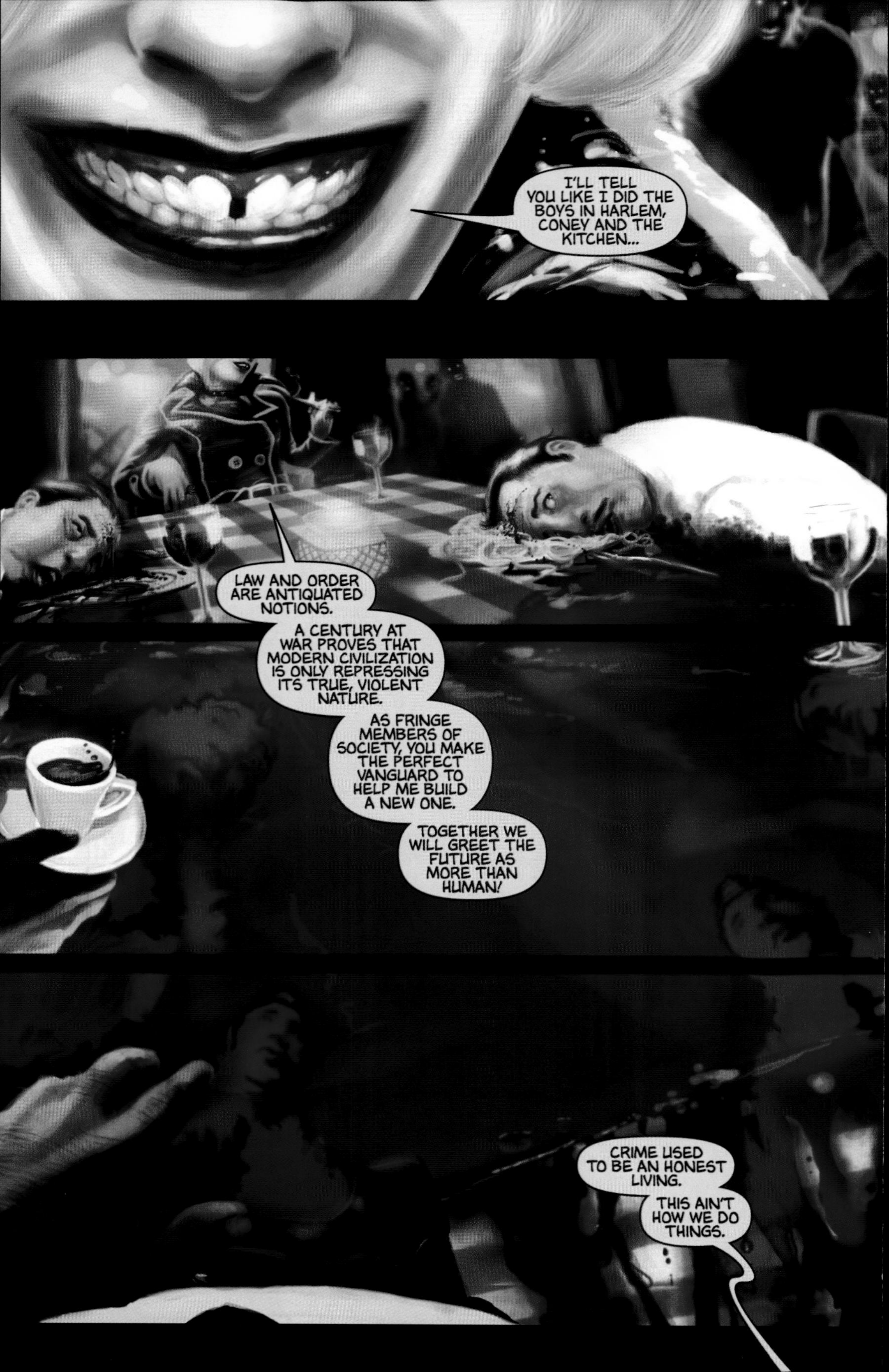
I'LL TELL YOU LIKE I DID THE BOYS IN HARLEM, CONEY AND THE KITCHEN...
LAW AND ORDER ARE ANTIQUATED NOTIONS.
A CENTURY AT WAR PROVES THAT MODERN CIVILIZATION IS ONLY REPRESSING ITS TRUE, VIOLENT NATURE.
AS FRINGE MEMBERS OF SOCIETY, YOU MAKE THE PERFECT VANGUARD TO HELP ME BUILD A NEW ONE.
TOGETHER WE WILL GREET THE FUTURE AS MORE THAN HUMAN!
CRIME USED TO BE AN HONEST LIVING.
THIS AIN'T HOW WE DO THINGS.

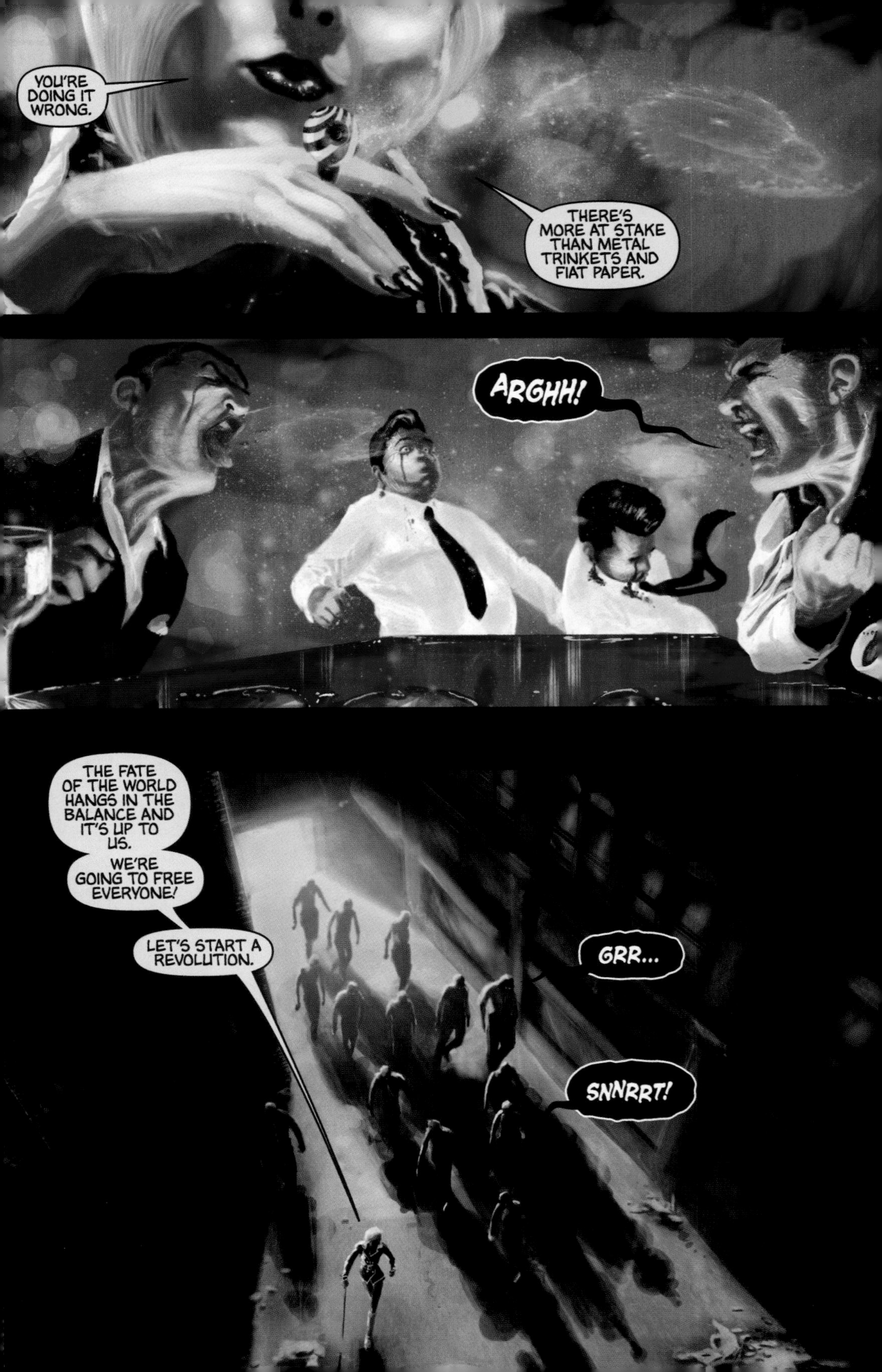
YOU'RE DOING IT WRONG.
THERE'S MORE AT STAKE THAN METAL TRINKETS AND FIAT PAPER.
ARGHH!
THE FATE OF THE WORLD HANGS IN THE BALANCE AND IT'S UP TO US.
WE'RE GOING TO FREE EVERYONE!
LET'S START A REVOLUTION.
GRR...
SNNRRT!

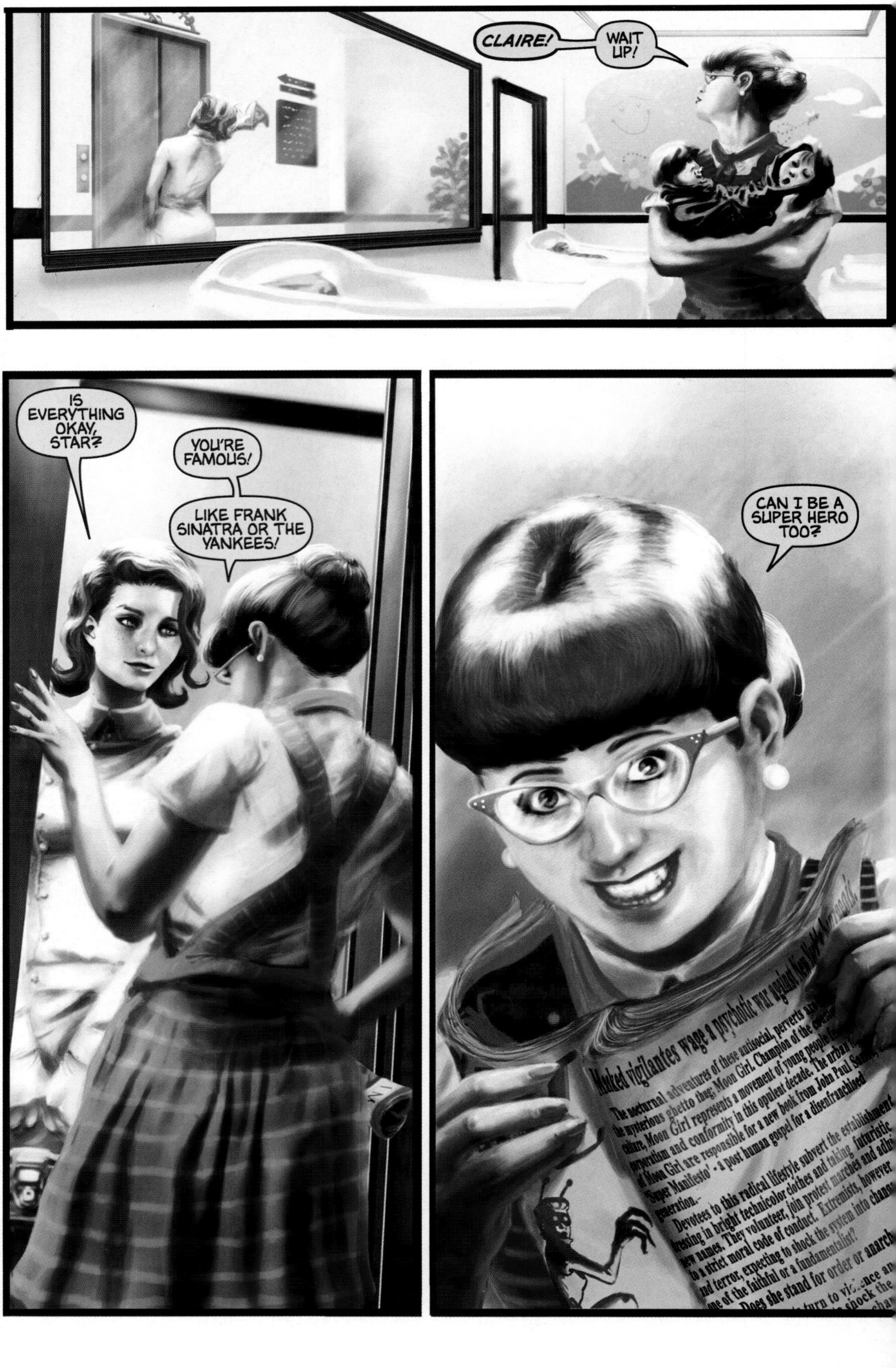
CLAIRE!
WAIT UP!
IS EVERYTHING OKAY, STAR?
YOU'RE FAMOUS!
LIKE FRANK SINATRA OR THE YANKEES!
CAN I BE A SUPER HERO TOO?

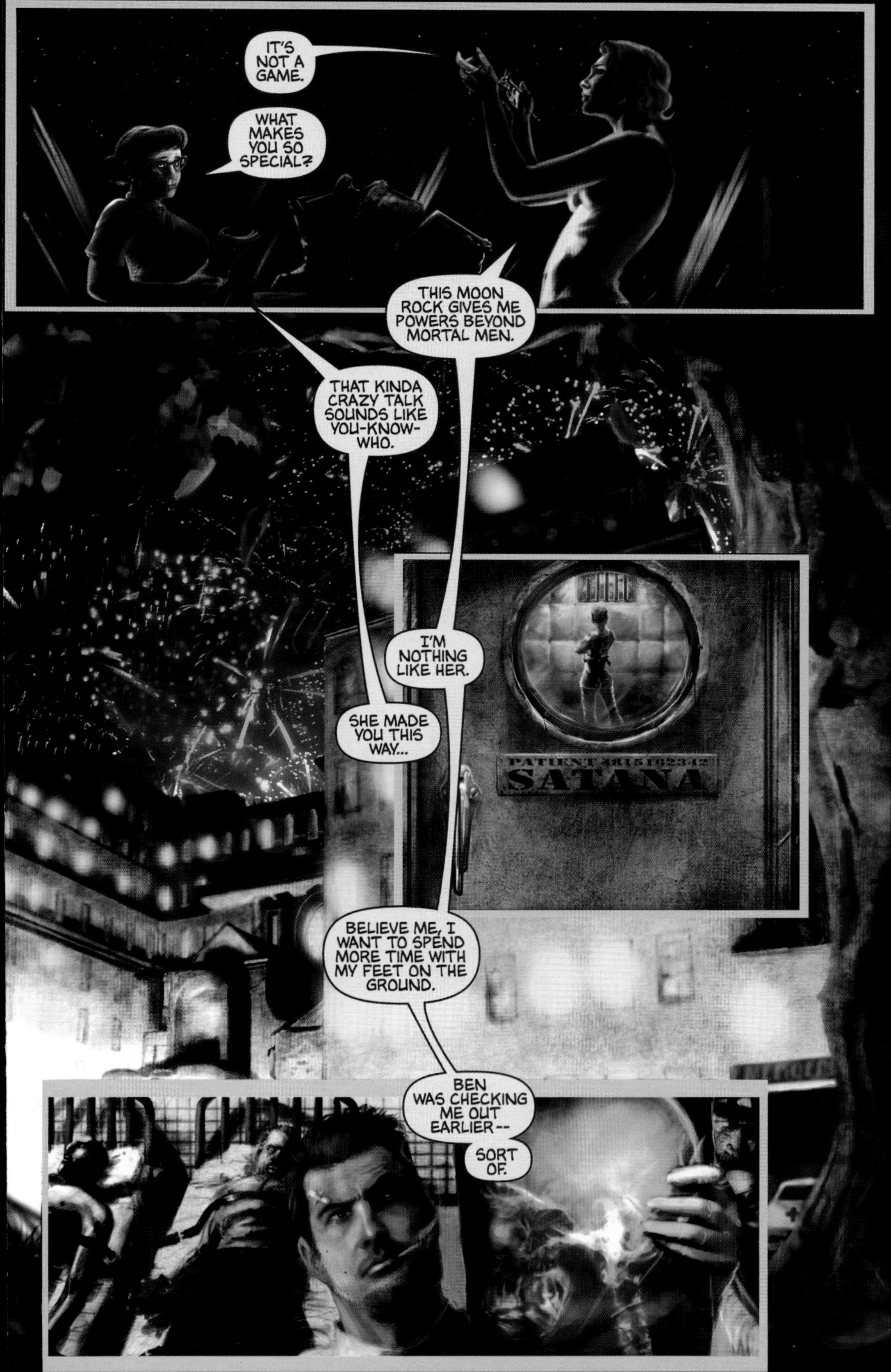
IT'S NOT A GAME.
WHAT MAKES YOU SO SPECIAL?
THIS MOON ROCK GIVES ME POWERS BEYOND MORTAL MEN.
THAT KINDA CRAZY TALK SOUNDS LIKE YOU-KNOW-WHO.
I'M NOTHING LIKE HER.
SHE MADE YOU THIS WAY...
PATIENT 4815162342
SATANA
BELIEVE ME, I WANT TO SPEND MORE TIME WITH MY FEET ON THE GROUND.
BEN WAS CHECKING ME OUT EARLIER--
SORT OF.

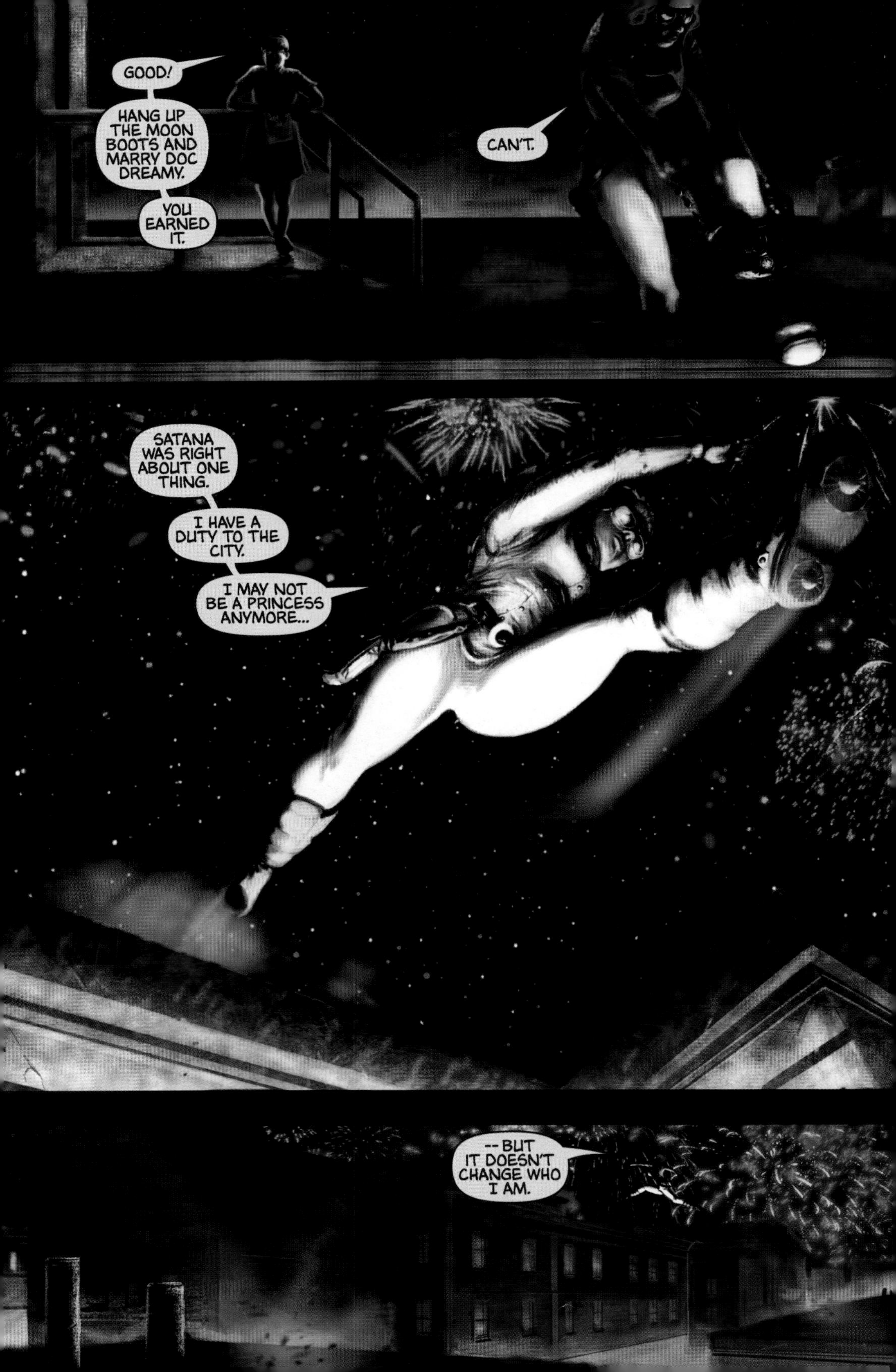
GOOD!
HANG UP THE MOON BOOTS AND MARRY DOC DREAMY.
YOU EARNED IT.
CAN'T.
SATANA WAS RIGHT ABOUT ONE THING.
I HAVE A DUTY TO THE CITY.
I MAY NOT BE A PRINCESS ANYMORE...
--BUT IT DOESN'T CHANGE WHO I AM.

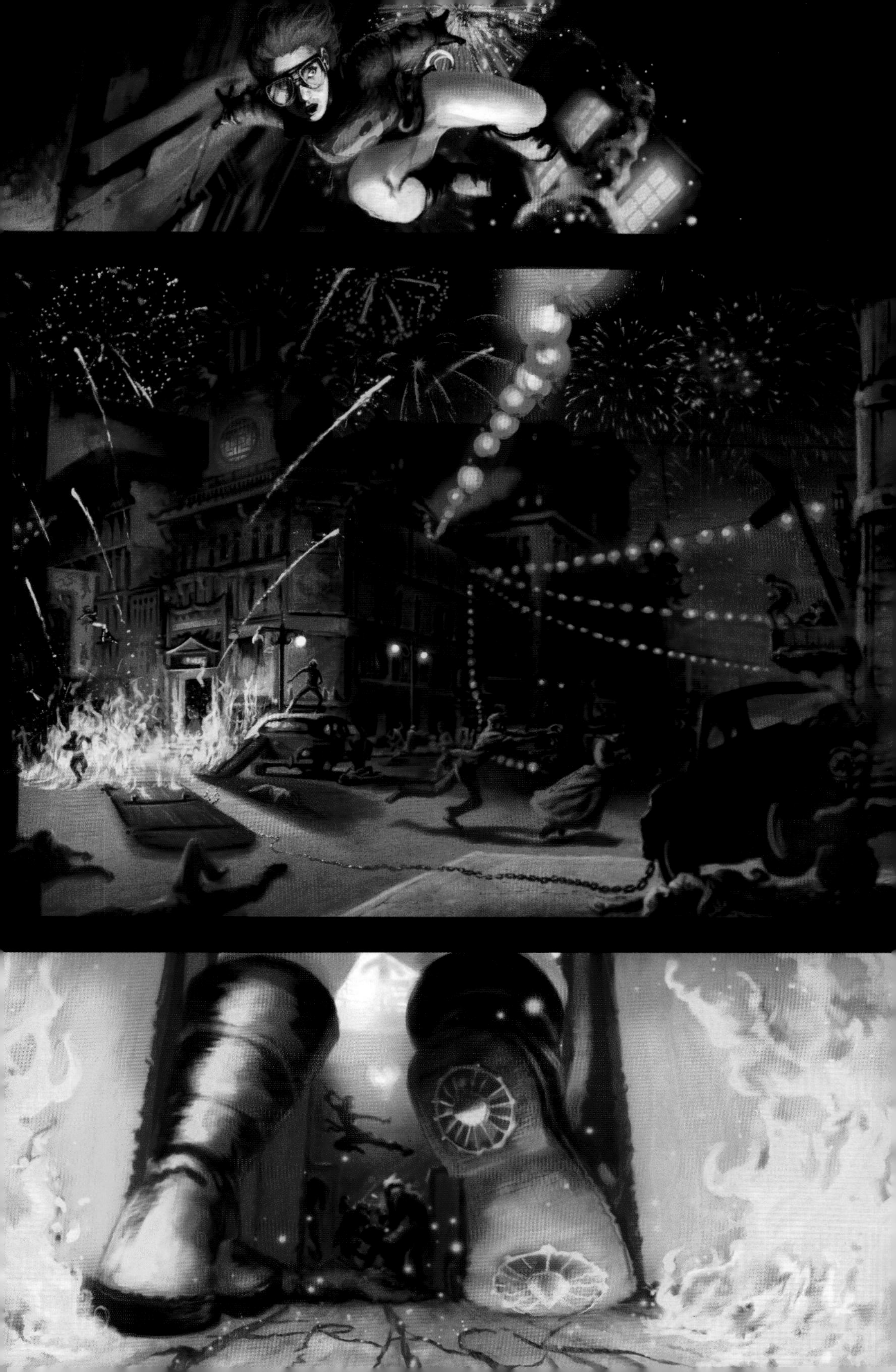

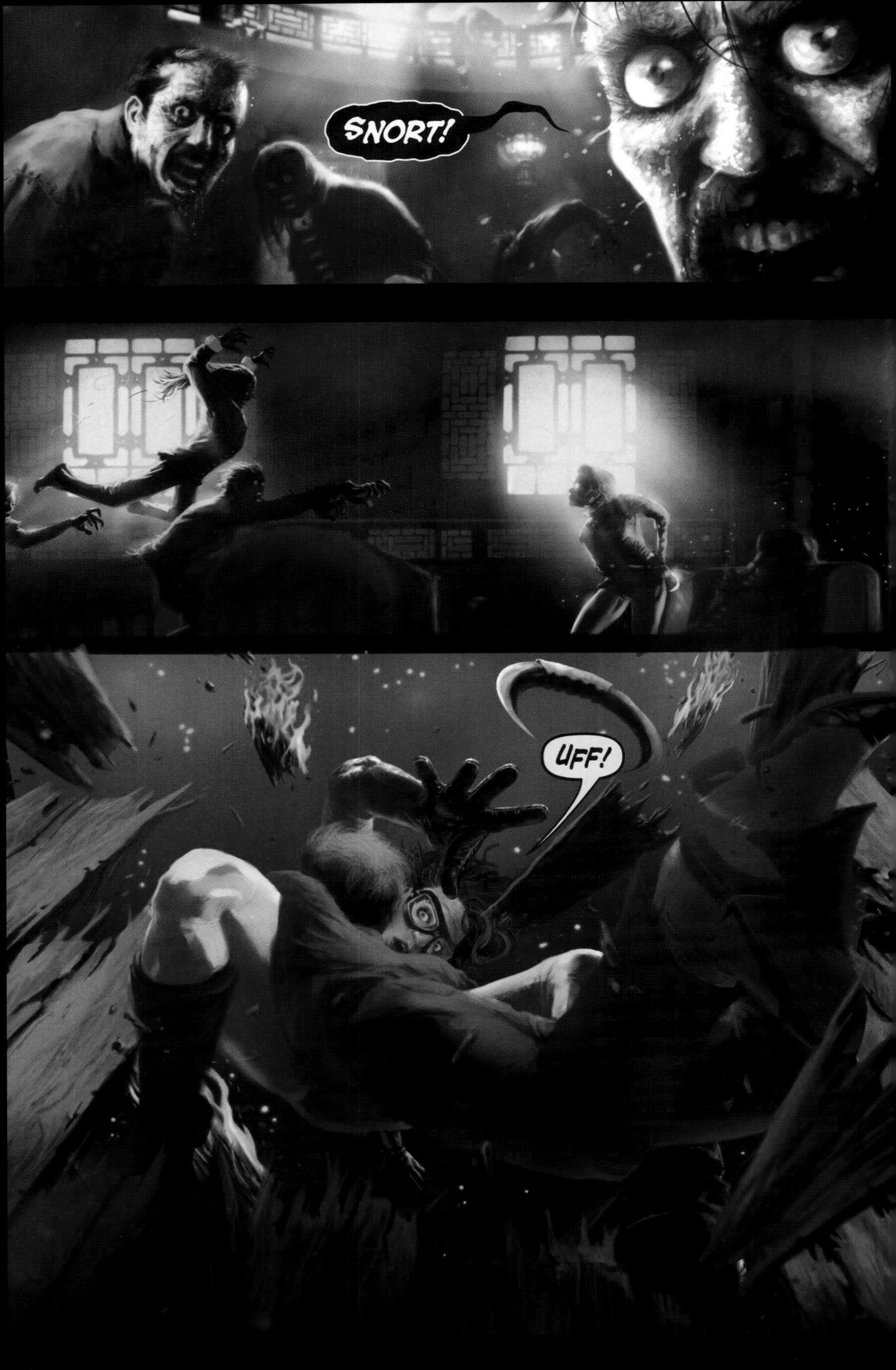
SNORT!
UFF!

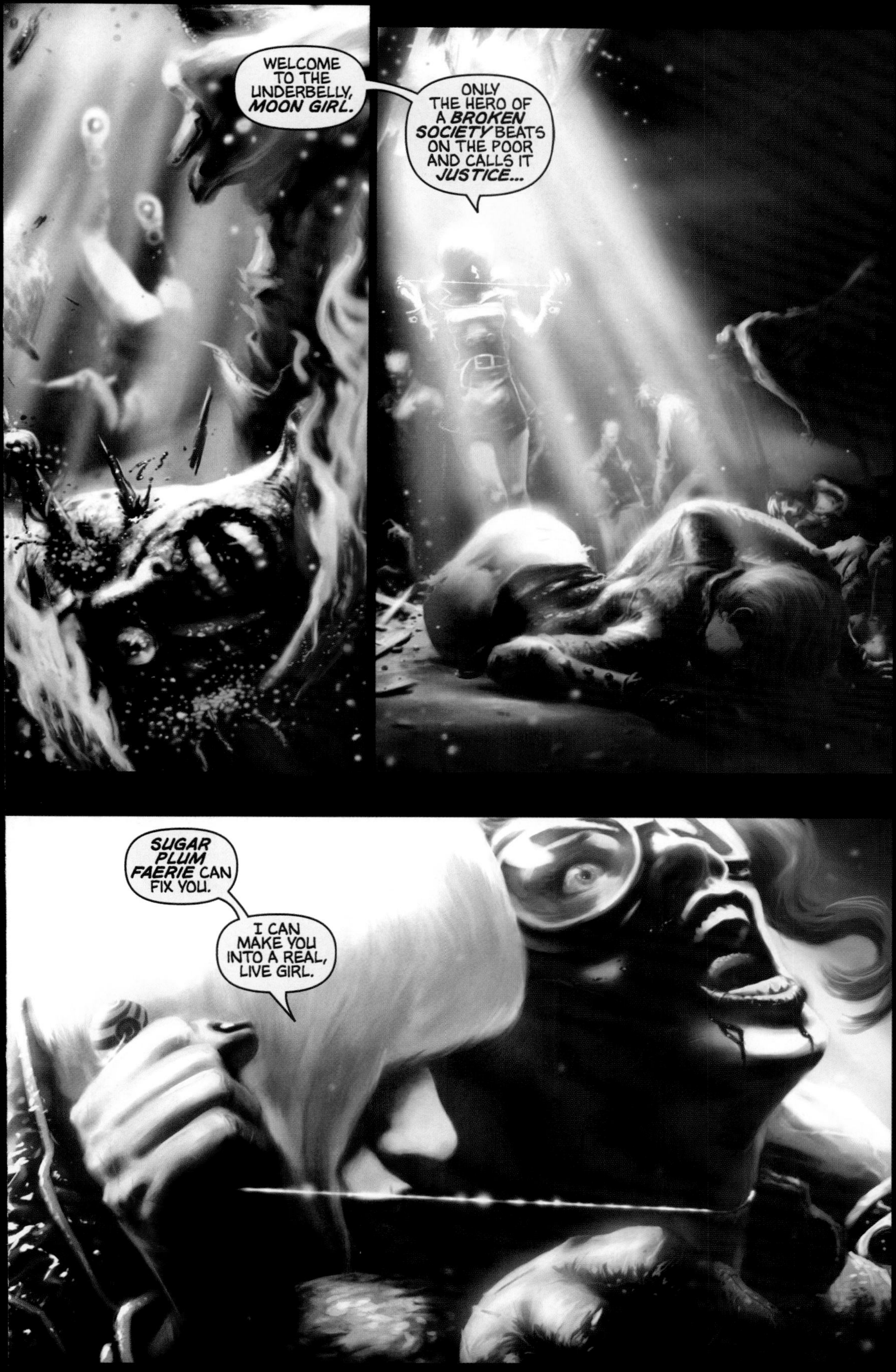
WELCOME TO THE UNDERBELLY, MOON GIRL.
ONLY THE HERO OF A BROKEN SOCIETY BEATS ON THE POOR AND CALLS IT JUSTICE...
SUGAR PLUM FAERIE CAN FIX YOU.
I CAN MAKE YOU INTO A REAL, LIVE GIRL.

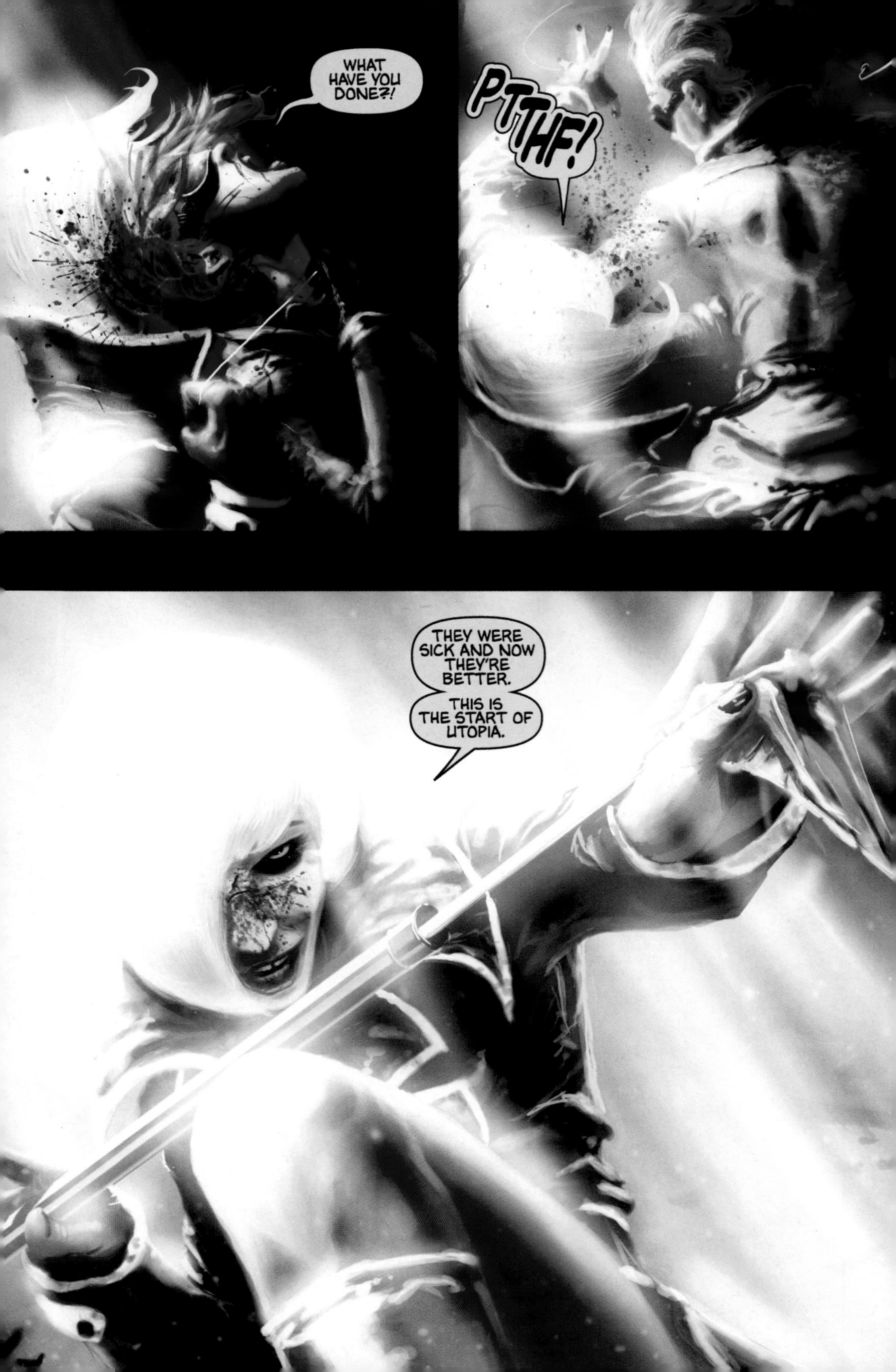
WHAT HAVE YOU DONE?!
PTTHF!
THEY WERE SICK AND NOW THEY'RE BETTER.
THIS IS THE START OF UTOPIA.

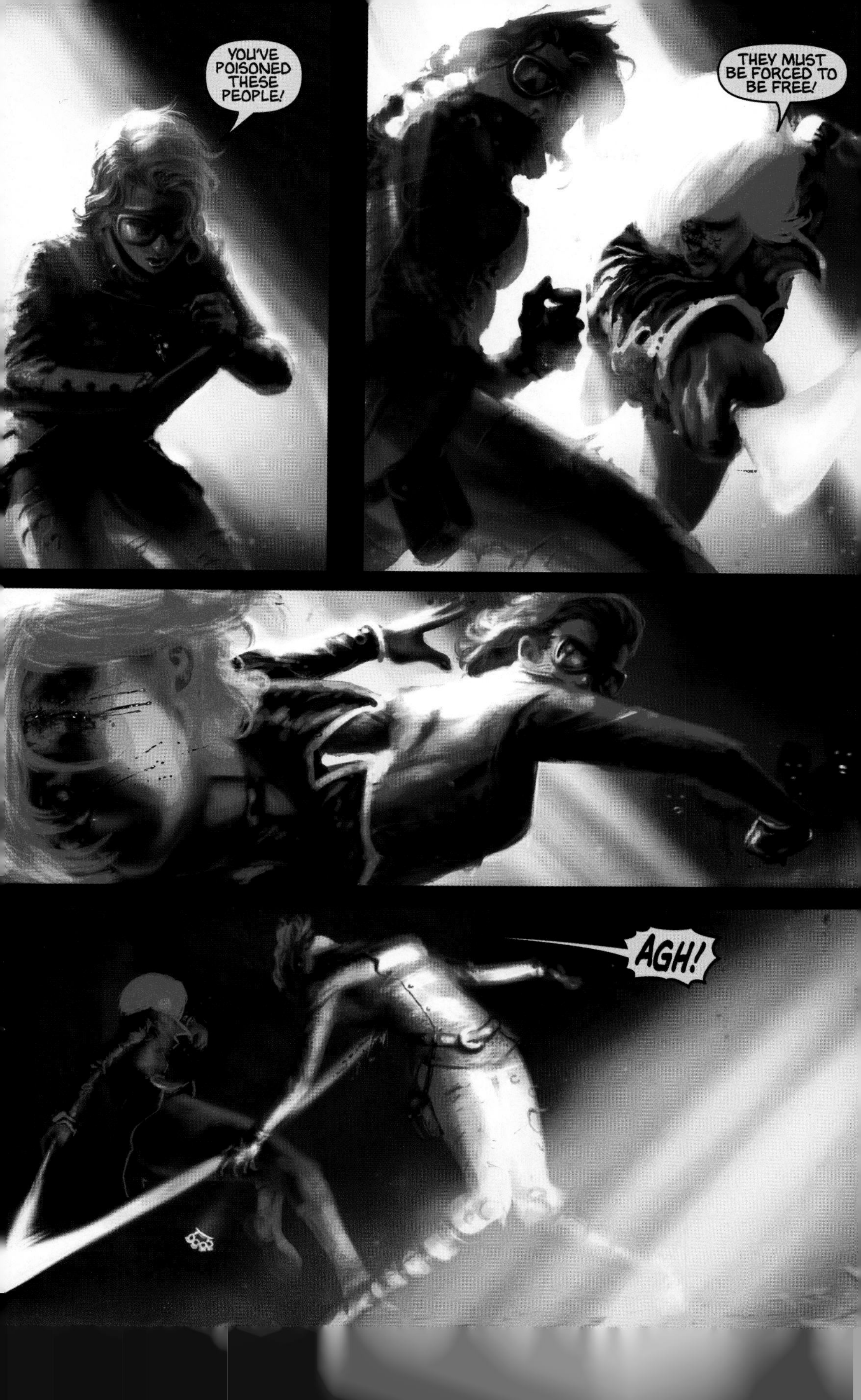
YOU'VE POISONED THESE PEOPLE!
THEY MUST BE FORCED TO BE FREE!
AGH!

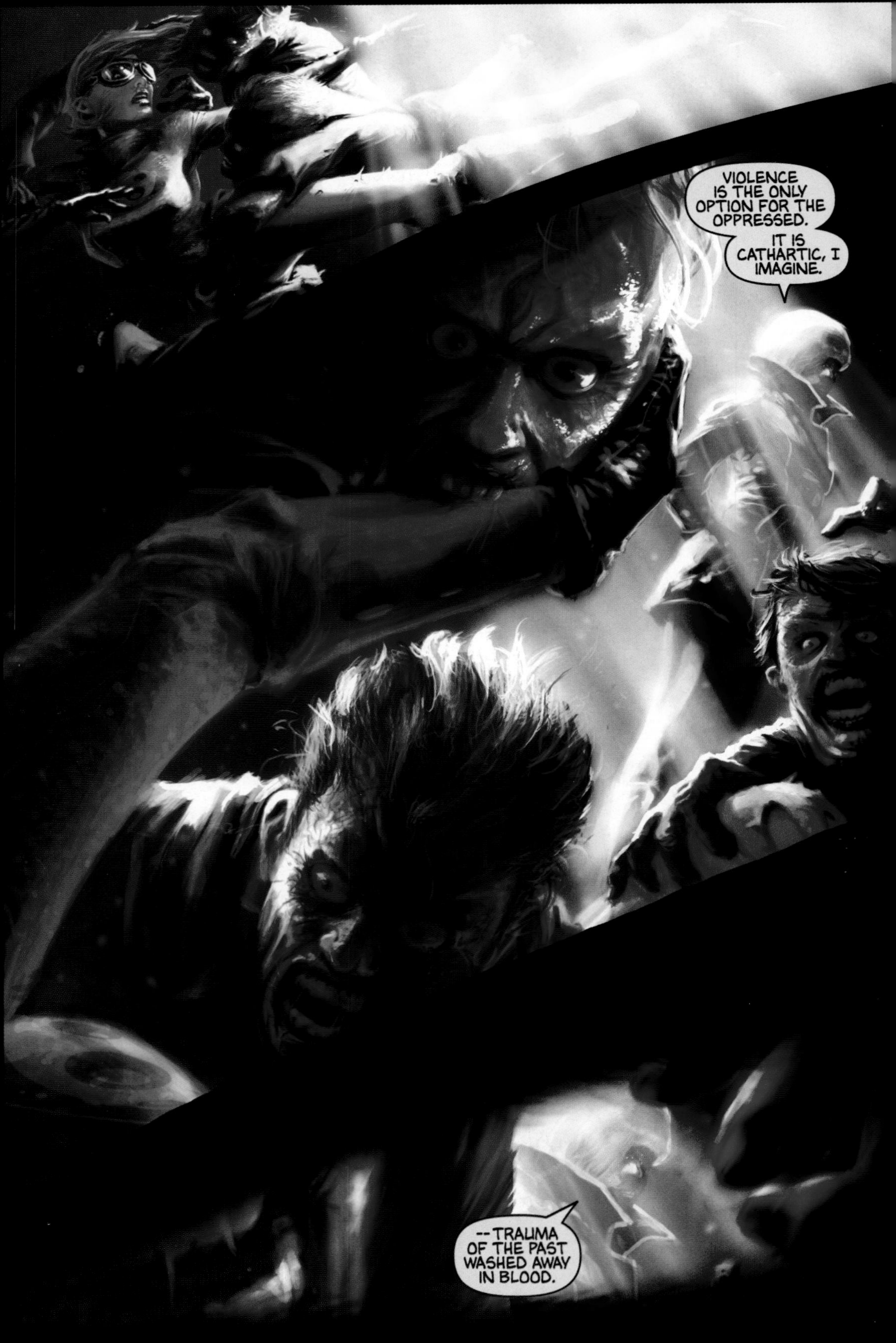
VIOLENCE IS THE ONLY OPTION FOR THE OPPRESSED.
IT IS CATHARTIC, I IMAGINE.
--TRAUMA OF THE PAST WASHED AWAY IN BLOOD.

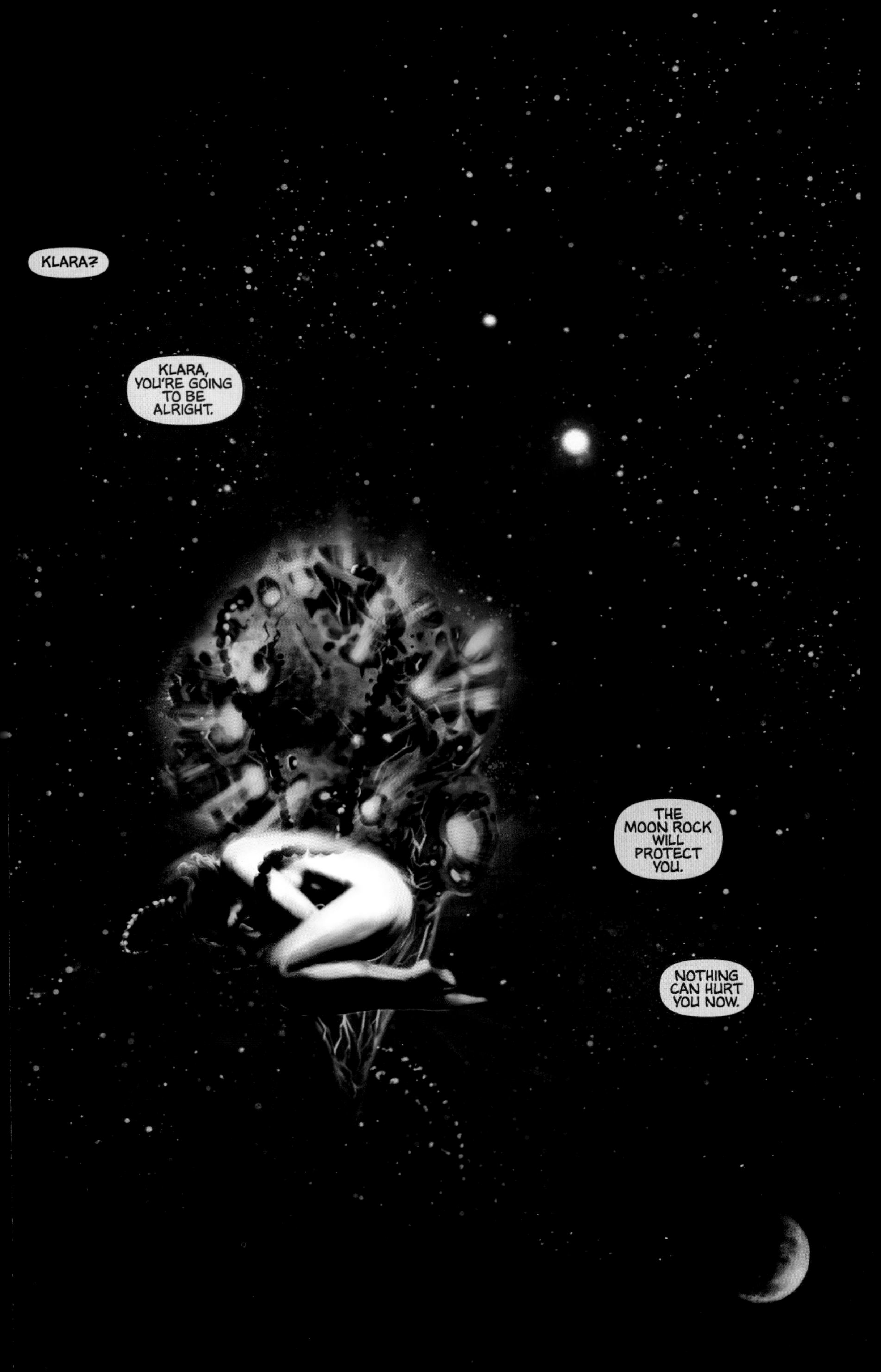
KLARA?
KLARA, YOU'RE GOING TO BE ALRIGHT.
THE MOON ROCK WILL PROTECT YOU.
NOTHING CAN HURT YOU NOW.

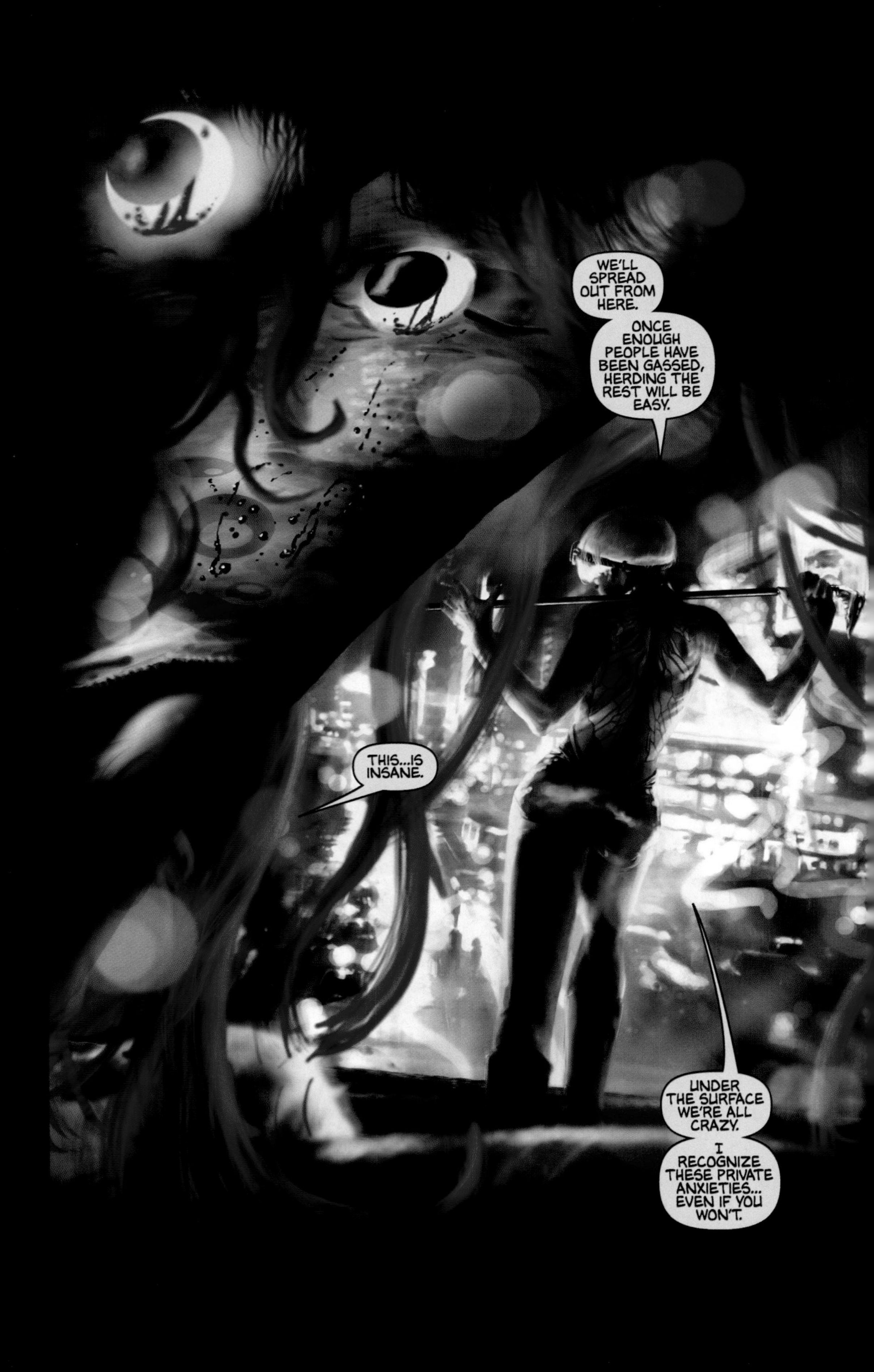
WE'LL SPREAD OUT FROM HERE.
ONCE ENOUGH PEOPLE HAVE BEEN GASSED, HERDING THE REST WILL BE EASY.
THIS...IS INSANE.
UNDER THE SURFACE WE'RE ALL CRAZY.
I RECOGNIZE THESE PRIVATE ANXIETIES... EVEN IF YOU WON'T.

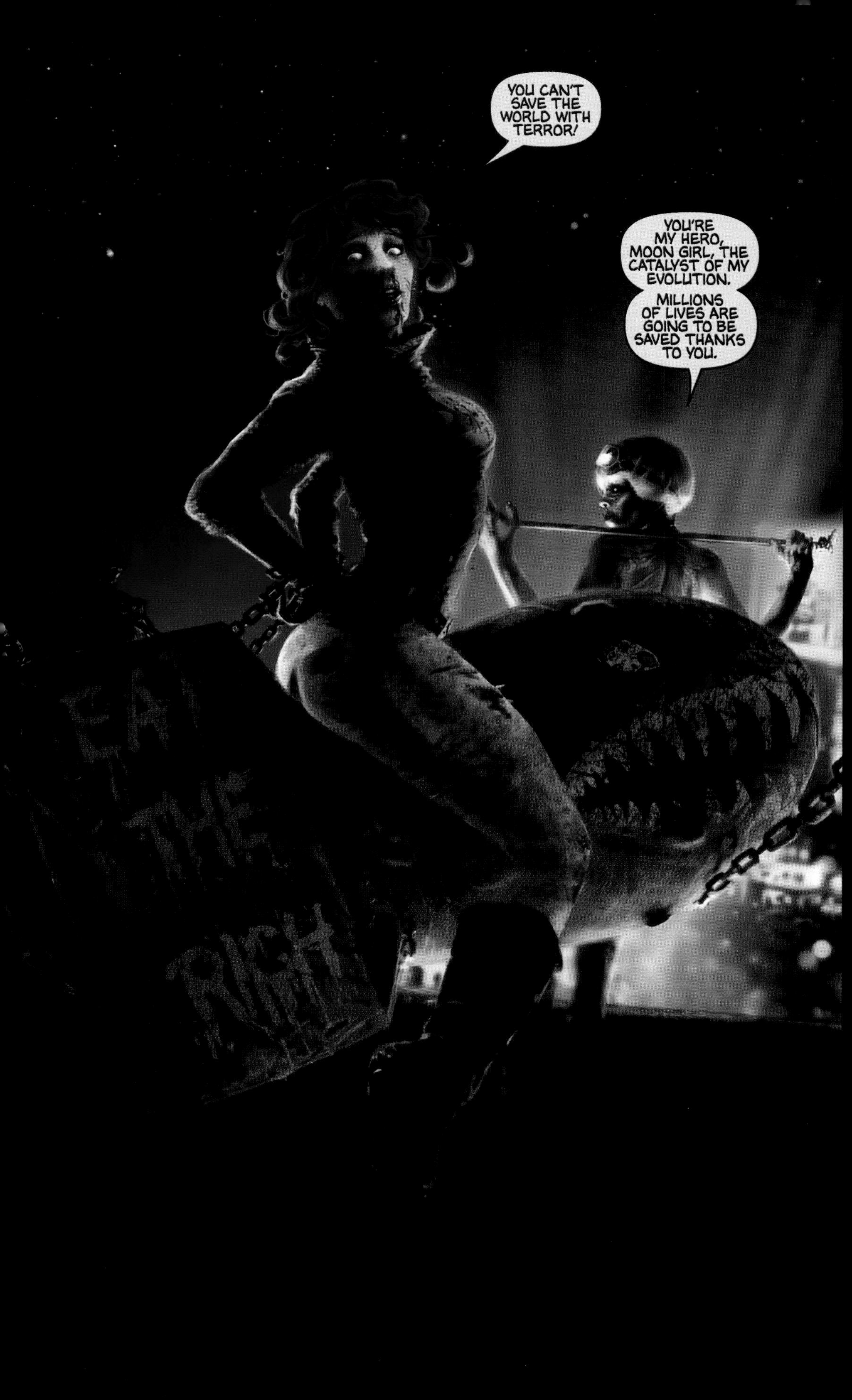
YOU CAN'T SAVE THE WORLD WITH TERROR!
YOU'RE MY HERO, MOON GIRL, THE CATALYST OF MY EVOLUTION.
MILLIONS OF LIVES ARE GOING TO BE SAVED THANKS TO YOU.

2

A MOON, A GIRL, A ROMANCE

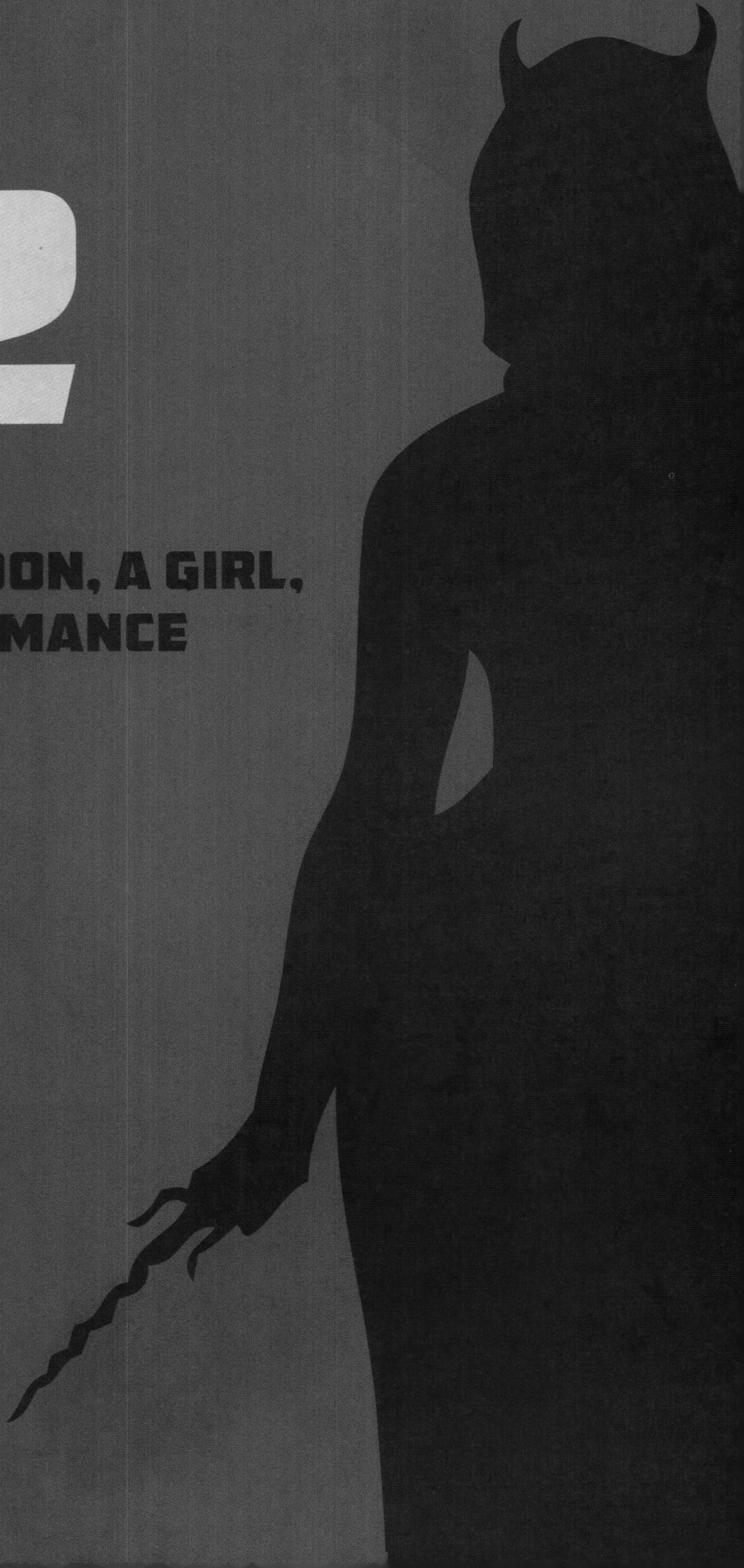

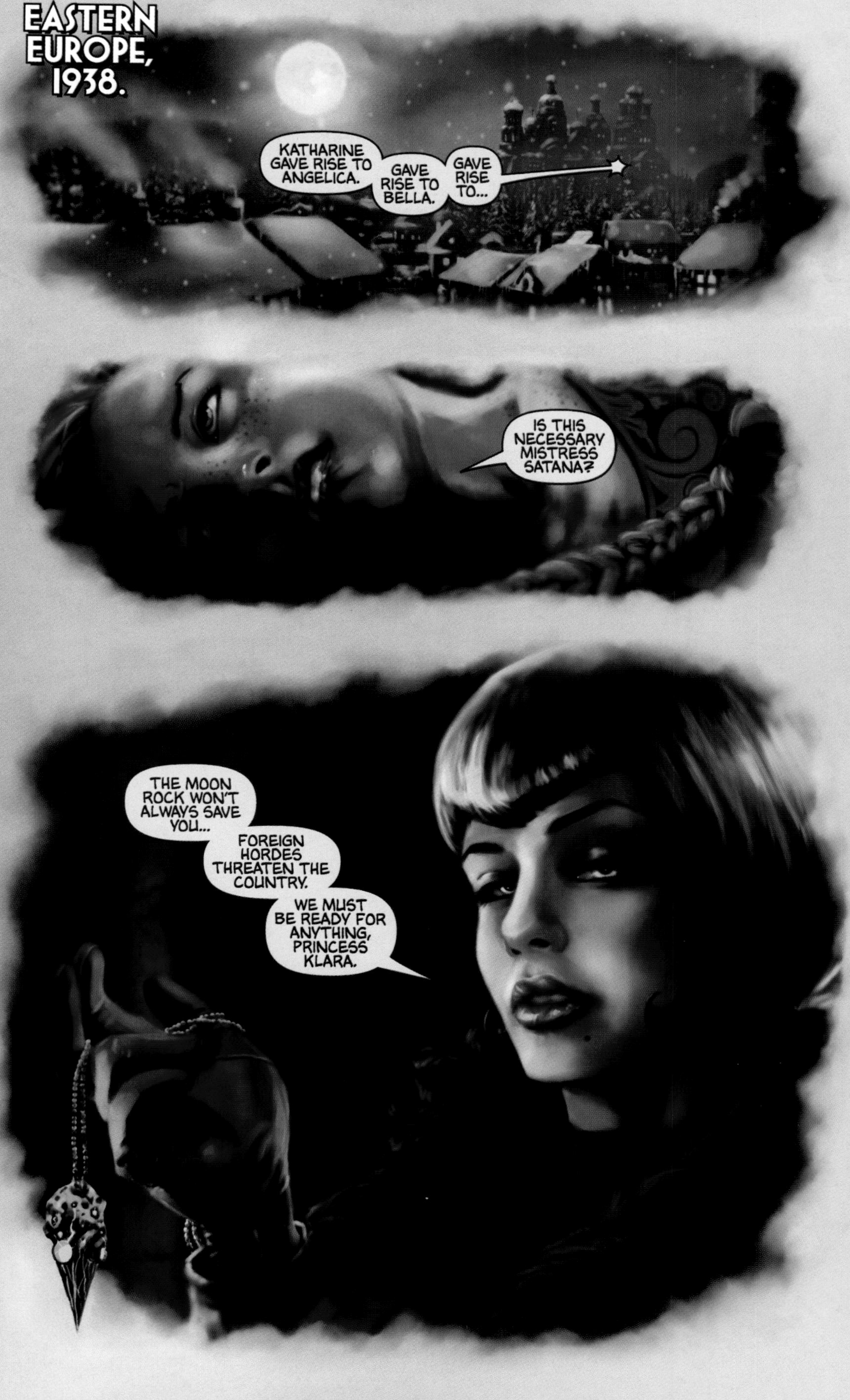
EASTERN EUROPE, 1938.
KATHARINE GAVE RISE TO ANGELICA.
GAVE RISE TO BELLA.
GAVE RISE TO...
IS THIS NECESSARY MISTRESS SATANA?
THE MOON ROCK WON'T ALWAYS SAVE YOU...
FOREIGN HORDES THREATEN THE COUNTRY.
WE MUST BE READY FOR ANYTHING, PRINCESS KLARA.

THESE GAMES DON'T MAKE ME A BETTER GENERAL.
NOT ALL BATTLES ARE FOUGHT IN FORMATION.
HER MAJESTY IS A WET NURSE, WISE MAN AND WARRIOR.

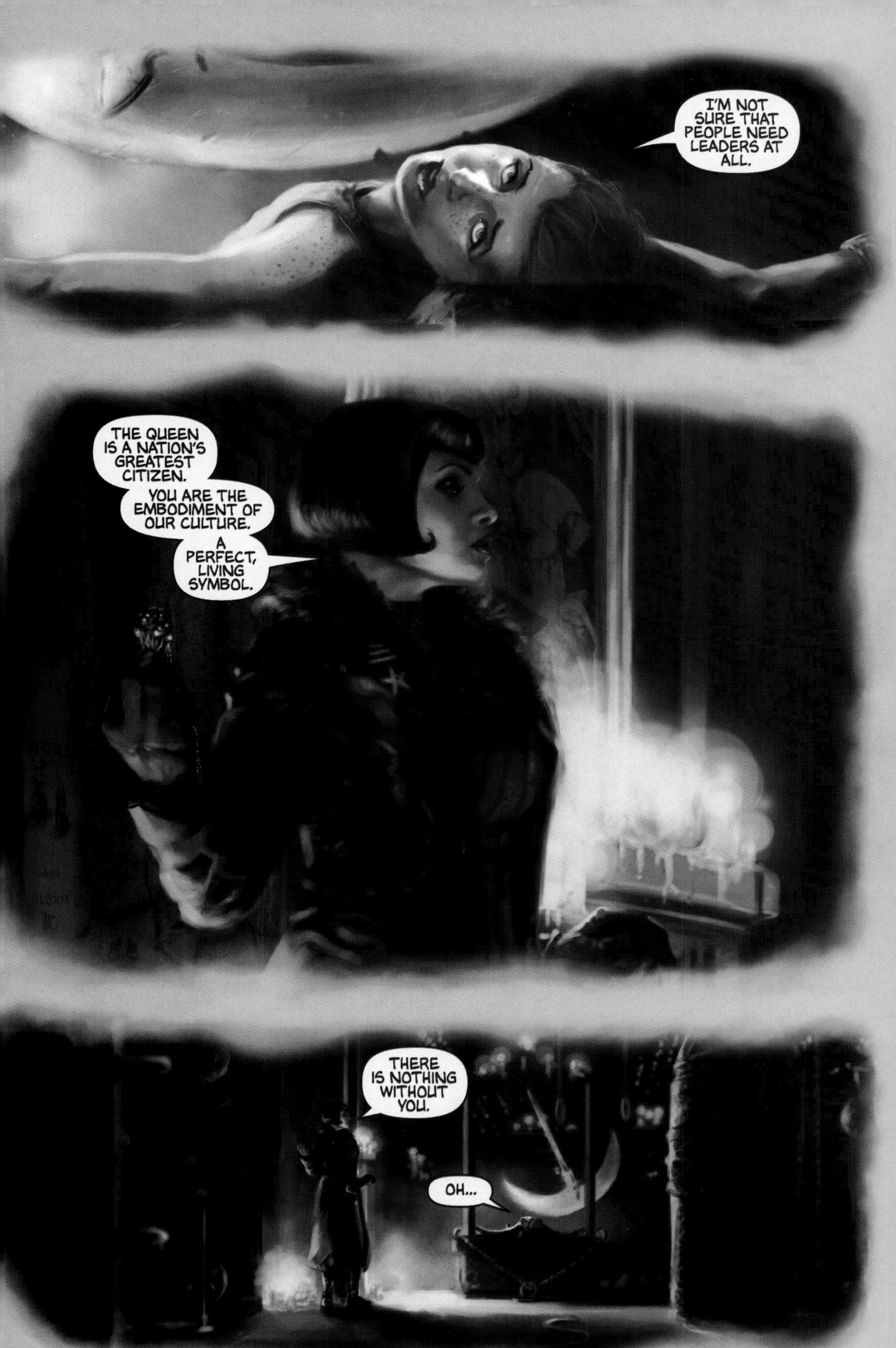
I'M NOT SURE THAT PEOPLE NEED LEADERS AT ALL.
THE QUEEN IS A NATION'S GREATEST CITIZEN.
YOU ARE THE EMBODIMENT OF OUR CULTURE.
A PERFECT, LIVING SYMBOL.
THERE IS NOTHING WITHOUT YOU.
OH...

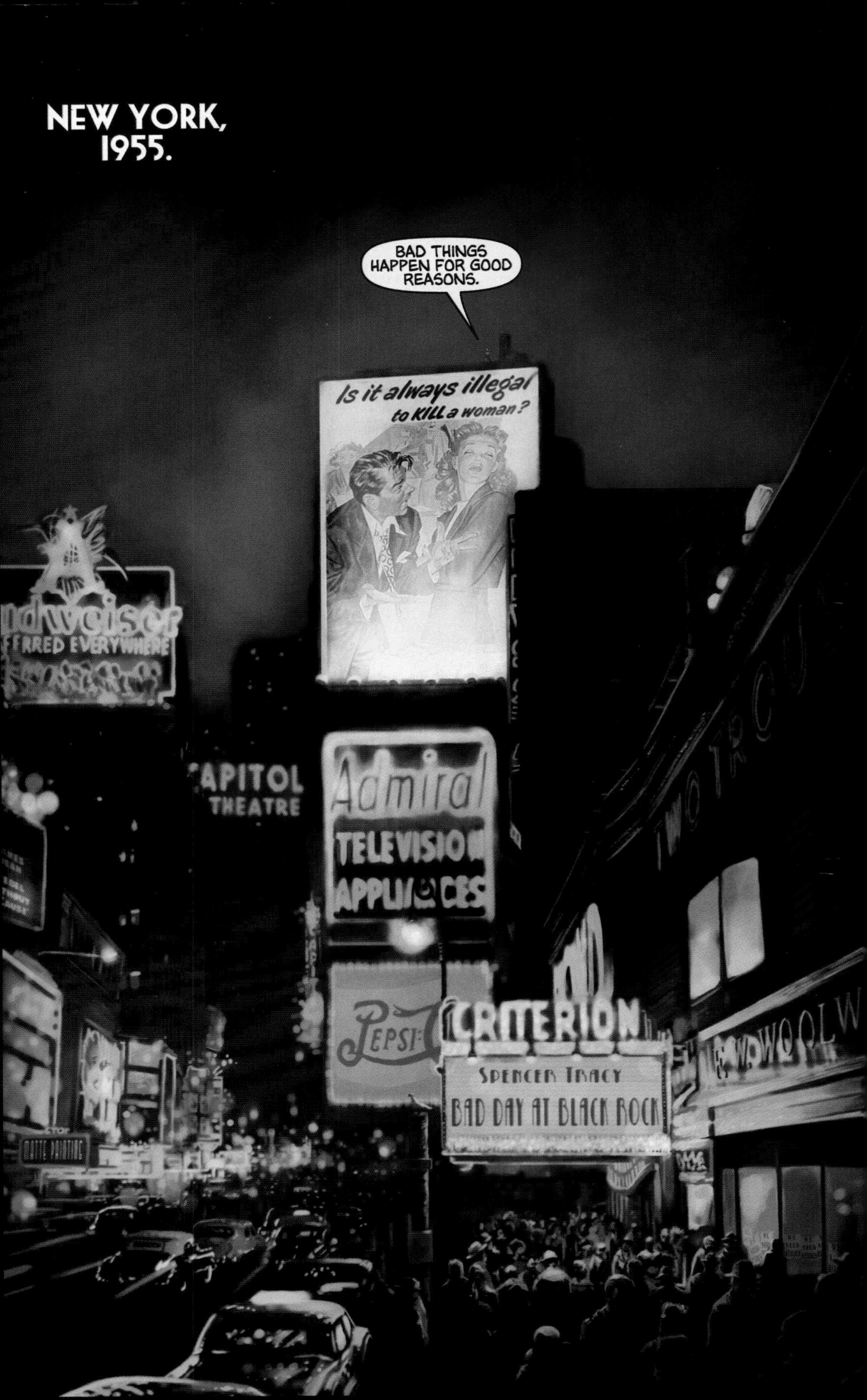
NEW YORK, 1955.
BAD THINGS HAPPEN FOR GOOD REASONS.
Is it always illegal to KILL a woman?
FERRED EVERYWHERE
APITOL THEATRE
Admiral
TELEVISION
CRITERION
SPENCER TRACY
BAD DAY AT BLACK ROCK
MATTE PAINTING

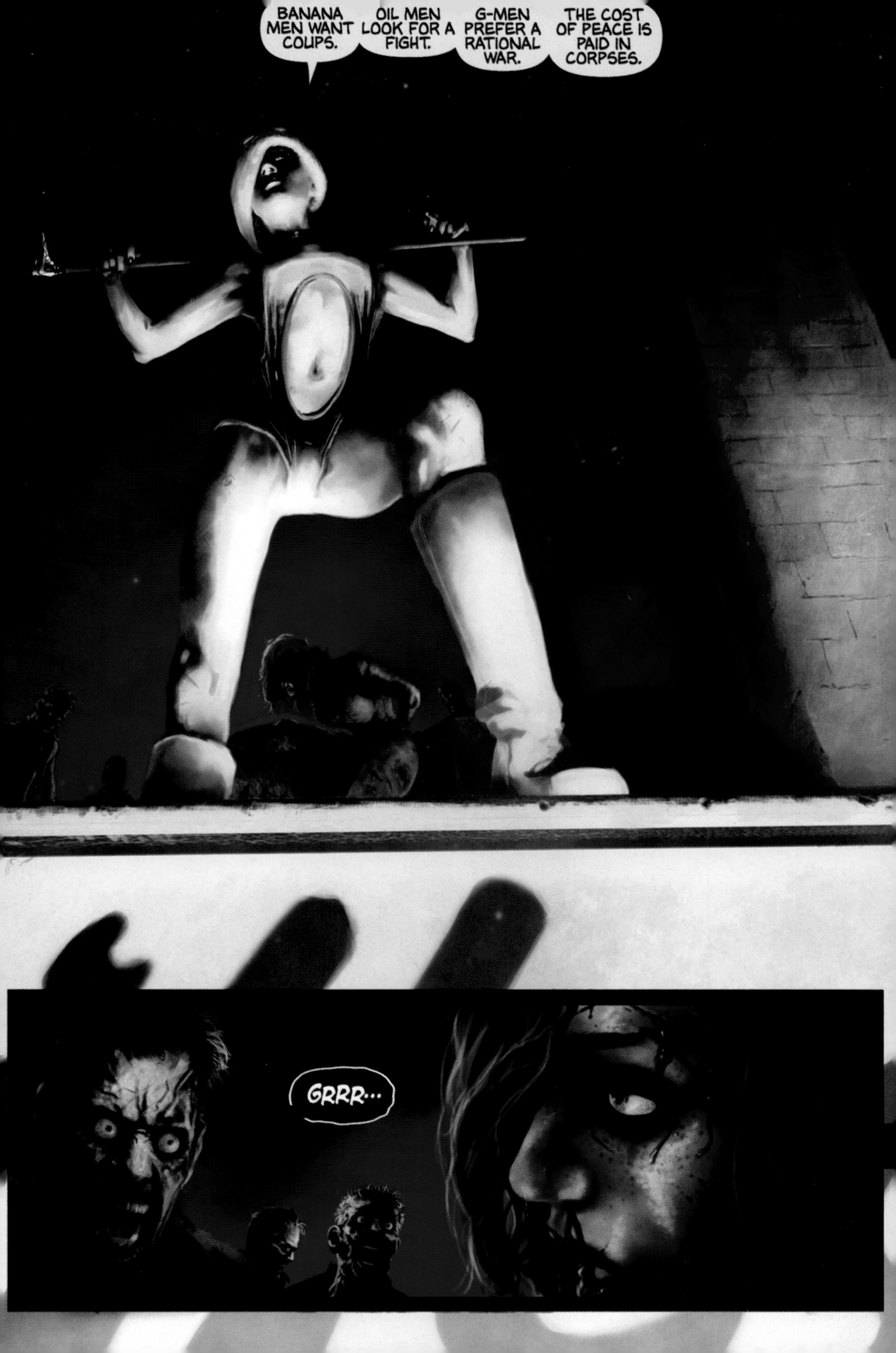
BANANA MEN WANT COUPS.
OIL MEN LOOK FOR A FIGHT.
G-MEN PREFER A RATIONAL WAR.
THE COST OF PEACE IS PAID IN CORPSES.
GRRR...

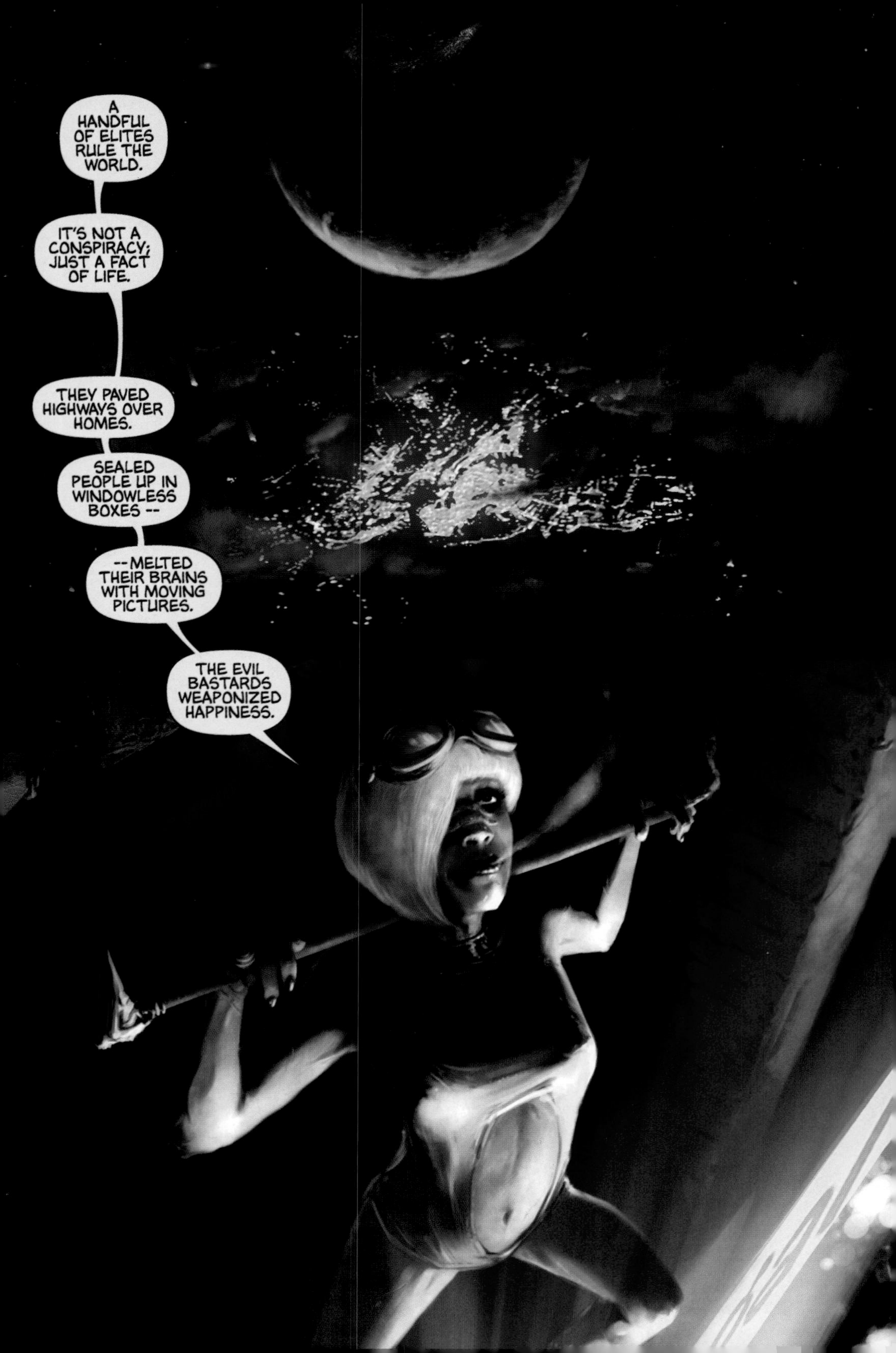
A HANDFUL OF ELITES RULE THE WORLD.
IT'S NOT A CONSPIRACY; JUST A FACT OF LIFE.
THEY PAVED HIGHWAYS OVER HOMES.
SEALED PEOPLE UP IN WINDOWLESS BOXES --
--MELTED THEIR BRAINS WITH MOVING PICTURES.
THE EVIL BASTARDS WEAPONIZED HAPPINESS.

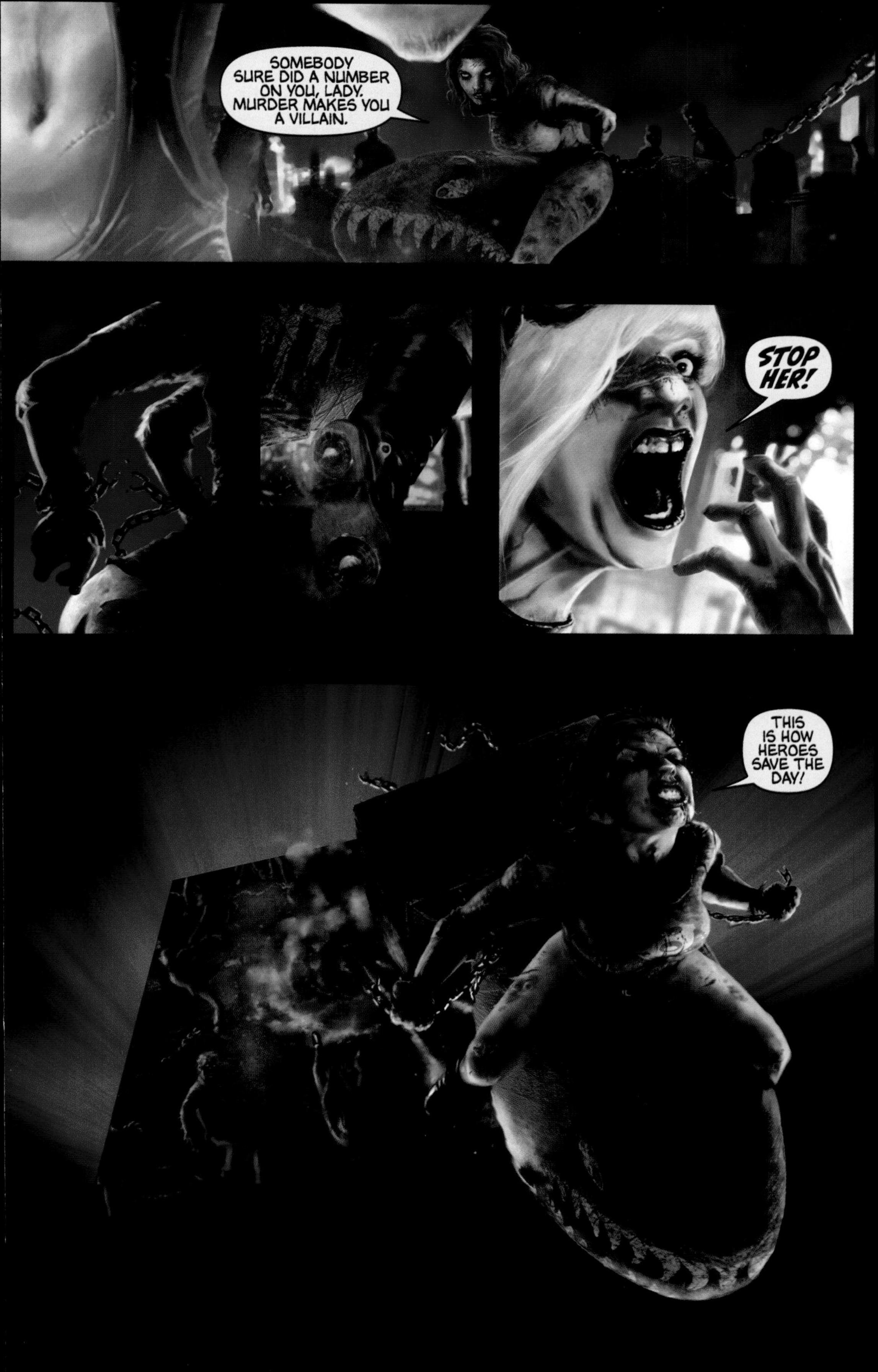
SOMEBODY SURE DID A NUMBER ON YOU, LADY. MURDER MAKES YOU A VILLAIN.
STOP HER!
THIS IS HOW HEROES SAVE THE DAY!

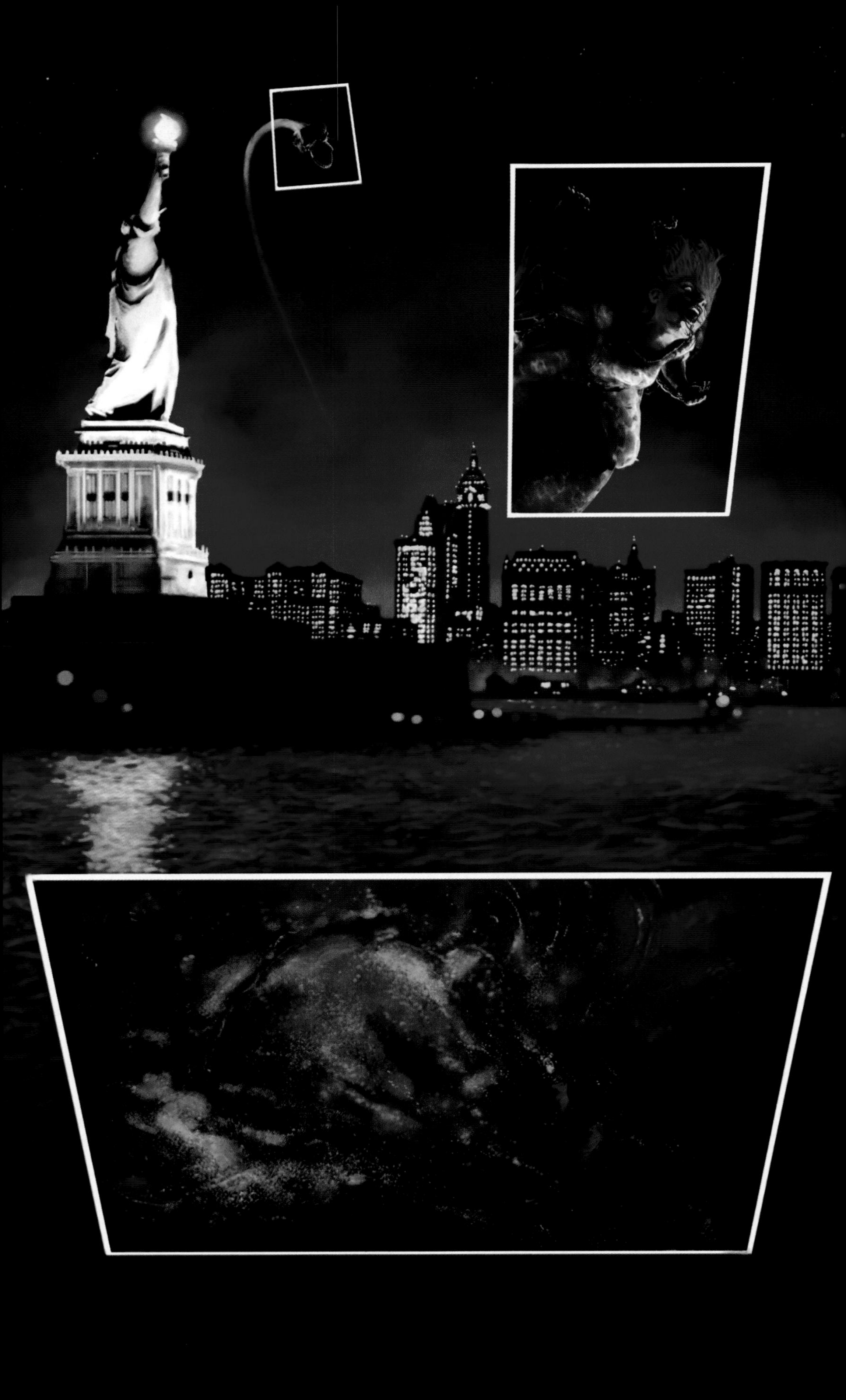

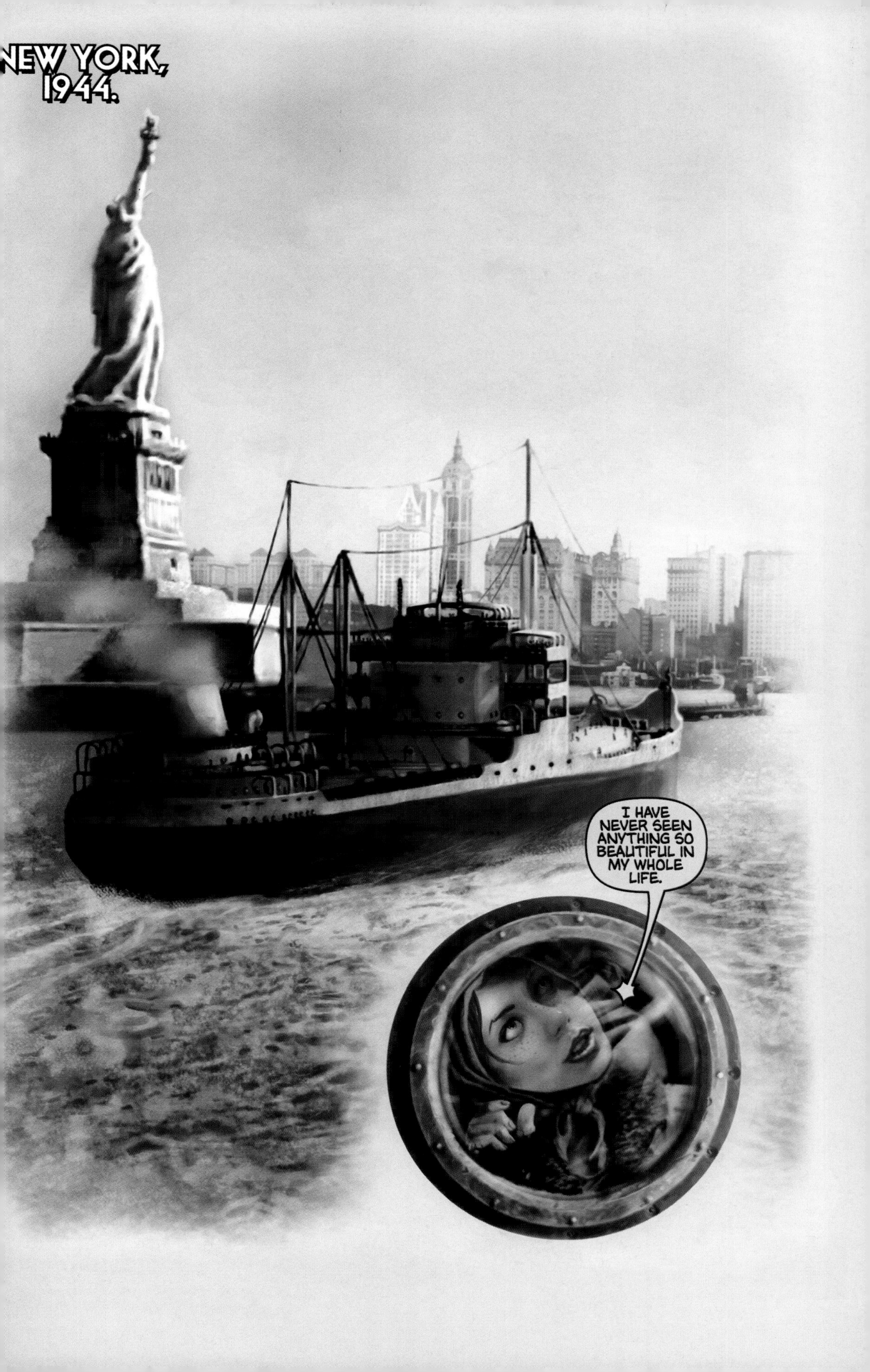
NEW YORK, 1944.
I HAVE NEVER SEEN ANYTHING SO BEAUTIFUL IN MY WHOLE LIFE.

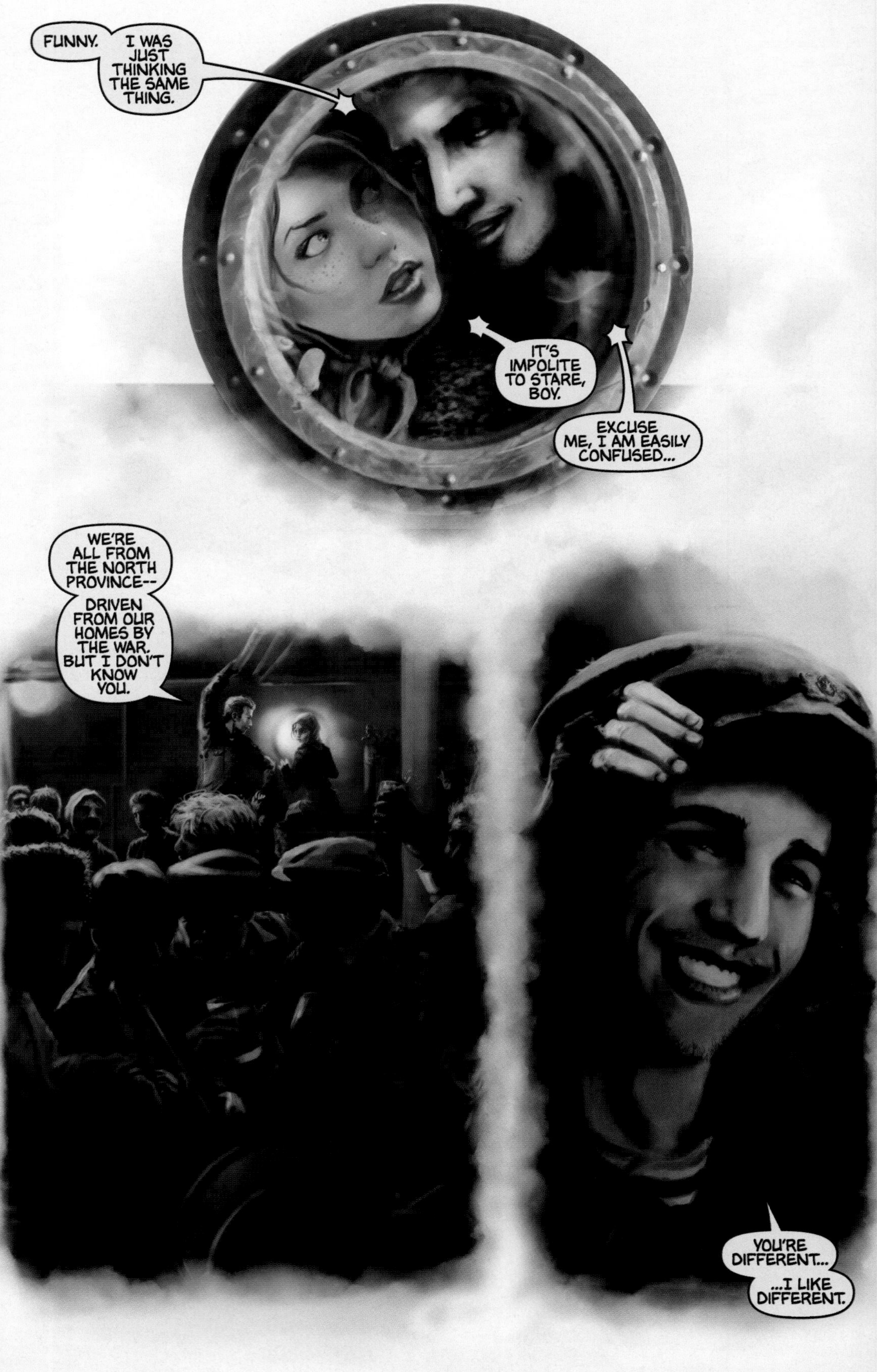
FUNNY.
I WAS JUST THINKING THE SAME THING.
IT'S IMPOLITE TO STARE, BOY.
EXCUSE ME, I AM EASILY CONFUSED...
WE'RE ALL FROM THE NORTH PROVINCE--
DRIVEN FROM OUR HOMES BY THE WAR. BUT I DON'T KNOW YOU.
YOU'RE DIFFERENT...
...I LIKE DIFFERENT.

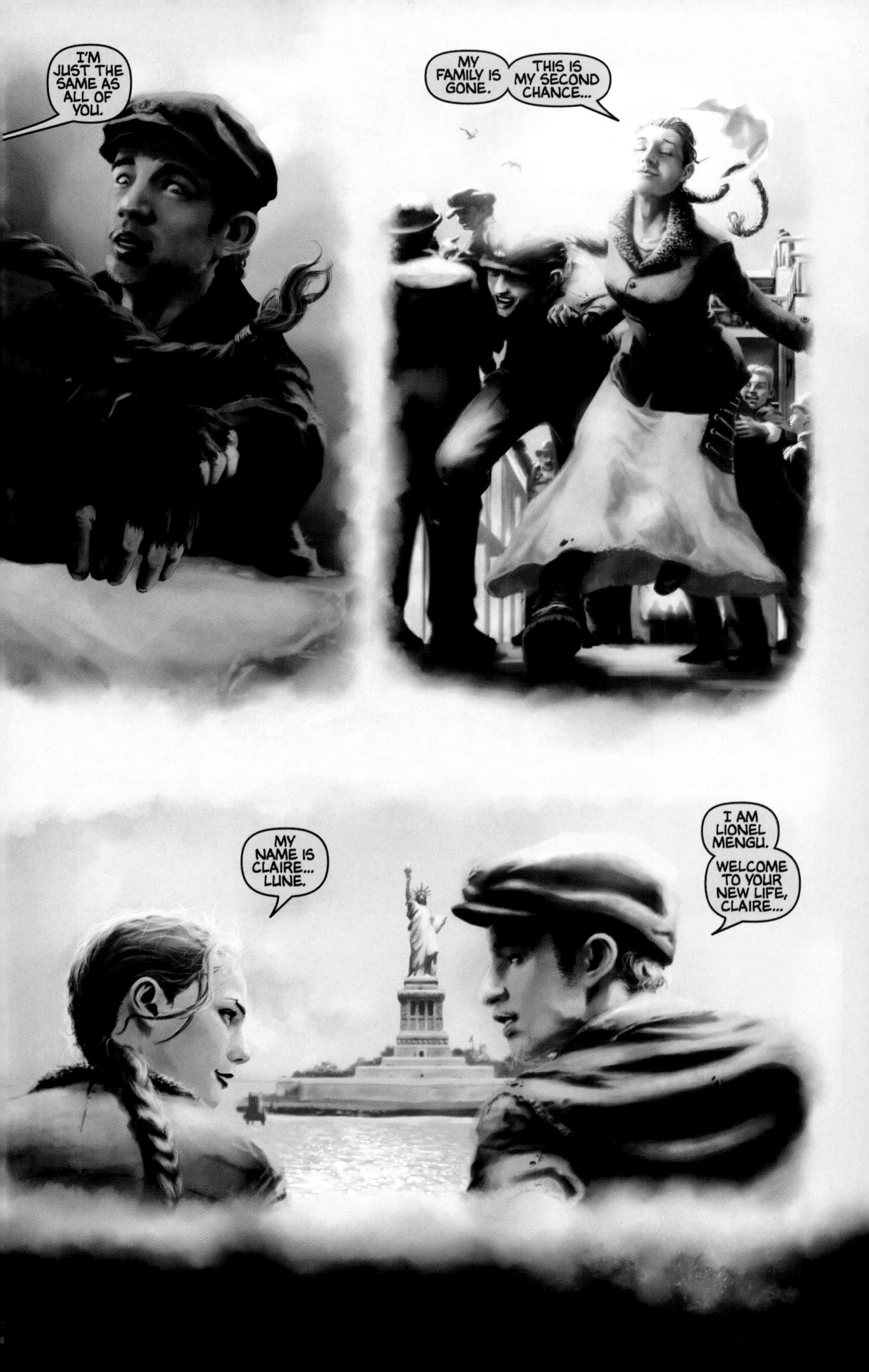
I'M JUST THE SAME AS ALL OF YOU.
MY FAMILY IS GONE.
THIS IS MY SECOND CHANCE...
MY NAME IS CLAIRE... LUNE.
I AM LIONEL MENGU.
WELCOME TO YOUR NEW LIFE, CLAIRE...

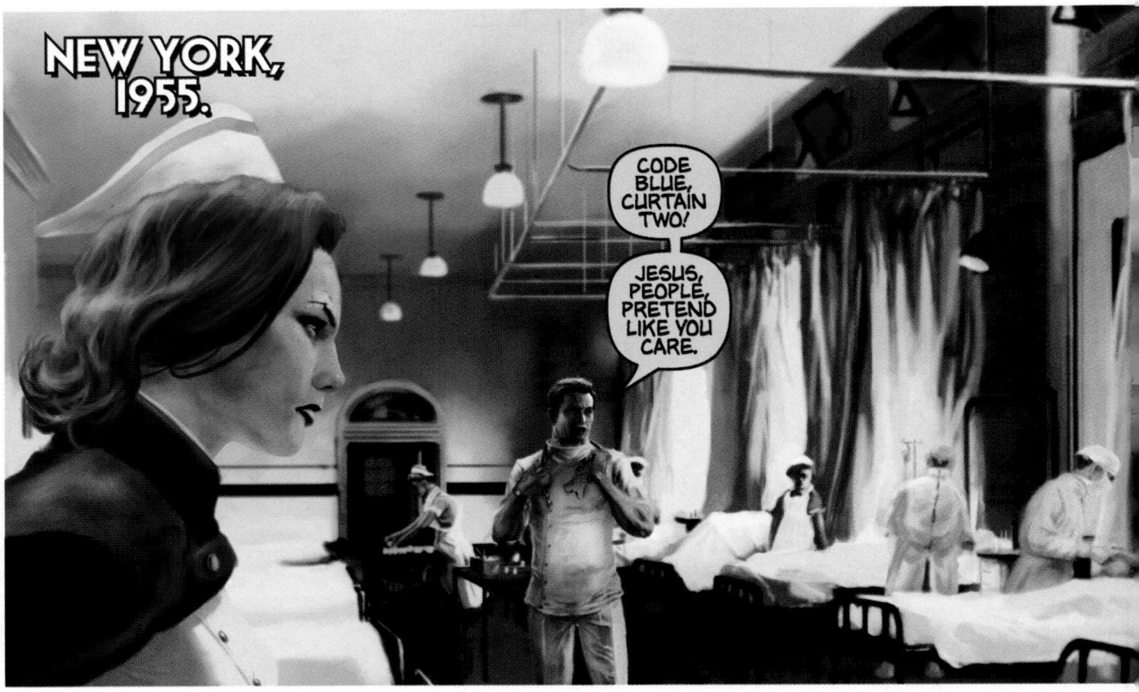
NEW YORK, 1955.
CODE BLUE, CURTAIN TWO!
JESUS, PEOPLE, PRETEND LIKE YOU CARE.

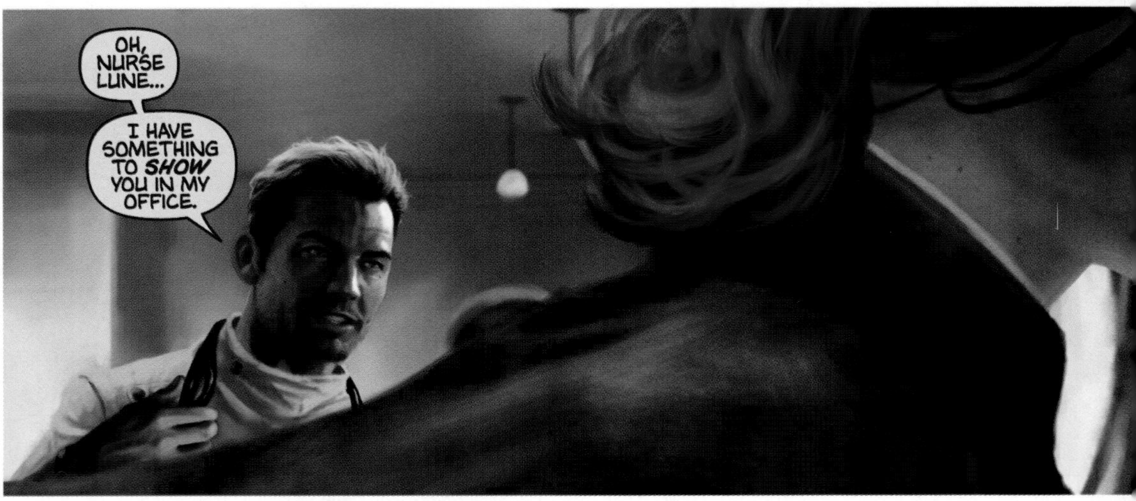
OH, NURSE LUNE...
I HAVE SOMETHING TO SHOW YOU IN MY OFFICE.

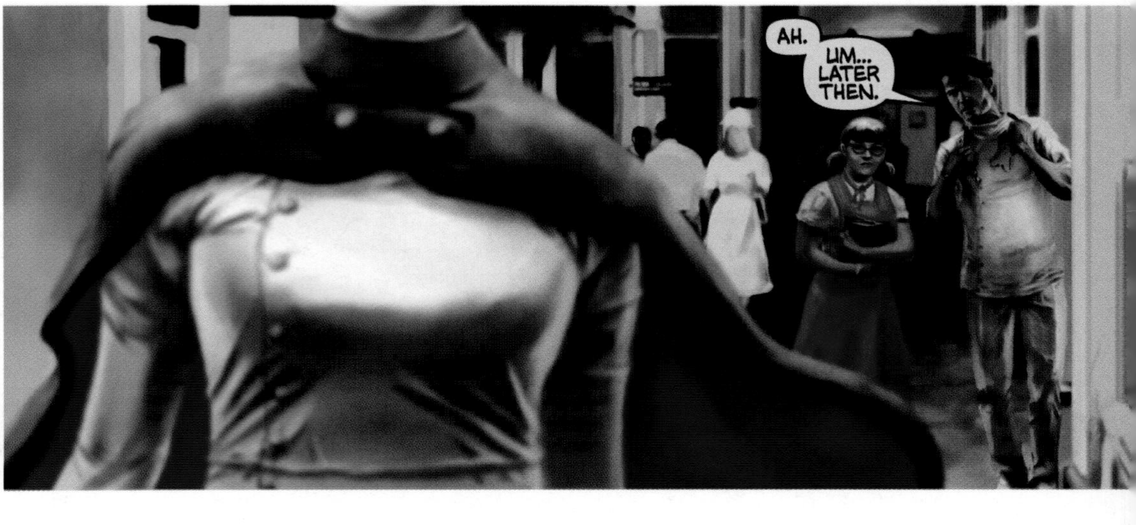
AH.
UM... LATER THEN.

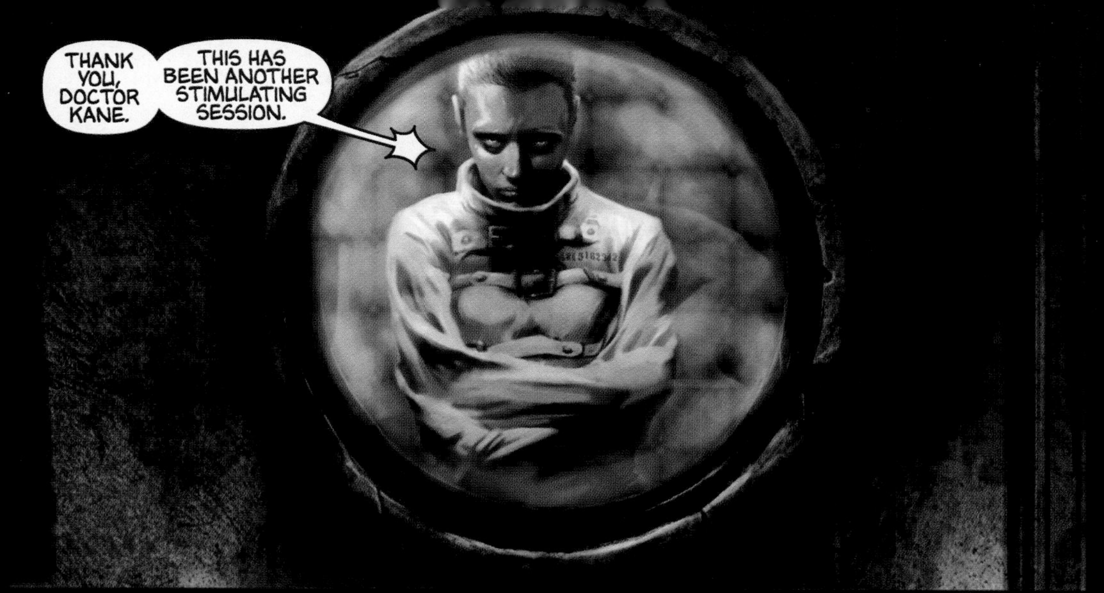
THANK YOU, DOCTOR KANE.
THIS HAS BEEN ANOTHER STIMULATING SESSION.
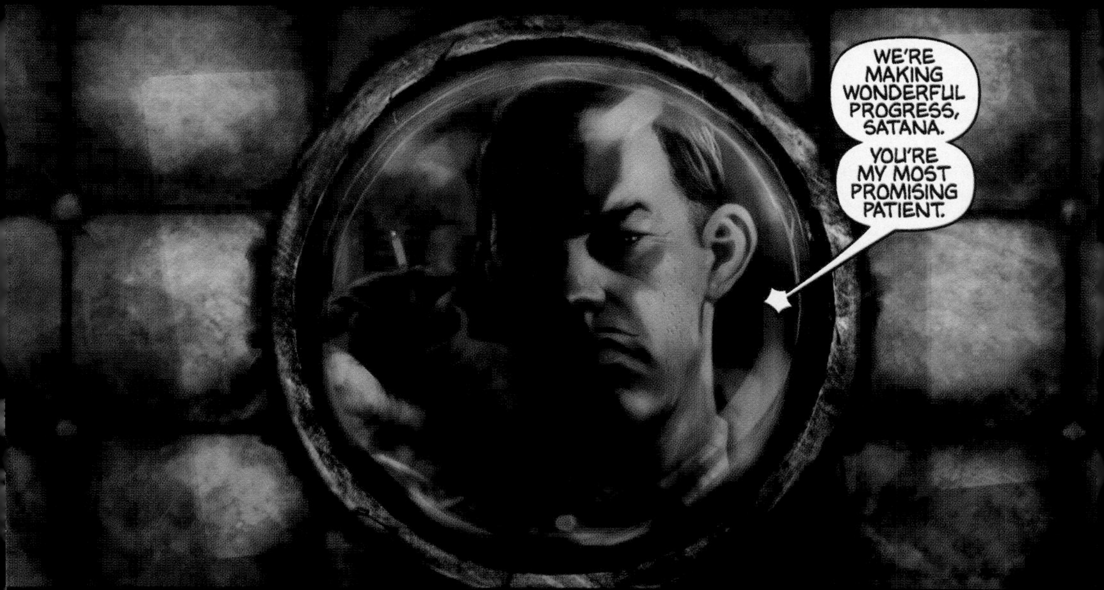
WE'RE MAKING WONDERFUL PROGRESS, SATANA.
YOU'RE MY MOST PROMISING PATIENT.
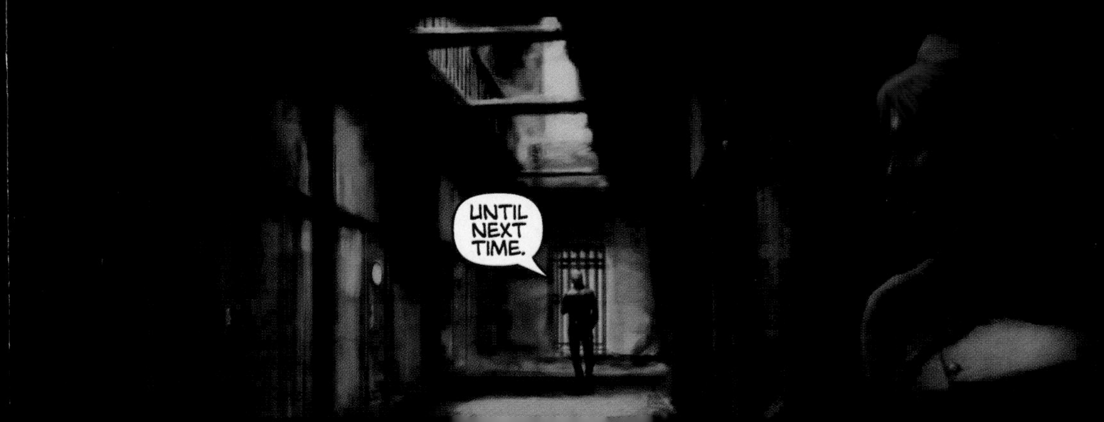
UNTIL NEXT TIME.

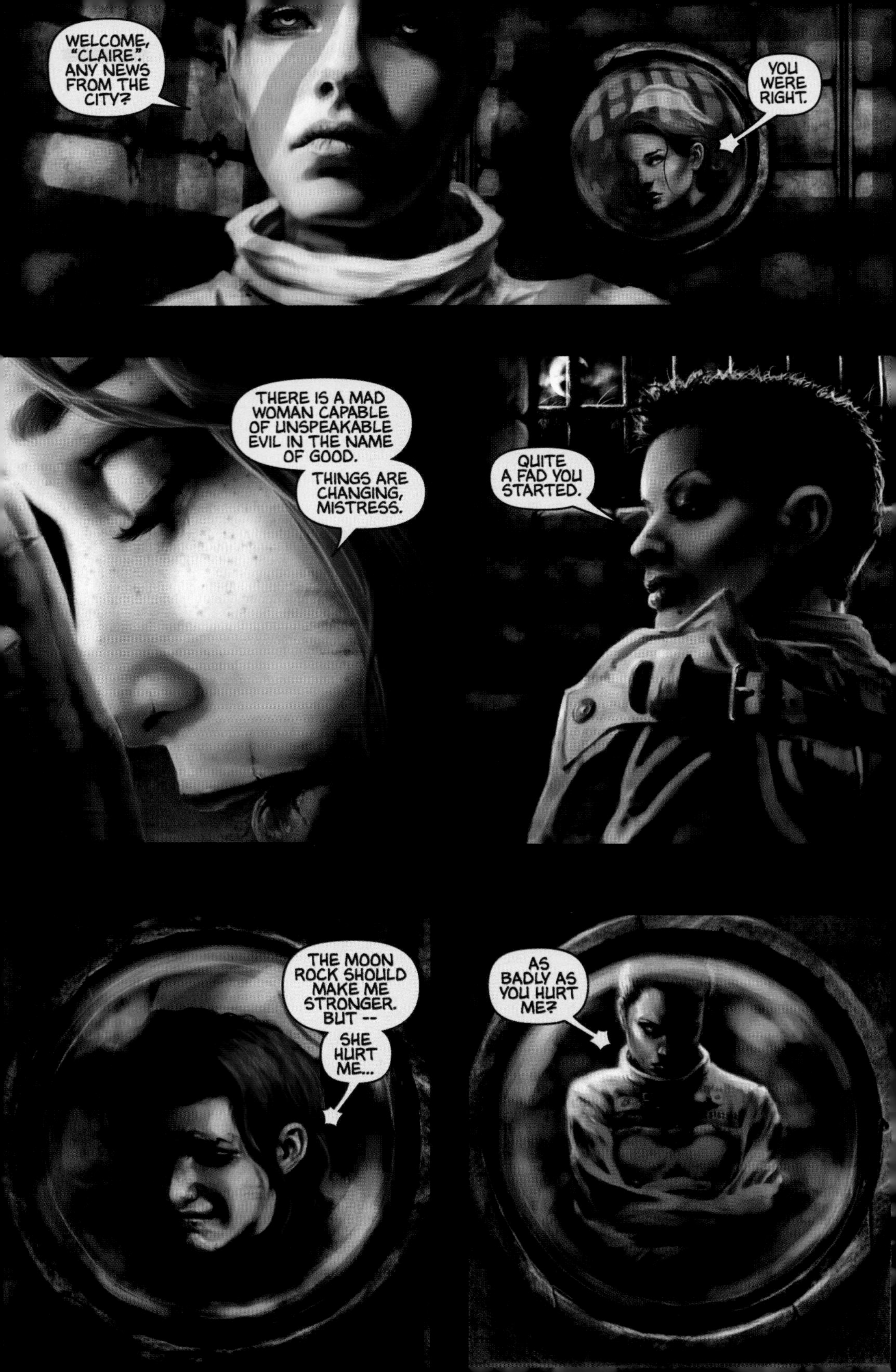
WELCOME, "CLAIRE". ANY NEWS FROM THE CITY?
YOU WERE RIGHT.
THERE IS A MAD WOMAN CAPABLE OF UNSPEAKABLE EVIL IN THE NAME OF GOOD.
THINGS ARE CHANGING, MISTRESS.
QUITE A FAD YOU STARTED.
THE MOON ROCK SHOULD MAKE ME STRONGER. BUT --
SHE HURT ME...
AS BADLY AS YOU HURT ME?

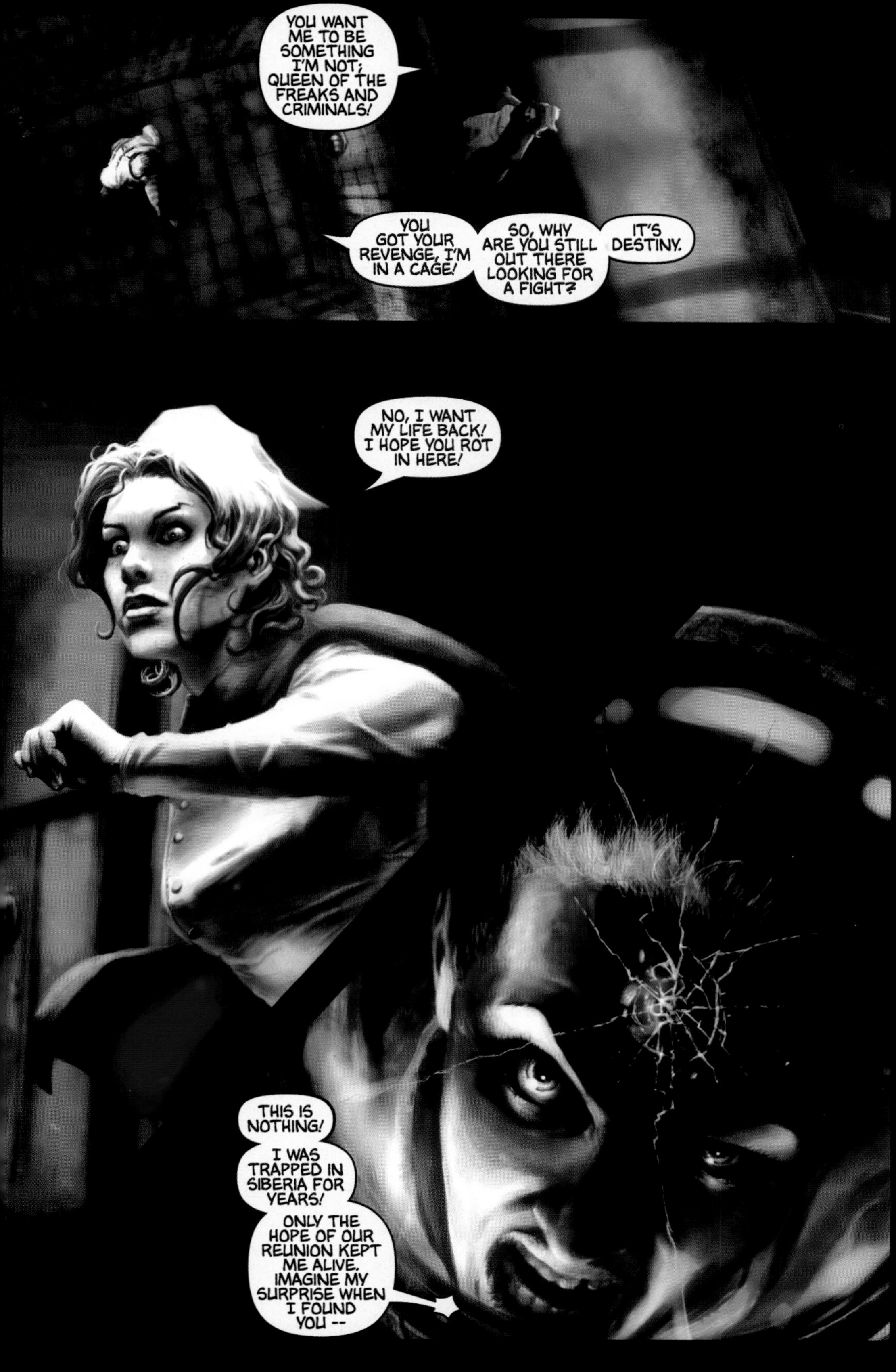
YOU WANT ME TO BE SOMETHING I'M NOT; QUEEN OF THE FREAKS AND CRIMINALS!
YOU GOT YOUR REVENGE, I'M IN A CAGE!
SO, WHY ARE YOU STILL OUT THERE LOOKING FOR A FIGHT?
IT'S DESTINY.
NO, I WANT MY LIFE BACK! I HOPE YOU ROT IN HERE!
THIS IS NOTHING!
I WAS TRAPPED IN SIBERIA FOR YEARS!
ONLY THE HOPE OF OUR REUNION KEPT ME ALIVE. IMAGINE MY SURPRISE WHEN I FOUND YOU --

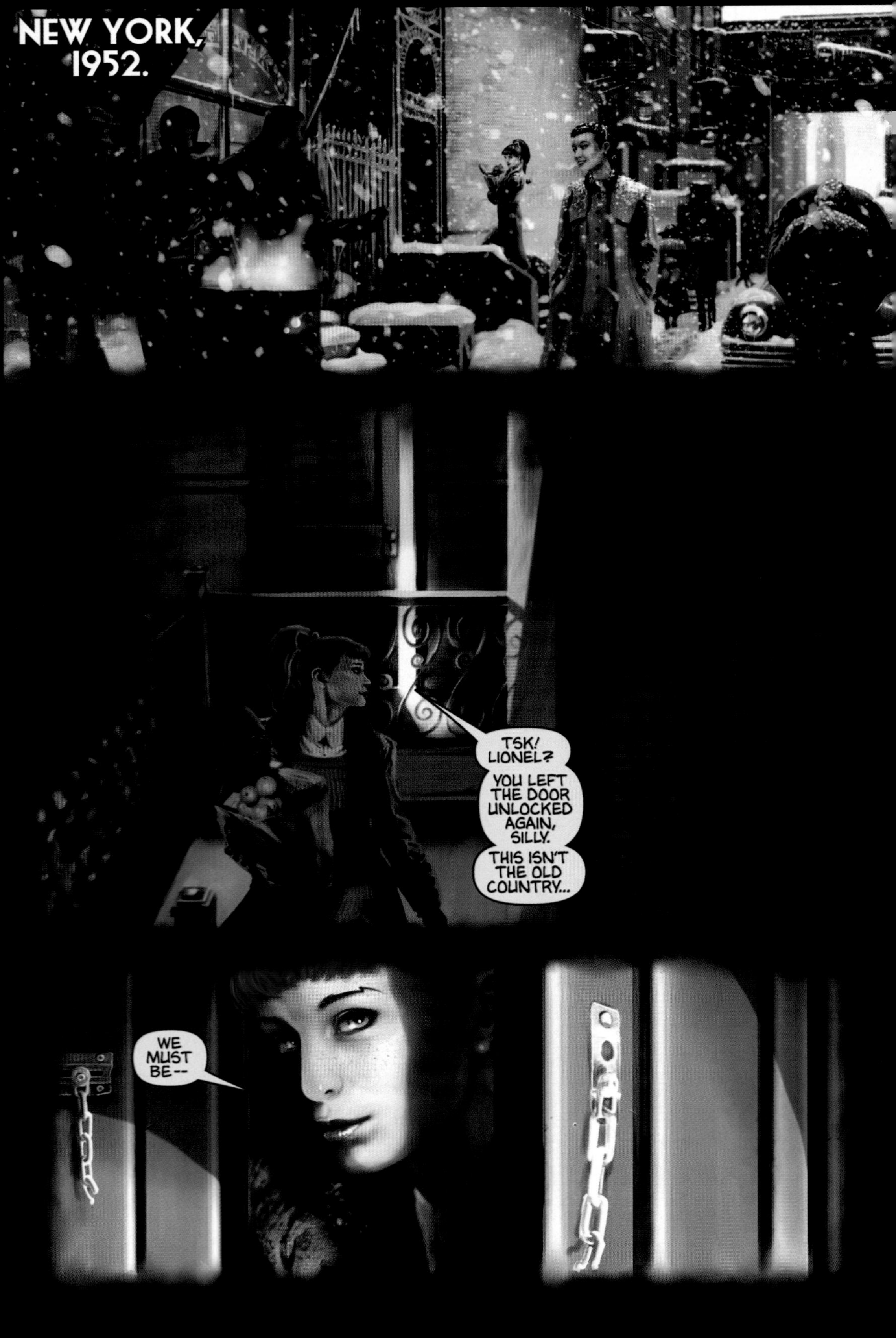
NEW YORK, 1952.
TSK! LIONEL?
YOU LEFT THE DOOR UNLOCKED AGAIN, SILLY.
THIS ISN'T THE OLD COUNTRY...
WE MUST BE--

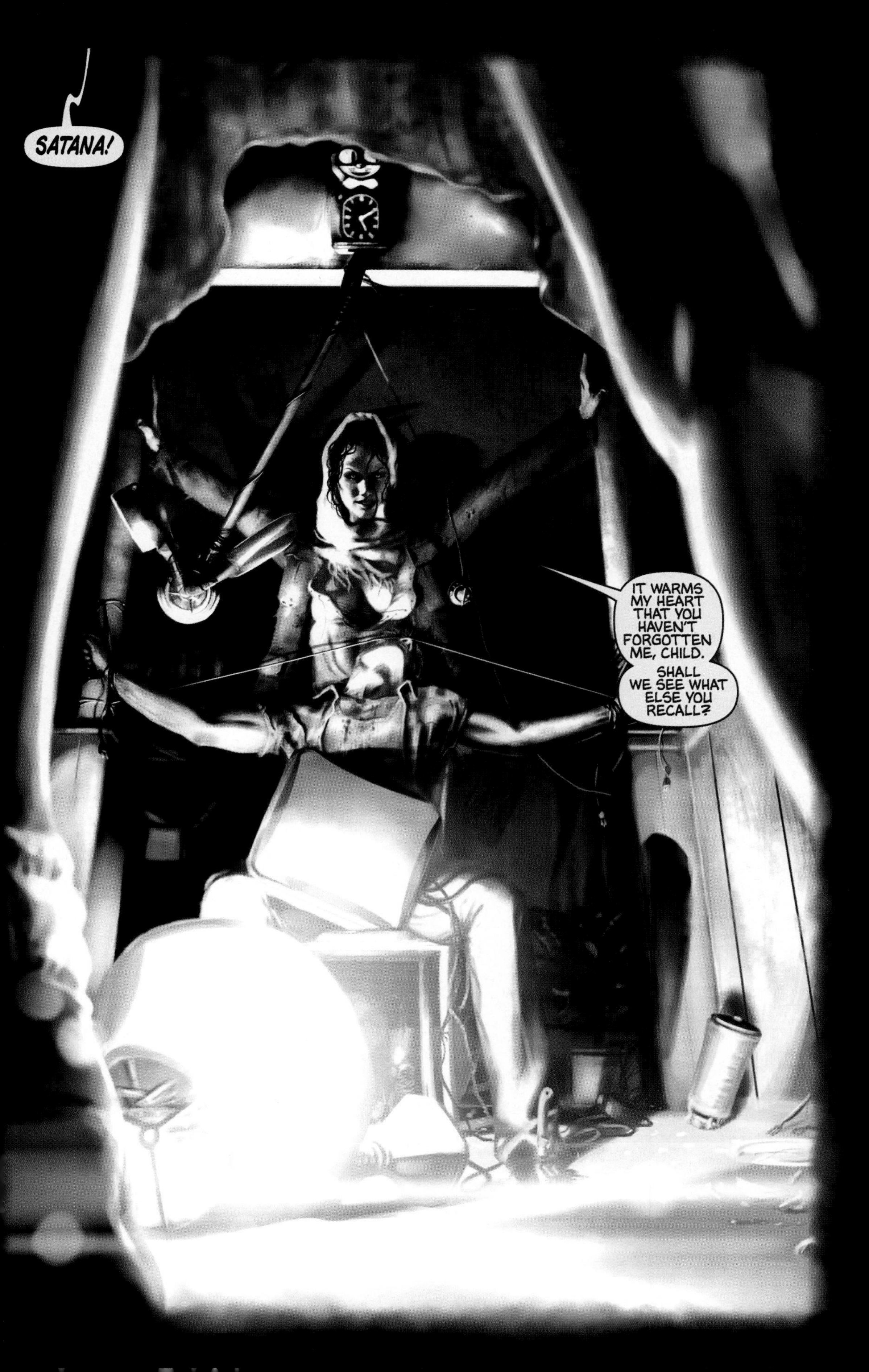
SATANA!
IT WARMS MY HEART THAT YOU HAVEN'T FORGOTTEN ME, CHILD.
SHALL WE SEE WHAT ELSE YOU RECALL?

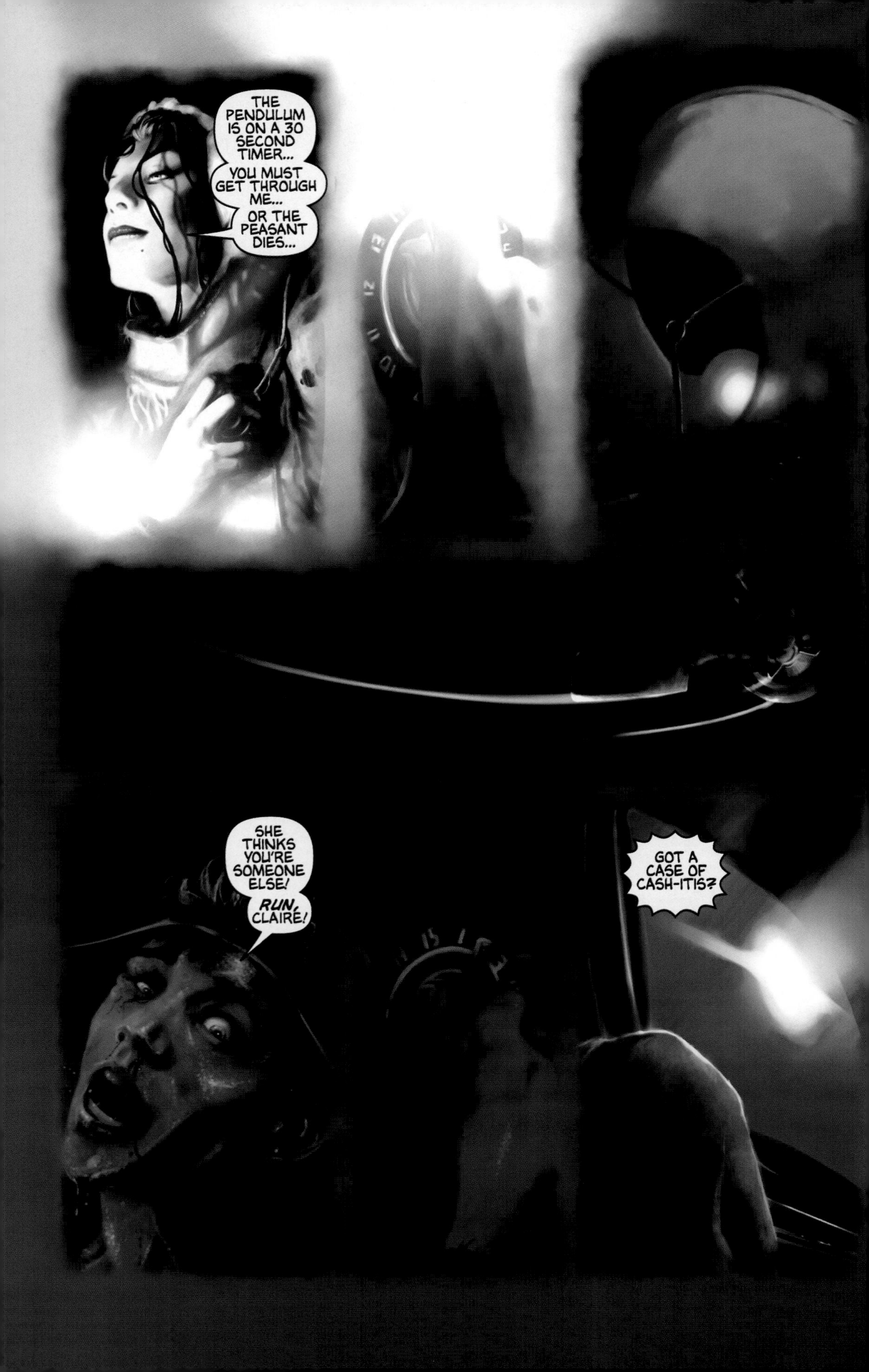
THE PENDULUM IS ON A 30 SECOND TIMER...
YOU MUST GET THROUGH ME...
OR THE PEASANT DIES...
SHE THINKS YOU'RE SOMEONE ELSE!
RUN, CLAIRE!
GOT A CASE OF CASH-ITIS?

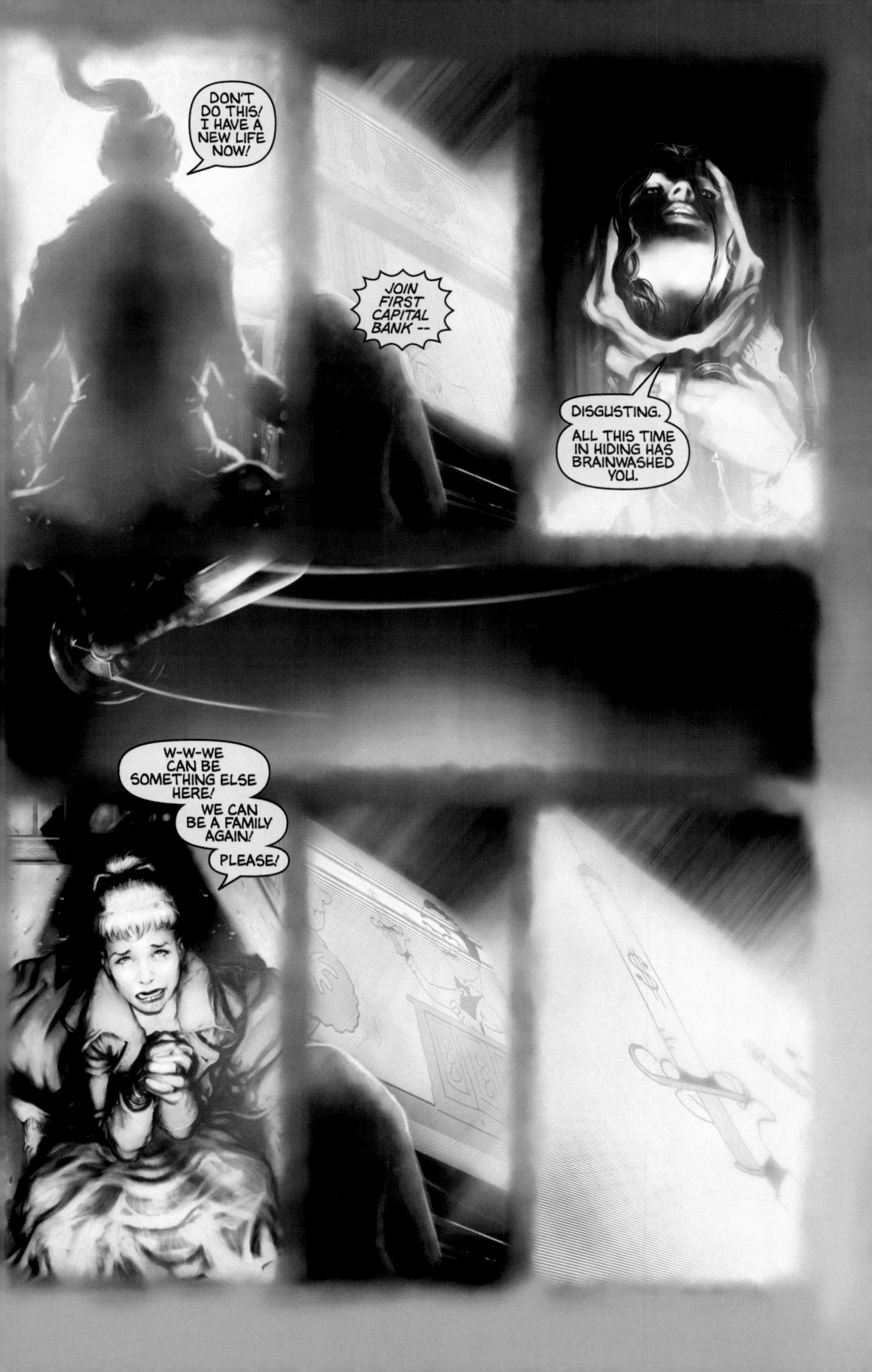
DON'T DO THIS! I HAVE A NEW LIFE NOW!
JOIN FIRST CAPITAL BANK --
DISGUSTING.
ALL THIS TIME IN HIDING HAS BRAINWASHED YOU.
W-W-WE CAN BE SOMETHING ELSE HERE!
WE CAN BE A FAMILY AGAIN!
PLEASE!

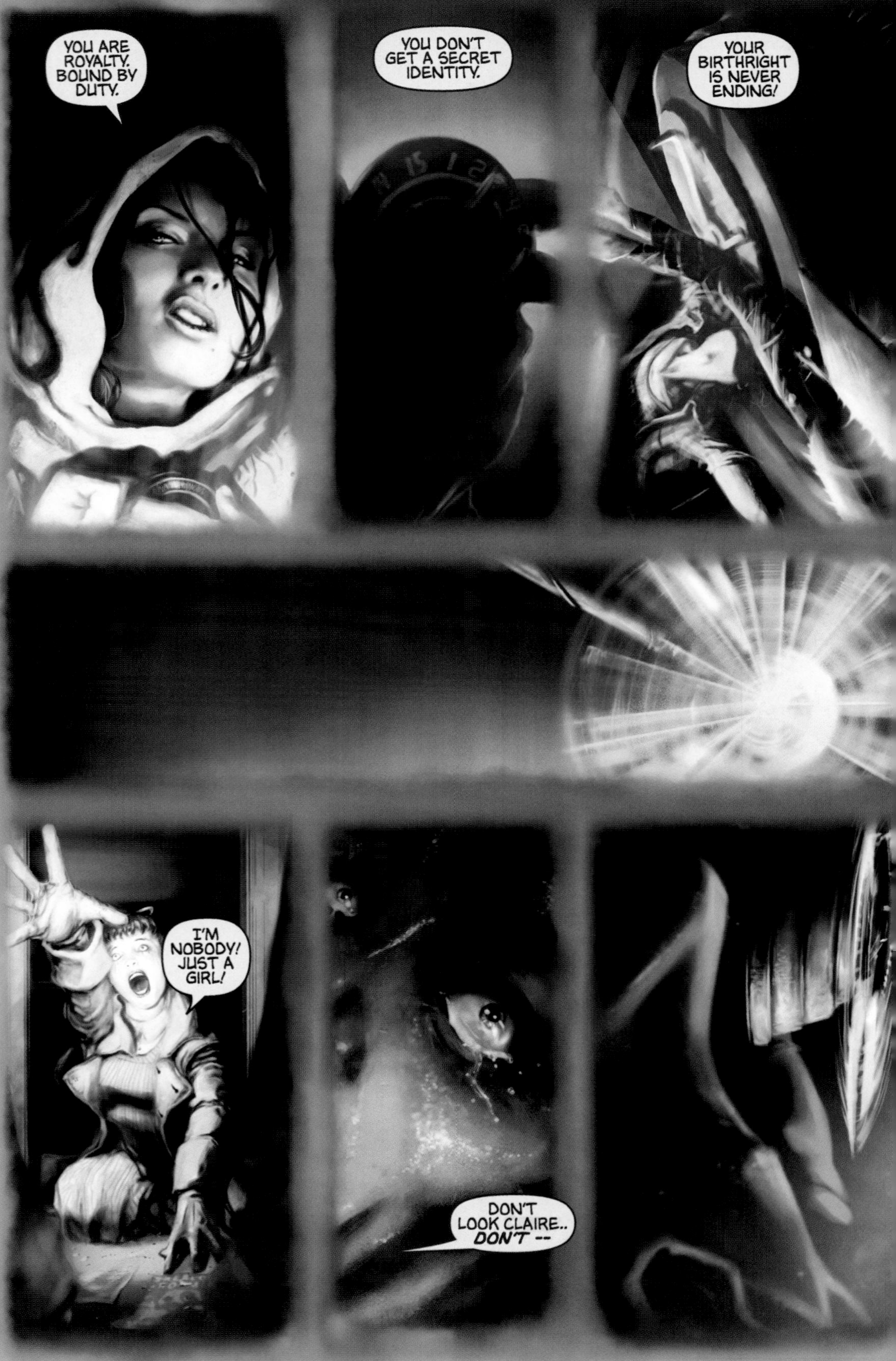
YOU ARE ROYALTY. BOUND BY DUTY.
YOU DON'T GET A SECRET IDENTITY.
YOUR BIRTHRIGHT IS NEVER ENDING!
I'M NOBODY! JUST A GIRL!
DON'T LOOK CLAIRE.. *DON'T* --

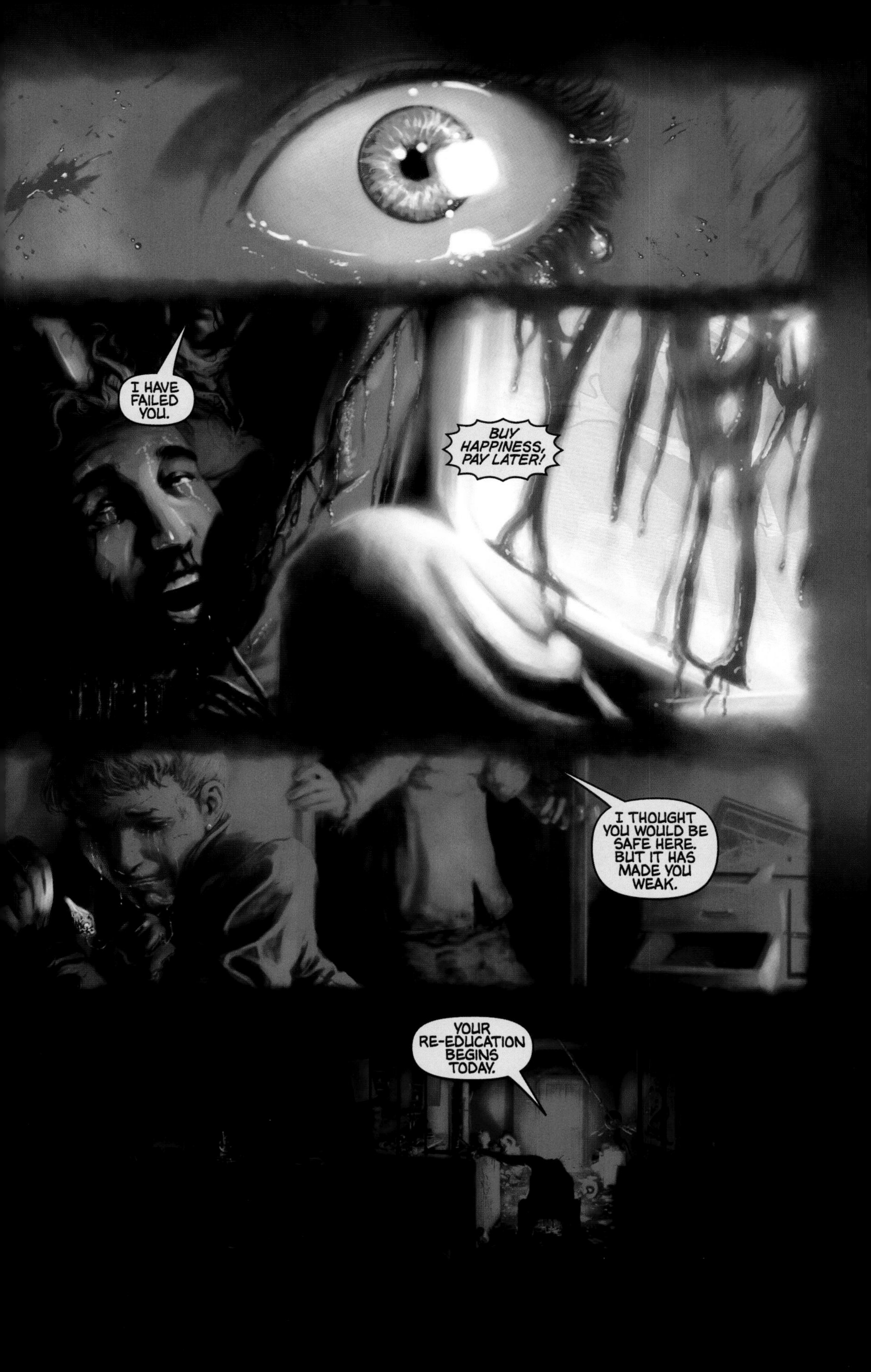
I HAVE FAILED YOU.
BUY HAPPINESS, PAY LATER!
I THOUGHT YOU WOULD BE SAFE HERE. BUT IT HAS MADE YOU WEAK.
YOUR RE-EDUCATION BEGINS TODAY.

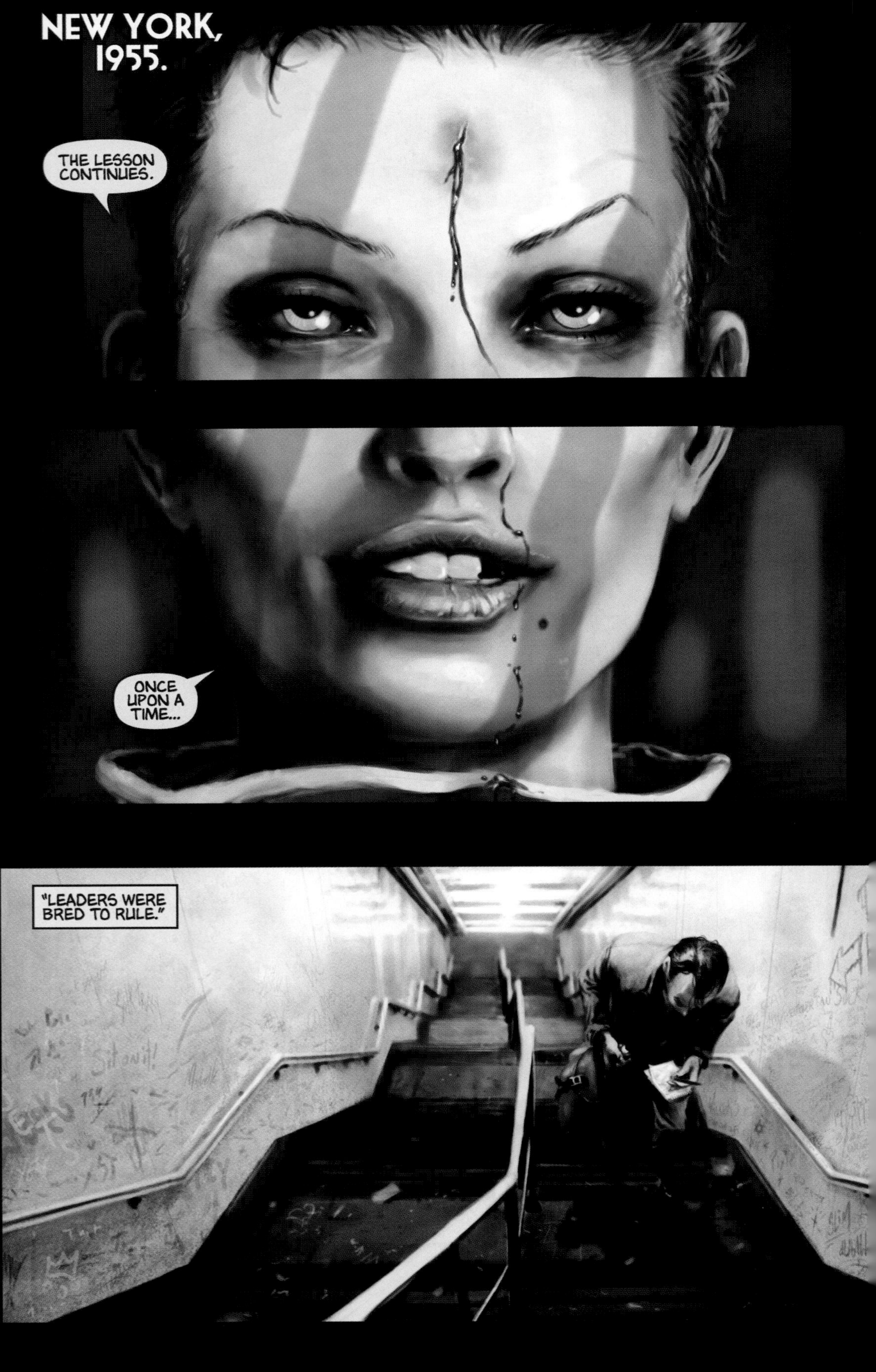
NEW YORK, 1955.
THE LESSON CONTINUES.
ONCE UPON A TIME...
"LEADERS WERE BRED TO RULE."

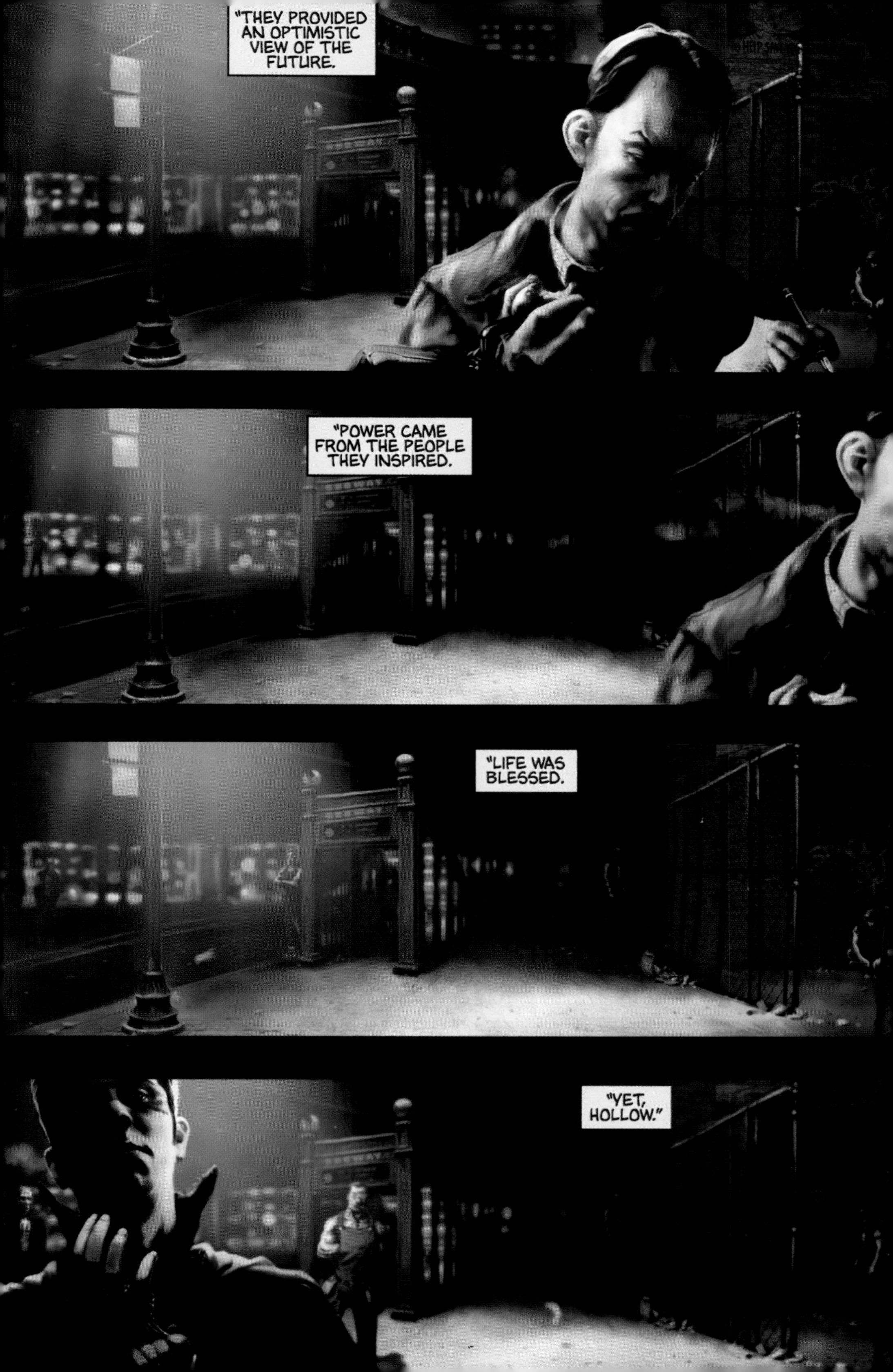
"THEY PROVIDED AN OPTIMISTIC VIEW OF THE FUTURE.
"POWER CAME FROM THE PEOPLE THEY INSPIRED.
"LIFE WAS BLESSED.
"YET, HOLLOW."

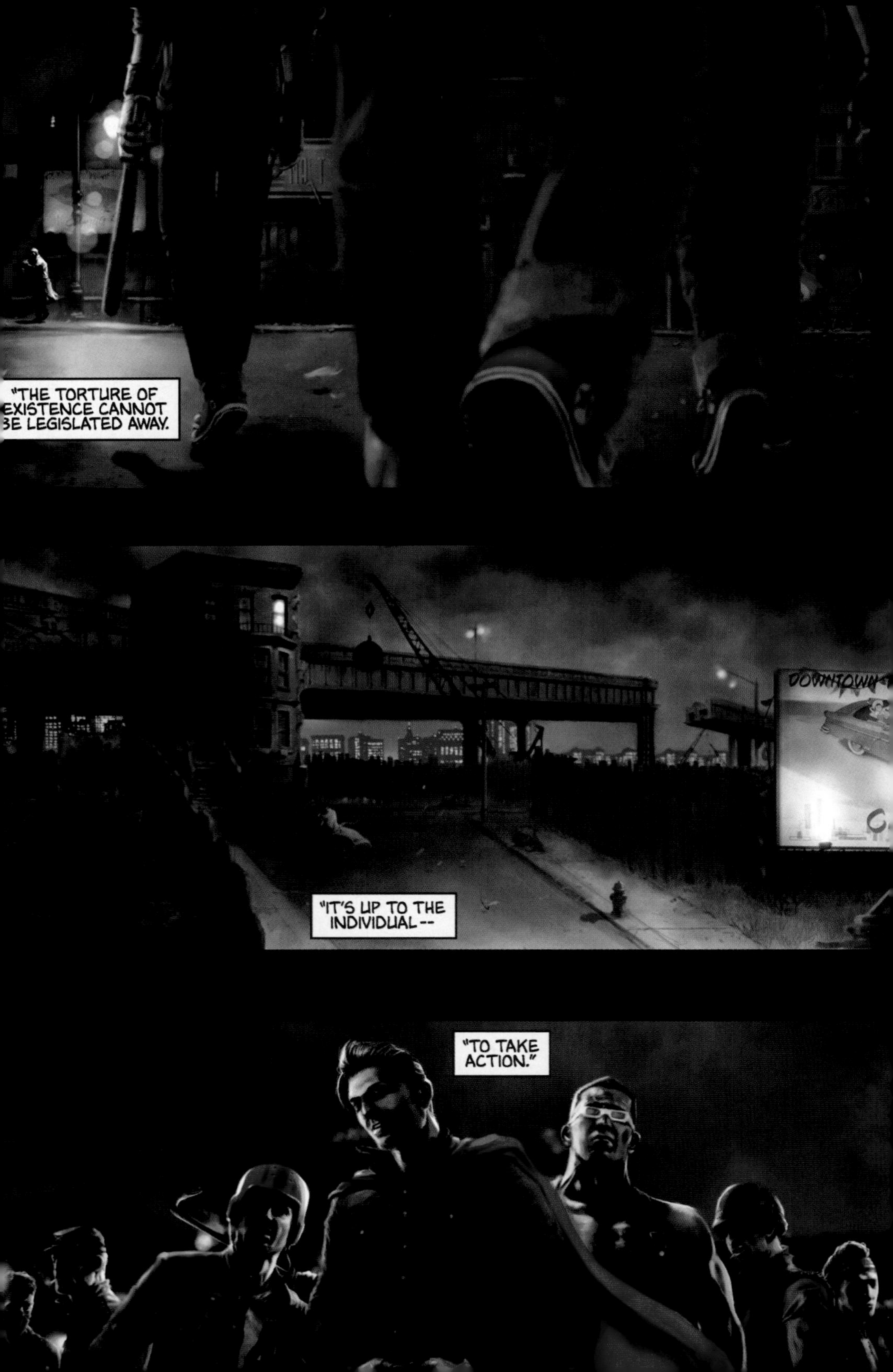
"THE TORTURE OF EXISTENCE CANNOT BE LEGISLATED AWAY.
DOWNTOWN
"IT'S UP TO THE INDIVIDUAL--
"TO TAKE ACTION."

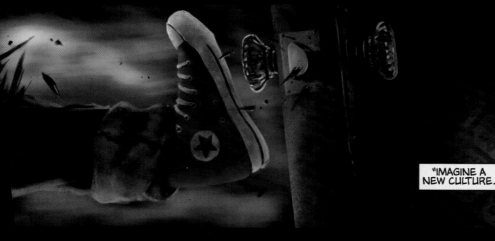

"IMAGINE A NEW CULTURE.

"ONE BUILT AROUND YOUR PERSONAL STRUGGLE.

"THE LAMB BECOMES THE LION TO LEAD THEM."

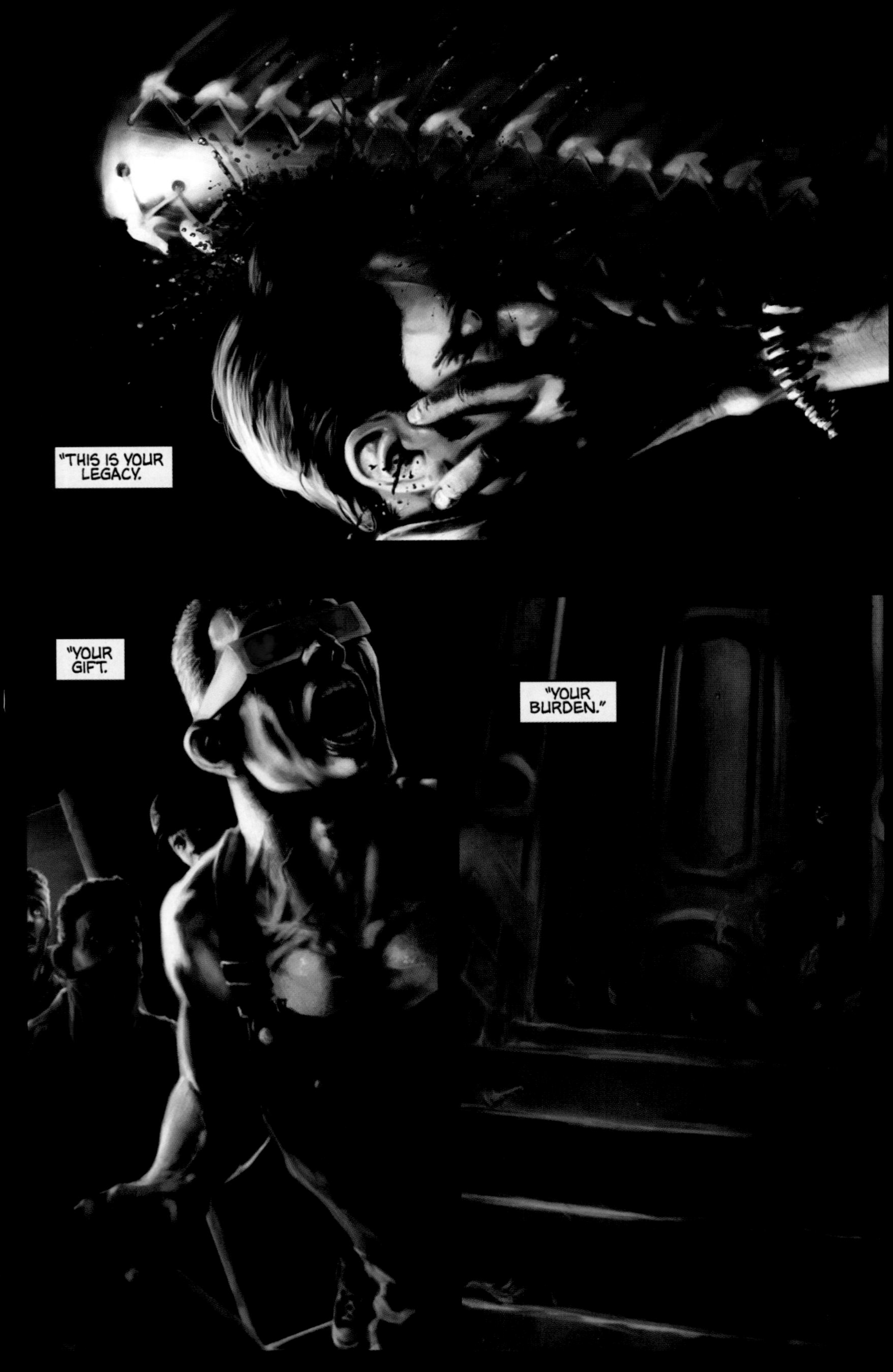
"THIS IS YOUR LEGACY.
"YOUR GIFT.
"YOUR BURDEN."

"LIKE A SEED ON THE WIND WE HAVE BEEN CARRIED HERE.

"AND SO I WILL BUILD YOU A NEW KINGDOM...

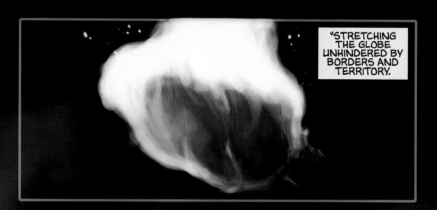

"STRETCHING THE GLOBE UNHINDERED BY BORDERS AND TERRITORY.

"THIS IS A NEW, WORLD ORDER BASED ON FAITH IN TRUTH AND JUSTICE; EVERYONE CAN BE A SUPER HERO."

BOW YOUR HEADS!

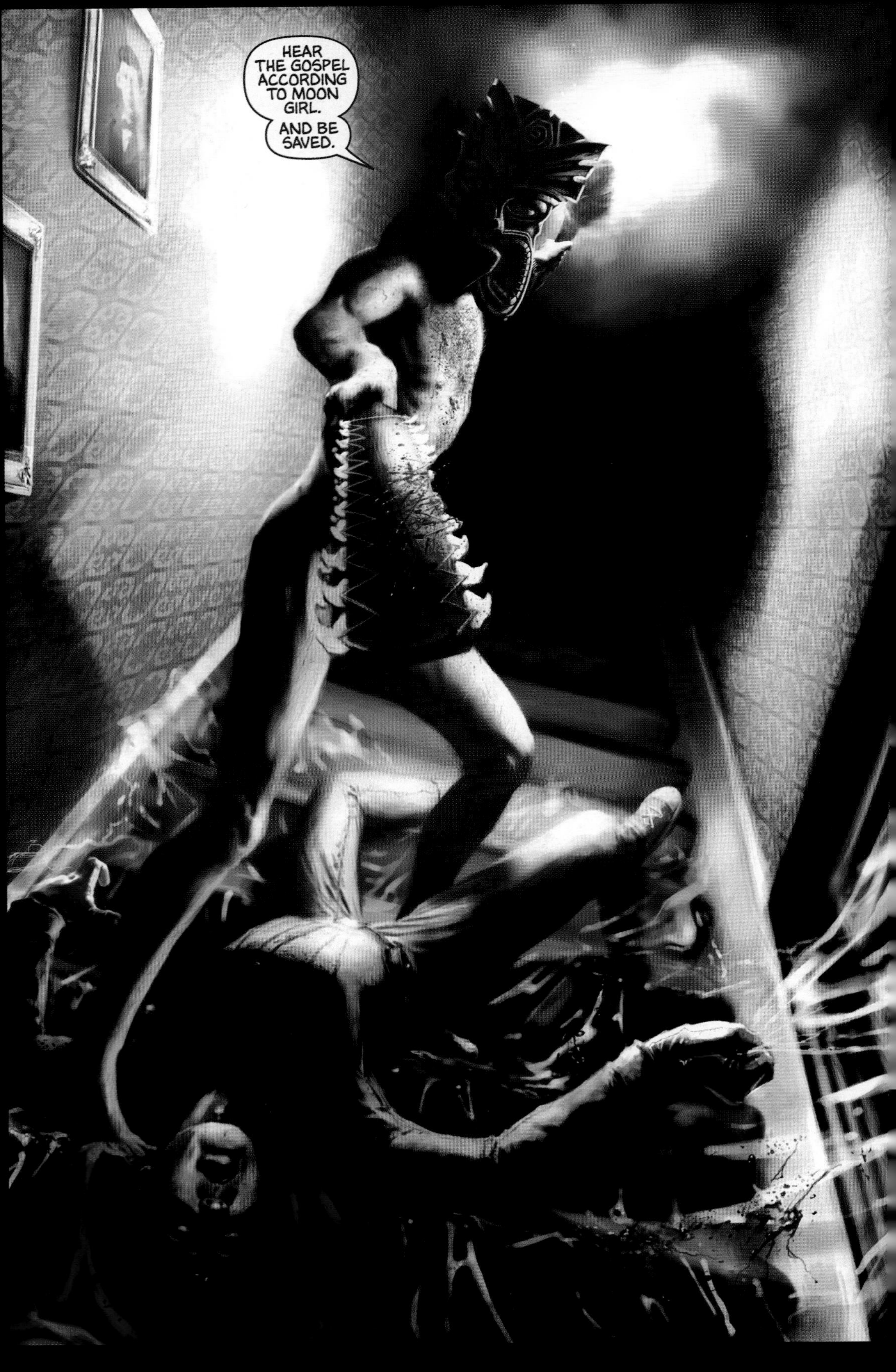
HEAR THE GOSPEL ACCORDING TO MOON GIRL.
AND BE SAVED.

3

MOON GIRL FIGHTS CRIME

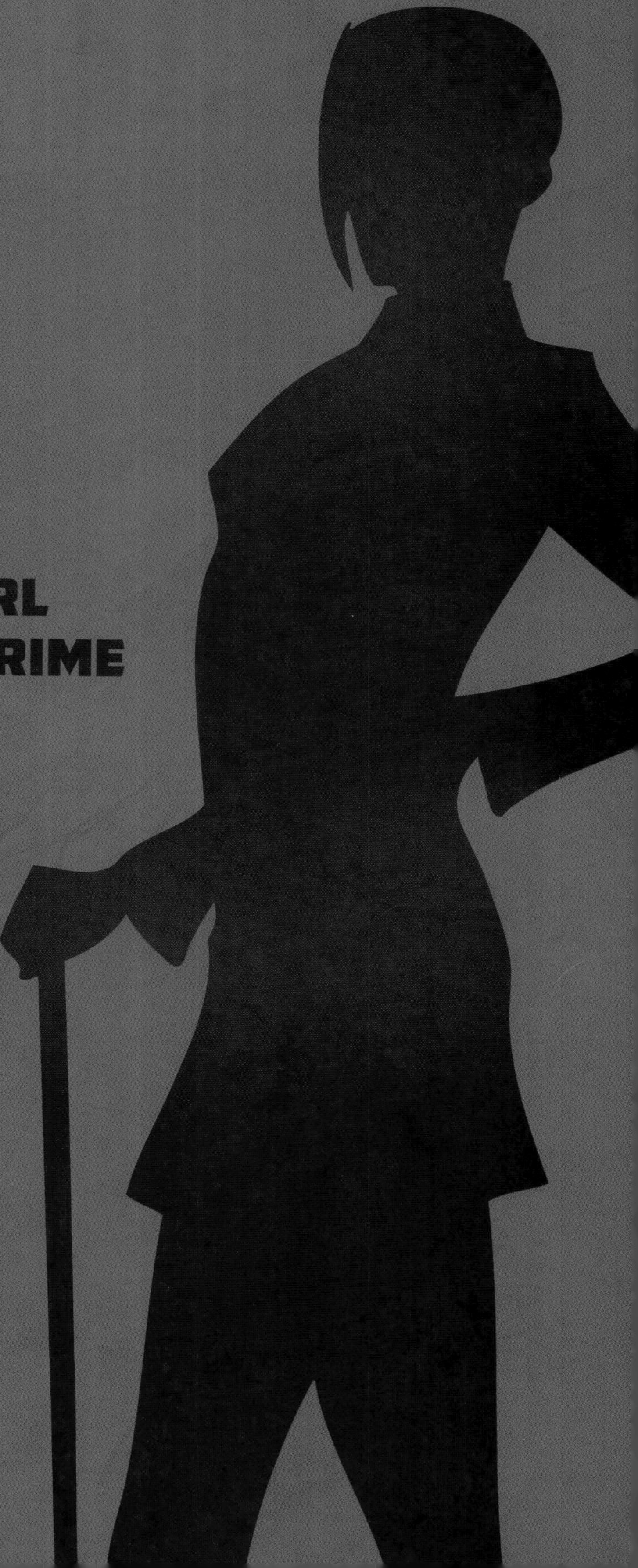

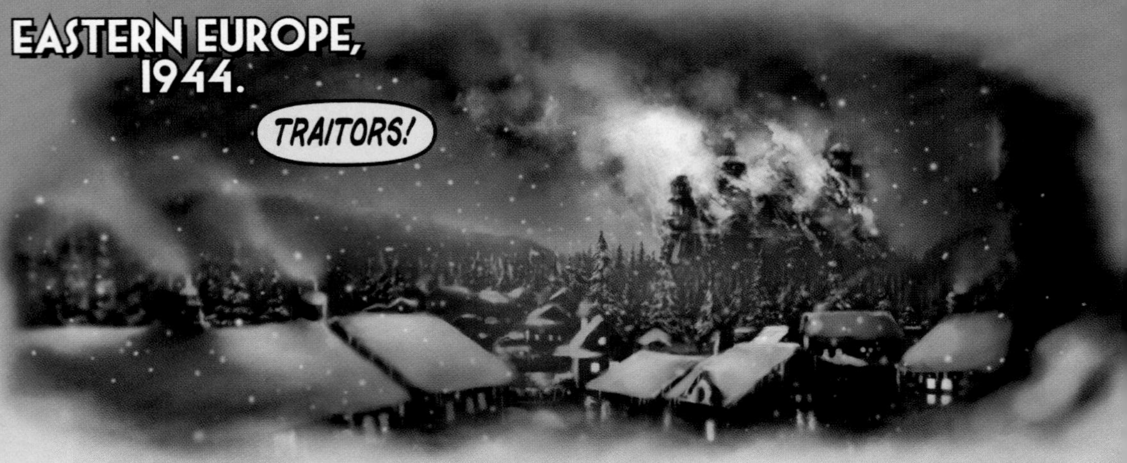
EASTERN EUROPE, 1944.
TRAITORS!

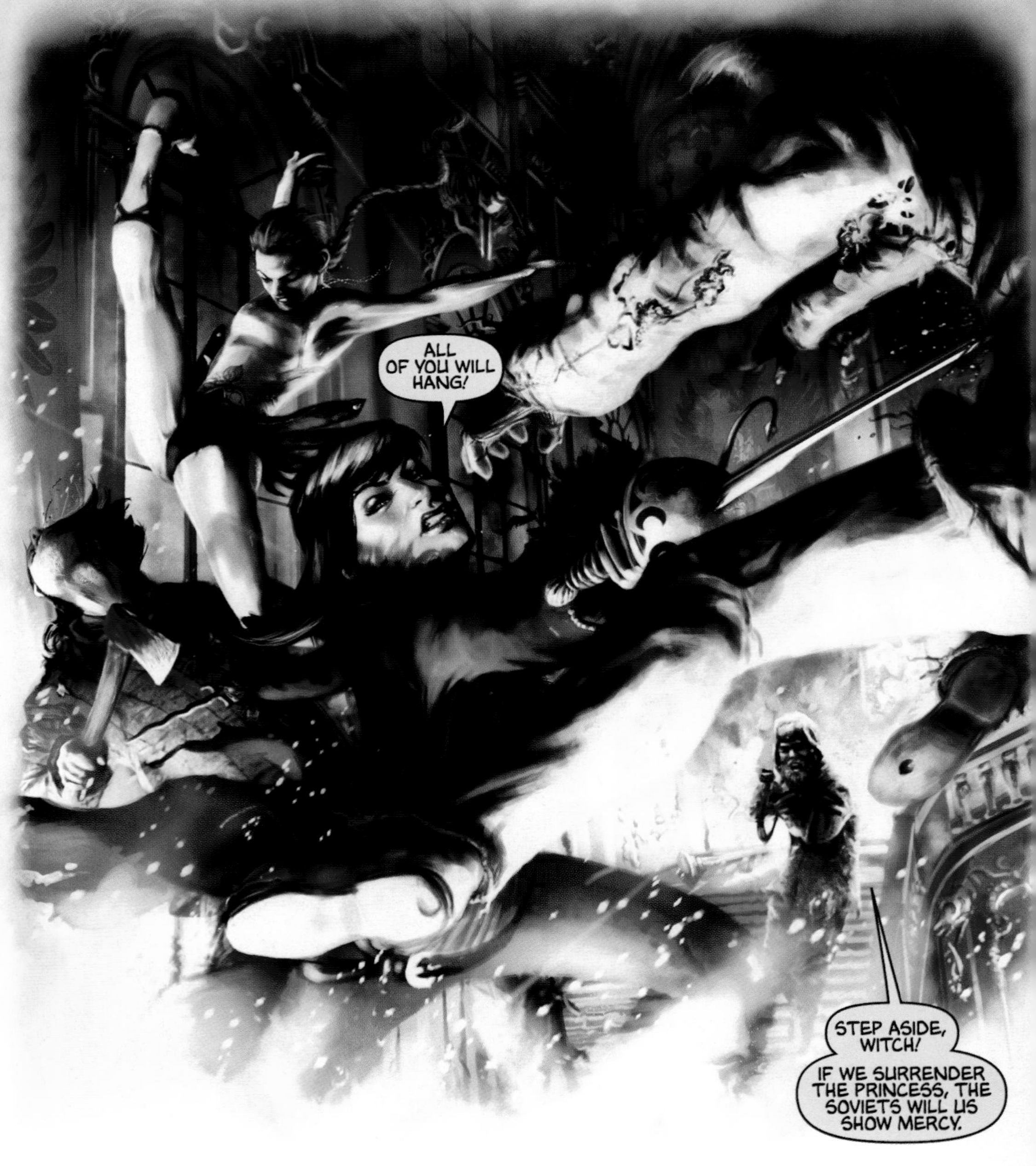
ALL OF YOU WILL HANG!
STEP ASIDE, WITCH!
IF WE SURRENDER THE PRINCESS, THE SOVIETS WILL US SHOW MERCY.

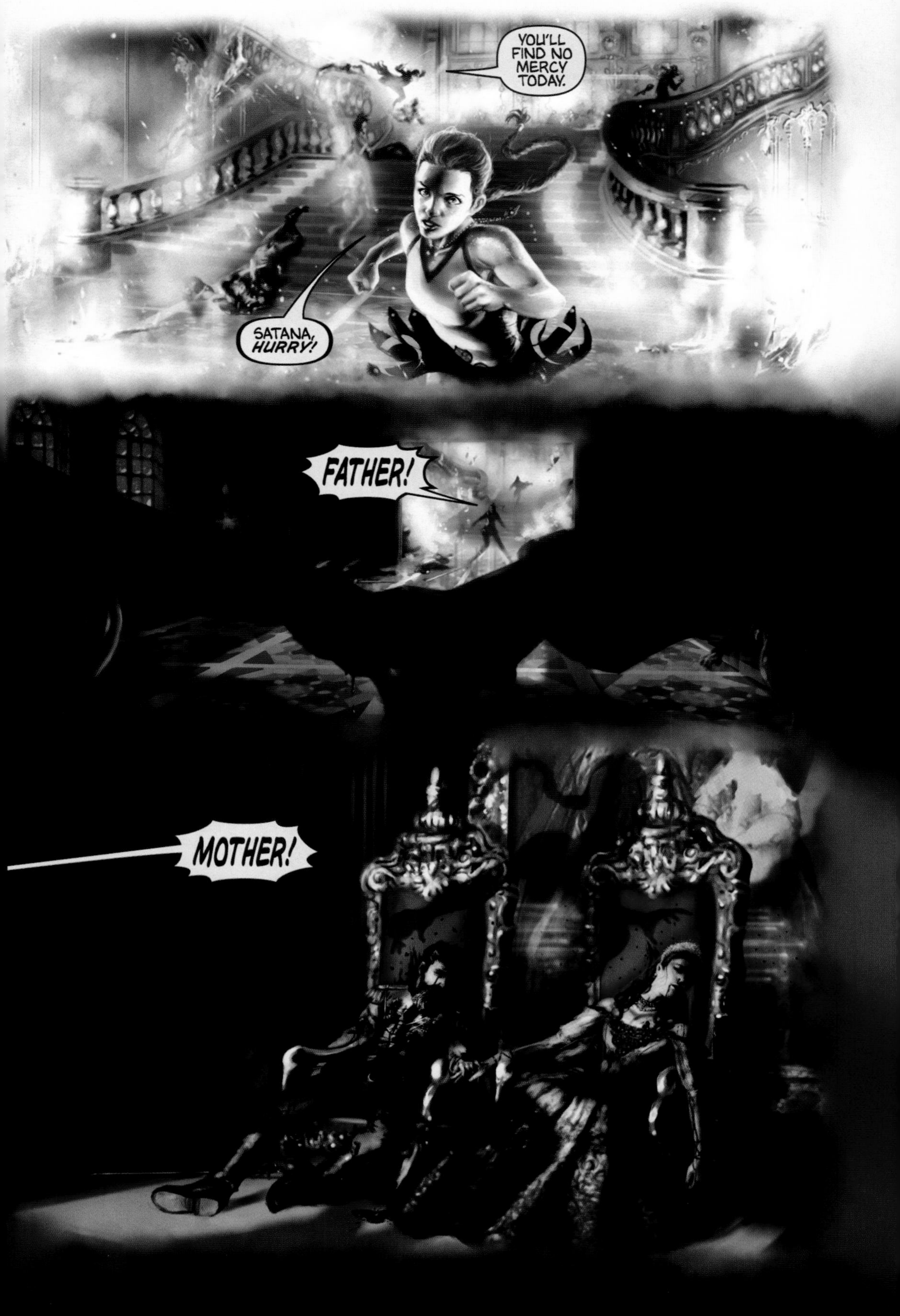
YOU'LL FIND NO MERCY TODAY.
SATANA, HURRY!
FATHER!
MOTHER!

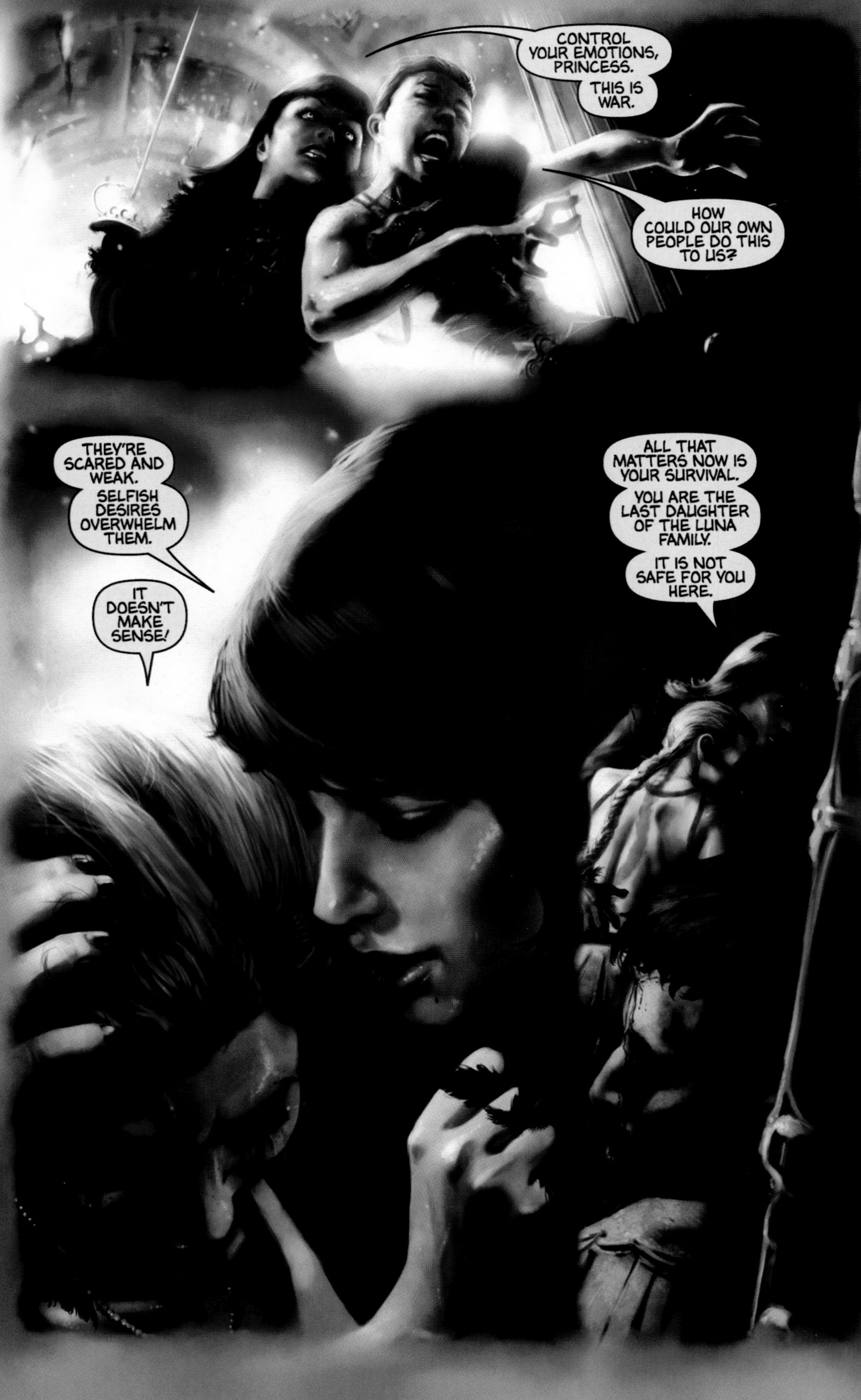
CONTROL YOUR EMOTIONS, PRINCESS.
THIS IS WAR.
HOW COULD OUR OWN PEOPLE DO THIS TO US?
THEY'RE SCARED AND WEAK.
SELFISH DESIRES OVERWHELM THEM.
IT DOESN'T MAKE SENSE!
ALL THAT MATTERS NOW IS YOUR SURVIVAL.
YOU ARE THE LAST DAUGHTER OF THE LUNA FAMILY.
IT IS NOT SAFE FOR YOU HERE.

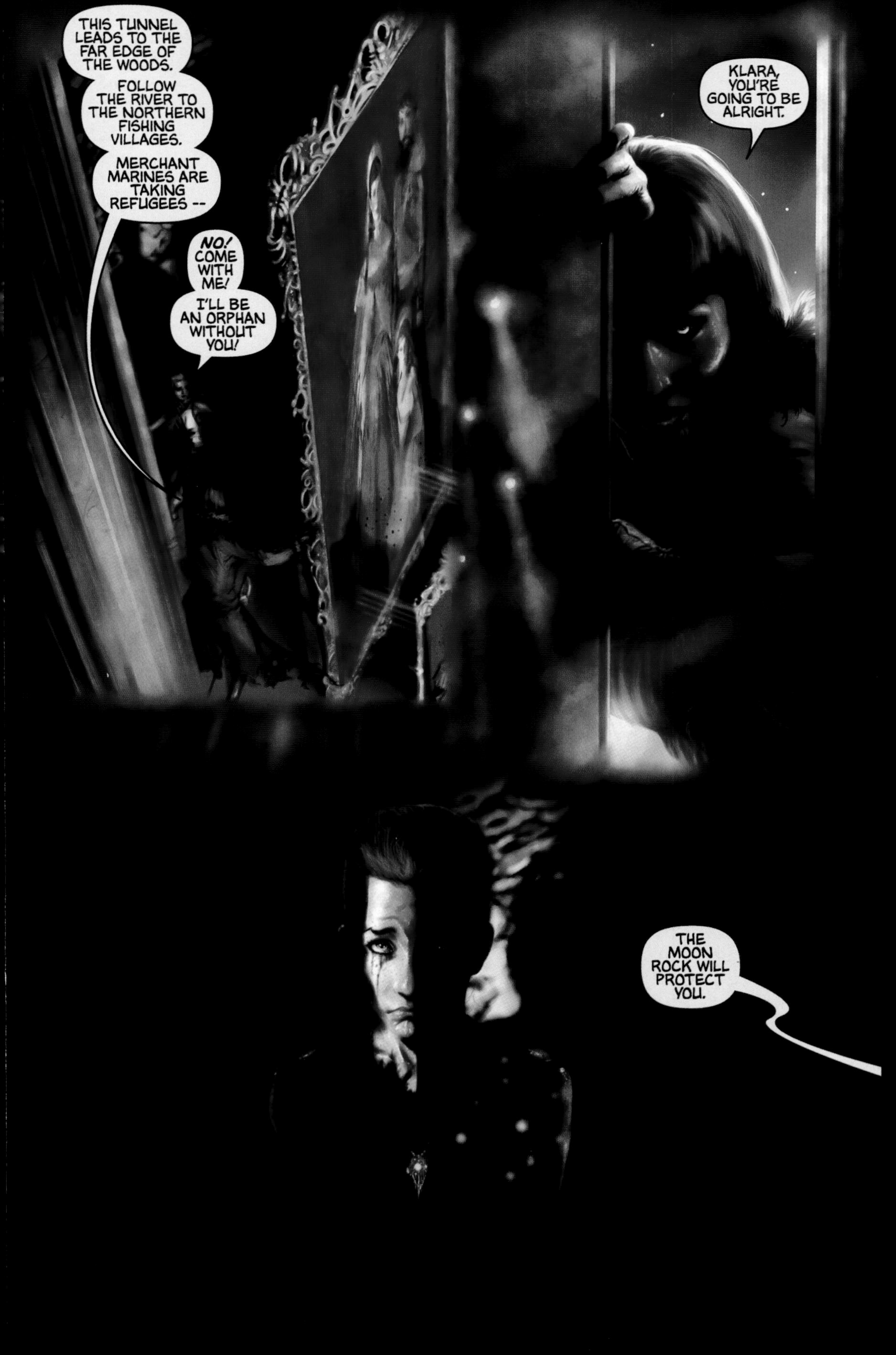
THIS TUNNEL LEADS TO THE FAR EDGE OF THE WOODS.
FOLLOW THE RIVER TO THE NORTHERN FISHING VILLAGES.
MERCHANT MARINES ARE TAKING REFUGEES --
NO! COME WITH ME!
I'LL BE AN ORPHAN WITHOUT YOU!
KLARA, YOU'RE GOING TO BE ALRIGHT.
THE MOON ROCK WILL PROTECT YOU.

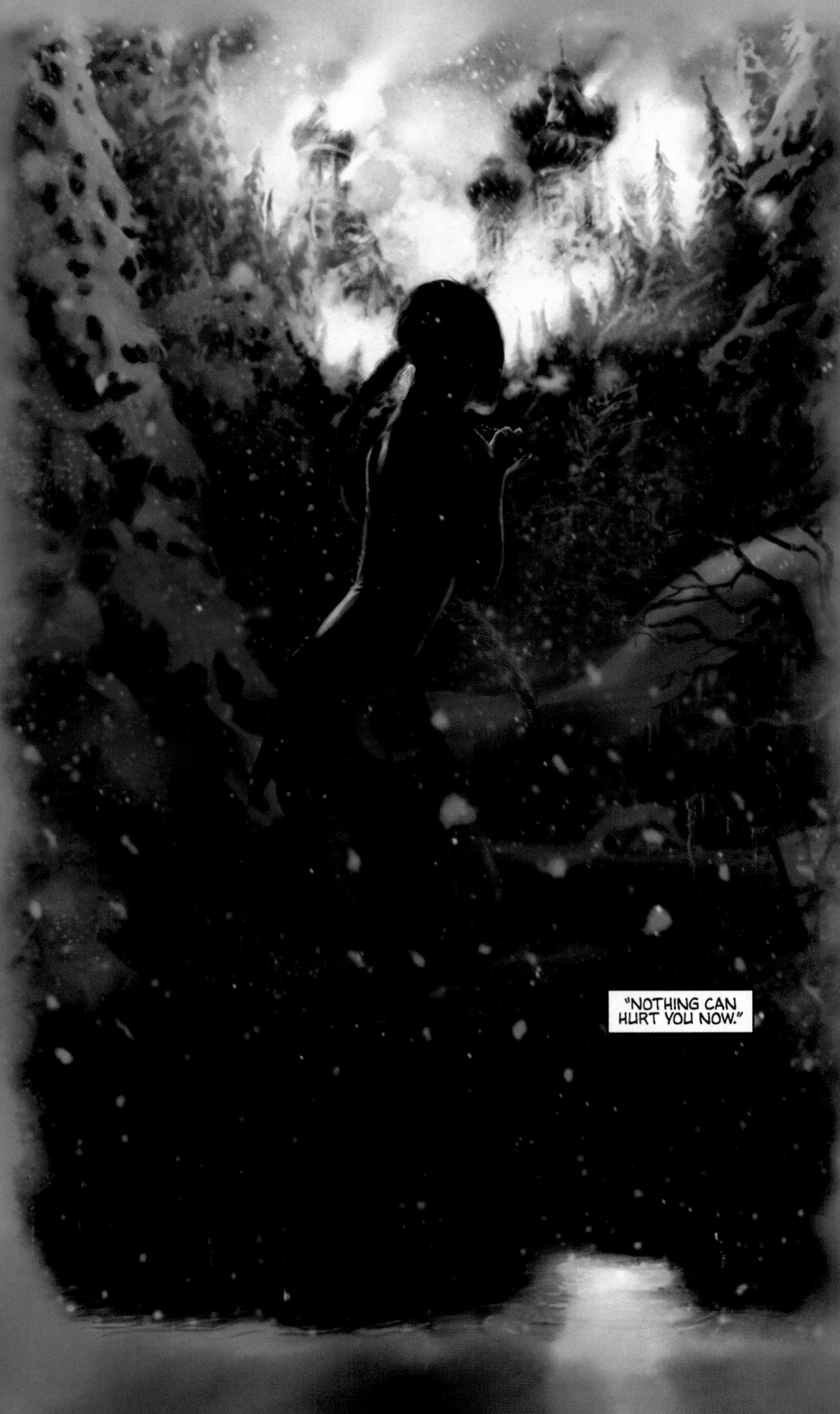
"NOTHING CAN HURT YOU NOW."

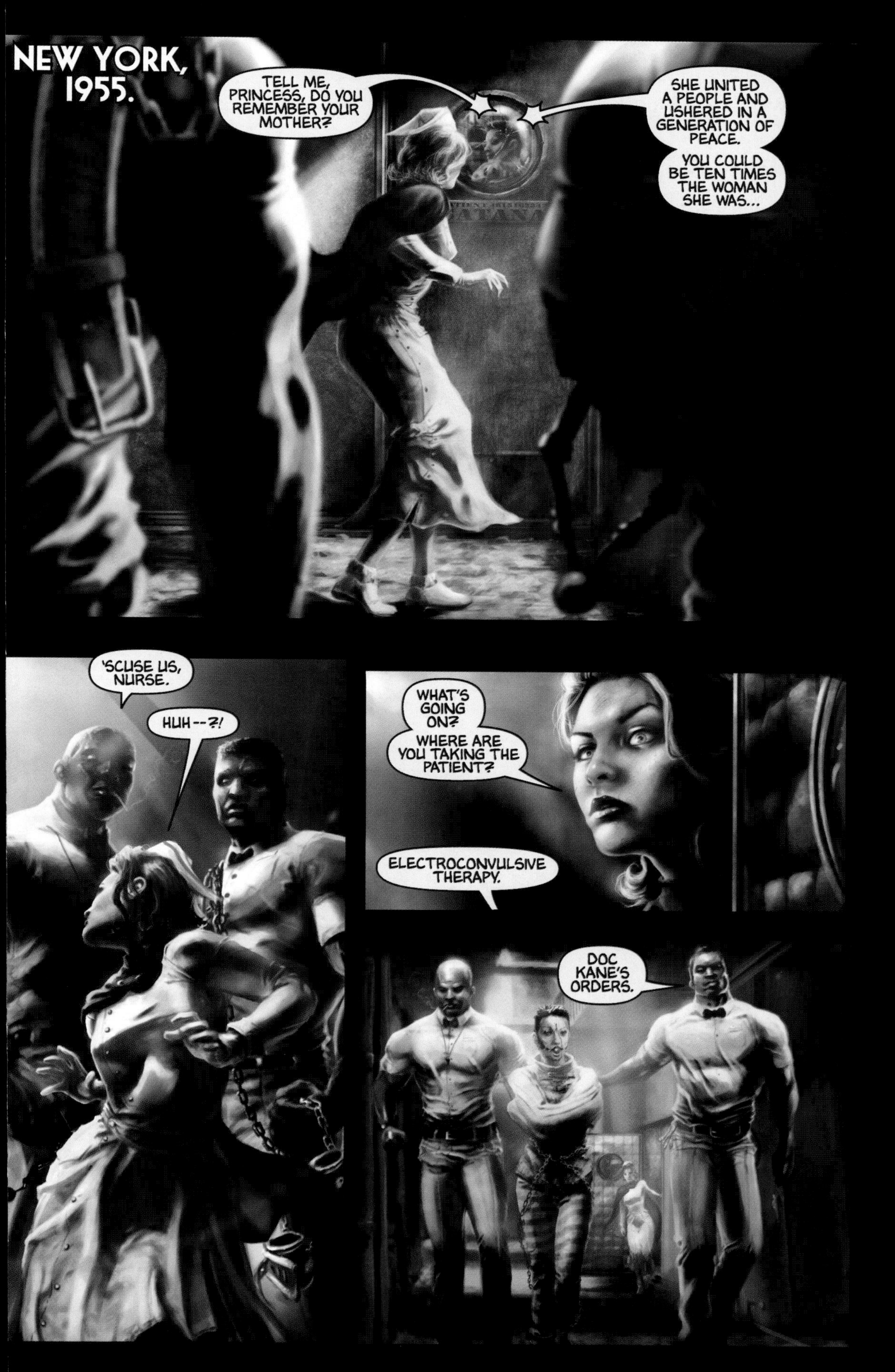
NEW YORK, 1955.
TELL ME, PRINCESS, DO YOU REMEMBER YOUR MOTHER?
SHE UNITED A PEOPLE AND USHERED IN A GENERATION OF PEACE.
YOU COULD BE TEN TIMES THE WOMAN SHE WAS...
'SCUSE US, NURSE.
HUH --?!
WHAT'S GOING ON?
WHERE ARE YOU TAKING THE PATIENT?
ELECTROCONVULSIVE THERAPY.
DOC KANE'S ORDERS.

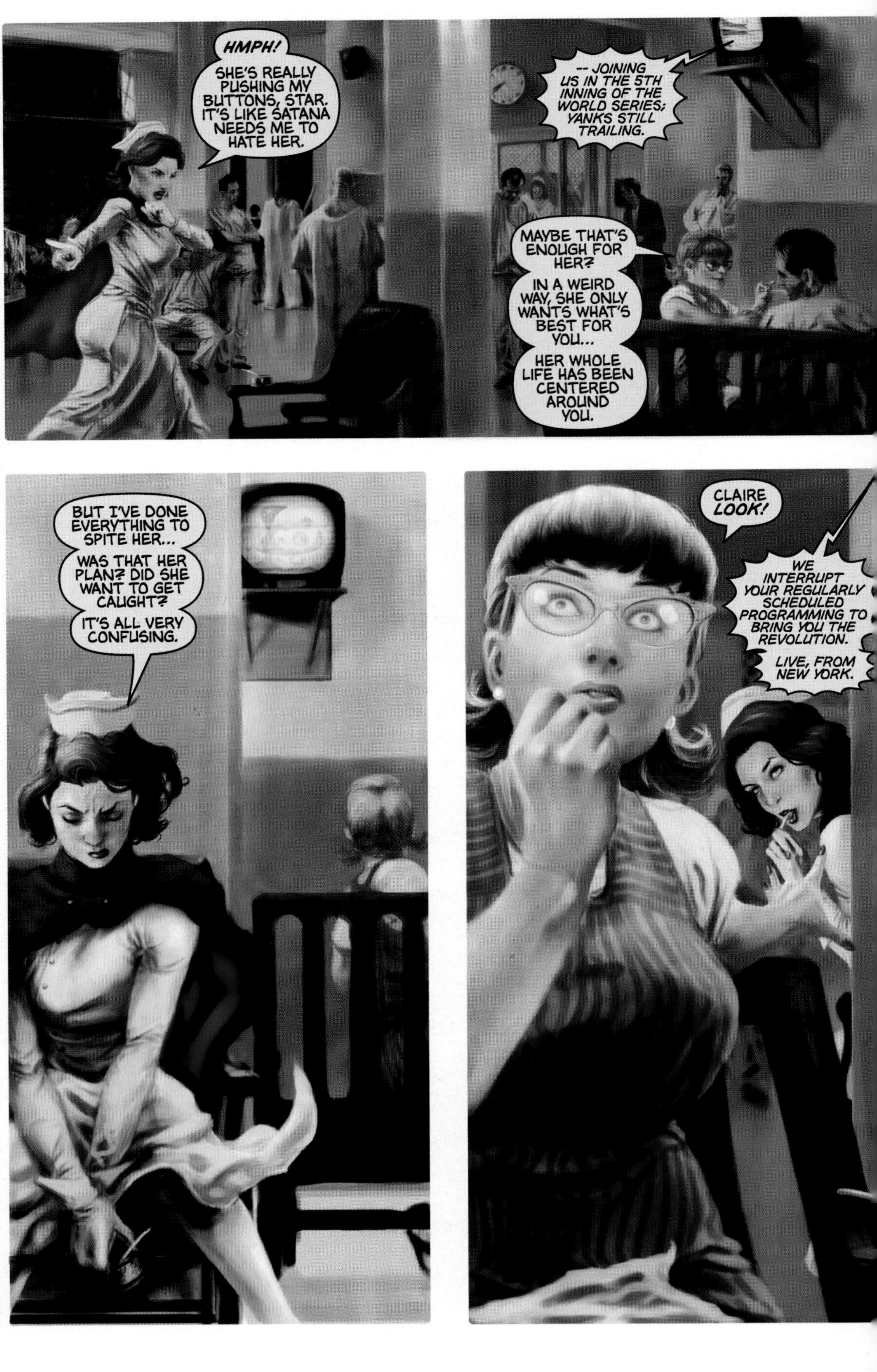
HMPH!
SHE'S REALLY PUSHING MY BUTTONS, STAR. IT'S LIKE SATANA NEEDS ME TO HATE HER.
-- JOINING US IN THE 5TH INNING OF THE WORLD SERIES; YANKS STILL TRAILING.
MAYBE THAT'S ENOUGH FOR HER?
IN A WEIRD WAY, SHE ONLY WANTS WHAT'S BEST FOR YOU...
HER WHOLE LIFE HAS BEEN CENTERED AROUND YOU.
BUT I'VE DONE EVERYTHING TO SPITE HER...
WAS THAT HER PLAN? DID SHE WANT TO GET CAUGHT?
IT'S ALL VERY CONFUSING.
CLAIRE LOOK!
WE INTERRUPT YOUR REGULARLY SCHEDULED PROGRAMMING TO BRING YOU THE REVOLUTION.
LIVE, FROM NEW YORK.

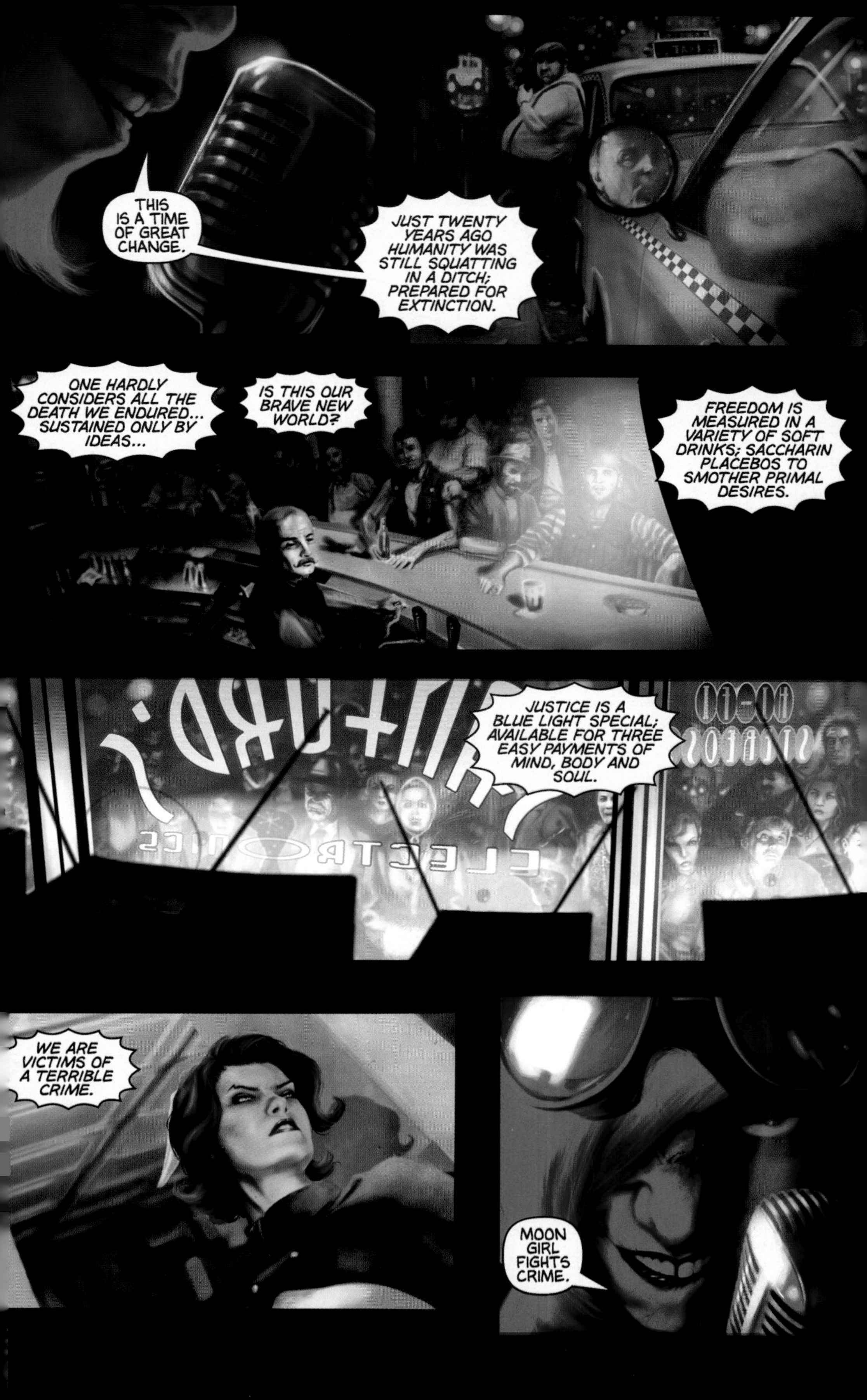

THIS IS A TIME OF GREAT CHANGE.
JUST TWENTY YEARS AGO HUMANITY WAS STILL SQUATTING IN A DITCH; PREPARED FOR EXTINCTION.
ONE HARDLY CONSIDERS ALL THE DEATH WE ENDURED... SUSTAINED ONLY BY IDEAS...
IS THIS OUR BRAVE NEW WORLD?
FREEDOM IS MEASURED IN A VARIETY OF SOFT DRINKS; SACCHARIN PLACEBOS TO SMOTHER PRIMAL DESIRES.
JUSTICE IS A BLUE LIGHT SPECIAL; AVAILABLE FOR THREE EASY PAYMENTS OF MIND, BODY AND SOUL.
WE ARE VICTIMS OF A TERRIBLE CRIME.
MOON GIRL FIGHTS CRIME.

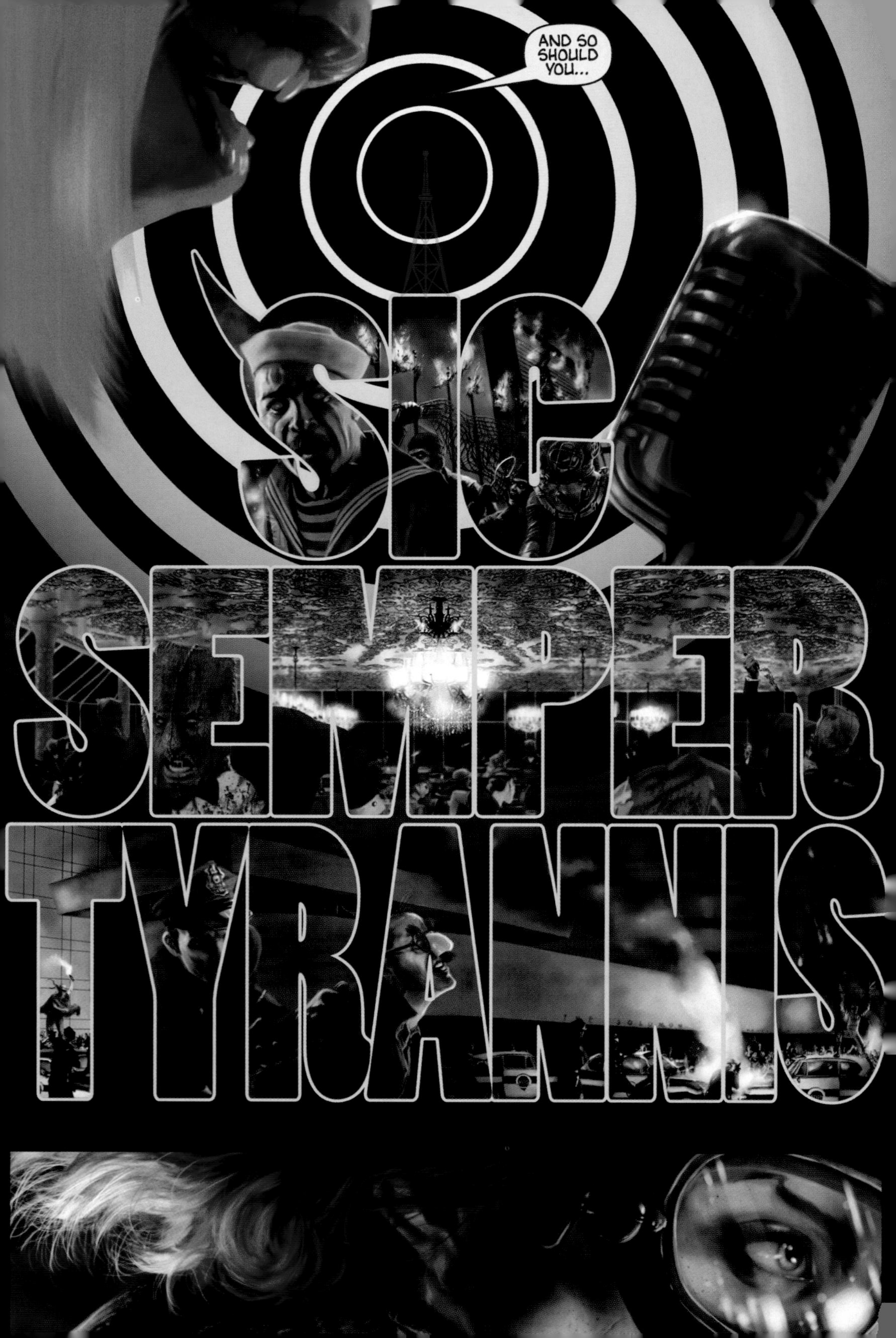
AND SO SHOULD YOU...
SIC SEMPER TYRANNIS

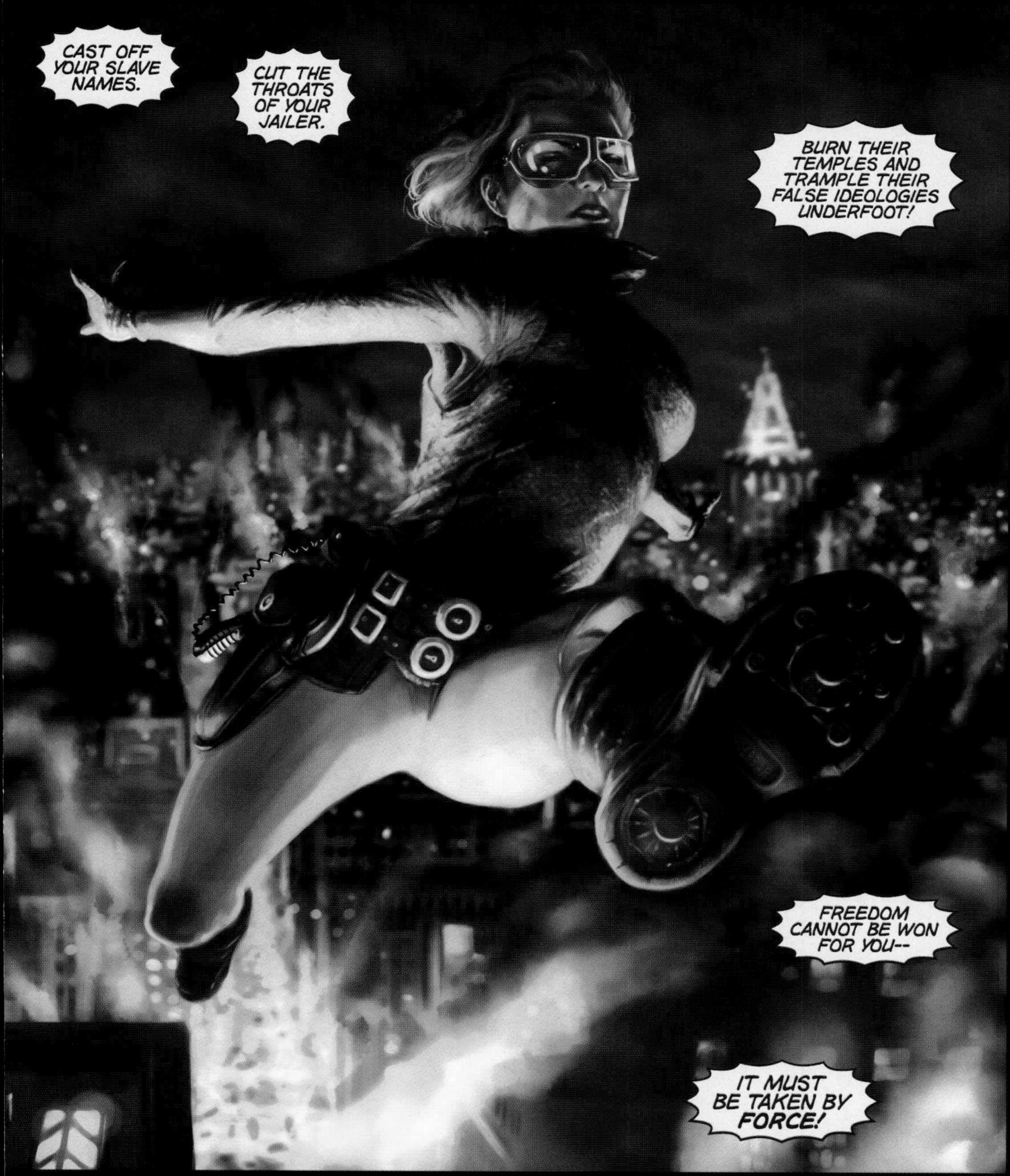
CAST OFF YOUR SLAVE NAMES.
CUT THE THROATS OF YOUR JAILER.
BURN THEIR TEMPLES AND TRAMPLE THEIR FALSE IDEOLOGIES UNDERFOOT!
FREEDOM CANNOT BE WON FOR YOU--
IT MUST BE TAKEN BY FORCE!

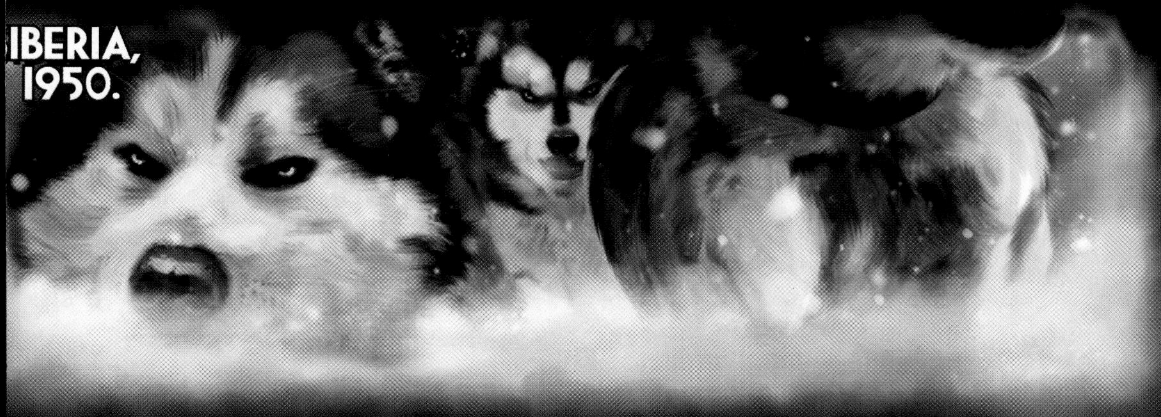
IBERIA, 1950.

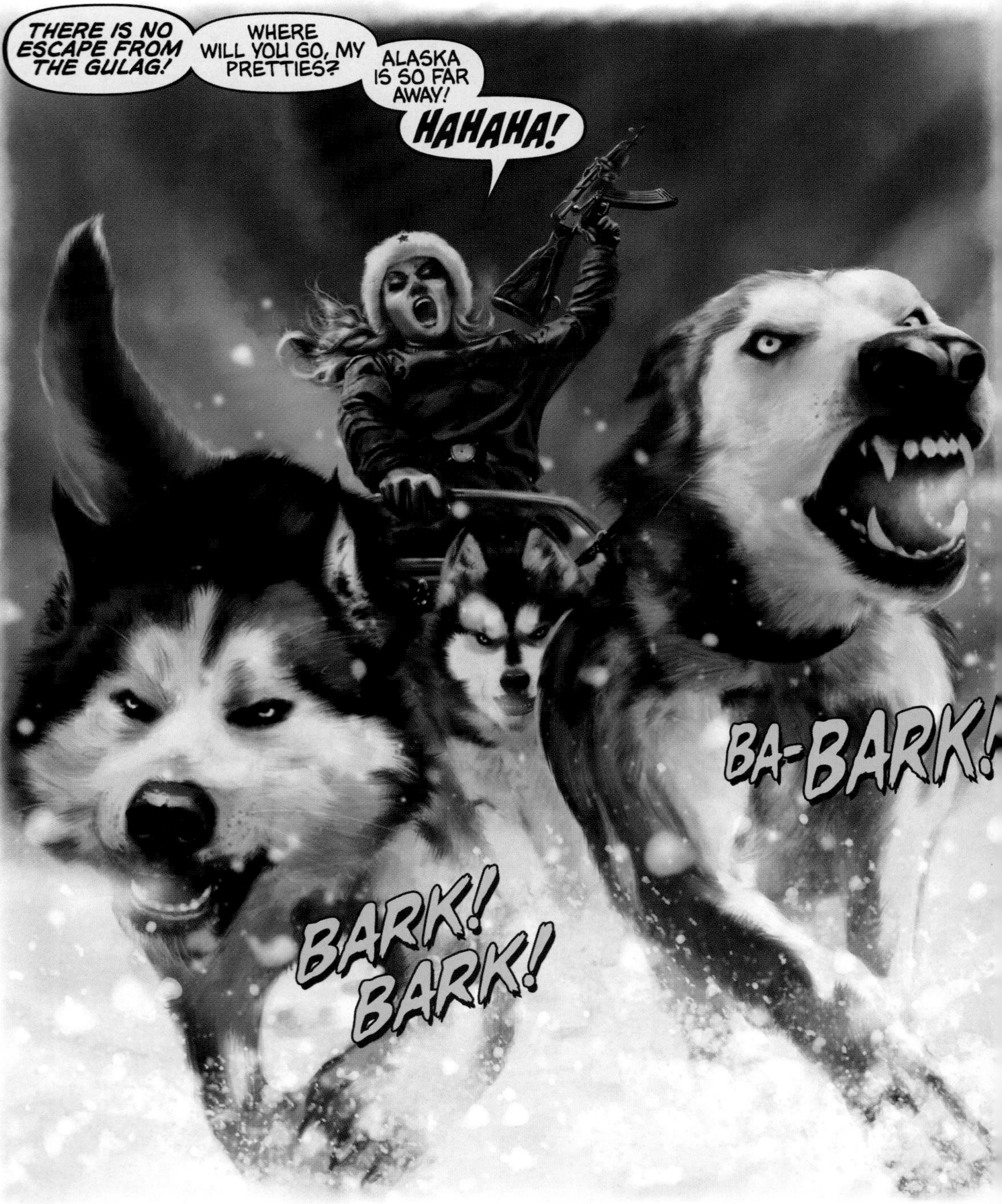
THERE IS NO ESCAPE FROM THE GULAG!
WHERE WILL YOU GO, MY PRETTIES?
ALASKA IS SO FAR AWAY!
HAHAHA!
BA-BARK!
BARK! BARK!

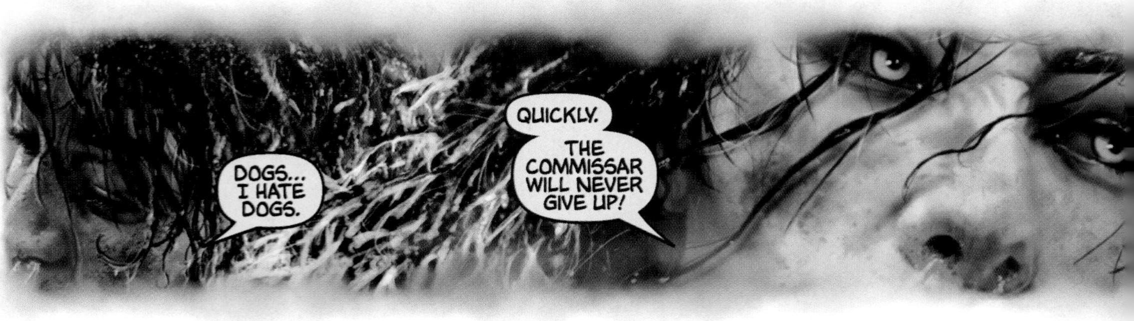
DOGS... I HATE DOGS.
QUICKLY.
THE COMMISSAR WILL NEVER GIVE UP!

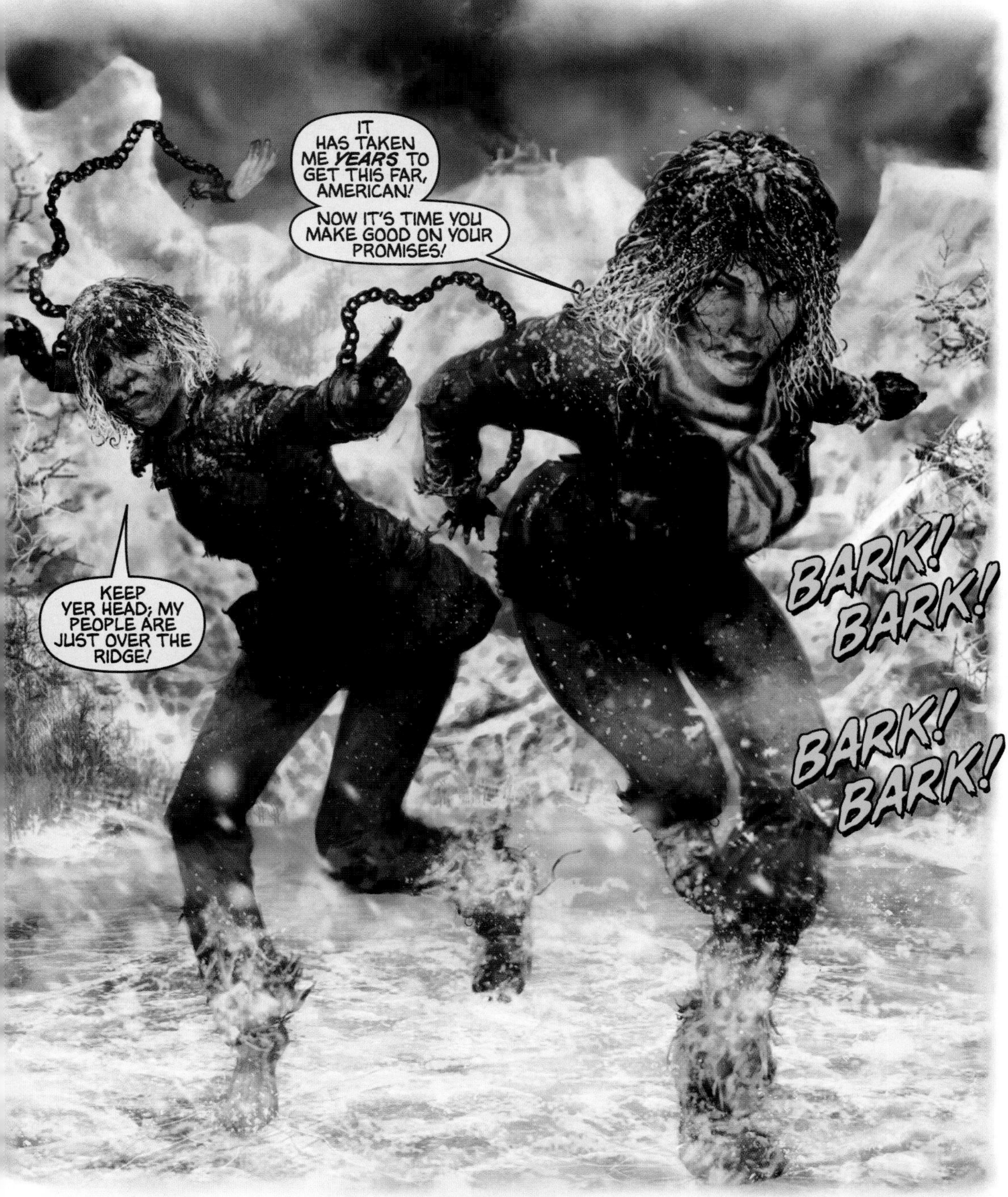
IT HAS TAKEN ME YEARS TO GET THIS FAR, AMERICAN!
NOW IT'S TIME YOU MAKE GOOD ON YOUR PROMISES!
KEEP YER HEAD; MY PEOPLE ARE JUST OVER THE RIDGE!
BARK! BARK!
BARK! BARK!
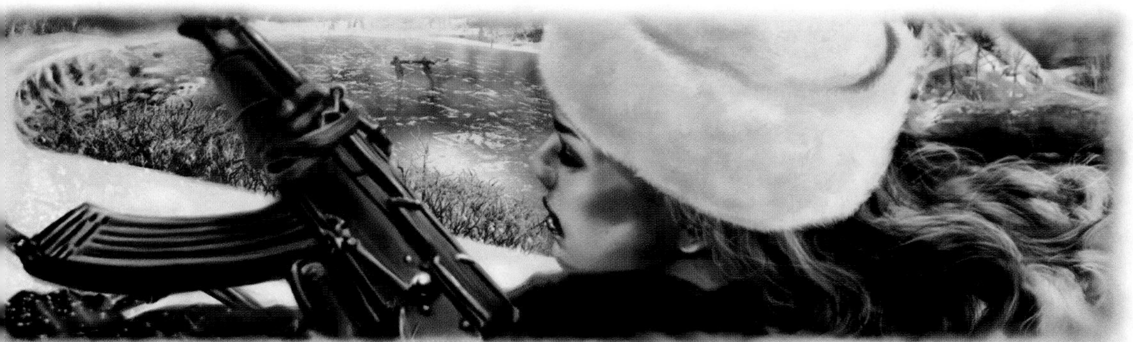

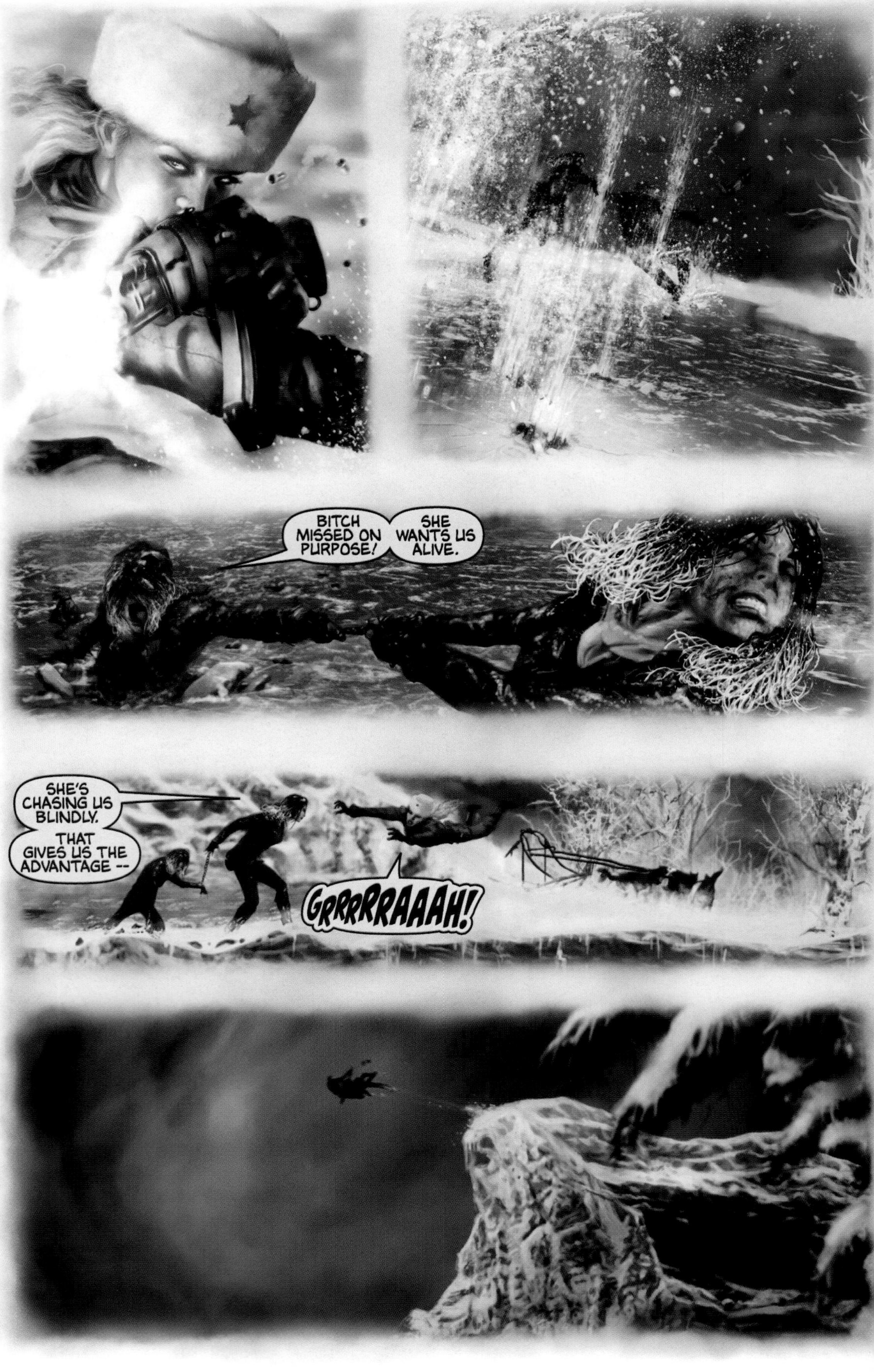
BITCH MISSED ON PURPOSE!
SHE WANTS US ALIVE.
SHE'S CHASING US BLINDLY.
THAT GIVES US THE ADVANTAGE --
GRRRRRAAAH!

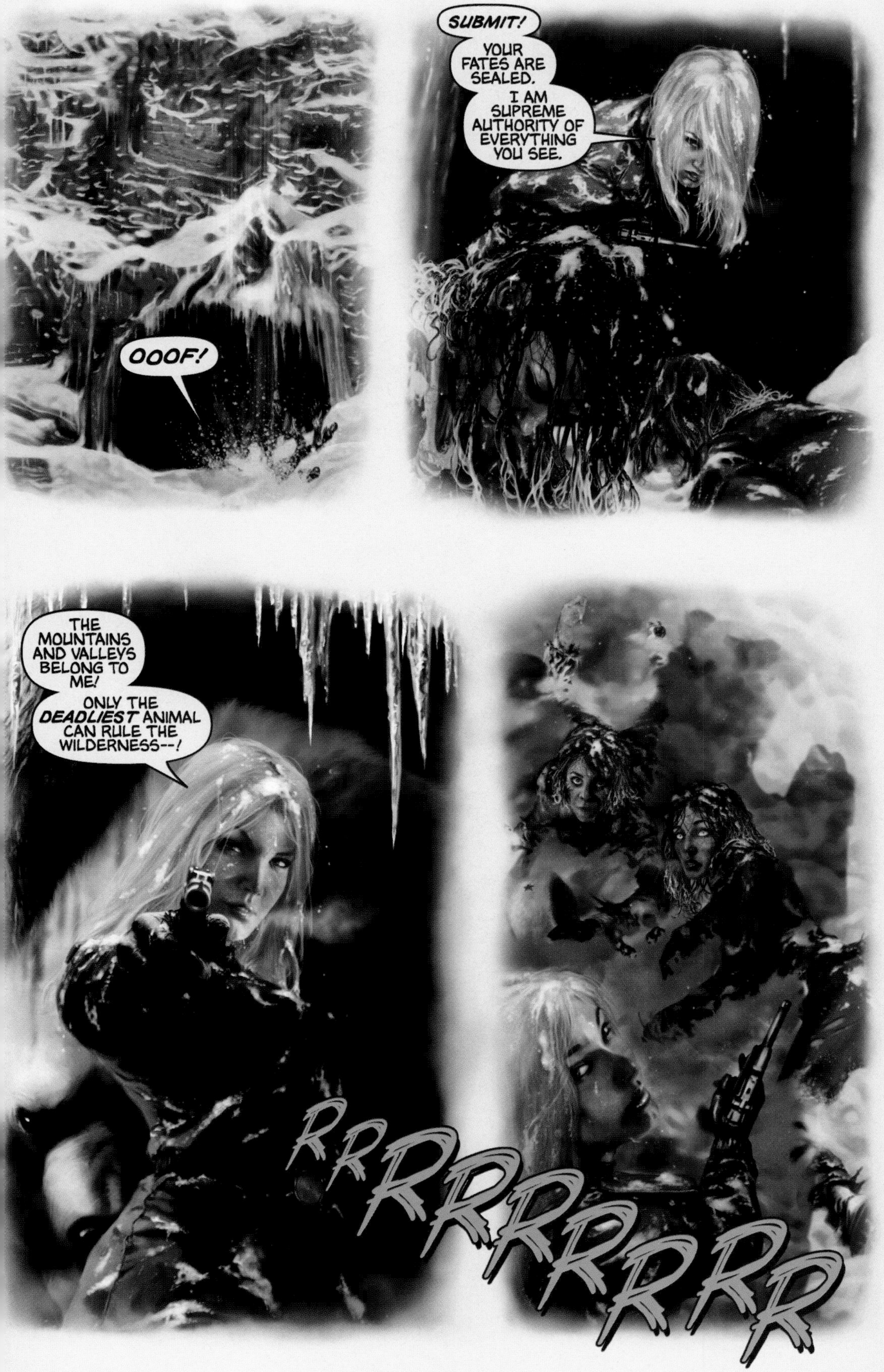
OOOF!
SUBMIT!
YOUR FATES ARE SEALED.
I AM SUPREME AUTHORITY OF EVERYTHING YOU SEE.
THE MOUNTAINS AND VALLEYS BELONG TO ME!
ONLY THE *DEADLIEST* ANIMAL CAN RULE THE WILDERNESS--!
RRRRRRRRRR

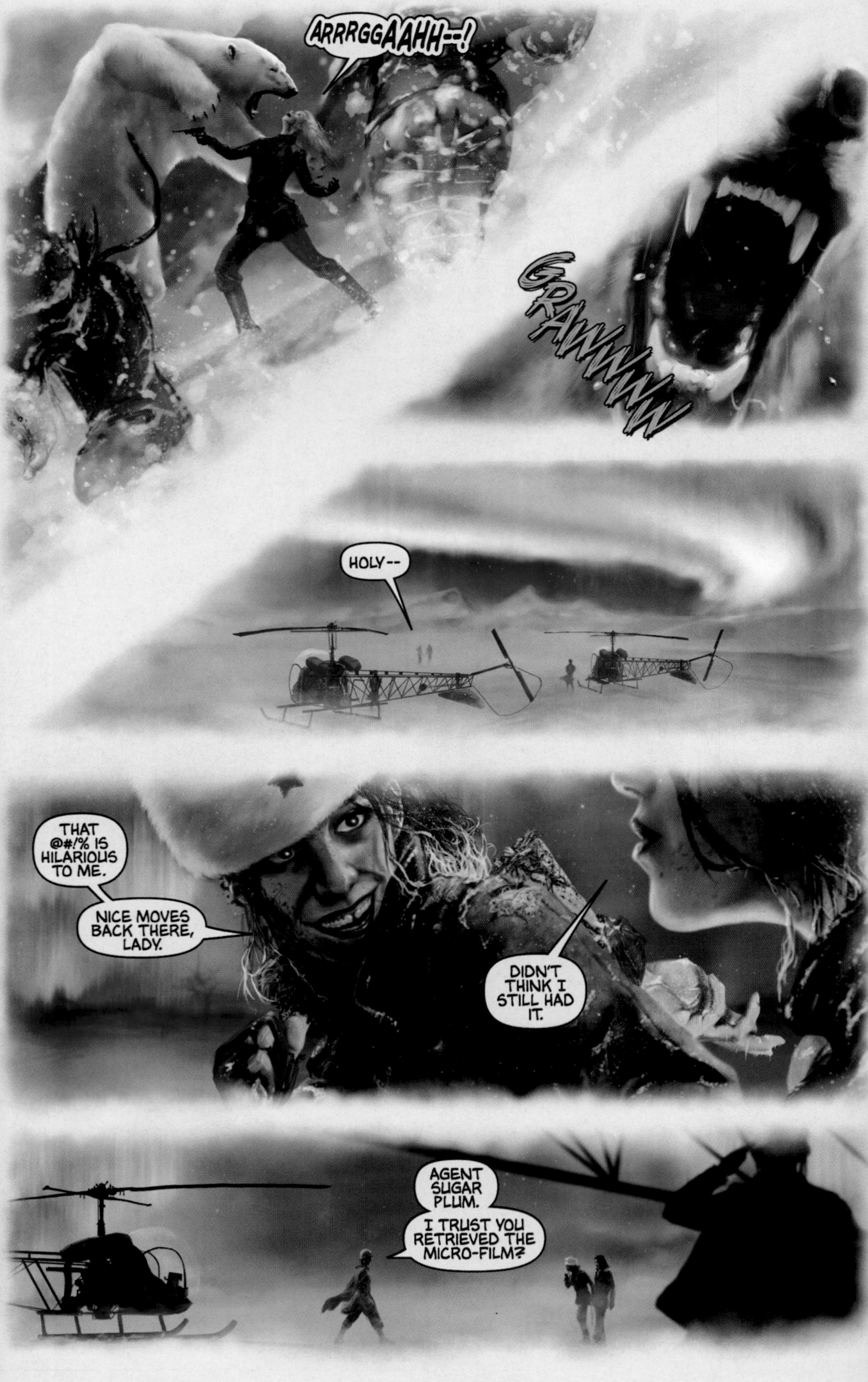
ARRRGGAAHH--!
GRAWWWW
HOLY--
THAT @#!% IS HILARIOUS TO ME.
NICE MOVES BACK THERE, LADY.
DIDN'T THINK I STILL HAD IT.
AGENT SUGAR PLUM.
I TRUST YOU RETRIEVED THE MICRO-FILM?

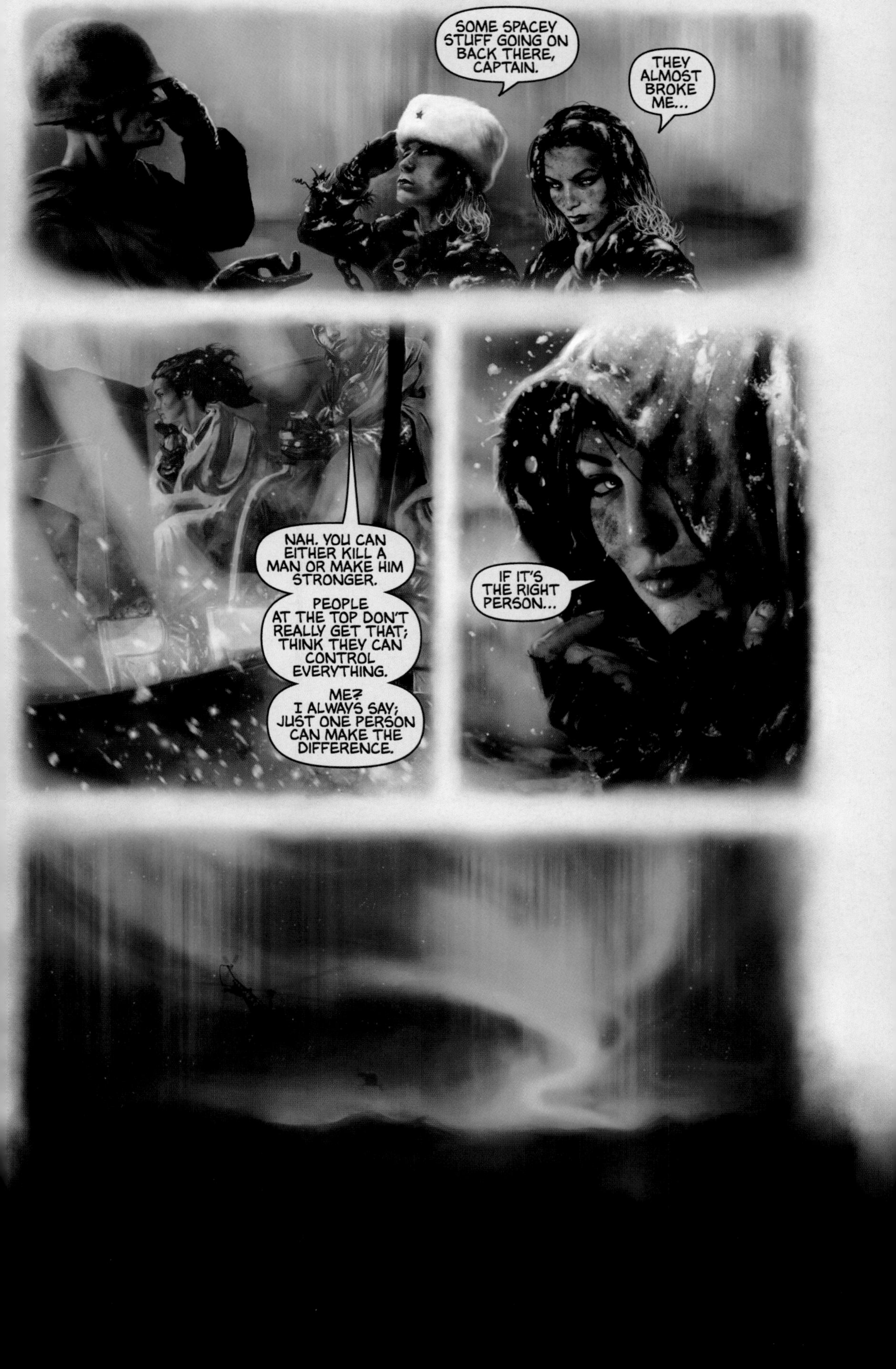
SOME SPACEY STUFF GOING ON BACK THERE, CAPTAIN.
THEY ALMOST BROKE ME...
NAH. YOU CAN EITHER KILL A MAN OR MAKE HIM STRONGER.
PEOPLE AT THE TOP DON'T REALLY GET THAT; THINK THEY CAN CONTROL EVERYTHING.
ME? I ALWAYS SAY; JUST ONE PERSON CAN MAKE THE DIFFERENCE.
IF IT'S THE RIGHT PERSON...

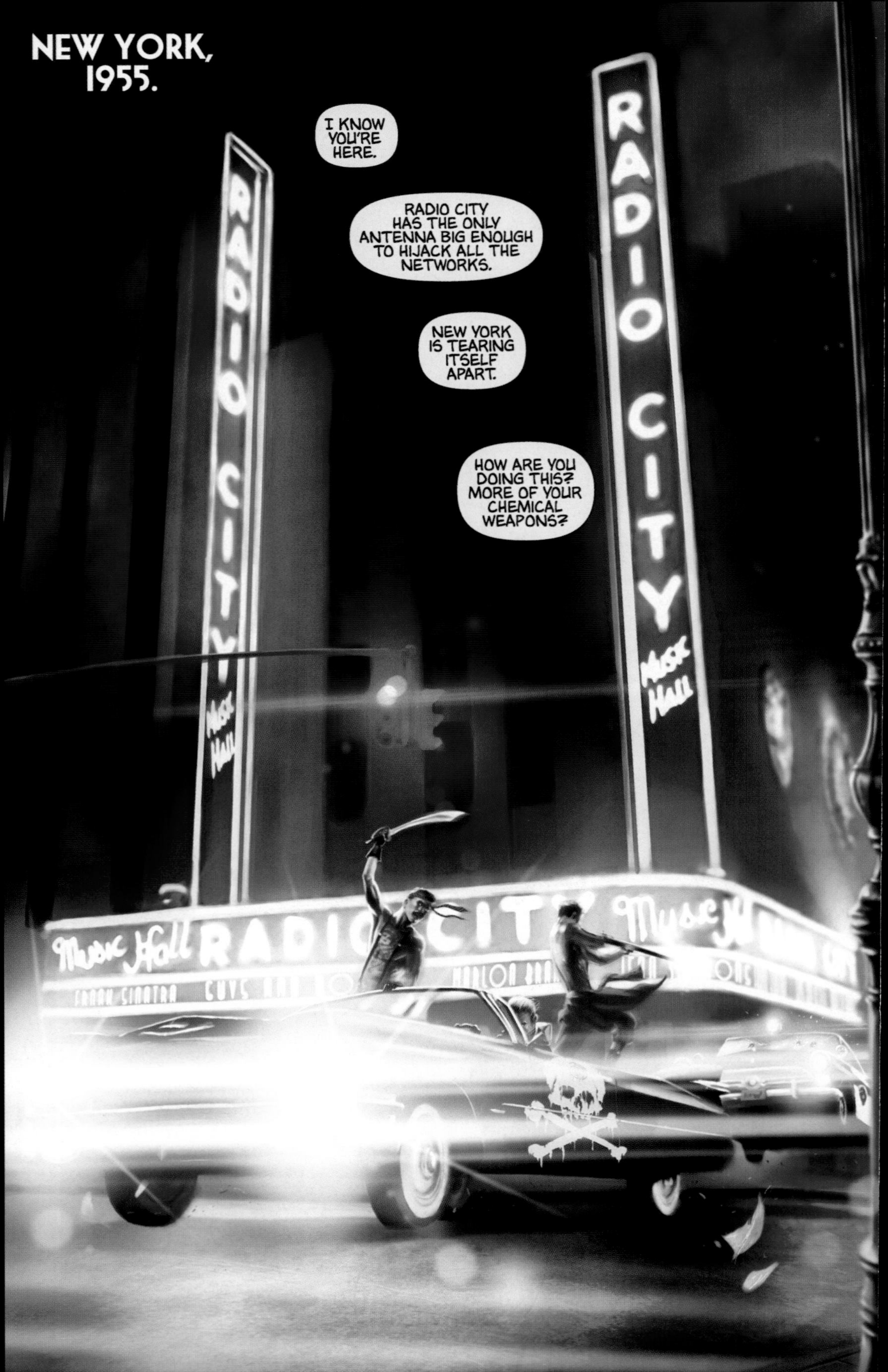
NEW YORK, 1955.
I KNOW YOU'RE HERE.
RADIO CITY HAS THE ONLY ANTENNA BIG ENOUGH TO HIJACK ALL THE NETWORKS.
NEW YORK IS TEARING ITSELF APART.
HOW ARE YOU DOING THIS? MORE OF YOUR CHEMICAL WEAPONS?
RADIO CITY
Music Hall
RADIO CITY
Music Hall
Music Hall RADIO CITY Music Hall

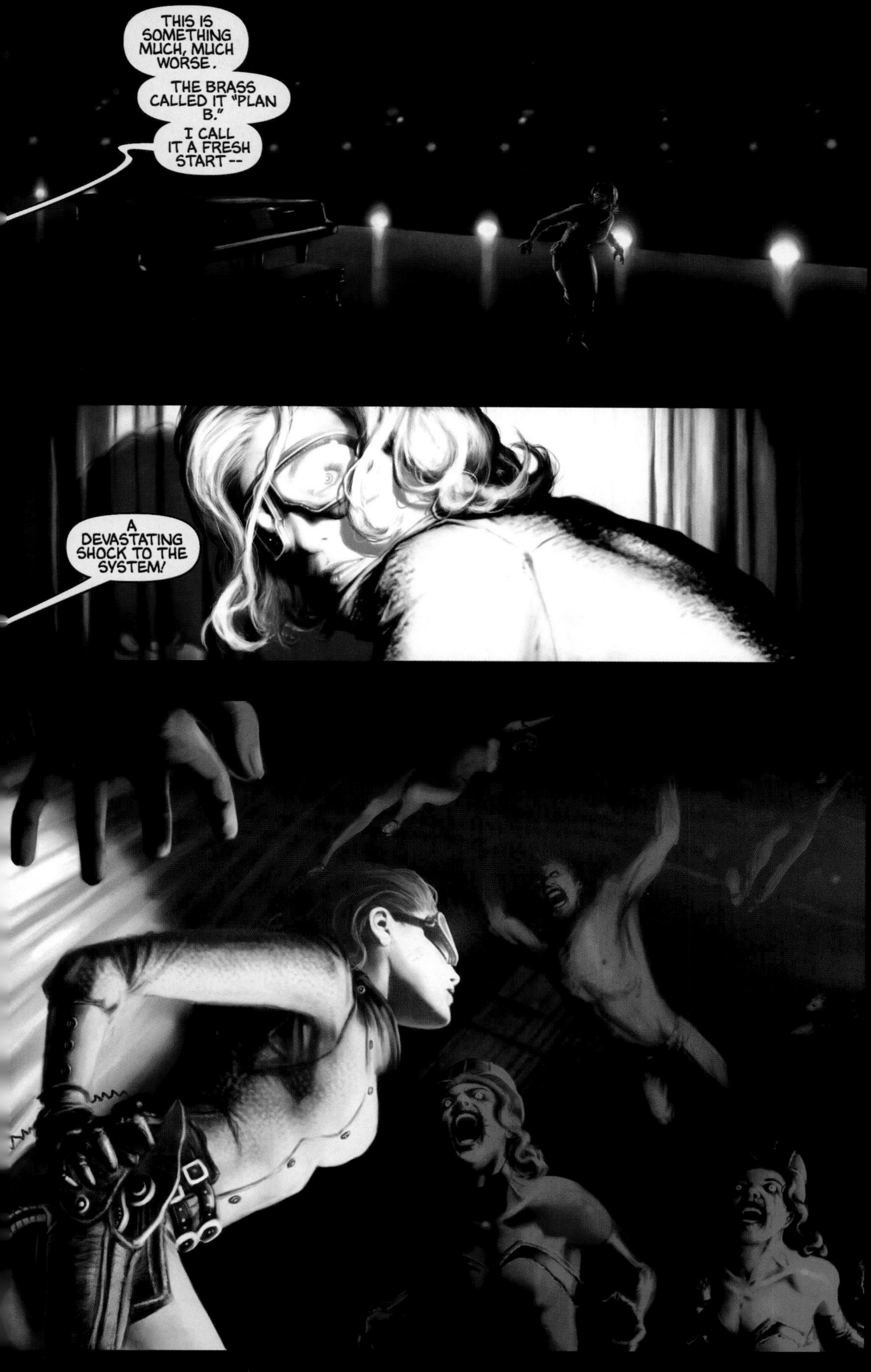
THIS IS SOMETHING MUCH, MUCH WORSE.
THE BRASS CALLED IT "PLAN B."
I CALL IT A FRESH START --
A DEVASTATING SHOCK TO THE SYSTEM!

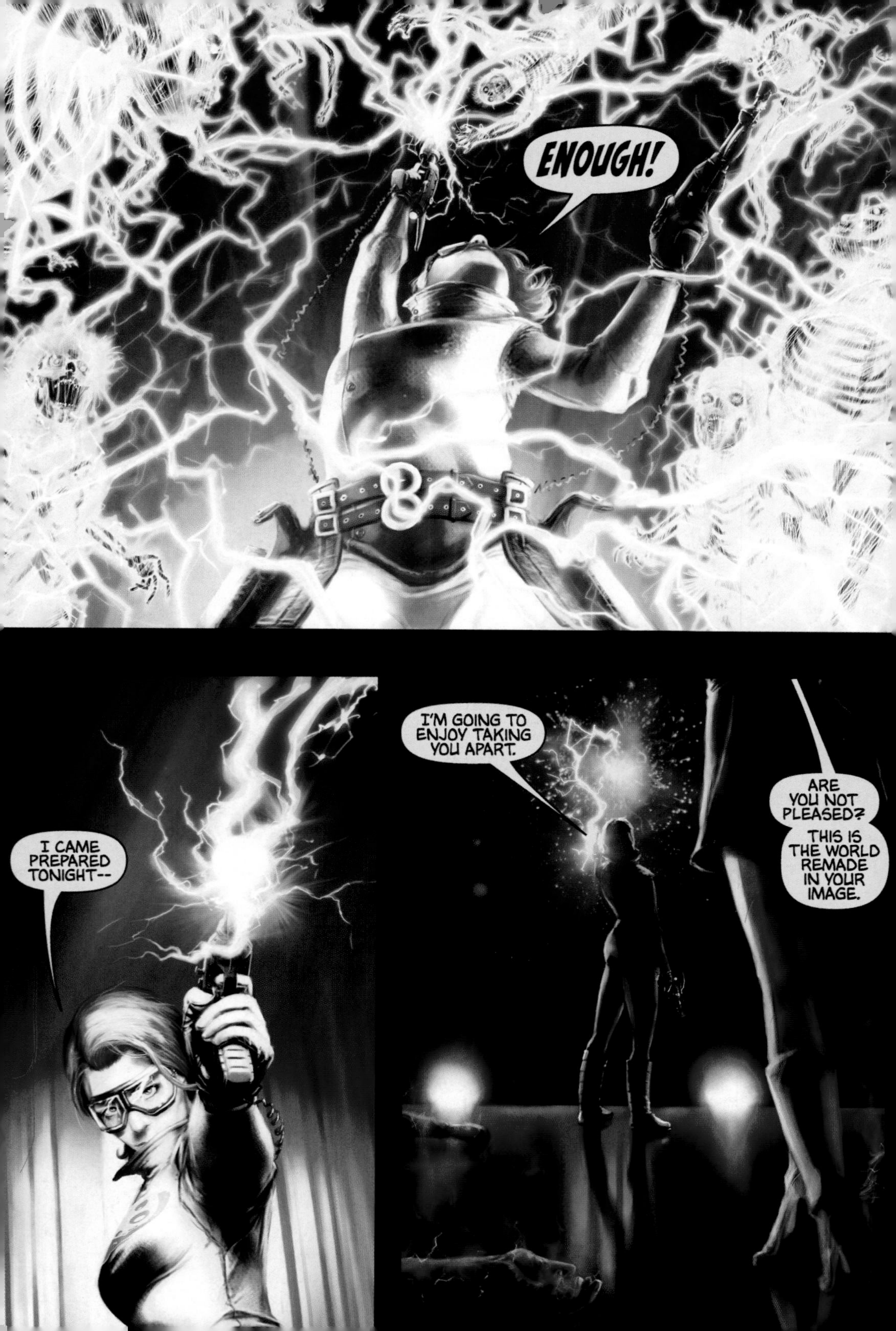
ENOUGH!
I CAME PREPARED TONIGHT--
I'M GOING TO ENJOY TAKING YOU APART.
ARE YOU NOT PLEASED?
THIS IS THE WORLD REMADE IN YOUR IMAGE.

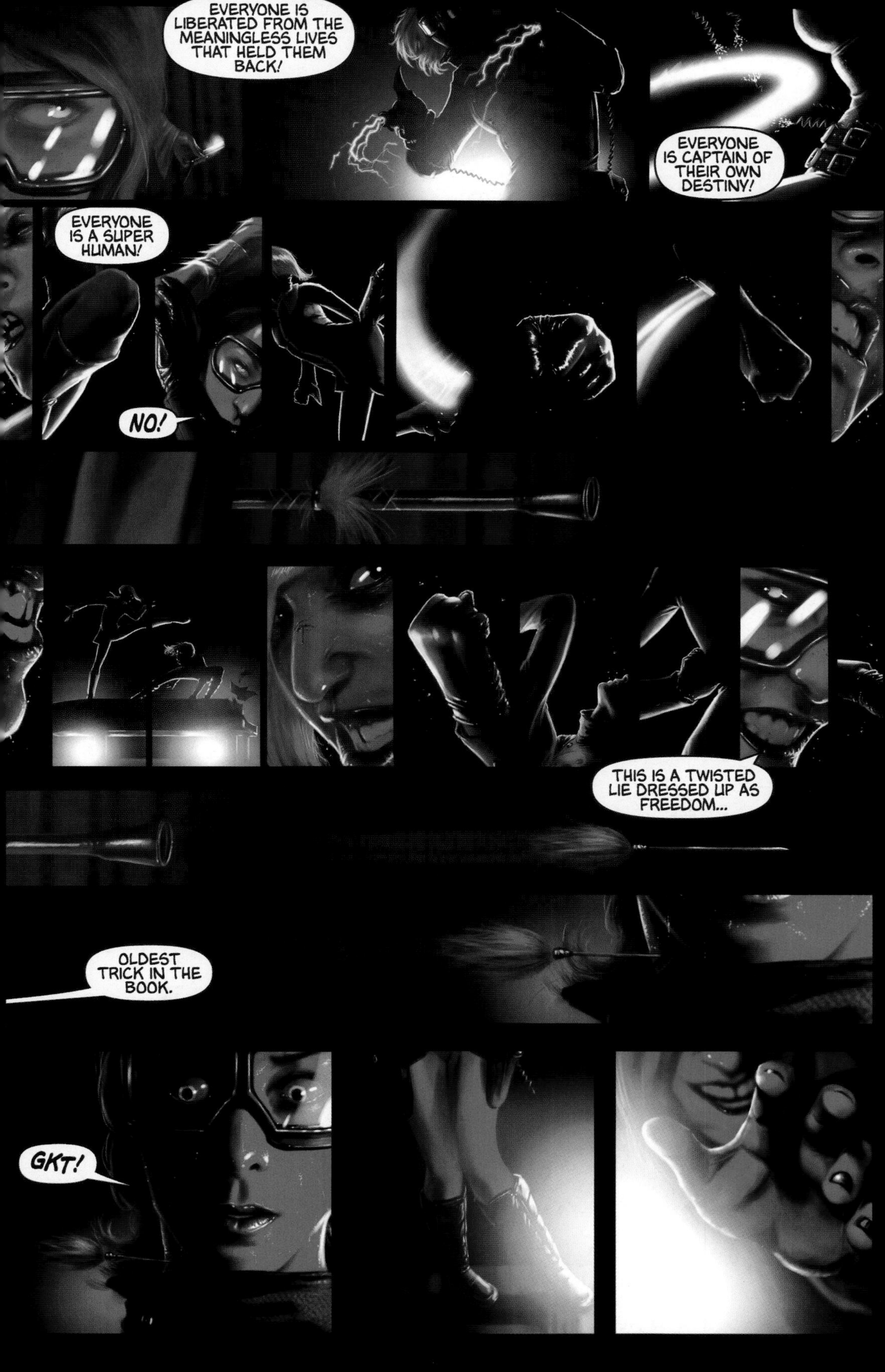
EVERYONE IS LIBERATED FROM THE MEANINGLESS LIVES THAT HELD THEM BACK!
EVERYONE IS CAPTAIN OF THEIR OWN DESTINY!
EVERYONE IS A SUPER HUMAN!
NO!
THIS IS A TWISTED LIE DRESSED UP AS FREEDOM...
OLDEST TRICK IN THE BOOK.
GKT!

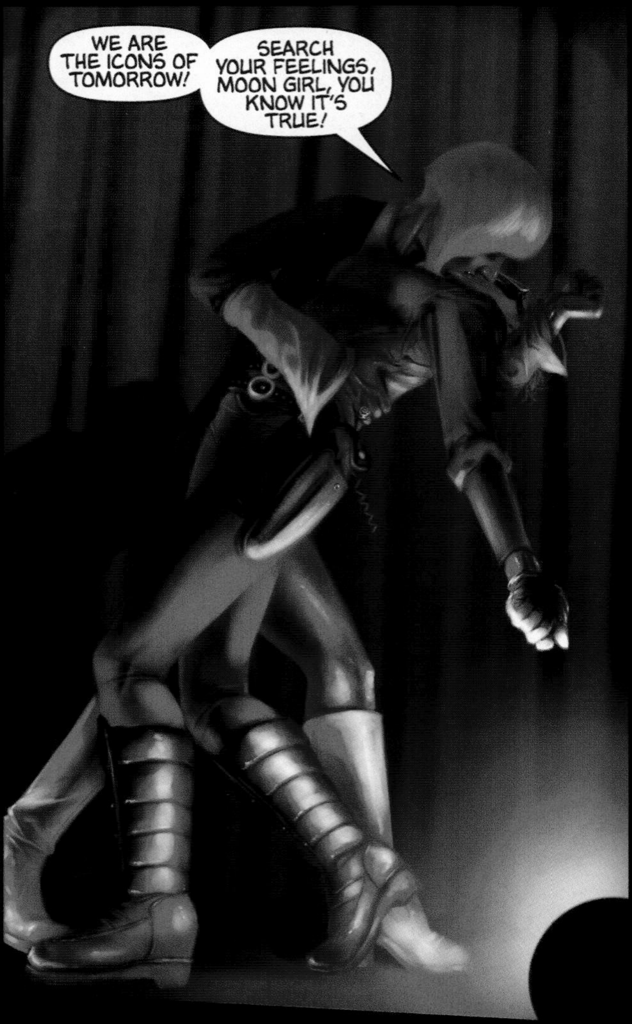
WE ARE THE ICONS OF TOMORROW!
SEARCH YOUR FEELINGS, MOON GIRL, YOU KNOW IT'S TRUE!

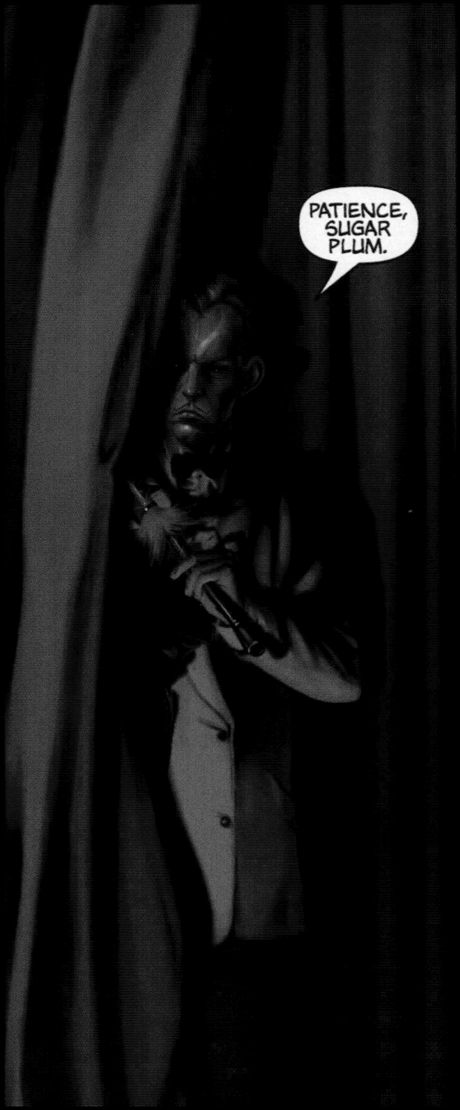
PATIENCE, SUGAR PLUM.

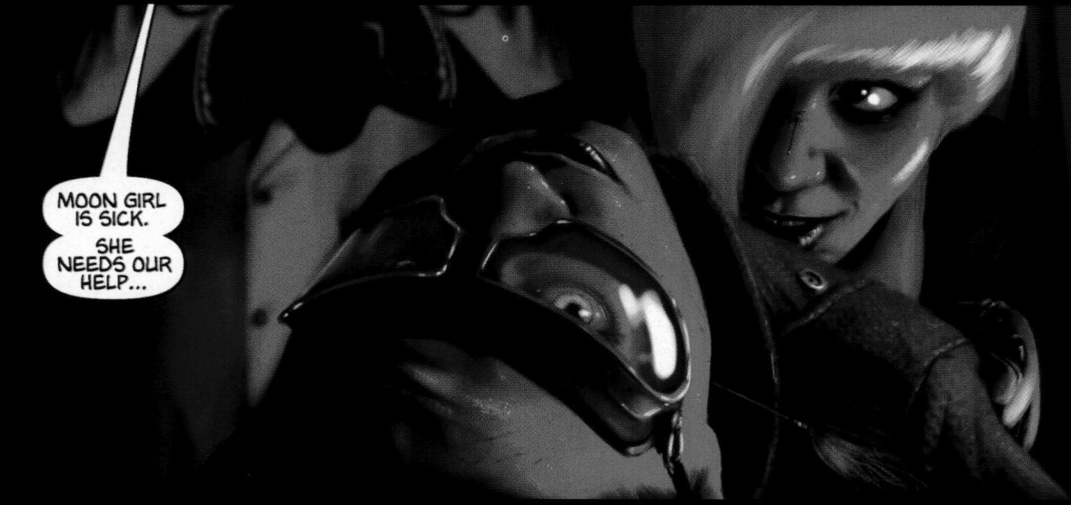
MOON GIRL IS SICK.
SHE NEEDS OUR HELP...

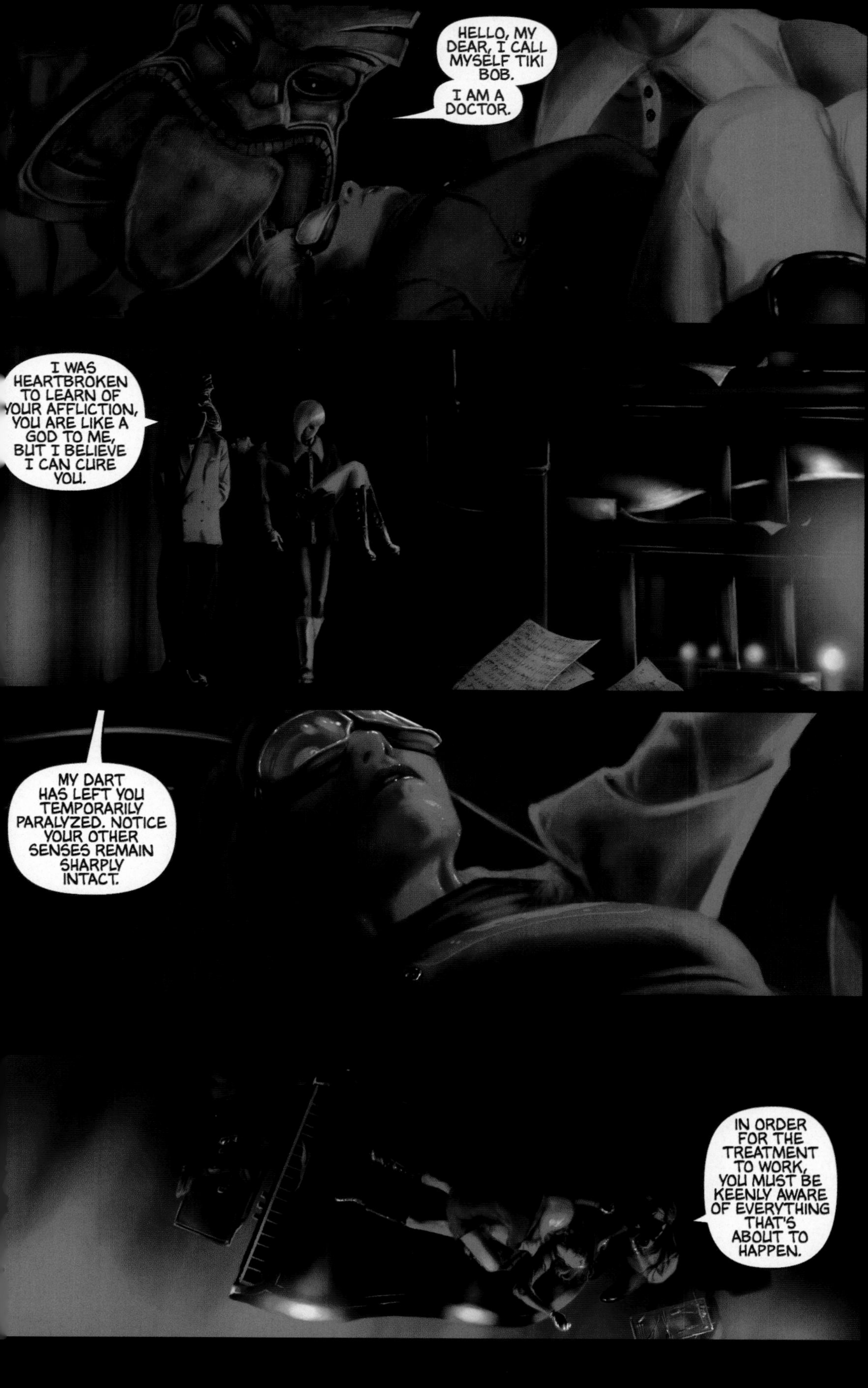
HELLO, MY DEAR, I CALL MYSELF TIKI BOB.
I AM A DOCTOR.
I WAS HEARTBROKEN TO LEARN OF YOUR AFFLICTION, YOU ARE LIKE A GOD TO ME, BUT I BELIEVE I CAN CURE YOU.
MY DART HAS LEFT YOU TEMPORARILY PARALYZED. NOTICE YOUR OTHER SENSES REMAIN SHARPLY INTACT.
IN ORDER FOR THE TREATMENT TO WORK, YOU MUST BE KEENLY AWARE OF EVERYTHING THAT'S ABOUT TO HAPPEN.

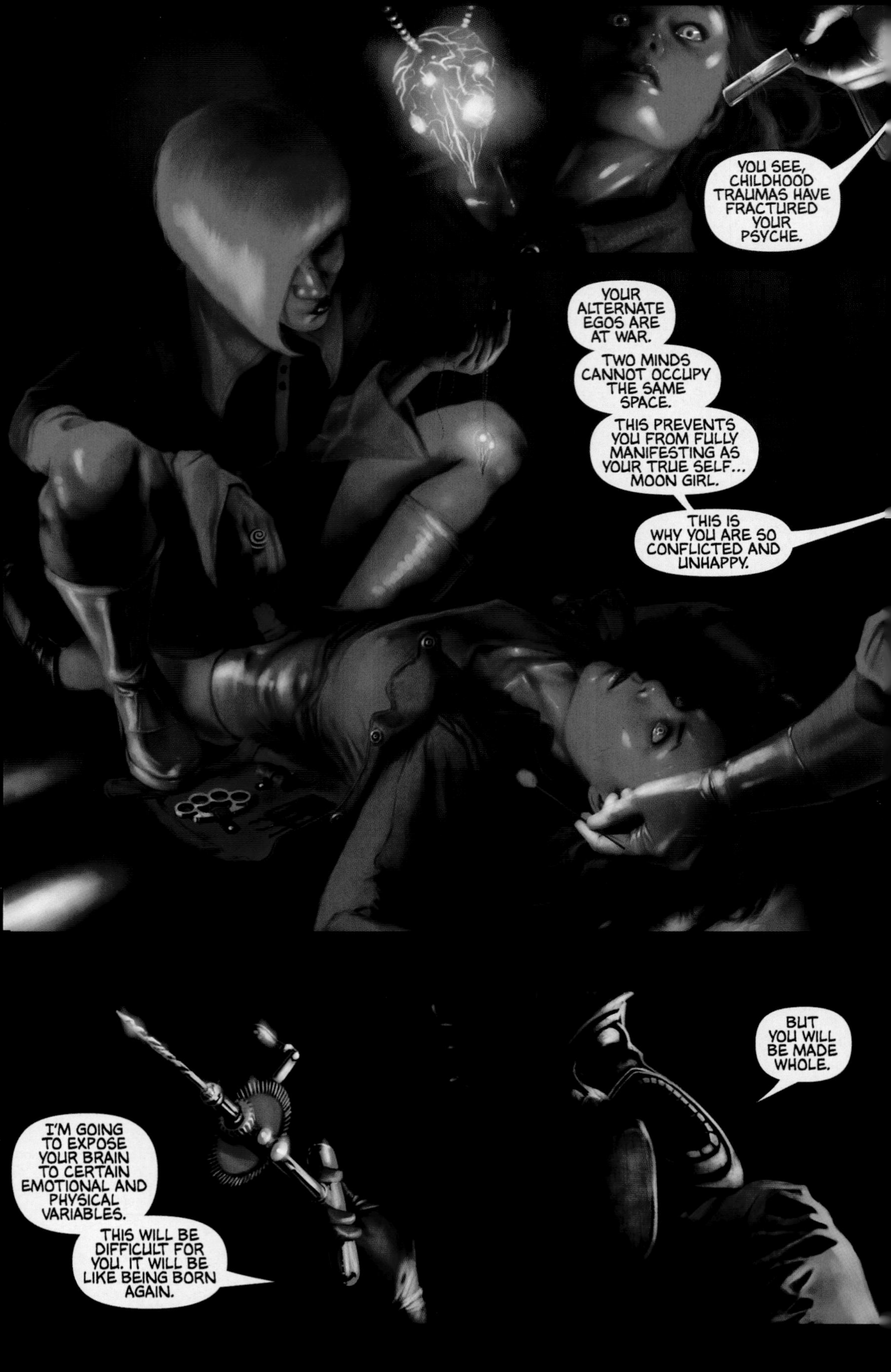
YOU SEE, CHILDHOOD TRAUMAS HAVE FRACTURED YOUR PSYCHE.
YOUR ALTERNATE EGOS ARE AT WAR.
TWO MINDS CANNOT OCCUPY THE SAME SPACE.
THIS PREVENTS YOU FROM FULLY MANIFESTING AS YOUR TRUE SELF... MOON GIRL.
THIS IS WHY YOU ARE SO CONFLICTED AND UNHAPPY.
BUT YOU WILL BE MADE WHOLE.
I'M GOING TO EXPOSE YOUR BRAIN TO CERTAIN EMOTIONAL AND PHYSICAL VARIABLES.
THIS WILL BE DIFFICULT FOR YOU. IT WILL BE LIKE BEING BORN AGAIN.

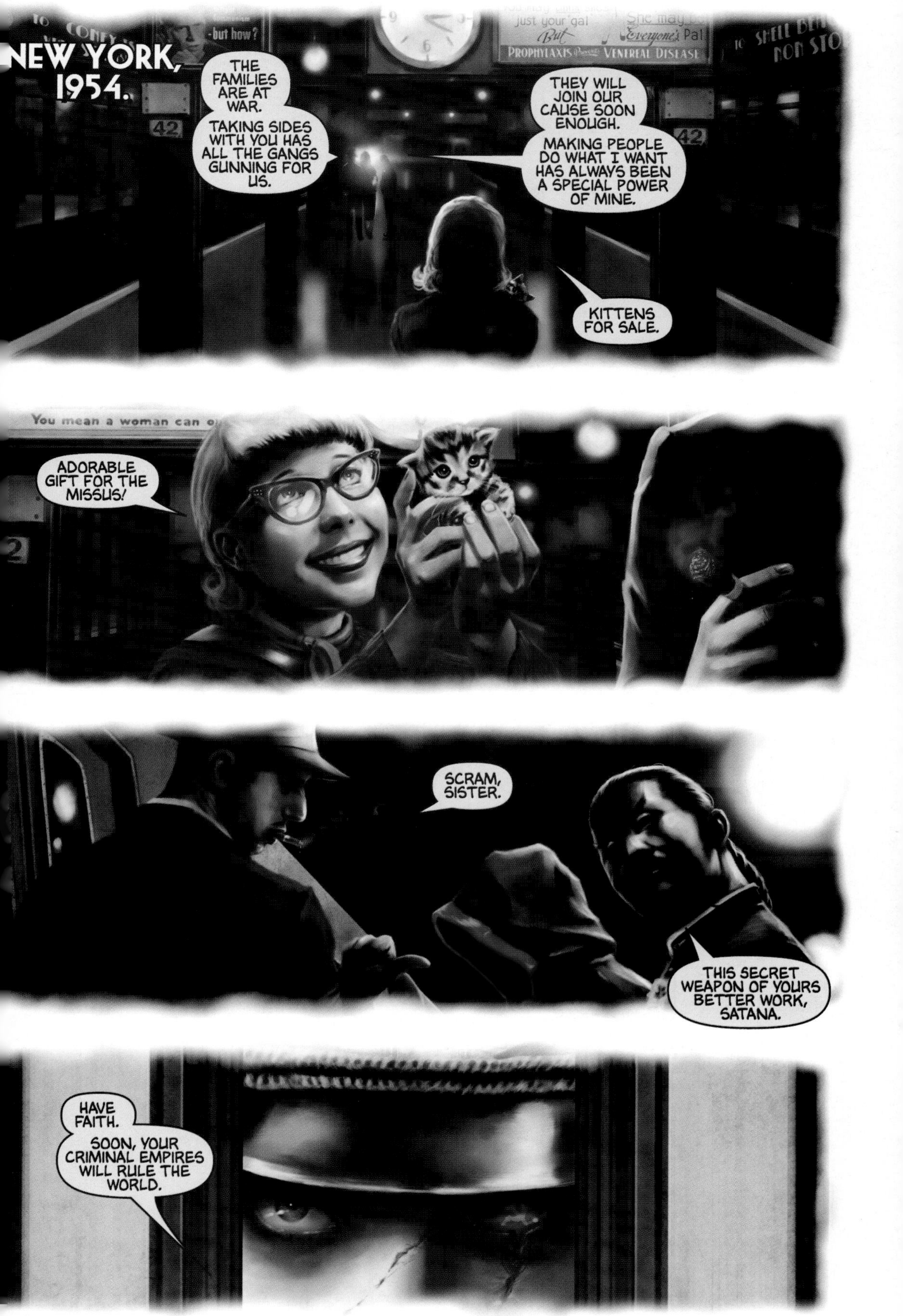
NEW YORK, 1954.
THE FAMILIES ARE AT WAR.
TAKING SIDES WITH YOU HAS ALL THE GANGS GUNNING FOR US.
THEY WILL JOIN OUR CAUSE SOON ENOUGH.
MAKING PEOPLE DO WHAT I WANT HAS ALWAYS BEEN A SPECIAL POWER OF MINE.
KITTENS FOR SALE.
ADORABLE GIFT FOR THE MISSUS!
SCRAM, SISTER.
THIS SECRET WEAPON OF YOURS BETTER WORK, SATANA.
HAVE FAITH.
SOON, YOUR CRIMINAL EMPIRES WILL RULE THE WORLD.

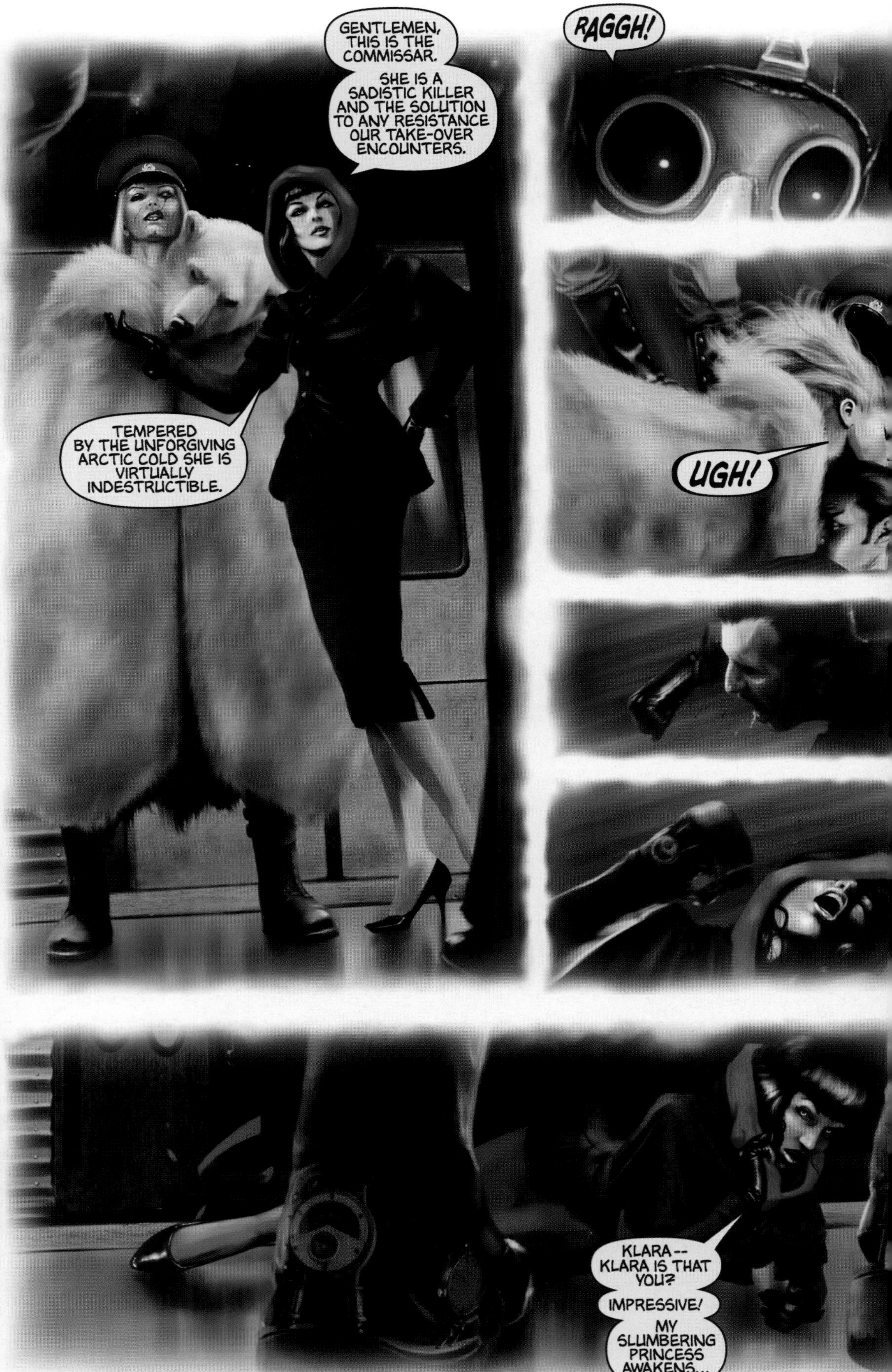
GENTLEMEN, THIS IS THE COMMISSAR.
SHE IS A SADISTIC KILLER AND THE SOLUTION TO ANY RESISTANCE OUR TAKE-OVER ENCOUNTERS.
TEMPERED BY THE UNFORGIVING ARCTIC COLD SHE IS VIRTUALLY INDESTRUCTIBLE.
RAGGH!
UGH!
KLARA-- KLARA IS THAT YOU?
IMPRESSIVE!
MY SLUMBERING PRINCESS AWAKENS...

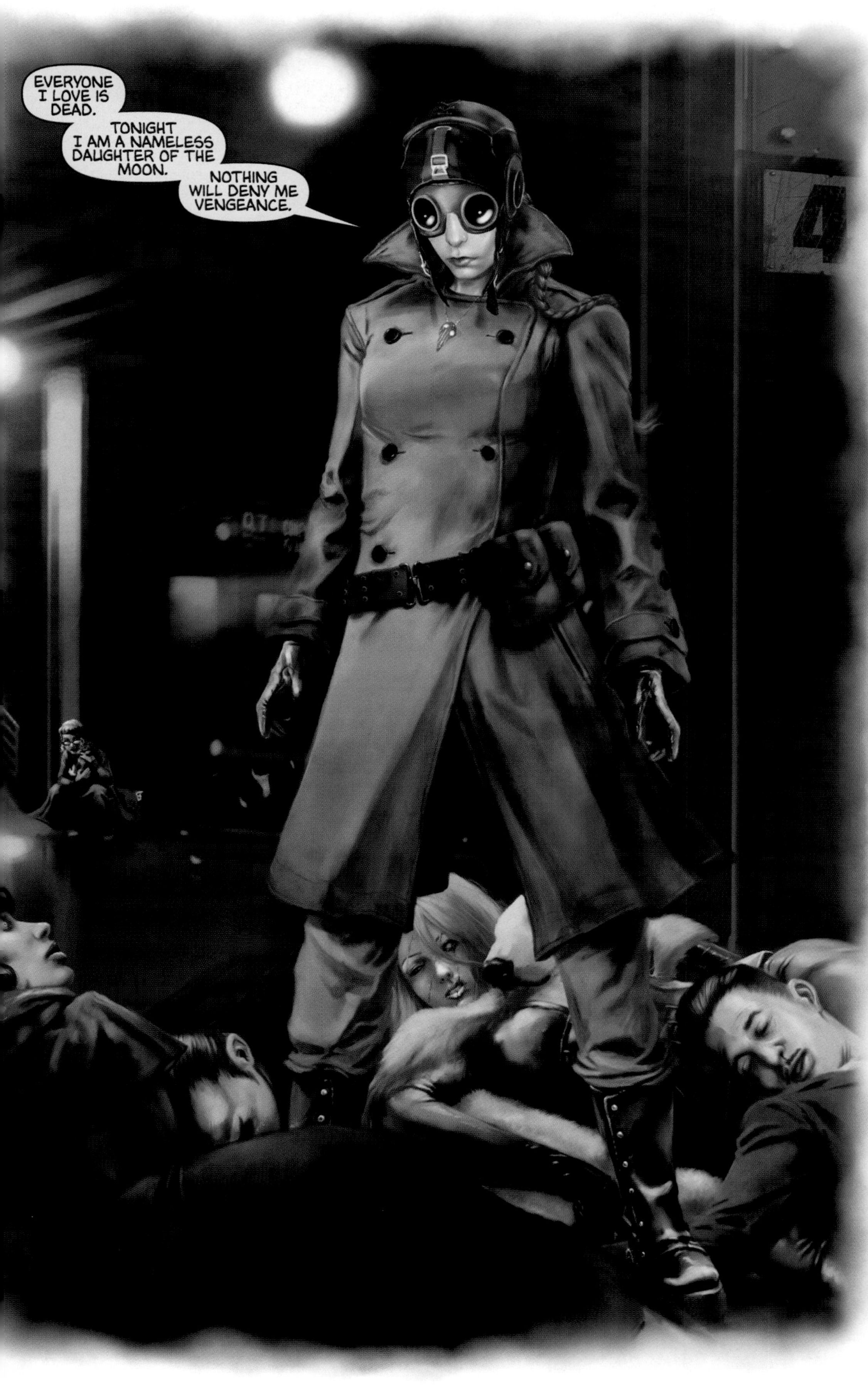
EVERYONE I LOVE IS DEAD.
TONIGHT I AM A NAMELESS DAUGHTER OF THE MOON.
NOTHING WILL DENY ME VENGEANCE.

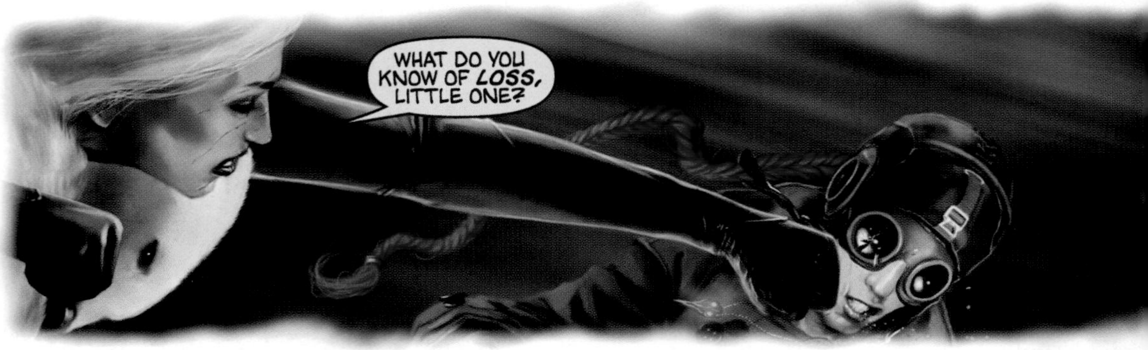
WHAT DO YOU KNOW OF *LOSS,* LITTLE ONE?
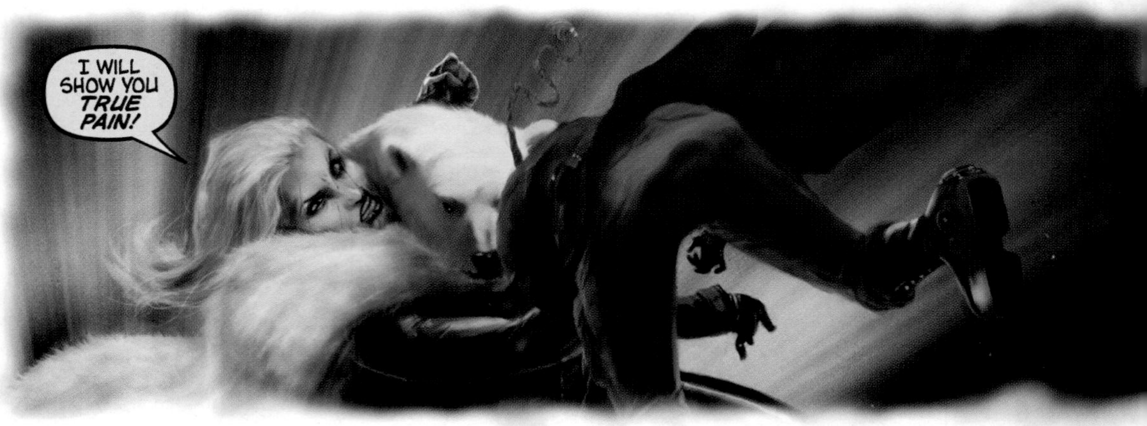
I WILL SHOW YOU *TRUE PAIN!*
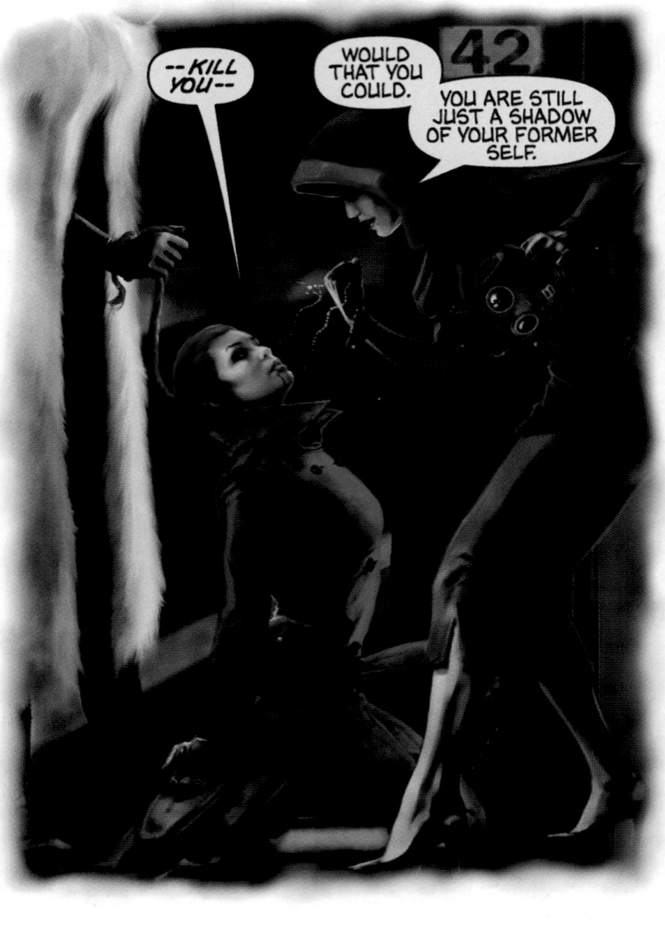
42
--*KILL YOU*--
WOULD THAT YOU COULD.
YOU ARE STILL JUST A SHADOW OF YOUR FORMER SELF.
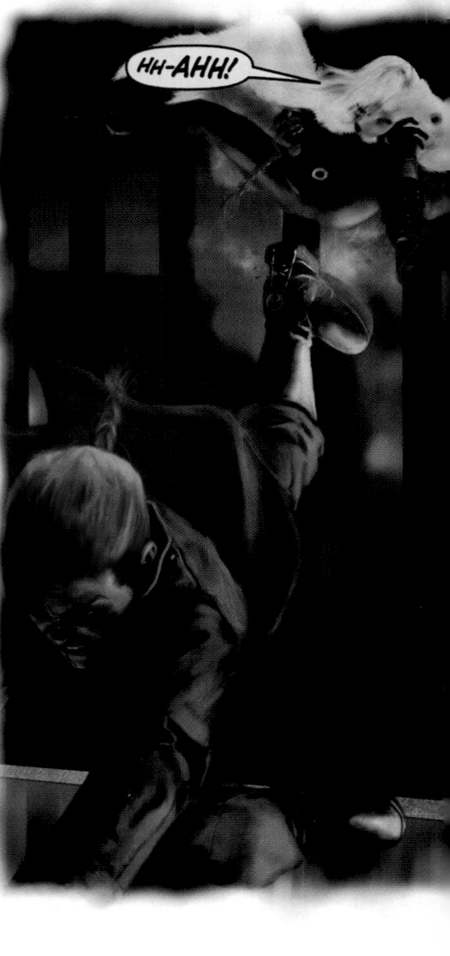
HH-AHH!

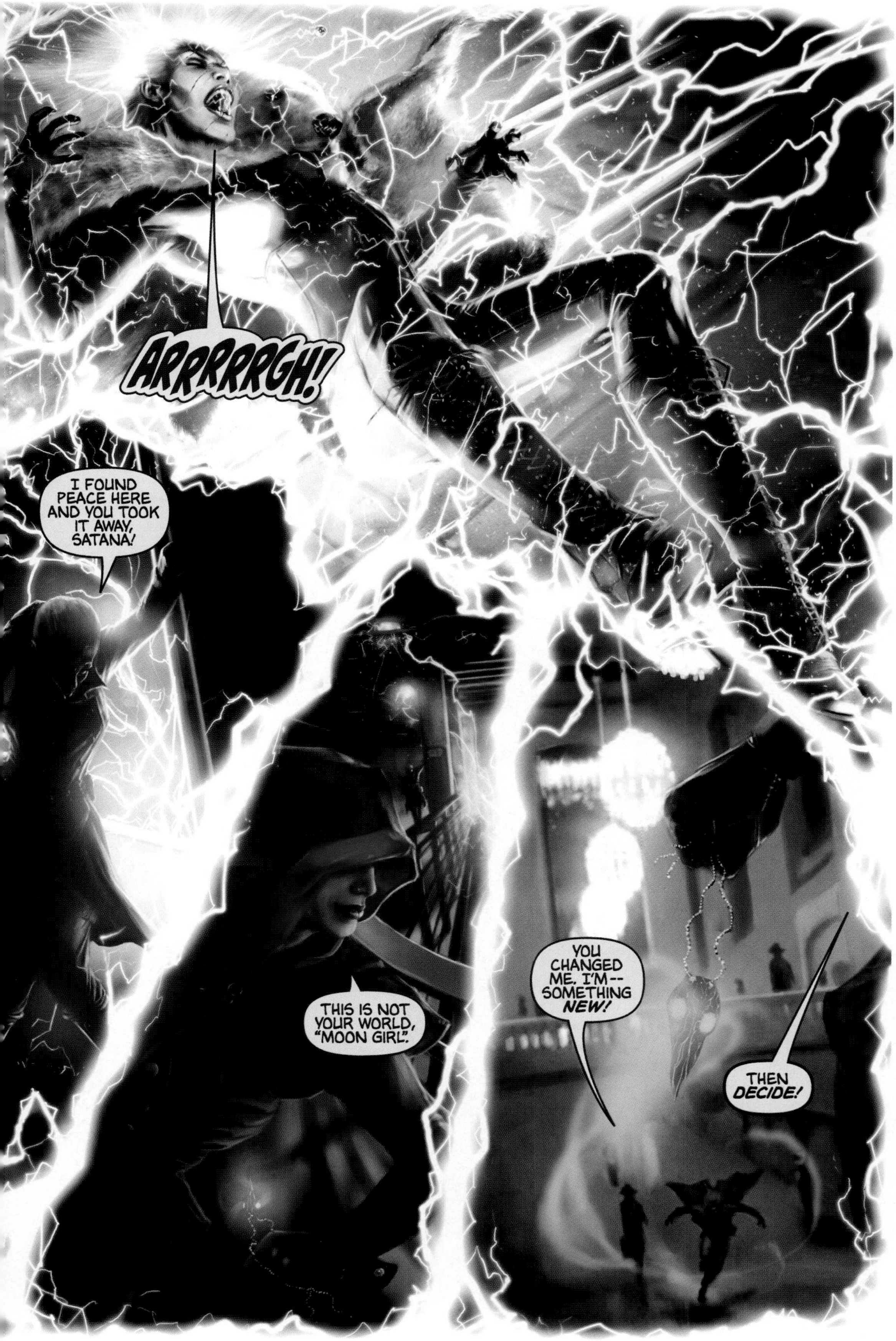
ARRRRRGH!
I FOUND PEACE HERE AND YOU TOOK IT AWAY, SATANA!
THIS IS NOT YOUR WORLD, "MOON GIRL."
YOU CHANGED ME. I'M-- SOMETHING NEW!
THEN DECIDE!

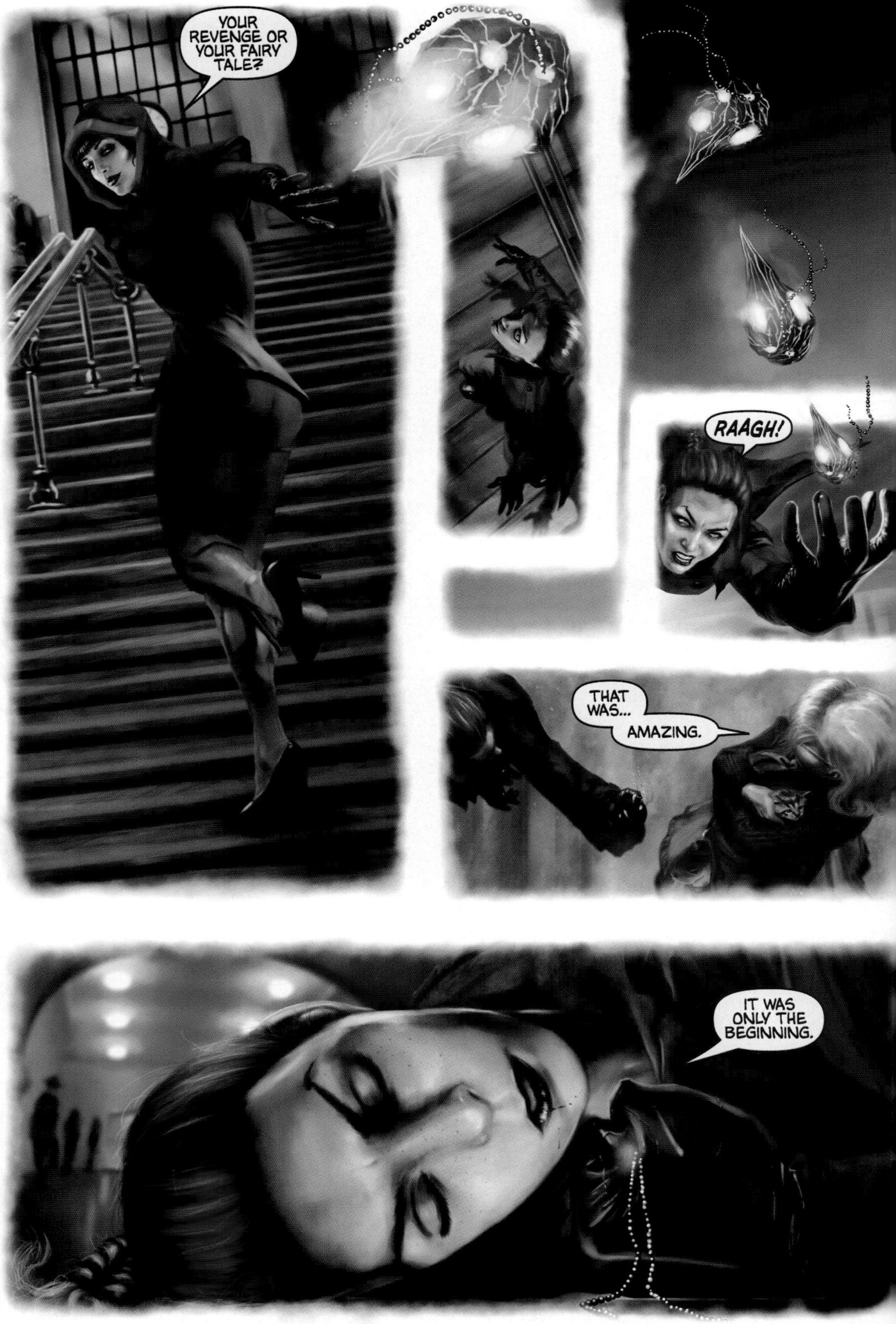
YOUR REVENGE OR YOUR FAIRY TALE?
RAAGH!
THAT WAS... AMAZING.
IT WAS ONLY THE BEGINNING.

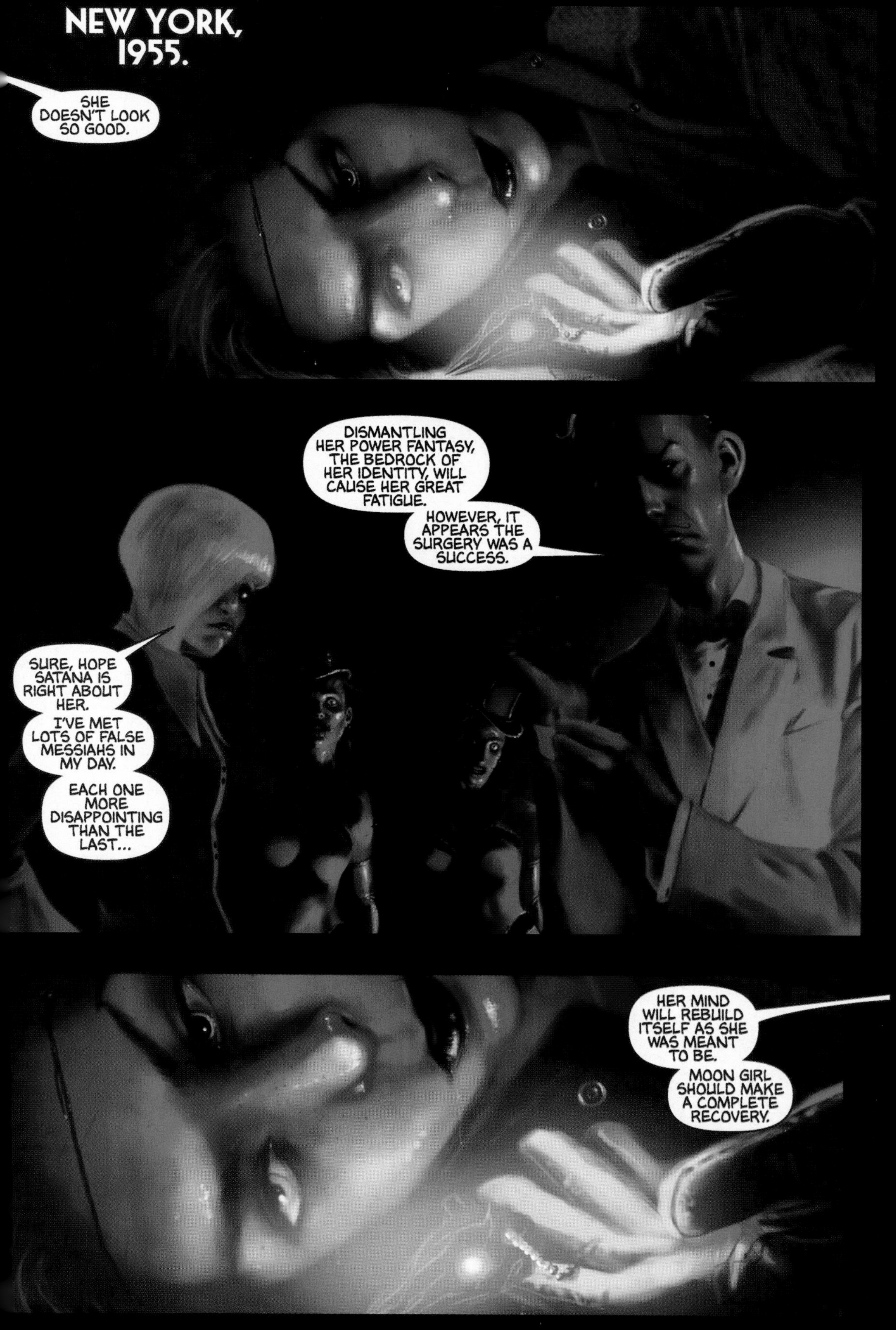
NEW YORK, 1955.
SHE DOESN'T LOOK SO GOOD.
DISMANTLING HER POWER FANTASY, THE BEDROCK OF HER IDENTITY, WILL CAUSE HER GREAT FATIGUE.
HOWEVER, IT APPEARS THE SURGERY WAS A SUCCESS.
SURE, HOPE SATANA IS RIGHT ABOUT HER.
I'VE MET LOTS OF FALSE MESSIAHS IN MY DAY.
EACH ONE MORE DISAPPOINTING THAN THE LAST...
HER MIND WILL REBUILD ITSELF AS SHE WAS MEANT TO BE.
MOON GIRL SHOULD MAKE A COMPLETE RECOVERY.

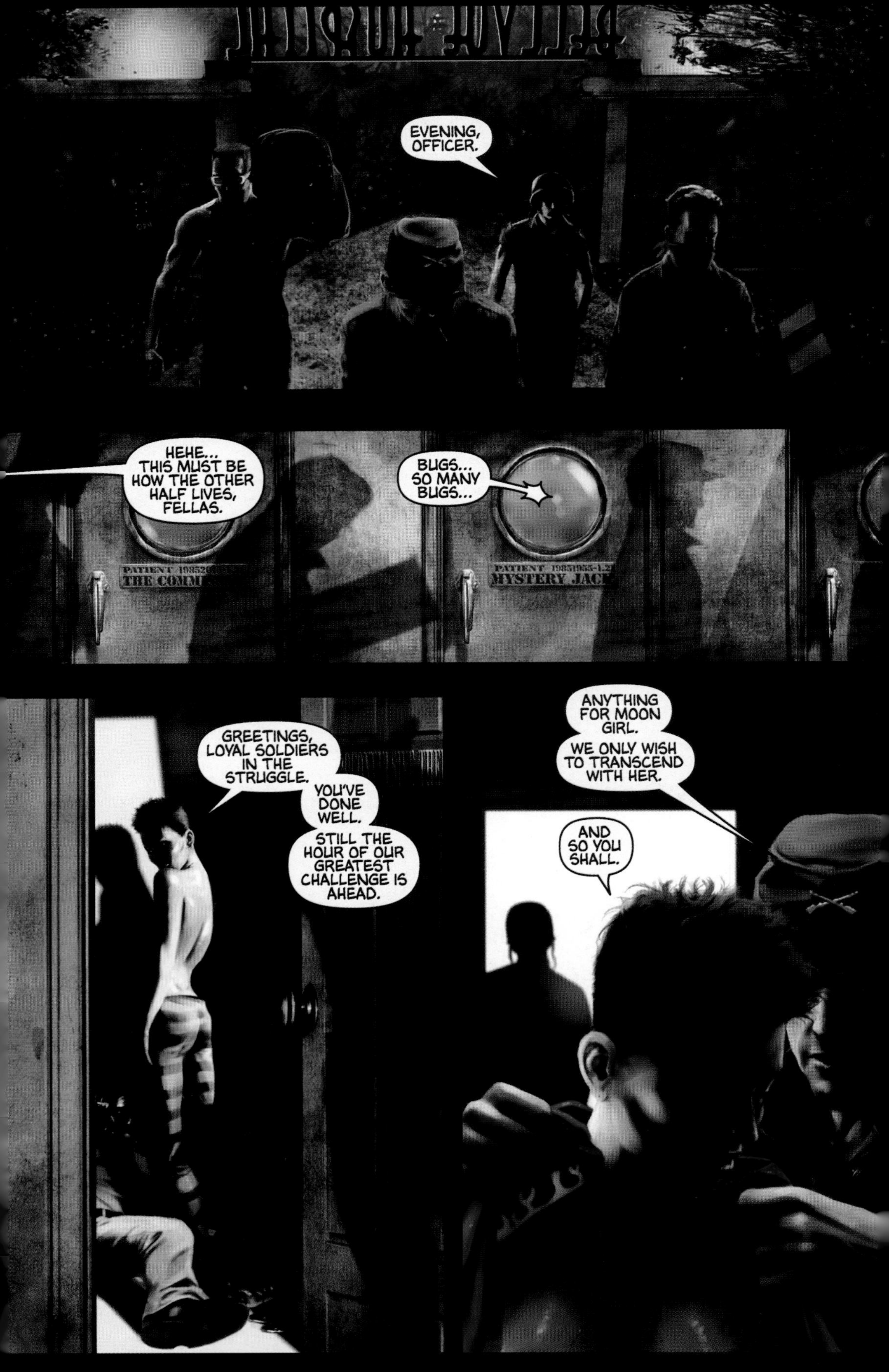
EVENING, OFFICER.
HEHE... THIS MUST BE HOW THE OTHER HALF LIVES, FELLAS.
BUGS... SO MANY BUGS...
GREETINGS, LOYAL SOLDIERS IN THE STRUGGLE.
YOU'VE DONE WELL.
STILL THE HOUR OF OUR GREATEST CHALLENGE IS AHEAD.
ANYTHING FOR MOON GIRL.
WE ONLY WISH TO TRANSCEND WITH HER.
AND SO YOU SHALL.

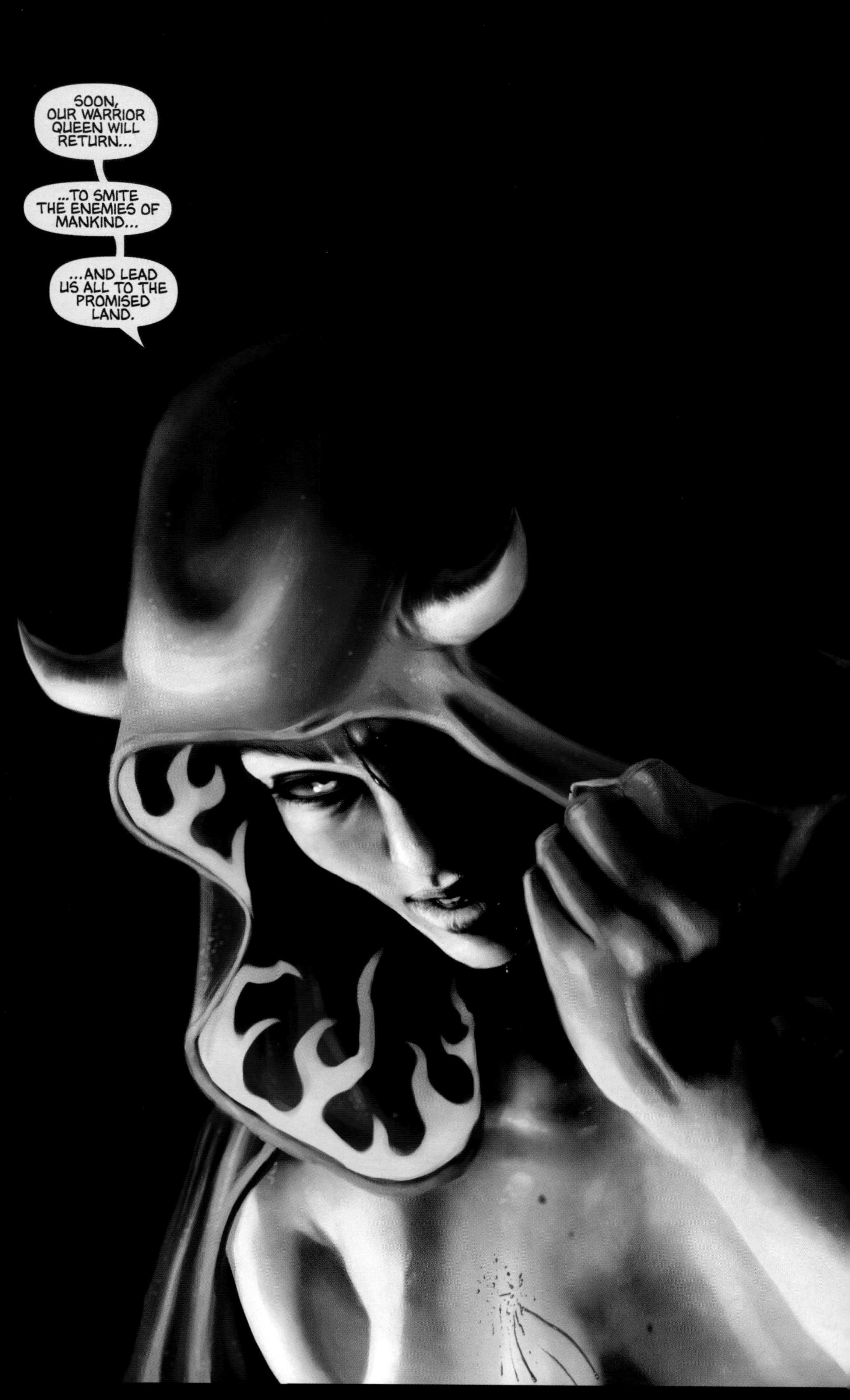
SOON, OUR WARRIOR QUEEN WILL RETURN...
...TO SMITE THE ENEMIES OF MANKIND...
...AND LEAD US ALL TO THE PROMISED LAND.

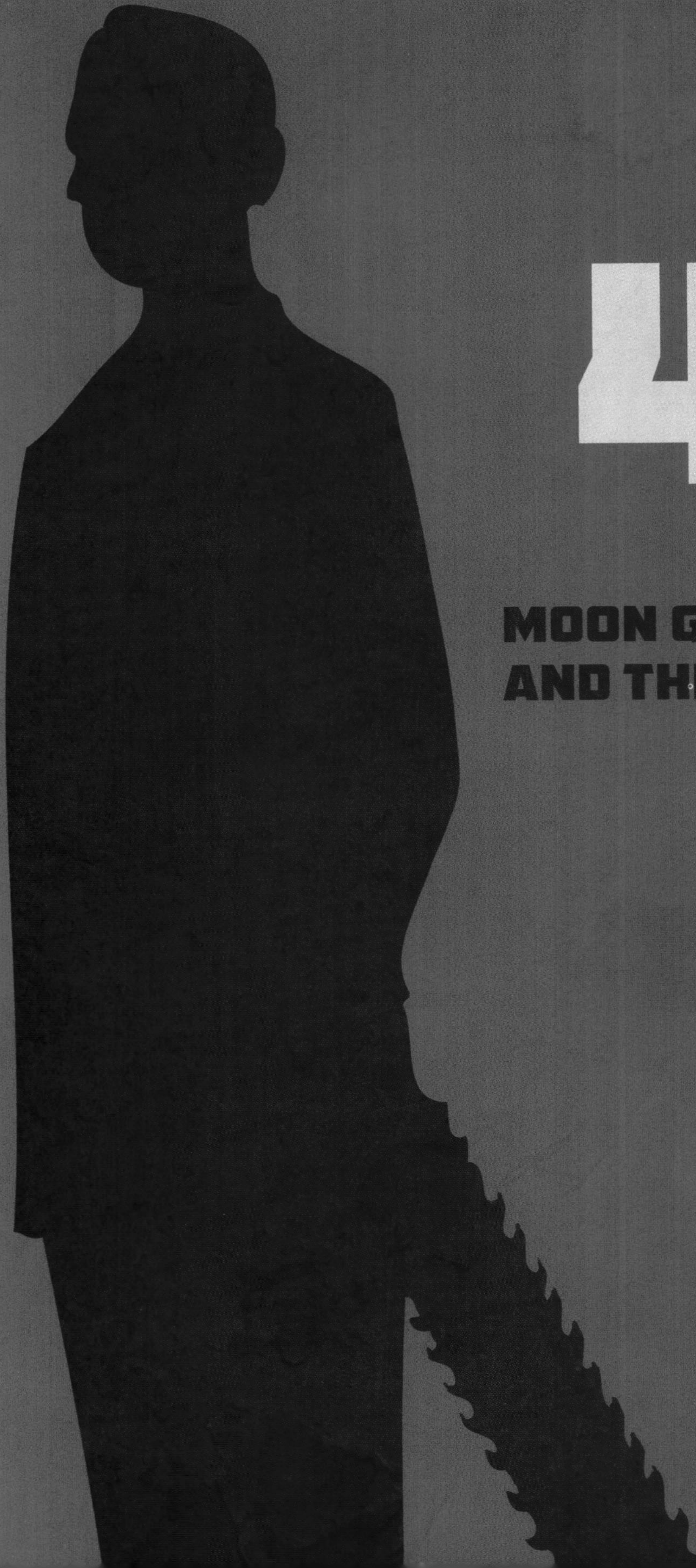

4

MOON GIRL AND THE PRINCE

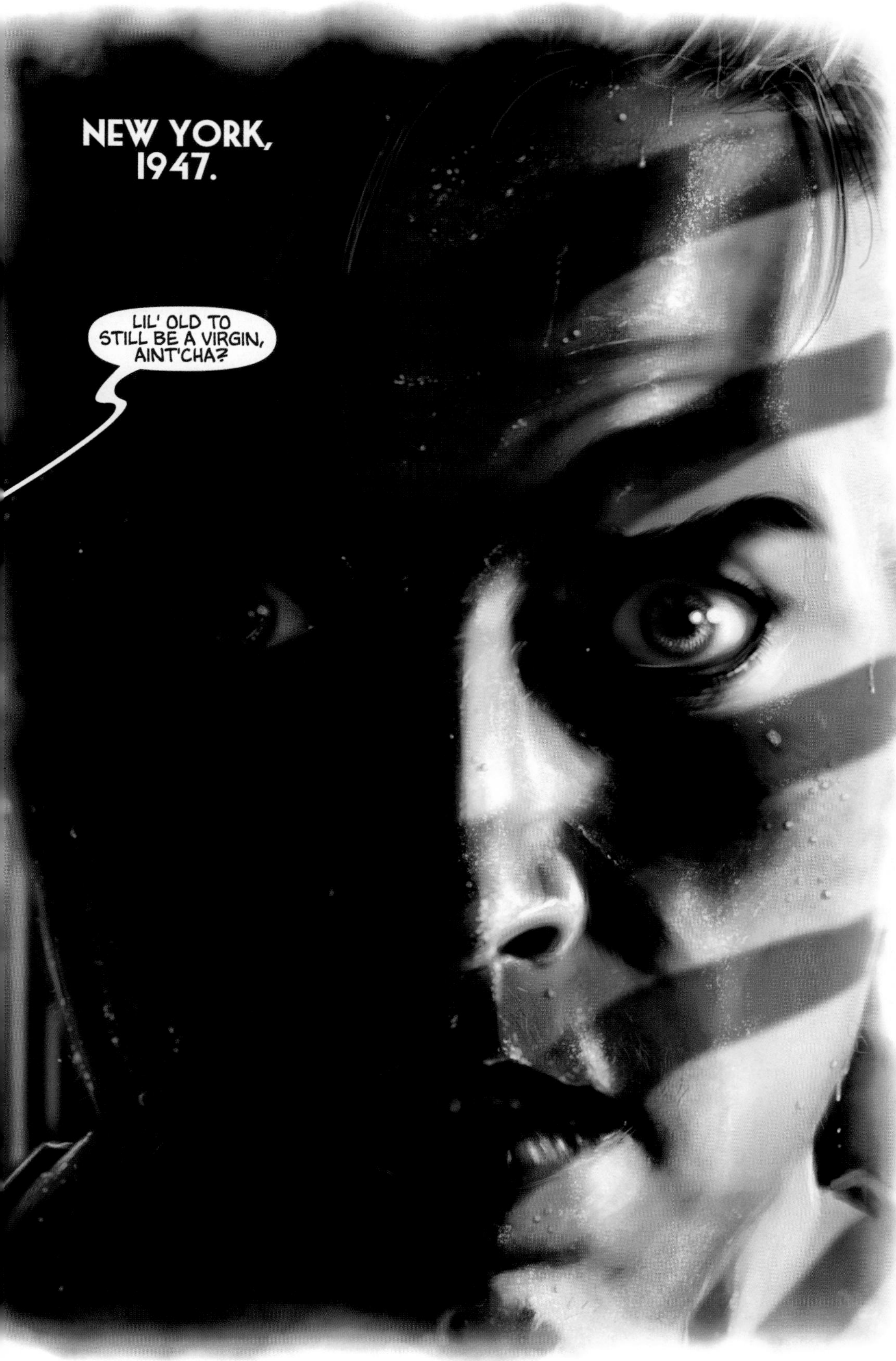
NEW YORK, 1947.
LIL' OLD TO STILL BE A VIRGIN, AINT'CHA?

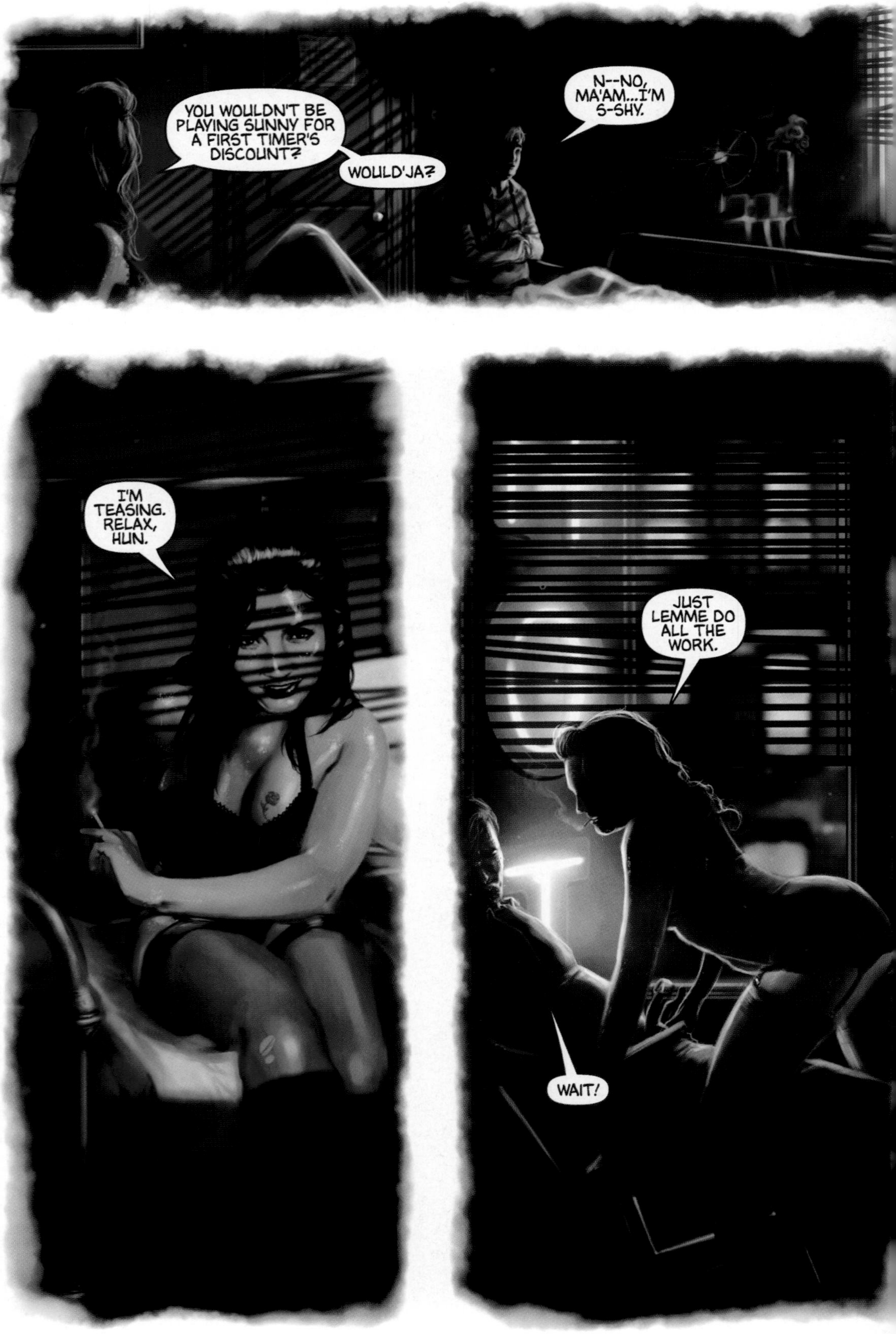
YOU WOULDN'T BE PLAYING SUNNY FOR A FIRST TIMER'S DISCOUNT?
WOULD'JA?
N--NO, MA'AM...I'M S-SHY.
I'M TEASING. RELAX, HUN.
JUST LEMME DO ALL THE WORK.
WAIT!

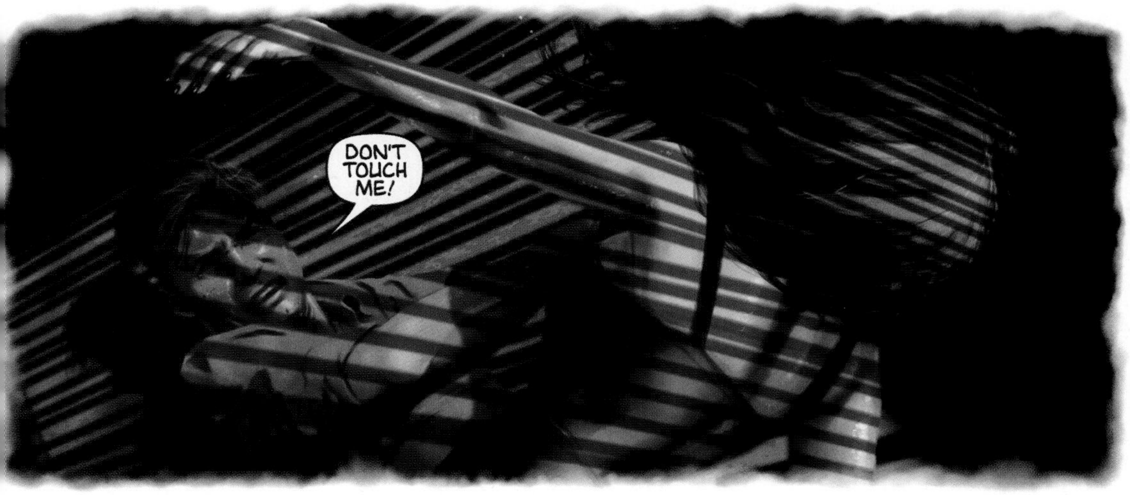
DON'T TOUCH ME!

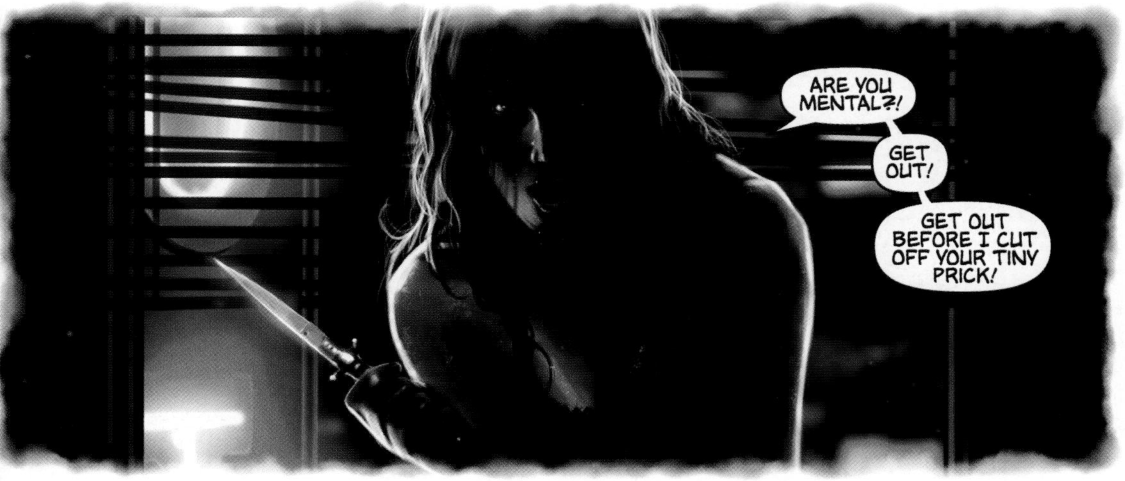
ARE YOU MENTAL?!
GET OUT!
GET OUT BEFORE I CUT OFF YOUR TINY PRICK!

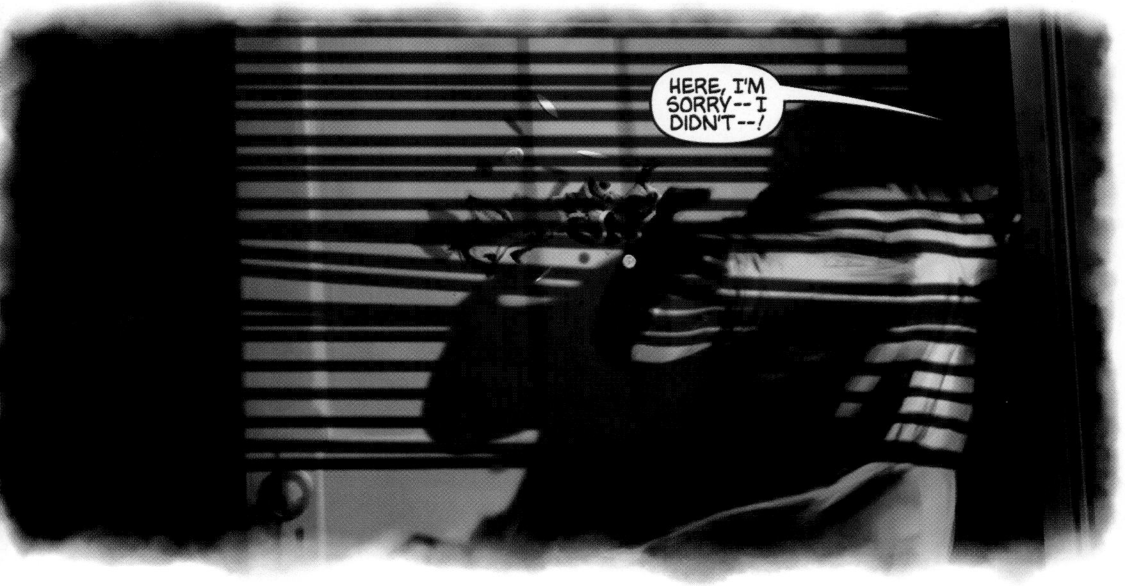
HERE, I'M SORRY-- I DIDN'T--!

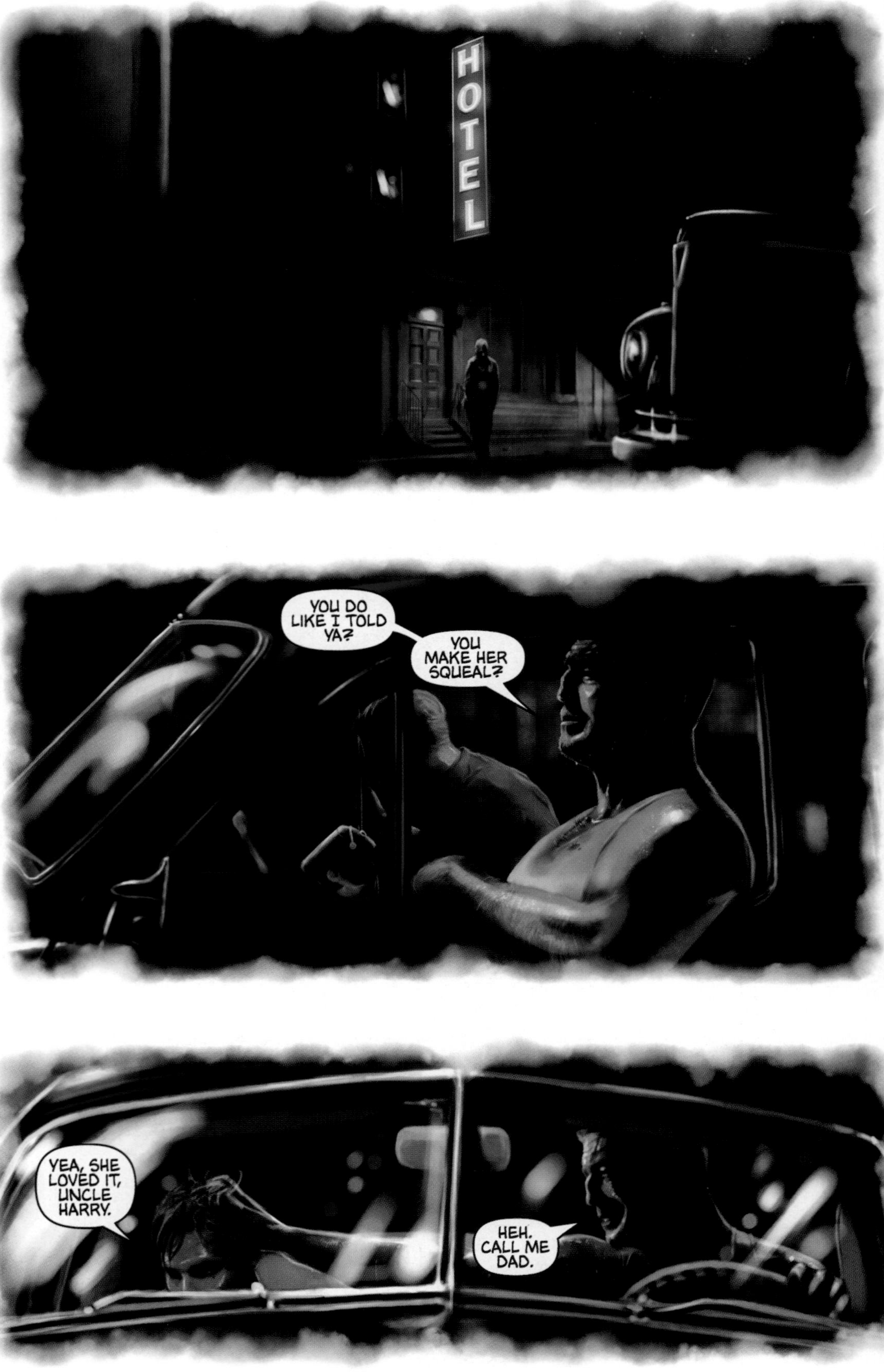
HOTEL
YOU DO LIKE I TOLD YA?
YOU MAKE HER SQUEAL?
YEA, SHE LOVED IT, UNCLE HARRY.
HEH. CALL ME DAD.

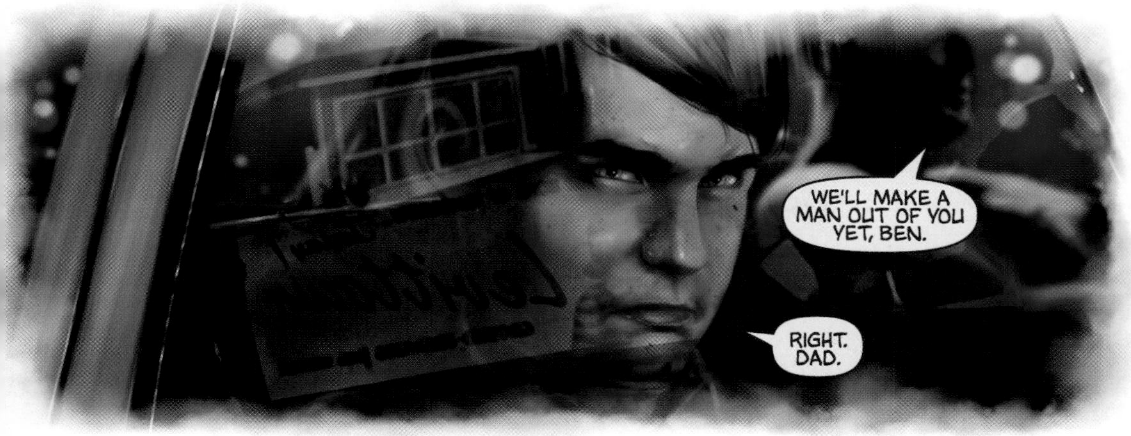
WE'LL MAKE A MAN OUT OF YOU YET, BEN.
RIGHT. DAD.

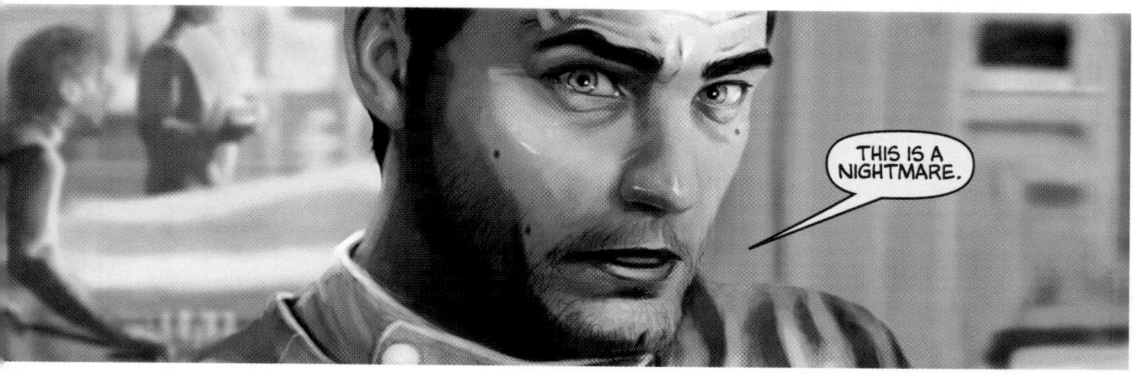
THIS IS A NIGHTMARE.

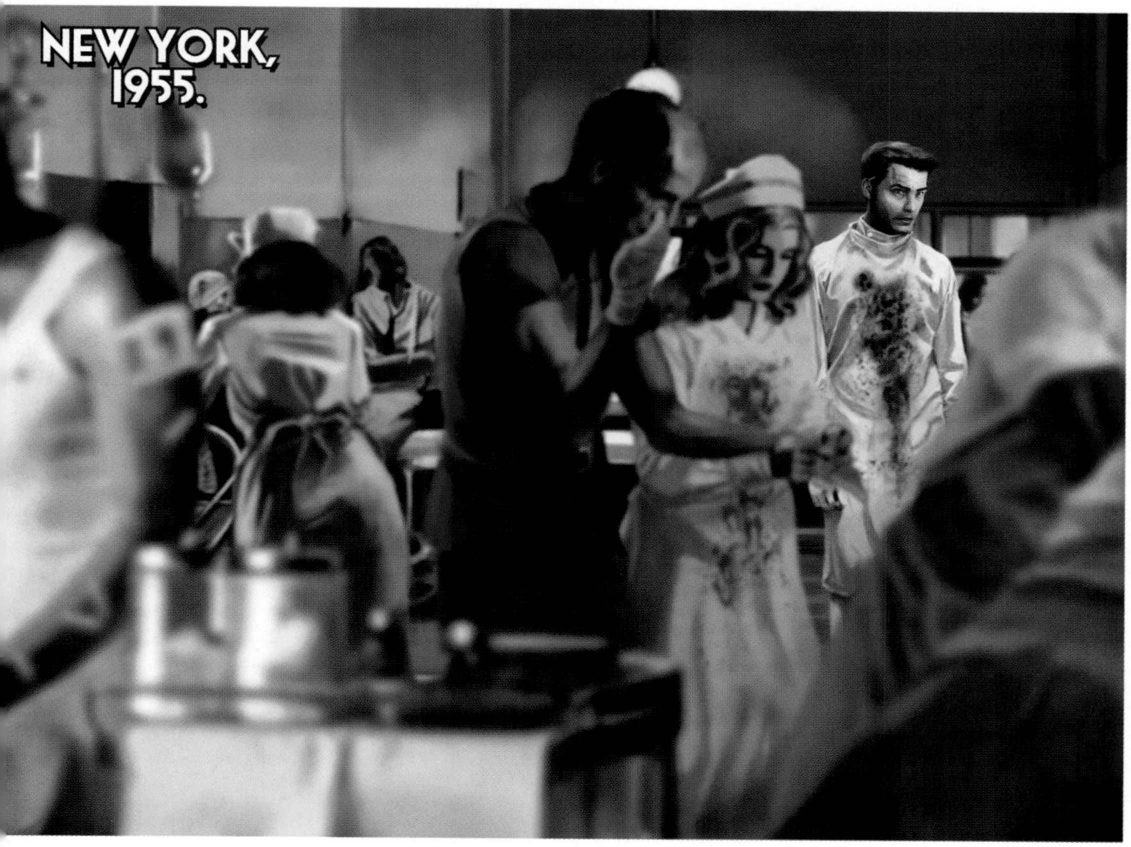
NEW YORK, 1955.

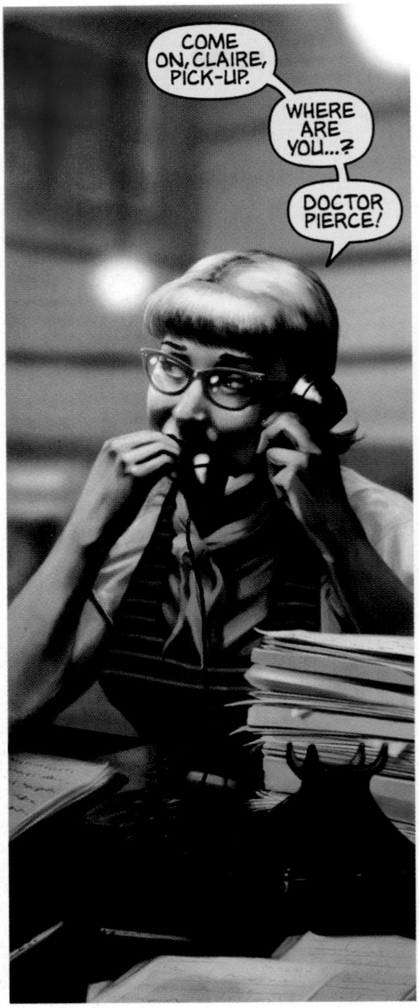
COME ON, CLAIRE, PICK-UP.
WHERE ARE YOU...?
DOCTOR PIERCE!

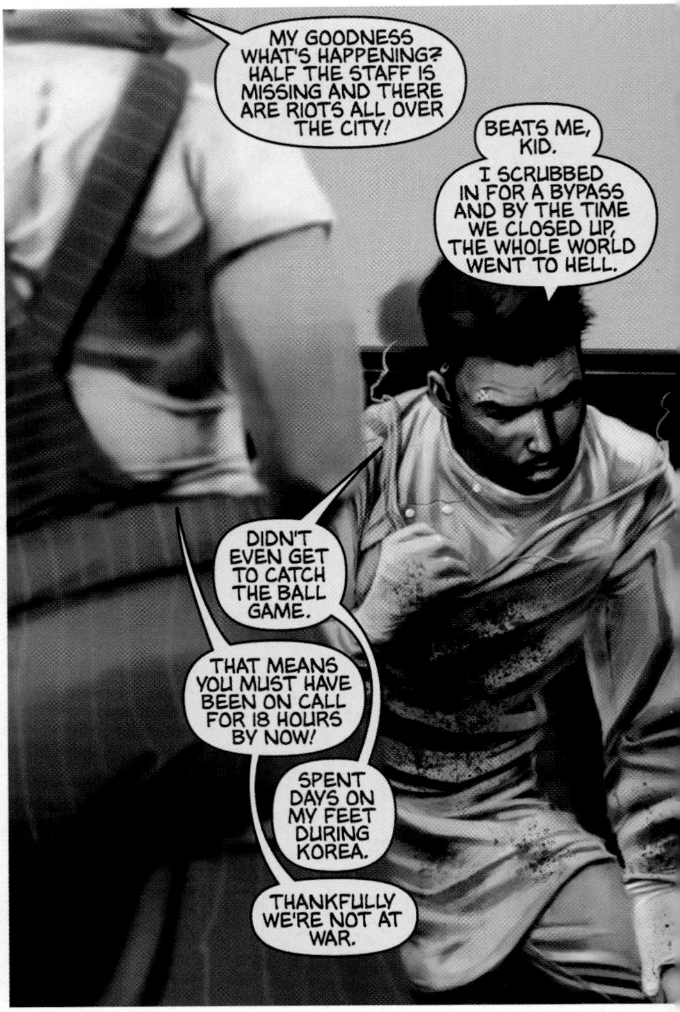
MY GOODNESS WHAT'S HAPPENING? HALF THE STAFF IS MISSING AND THERE ARE RIOTS ALL OVER THE CITY!
BEATS ME, KID.
I SCRUBBED IN FOR A BYPASS AND BY THE TIME WE CLOSED UP, THE WHOLE WORLD WENT TO HELL.
DIDN'T EVEN GET TO CATCH THE BALL GAME.
THAT MEANS YOU MUST HAVE BEEN ON CALL FOR 18 HOURS BY NOW!
SPENT DAYS ON MY FEET DURING KOREA.
THANKFULLY WE'RE NOT AT WAR.

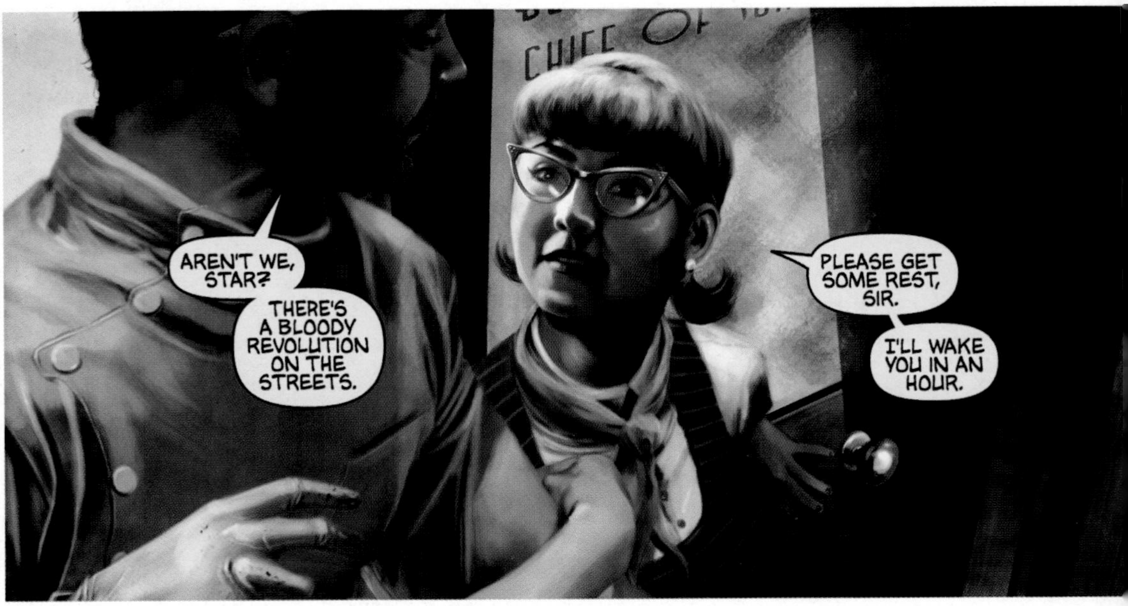
AREN'T WE, STAR?
THERE'S A BLOODY REVOLUTION ON THE STREETS.
PLEASE GET SOME REST, SIR.
I'LL WAKE YOU IN AN HOUR.

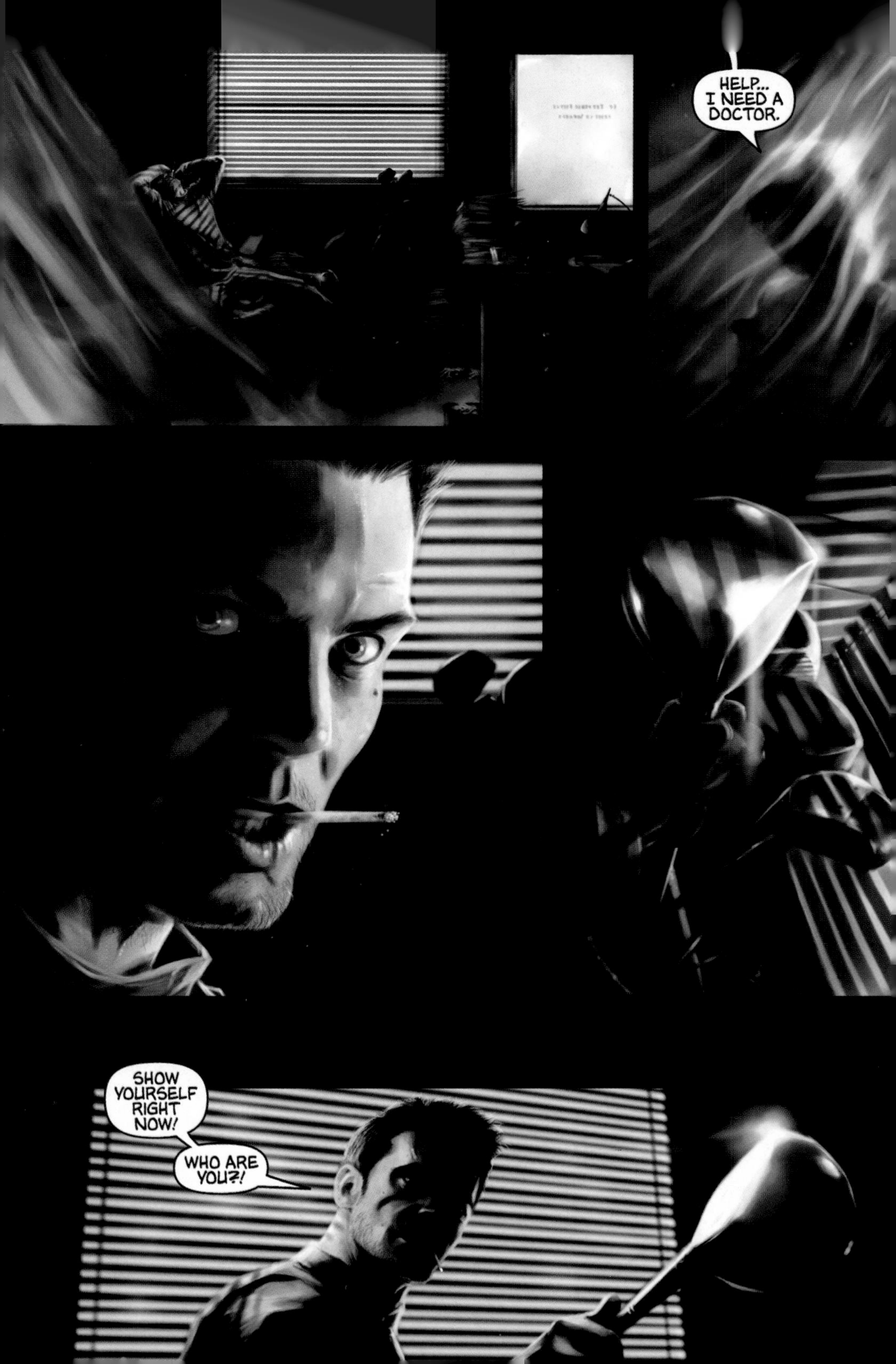
HELP... I NEED A DOCTOR.
SHOW YOURSELF RIGHT NOW!
WHO ARE YOU?!

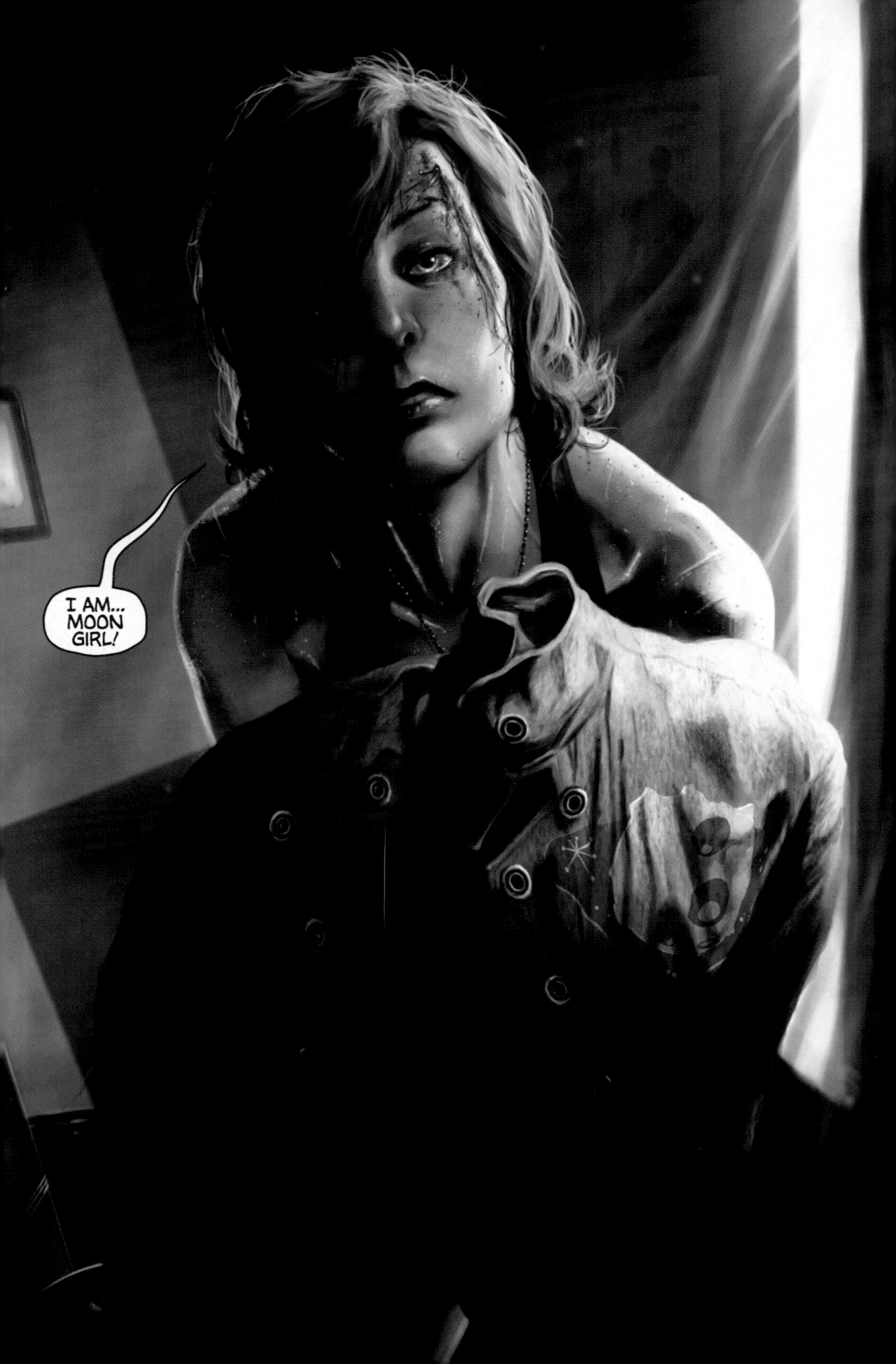
I AM... MOON GIRL!

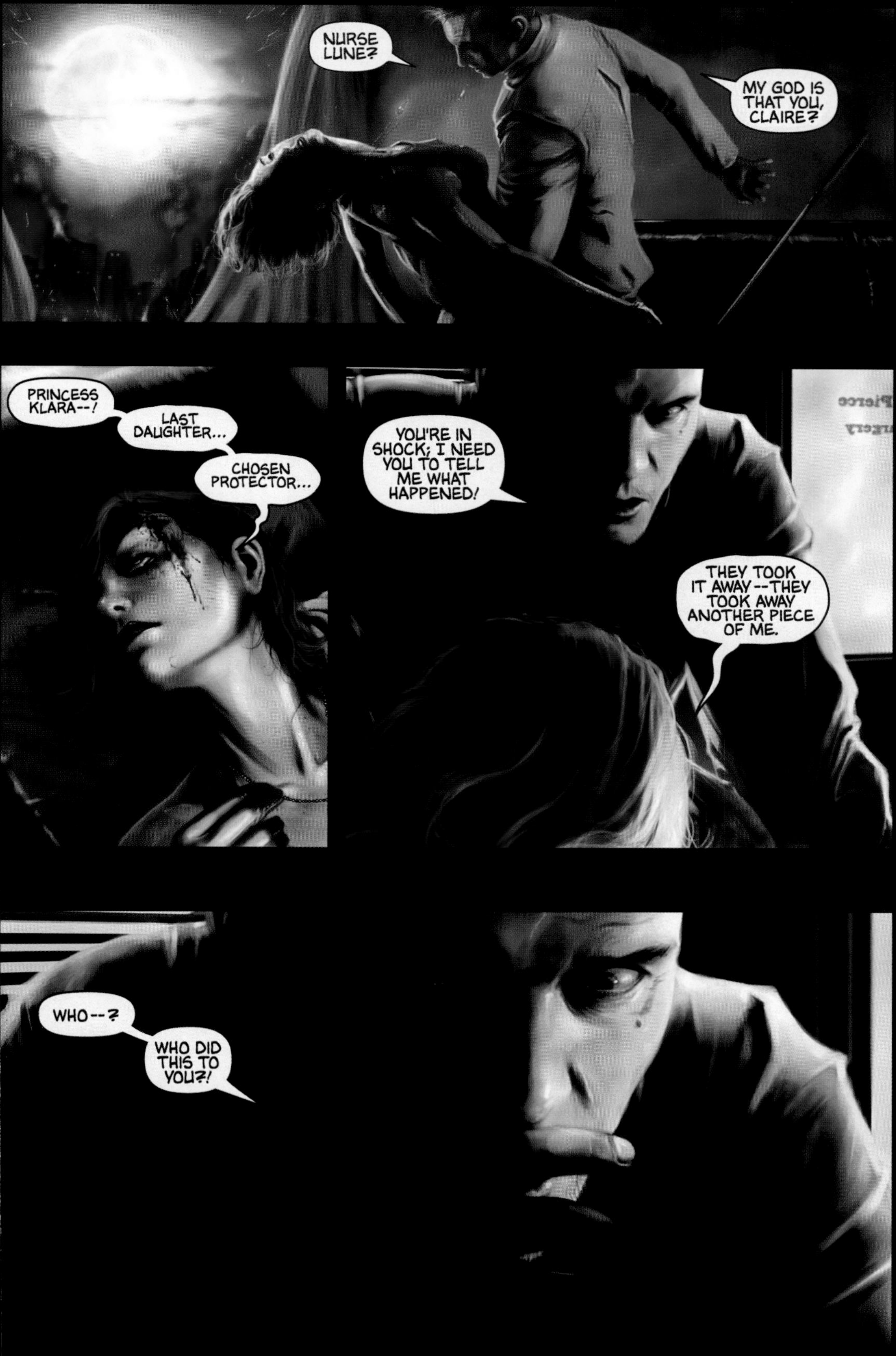
NURSE LUNE?
MY GOD IS THAT YOU, CLAIRE?
PRINCESS KLARA--!
LAST DAUGHTER...
CHOSEN PROTECTOR...
YOU'RE IN SHOCK; I NEED YOU TO TELL ME WHAT HAPPENED!
THEY TOOK IT AWAY--THEY TOOK AWAY ANOTHER PIECE OF ME.
WHO--?
WHO DID THIS TO YOU?!

SOUTH KOREA,
1951.

GOOD vs evil

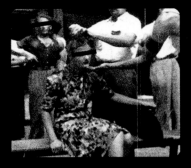

the Police Ma

in Your Min

Kill

Hell

is

Other People

H an Beings

lways

You

WE'VE HAD SUBSTANTIAL SUCCESS AT CONDITIONING VOLUNTEERS WITH SURGERY AND CHEMICAL GASSES.

HOWEVER, WITH SUBLIMINAL PSYCHOTHERAPY WE'LL BE ABLE TO CONQUER WHOLE NATIONS BEFORE EVER PUTTING A BOOT ON THE GROUND.

HYPNOTIC SUGGESTIONS HIDDEN WITHIN RADIO AND TELEVISION PROGRAMS ARE PLANTED DEEP WITHIN THE SUBCONSCIOUS.

A COMMAND PHRASE ACTIVATES A COMPLETELY OBEDIENT ARMY OF RIGHTEOUS SOLDIERS RISING UP FROM WITHIN THE ENEMY'S CIVILIAN POPULATION.

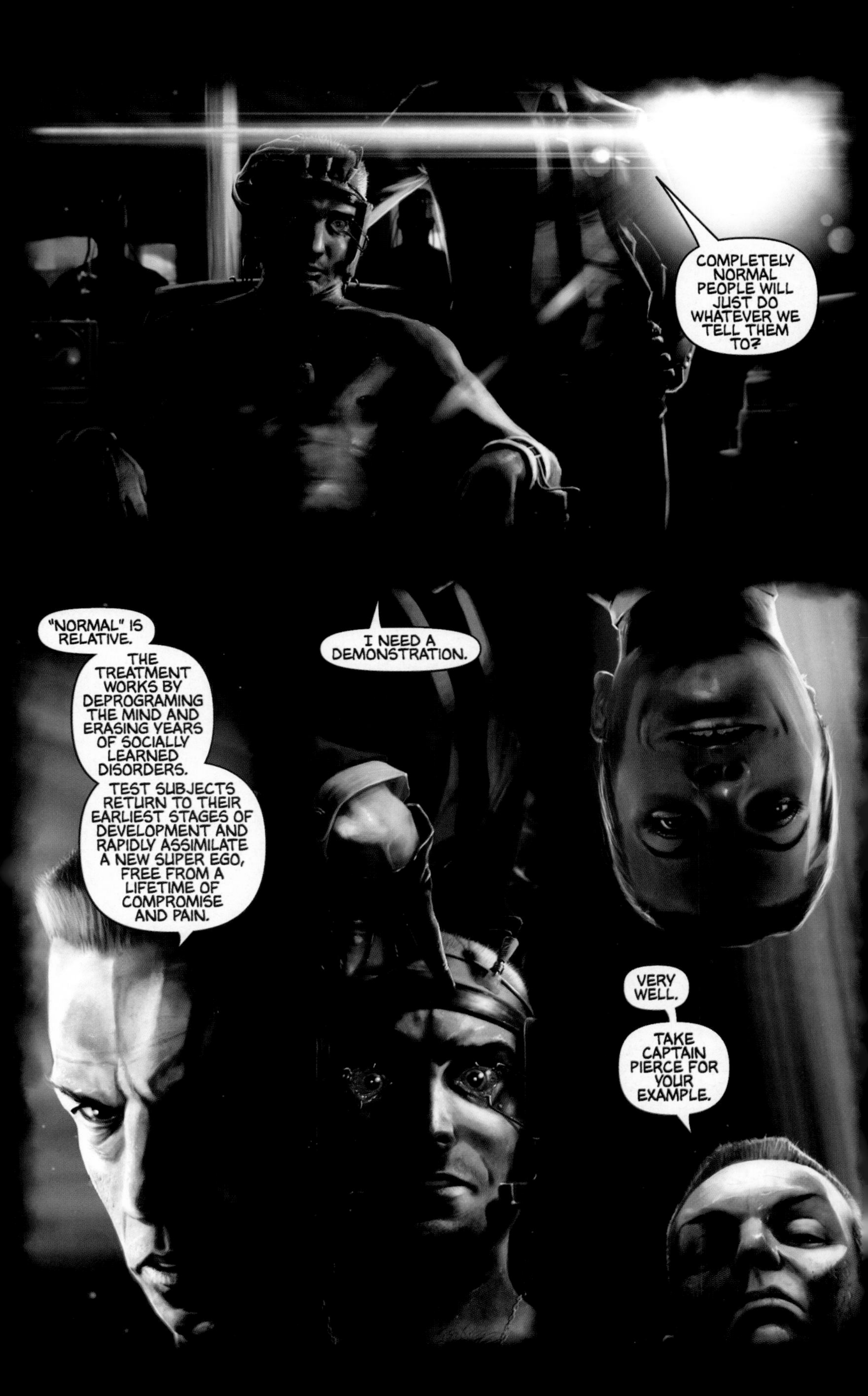
COMPLETELY NORMAL PEOPLE WILL JUST DO WHATEVER WE TELL THEM TO?
I NEED A DEMONSTRATION.
"NORMAL" IS RELATIVE.
THE TREATMENT WORKS BY DEPROGRAMING THE MIND AND ERASING YEARS OF SOCIALLY LEARNED DISORDERS.
TEST SUBJECTS RETURN TO THEIR EARLIEST STAGES OF DEVELOPMENT AND RAPIDLY ASSIMILATE A NEW SUPER EGO, FREE FROM A LIFETIME OF COMPROMISE AND PAIN.
VERY WELL.
TAKE CAPTAIN PIERCE FOR YOUR EXAMPLE.

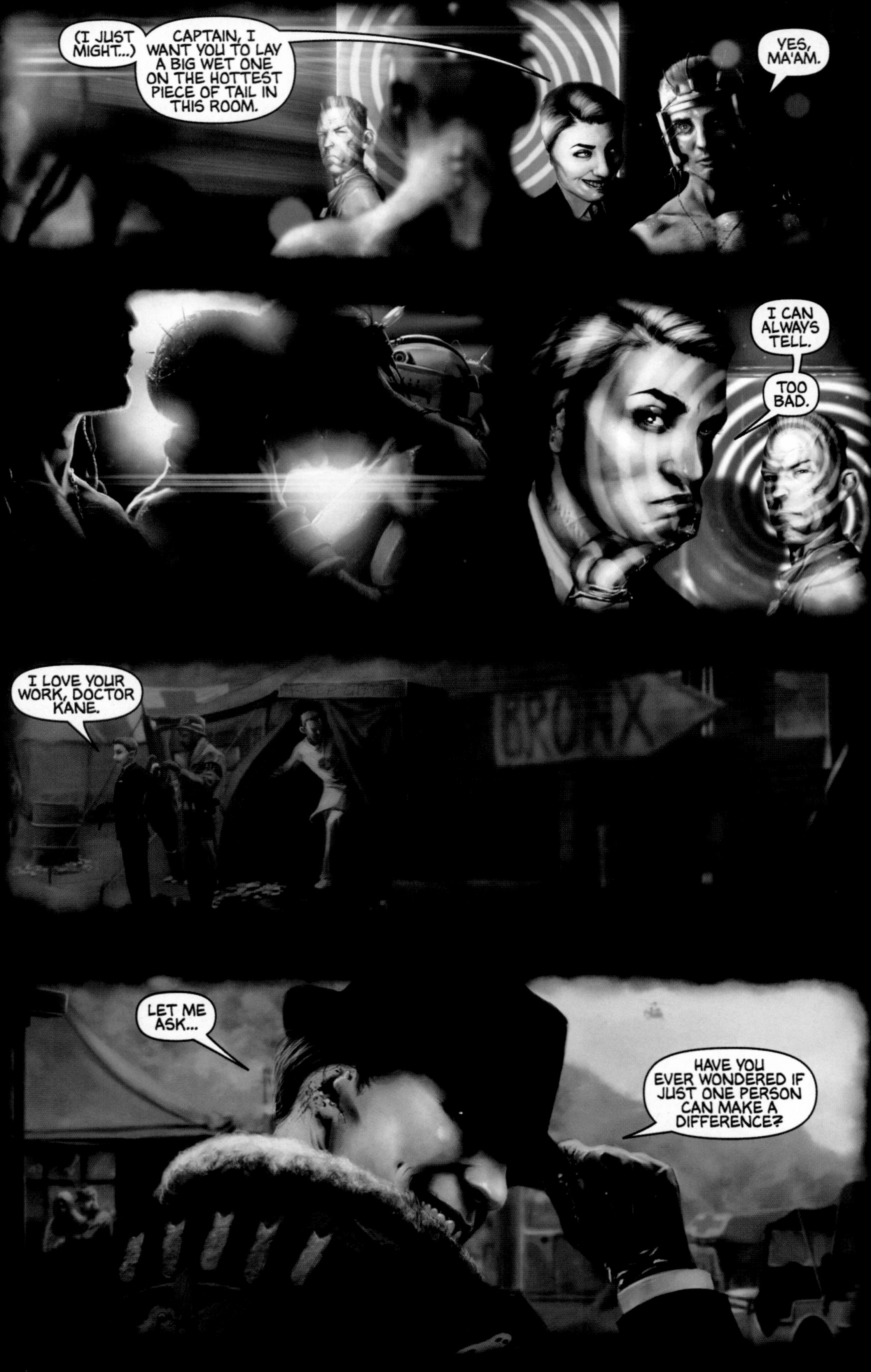
(I JUST MIGHT...)
CAPTAIN, I WANT YOU TO LAY A BIG WET ONE ON THE HOTTEST PIECE OF TAIL IN THIS ROOM.
YES, MA'AM.
I CAN ALWAYS TELL.
TOO BAD.
I LOVE YOUR WORK, DOCTOR KANE.
BRONX
LET ME ASK...
HAVE YOU EVER WONDERED IF JUST ONE PERSON CAN MAKE A DIFFERENCE?

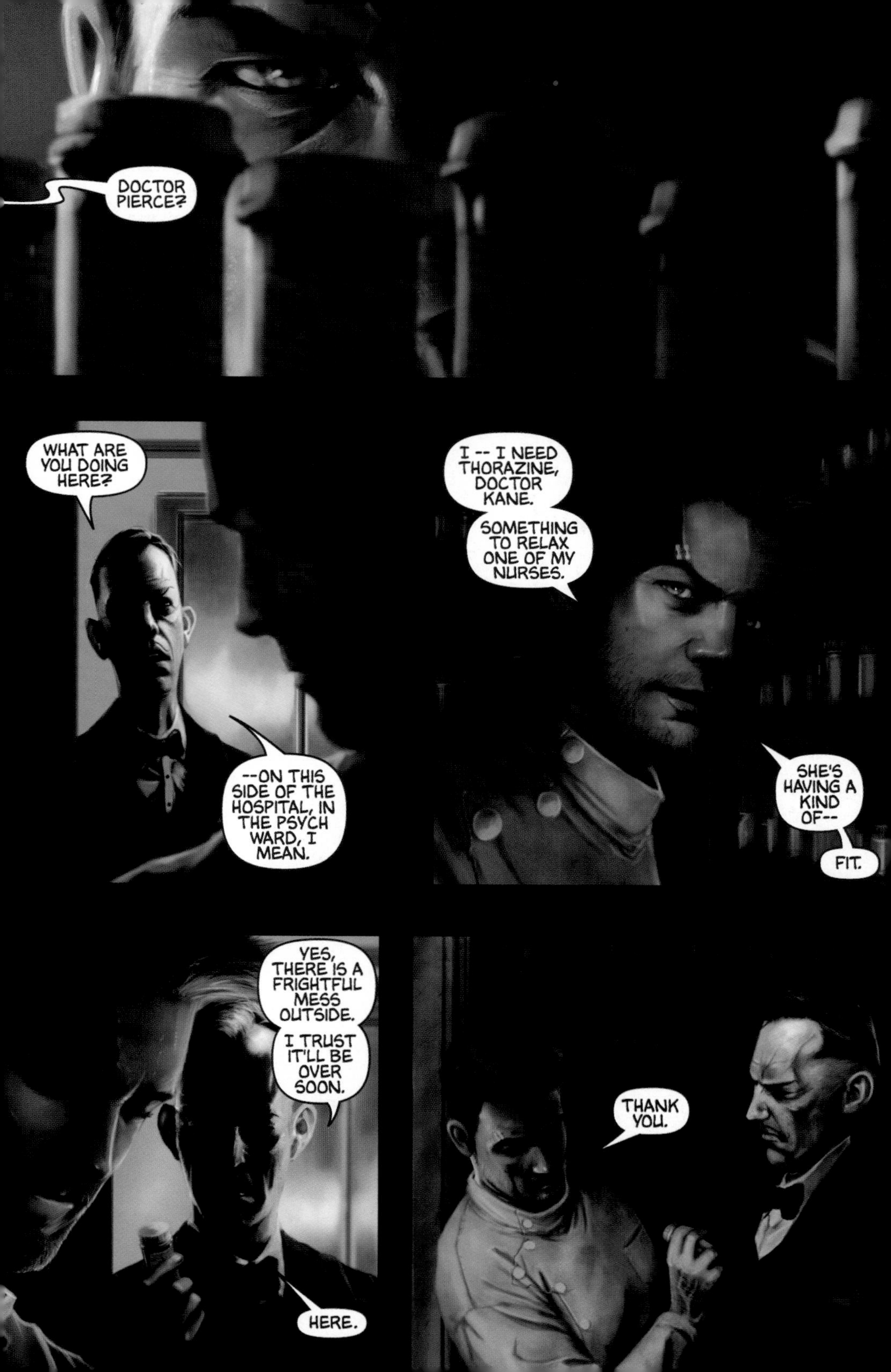
DOCTOR PIERCE?
WHAT ARE YOU DOING HERE?
--ON THIS SIDE OF THE HOSPITAL, IN THE PSYCH WARD, I MEAN.
I -- I NEED THORAZINE, DOCTOR KANE.
SOMETHING TO RELAX ONE OF MY NURSES.
SHE'S HAVING A KIND OF--
FIT.
YES, THERE IS A FRIGHTFUL MESS OUTSIDE.
I TRUST IT'LL BE OVER SOON.
HERE.
THANK YOU.

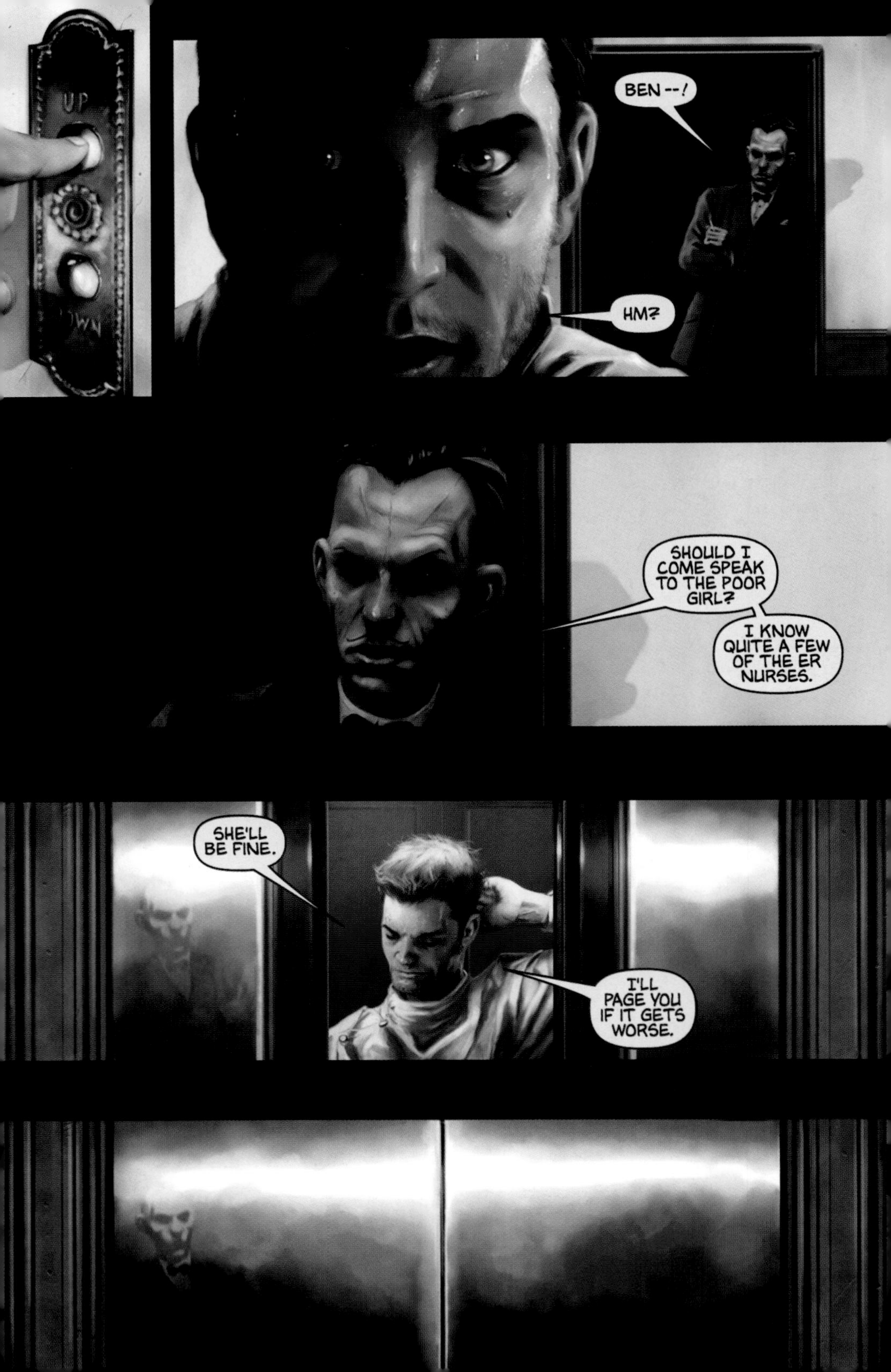
UP
BEN --!
HM?
SHOULD I COME SPEAK TO THE POOR GIRL?
I KNOW QUITE A FEW OF THE ER NURSES.
SHE'LL BE FINE.
I'LL PAGE YOU IF IT GETS WORSE.

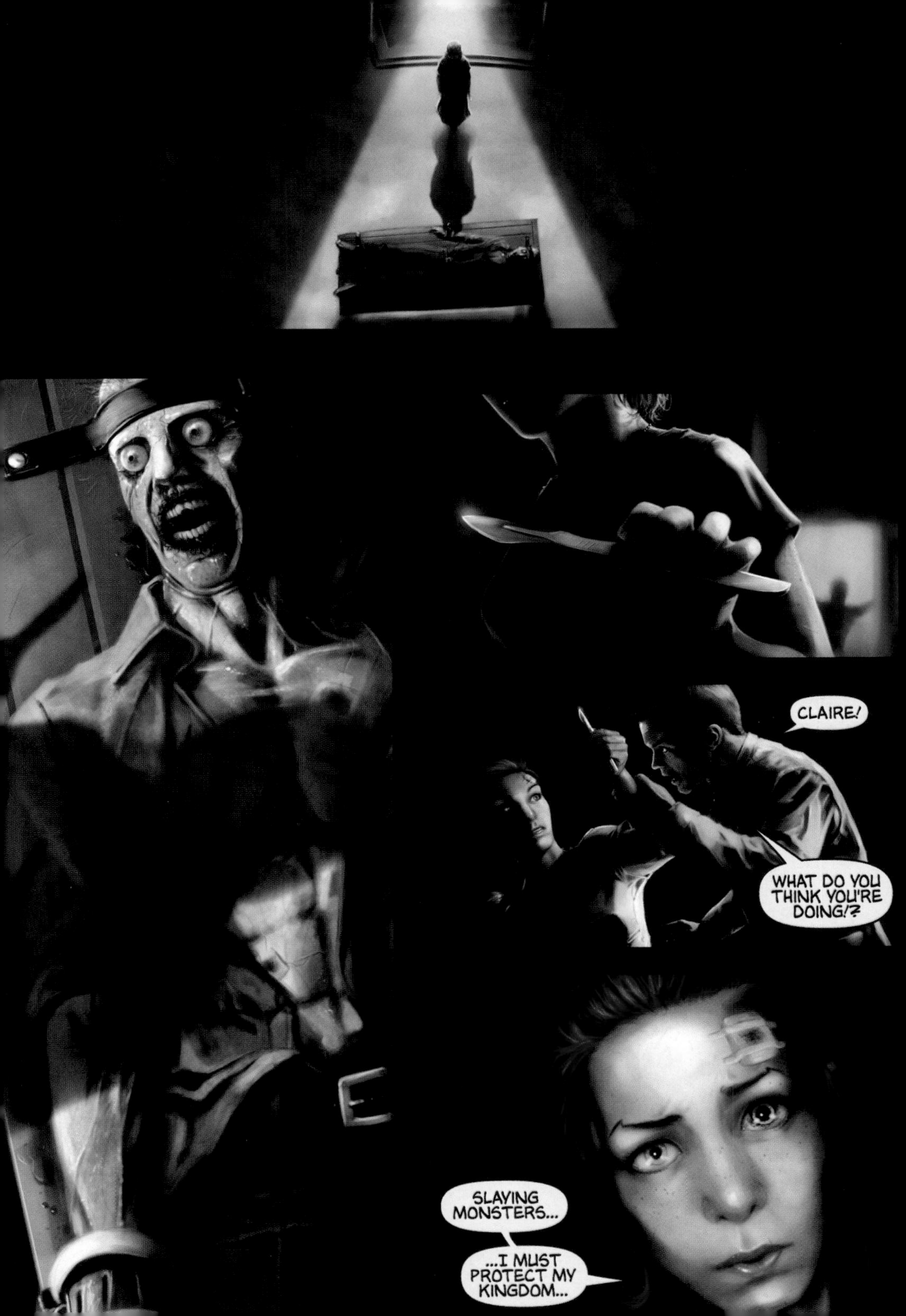
CLAIRE!
WHAT DO YOU THINK YOU'RE DOING!?
SLAYING MONSTERS...
...I MUST PROTECT MY KINGDOM...

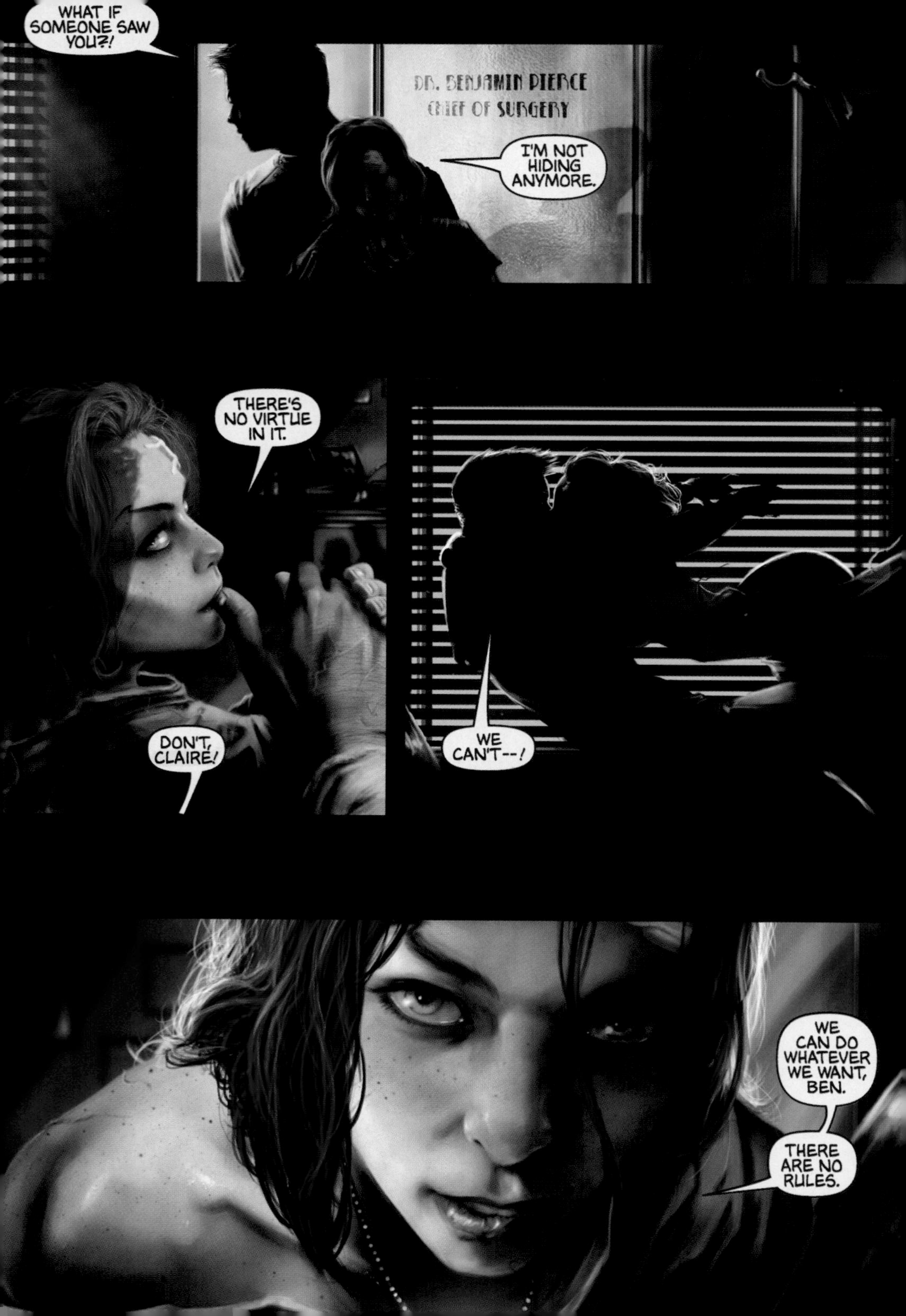
WHAT IF SOMEONE SAW YOU?!
DR. BENJAMIN PIERCE
CHIEF OF SURGERY
I'M NOT HIDING ANYMORE.
THERE'S NO VIRTUE IN IT.
DON'T, CLAIRE!
WE CAN'T--!
WE CAN DO WHATEVER WE WANT, BEN.
THERE ARE NO RULES.

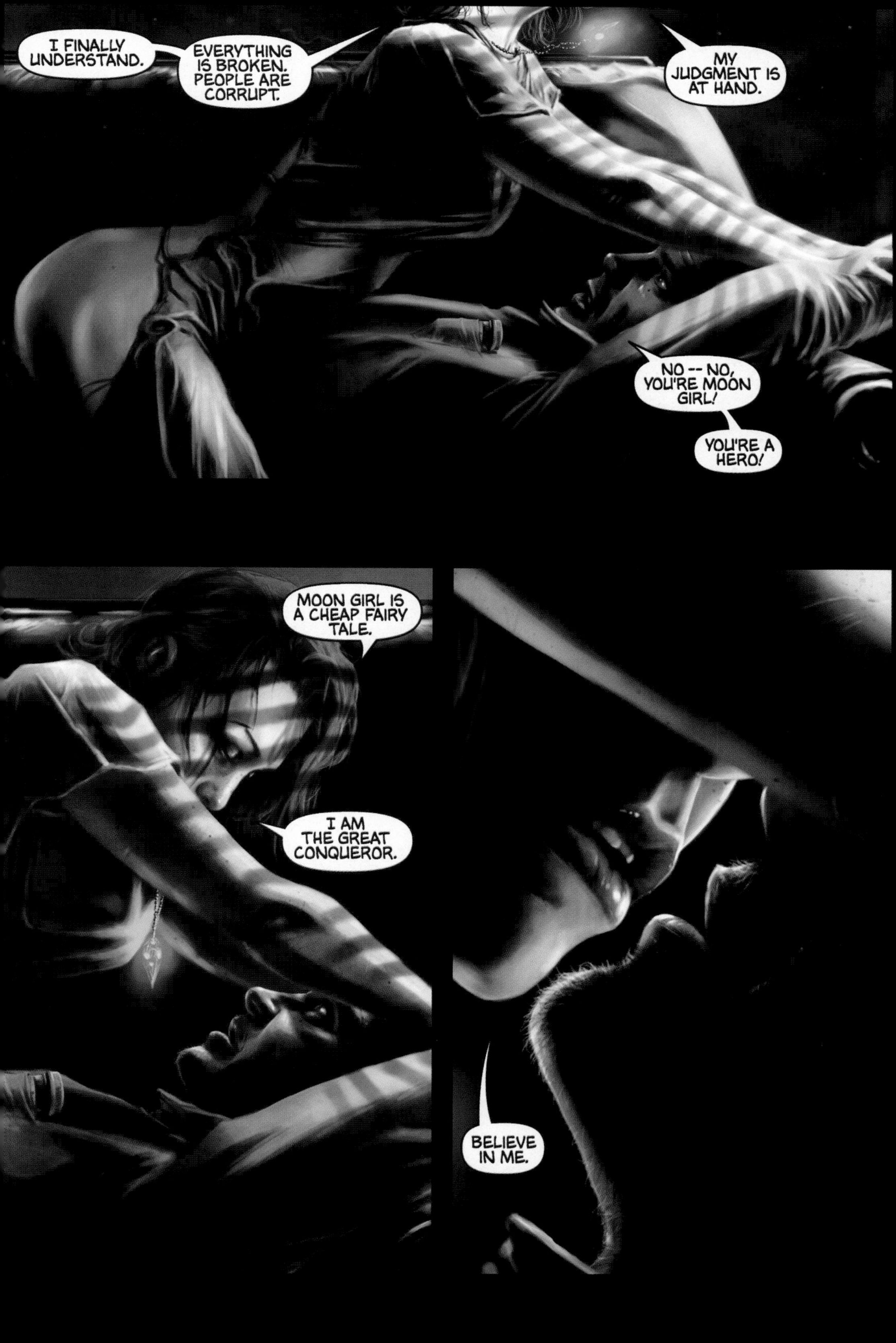
I FINALLY UNDERSTAND.
EVERYTHING IS BROKEN. PEOPLE ARE CORRUPT.
MY JUDGMENT IS AT HAND.
NO -- NO, YOU'RE MOON GIRL!
YOU'RE A HERO!
MOON GIRL IS A CHEAP FAIRY TALE.
I AM THE GREAT CONQUEROR.
BELIEVE IN ME.

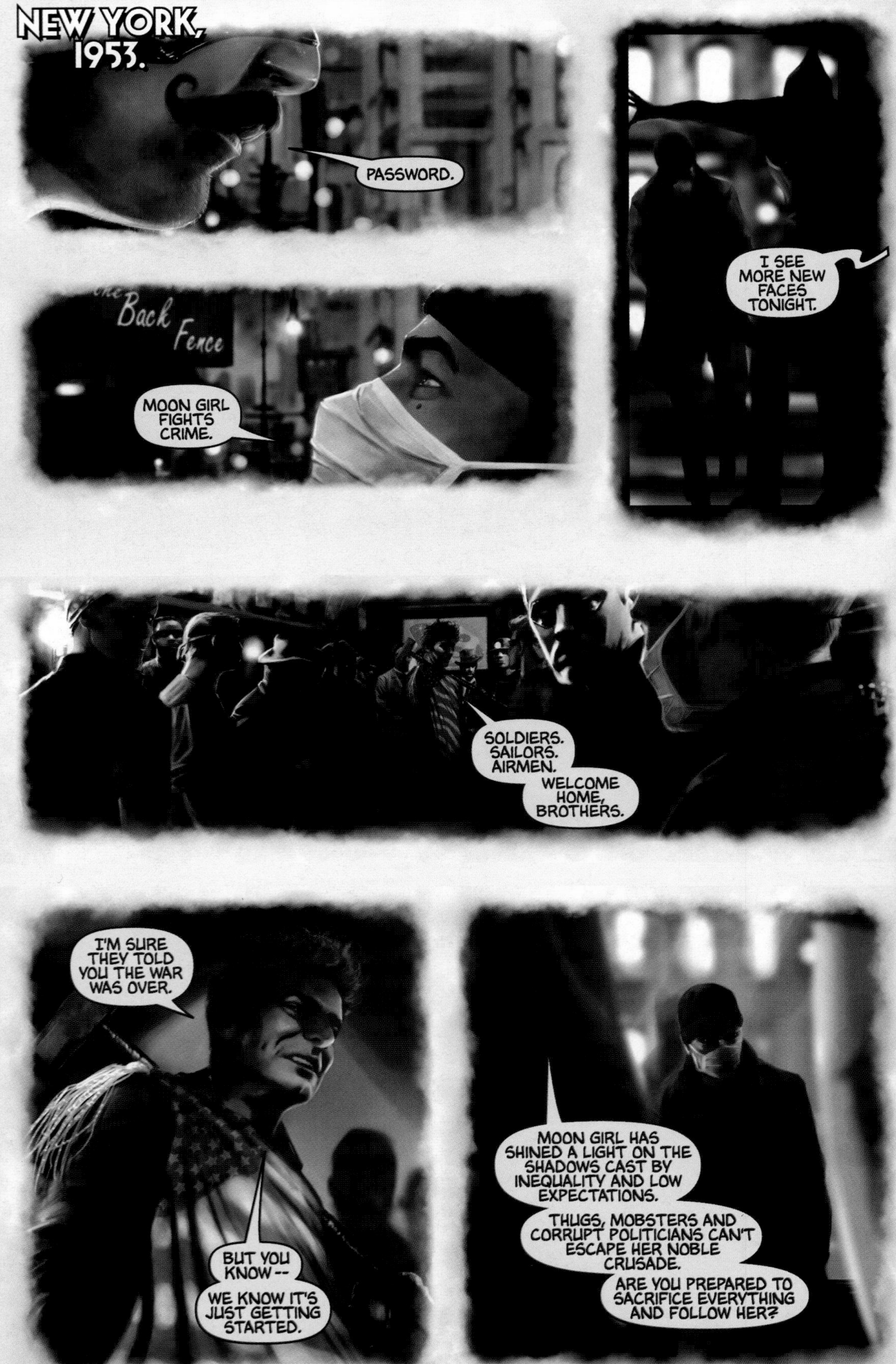
NEW YORK, 1953.
PASSWORD.
I SEE MORE NEW FACES TONIGHT.
Back Fence
MOON GIRL FIGHTS CRIME.
SOLDIERS. SAILORS. AIRMEN.
WELCOME HOME, BROTHERS.
I'M SURE THEY TOLD YOU THE WAR WAS OVER.
BUT YOU KNOW --
WE KNOW IT'S JUST GETTING STARTED.
MOON GIRL HAS SHINED A LIGHT ON THE SHADOWS CAST BY INEQUALITY AND LOW EXPECTATIONS.
THUGS, MOBSTERS AND CORRUPT POLITICIANS CAN'T ESCAPE HER NOBLE CRUSADE.
ARE YOU PREPARED TO SACRIFICE EVERYTHING AND FOLLOW HER?

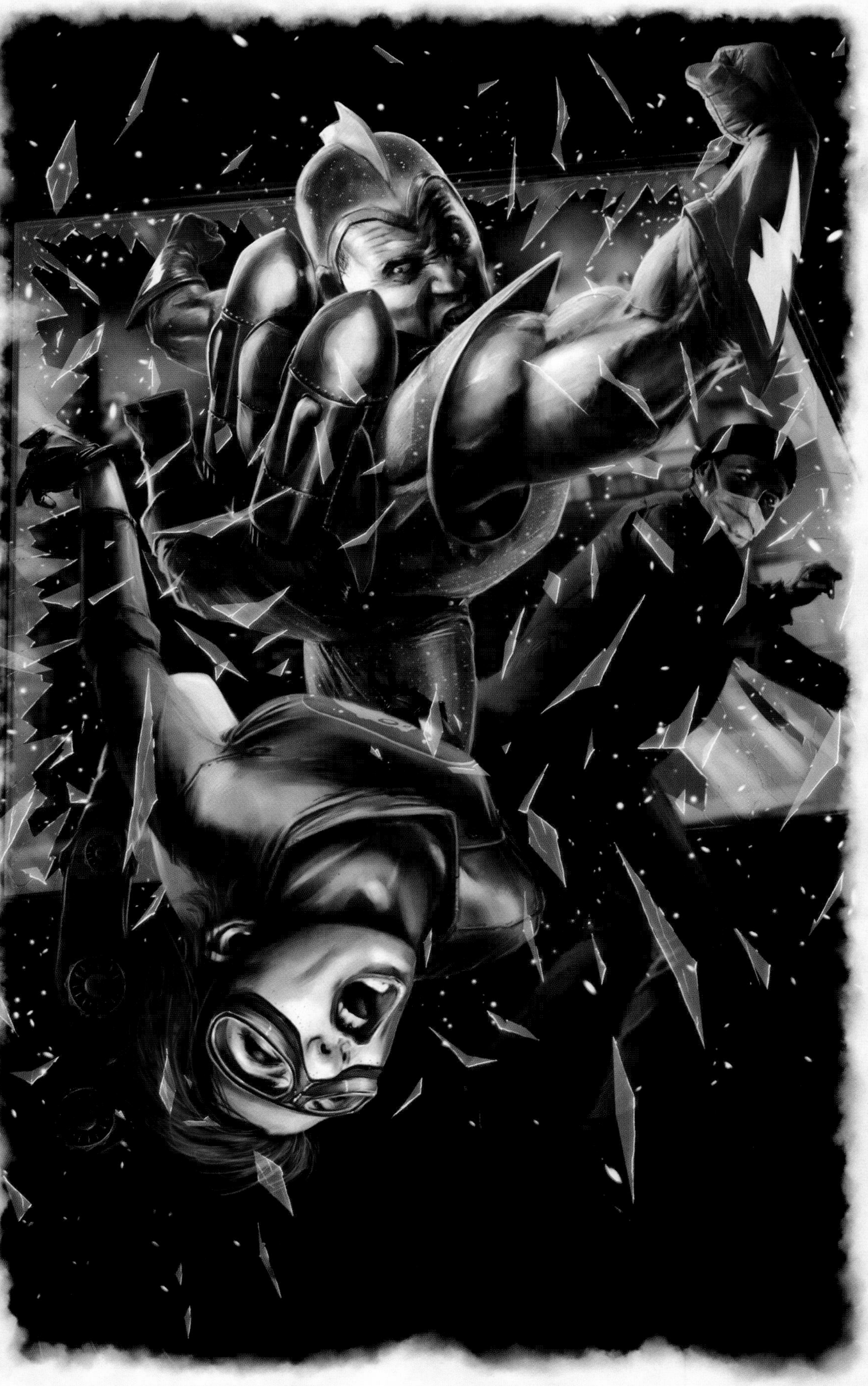

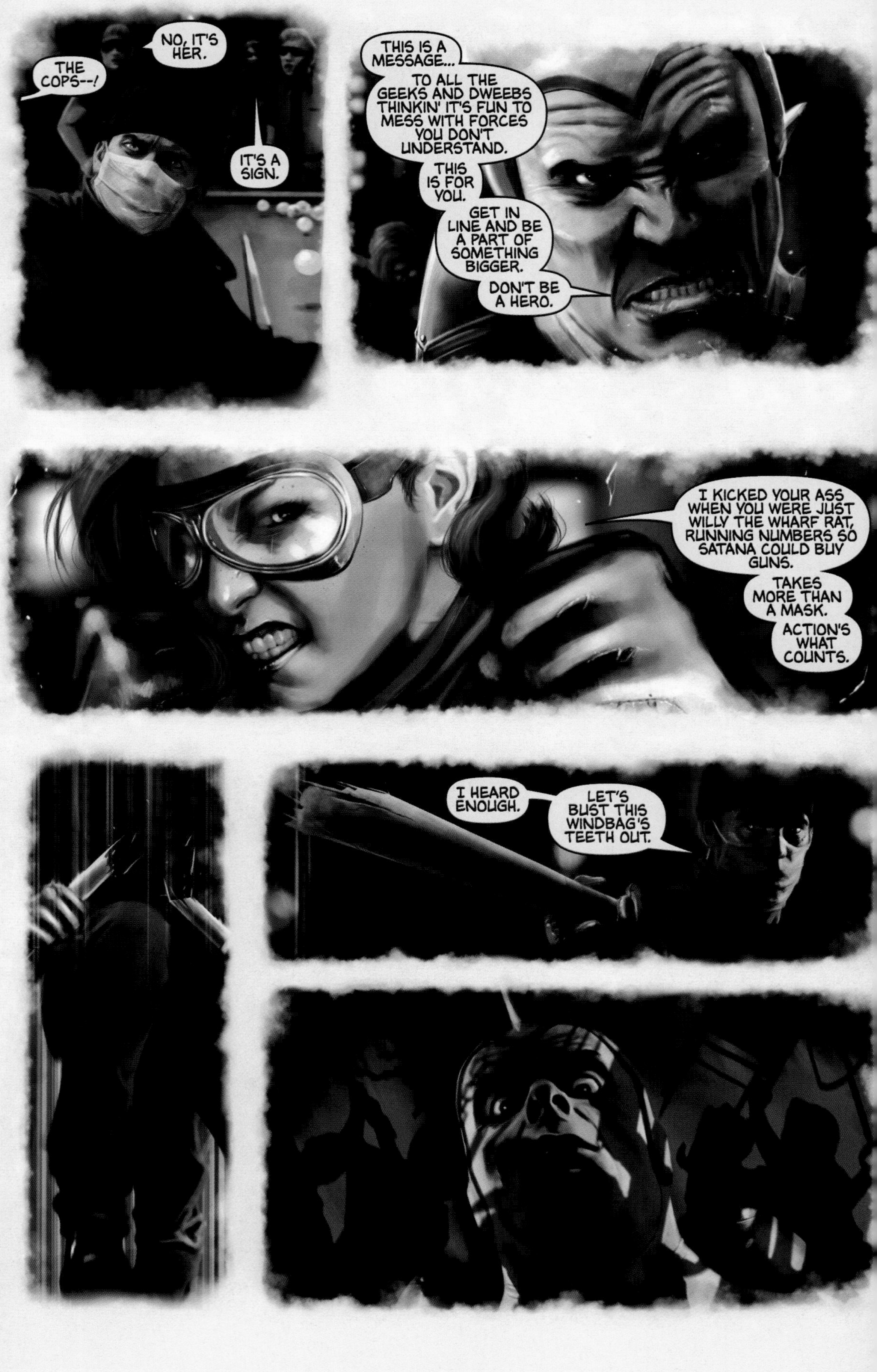
THE COPS--!
NO, IT'S HER.
IT'S A SIGN.
THIS IS A MESSAGE...
TO ALL THE GEEKS AND DWEEBS THINKIN' IT'S FUN TO MESS WITH FORCES YOU DON'T UNDERSTAND.
THIS IS FOR YOU.
GET IN LINE AND BE A PART OF SOMETHING BIGGER.
DON'T BE A HERO.
I KICKED YOUR ASS WHEN YOU WERE JUST WILLY THE WHARF RAT, RUNNING NUMBERS SO SATANA COULD BUY GUNS.
TAKES MORE THAN A MASK.
ACTION'S WHAT COUNTS.
I HEARD ENOUGH.
LET'S BUST THIS WINDBAG'S TEETH OUT.

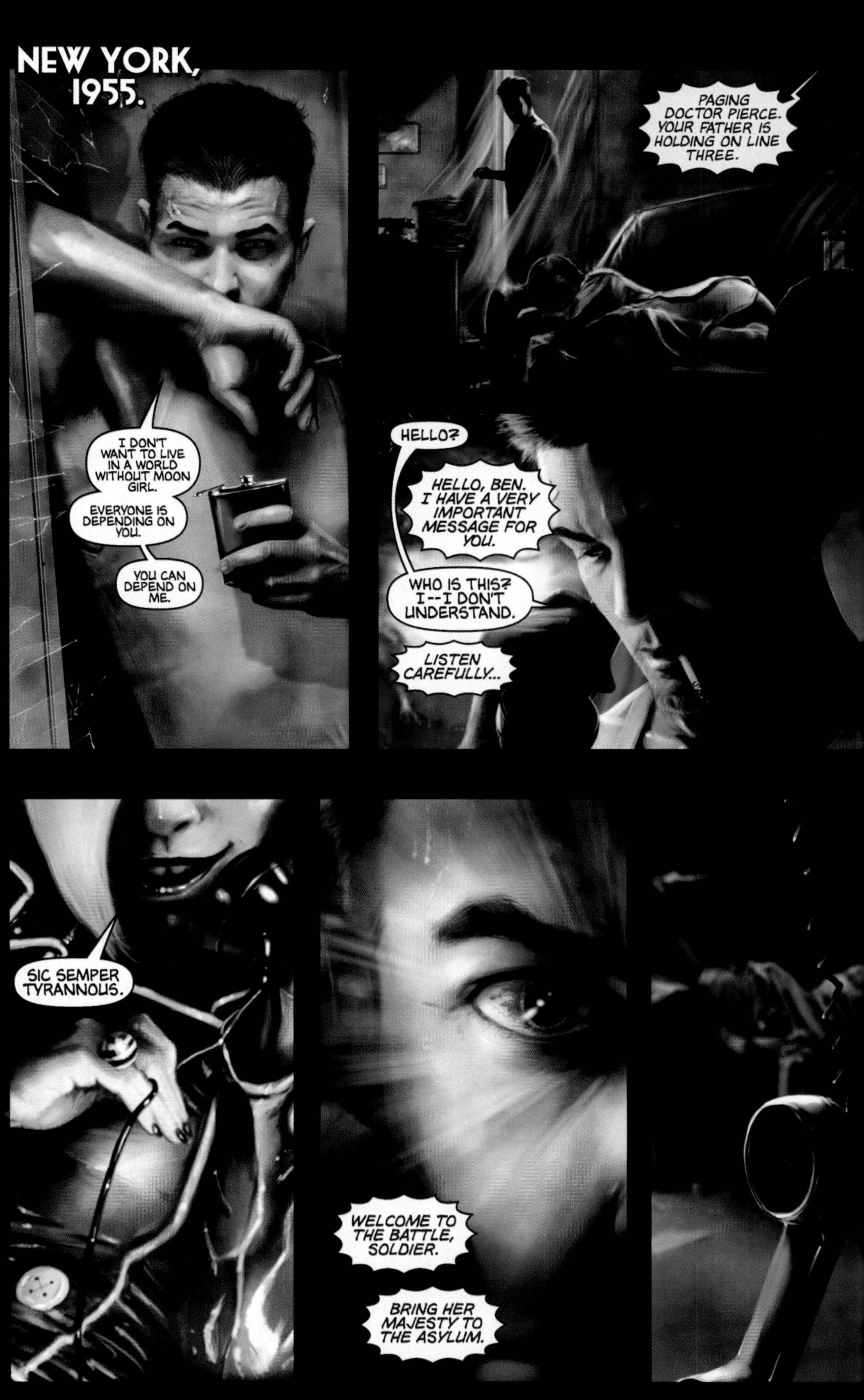
NEW YORK, 1955.
PAGING DOCTOR PIERCE. YOUR FATHER IS HOLDING ON LINE THREE.
I DON'T WANT TO LIVE IN A WORLD WITHOUT MOON GIRL.
EVERYONE IS DEPENDING ON YOU.
YOU CAN DEPEND ON ME.
HELLO?
HELLO, BEN. I HAVE A VERY IMPORTANT MESSAGE FOR YOU.
WHO IS THIS? I--I DON'T UNDERSTAND.
LISTEN CAREFULLY...
SIC SEMPER TYRANNOUS.
WELCOME TO THE BATTLE, SOLDIER.
BRING HER MAJESTY TO THE ASYLUM.

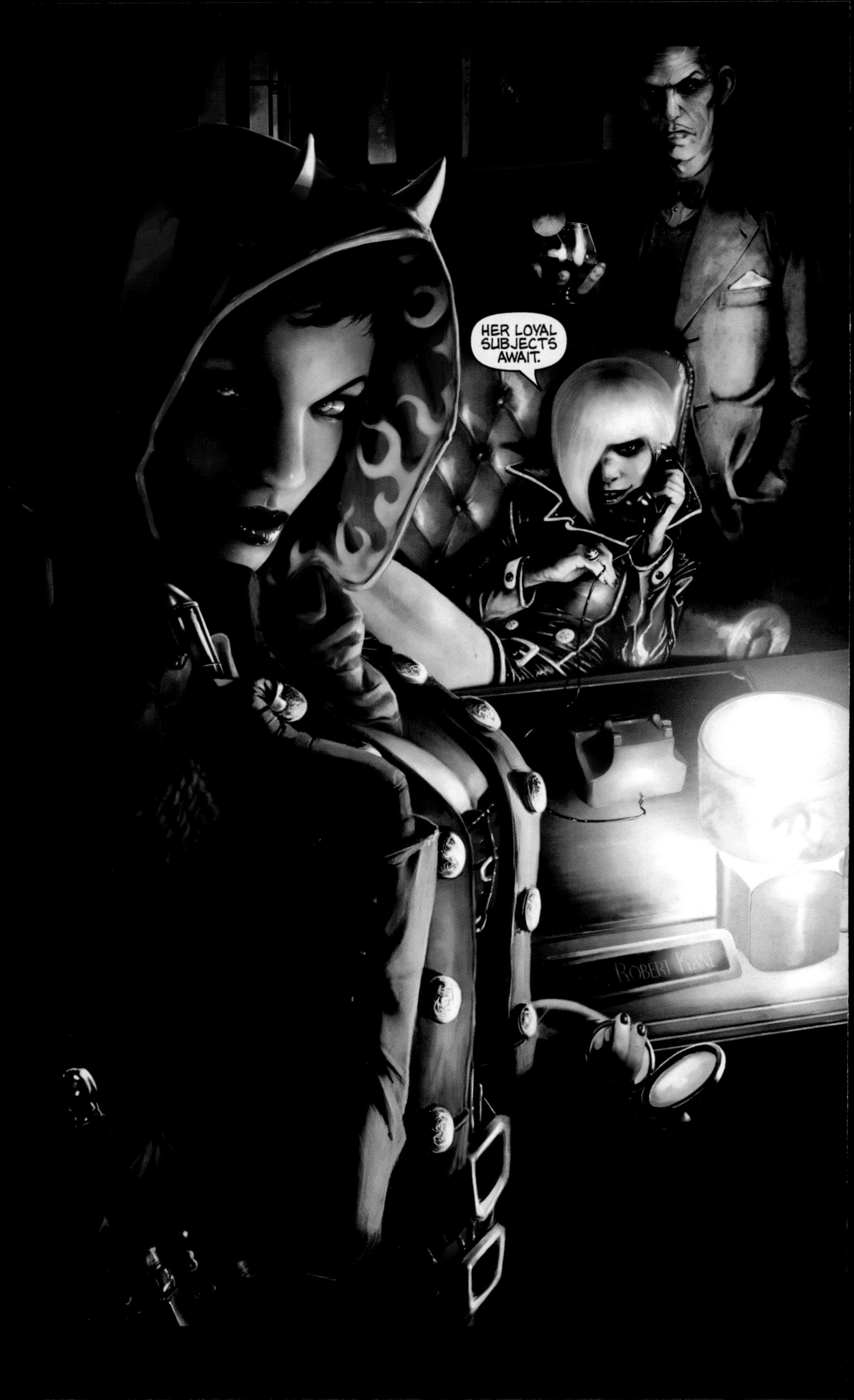
HER LOYAL SUBJECTS AWAIT.
ROBERT KANE

5

WEIRD FANTASY

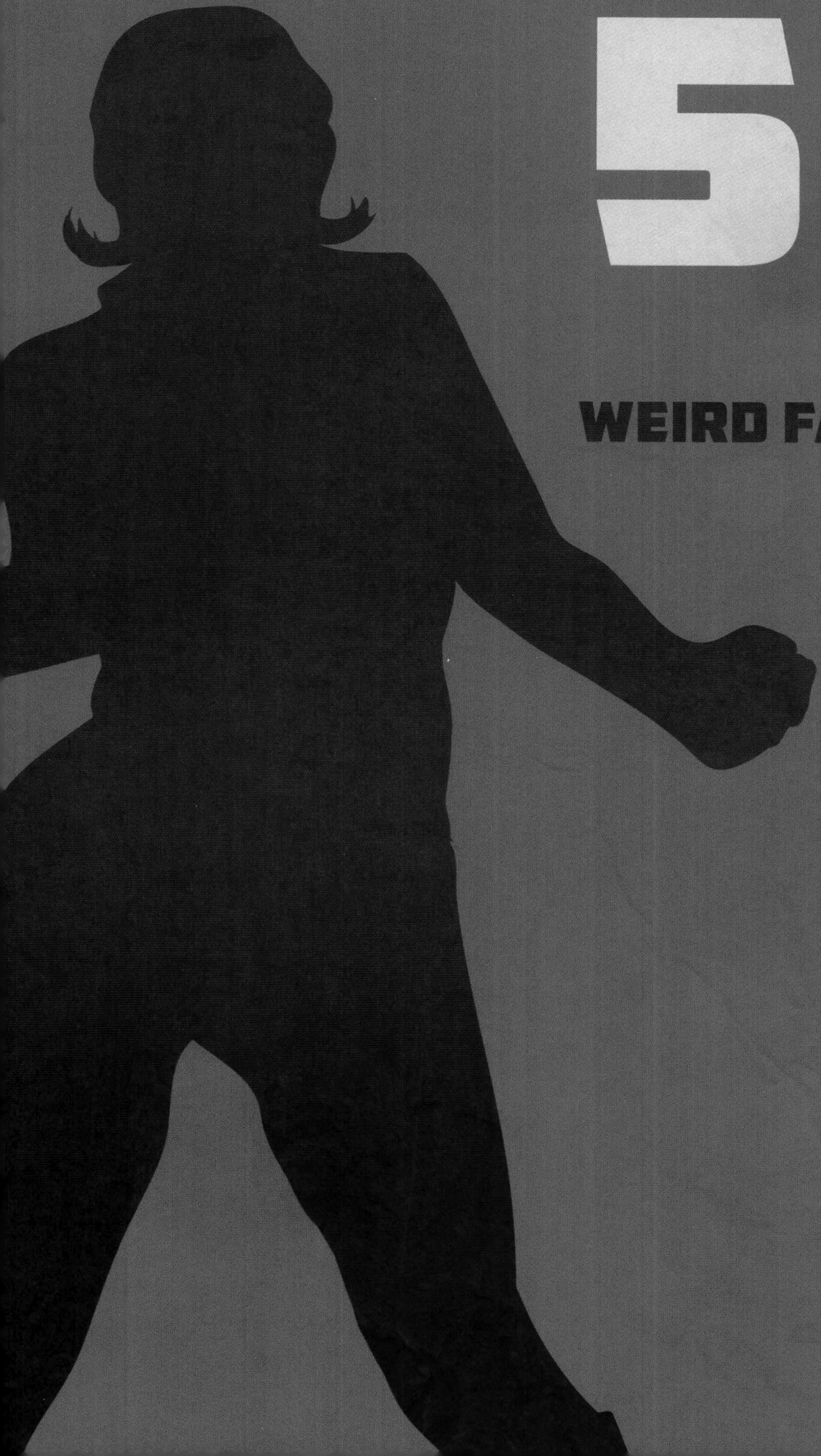

WHERE IS EVERYONE?!

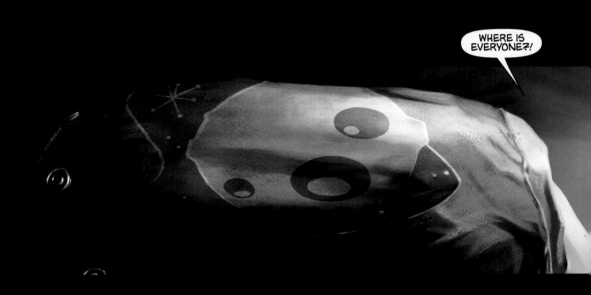

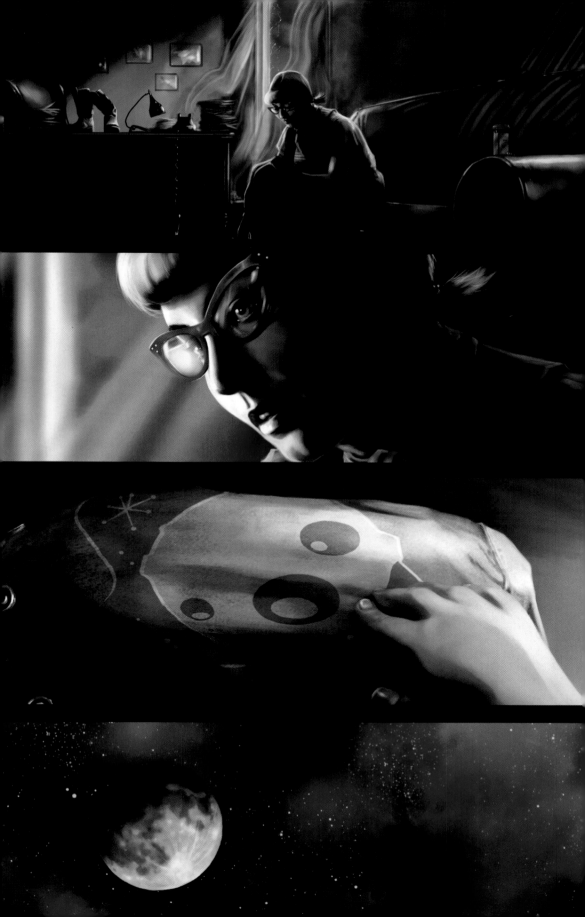

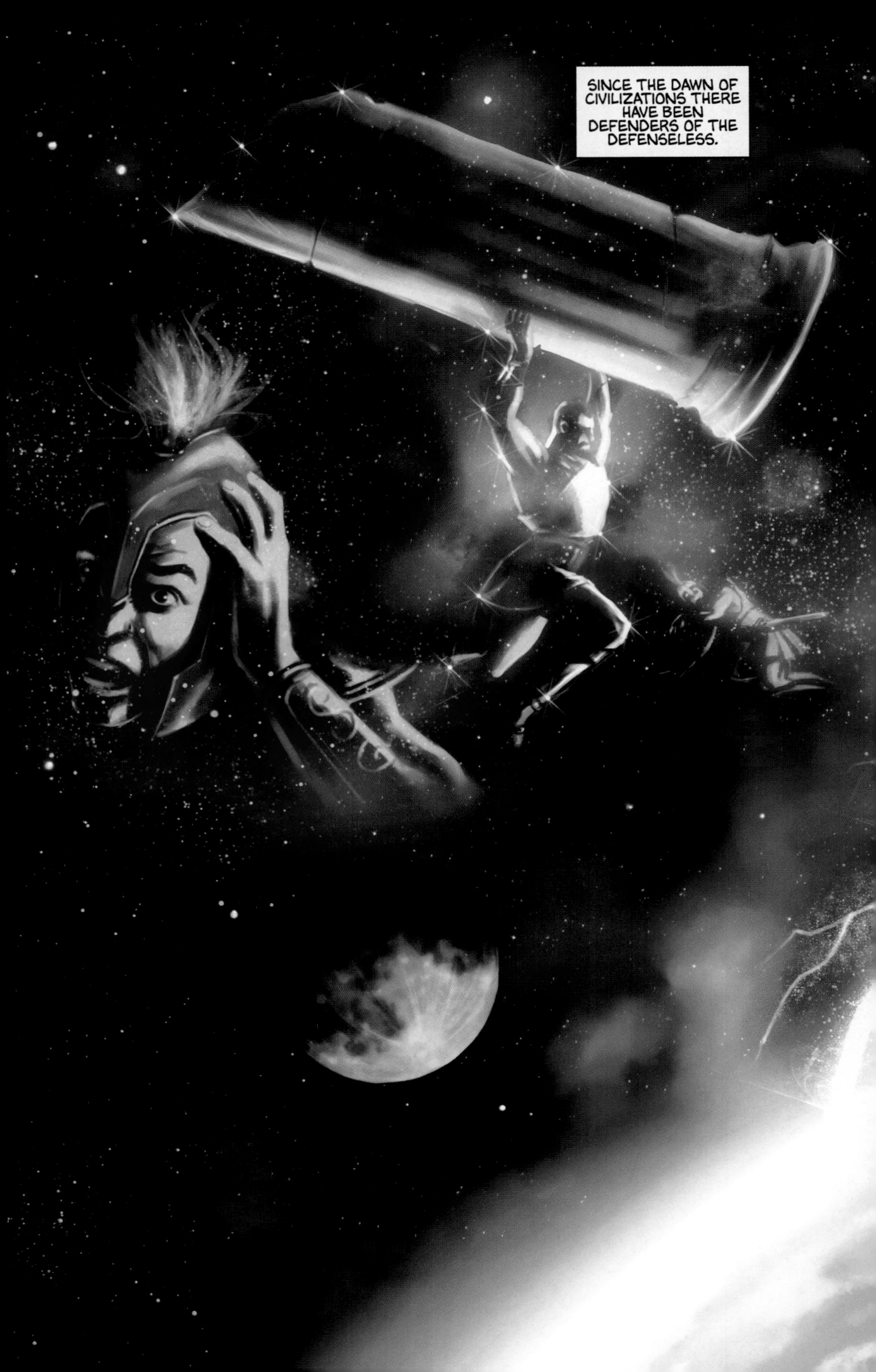
SINCE THE DAWN OF CIVILIZATIONS THERE HAVE BEEN DEFENDERS OF THE DEFENSELESS.

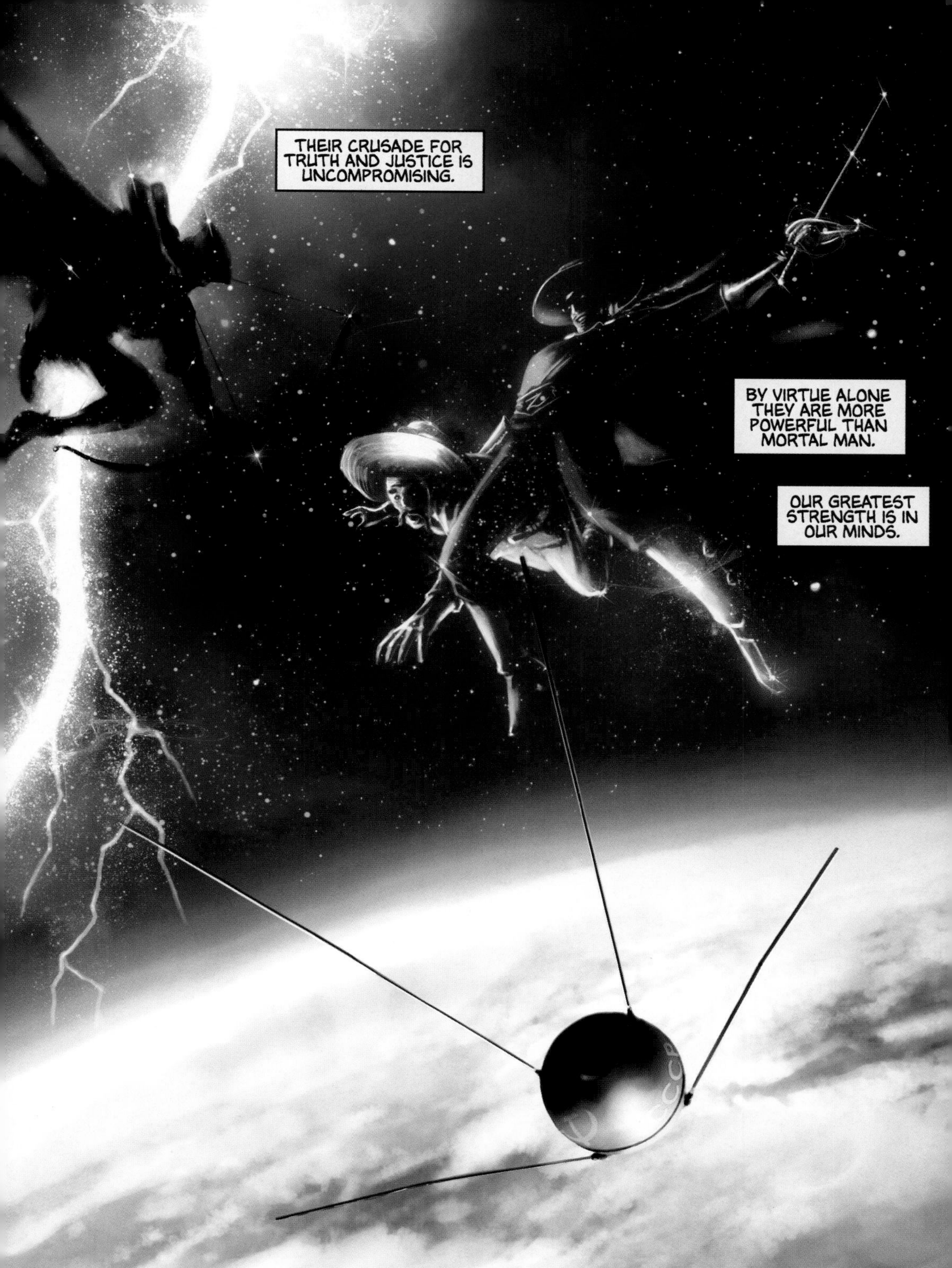
THEIR CRUSADE FOR TRUTH AND JUSTICE IS UNCOMPROMISING.
BY VIRTUE ALONE THEY ARE MORE POWERFUL THAN MORTAL MAN.
OUR GREATEST STRENGTH IS IN OUR MINDS.
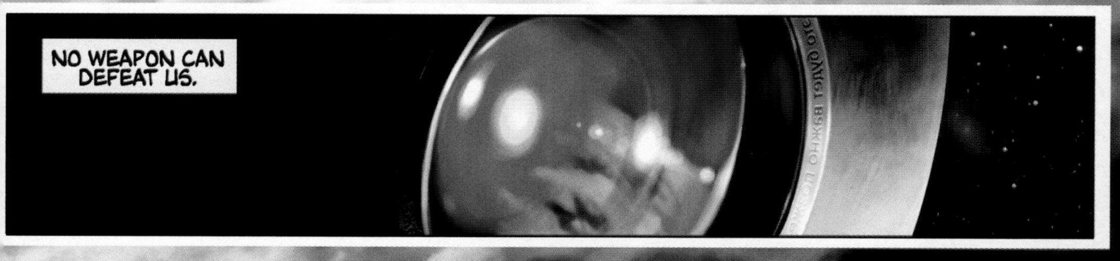
NO WEAPON CAN DEFEAT US.

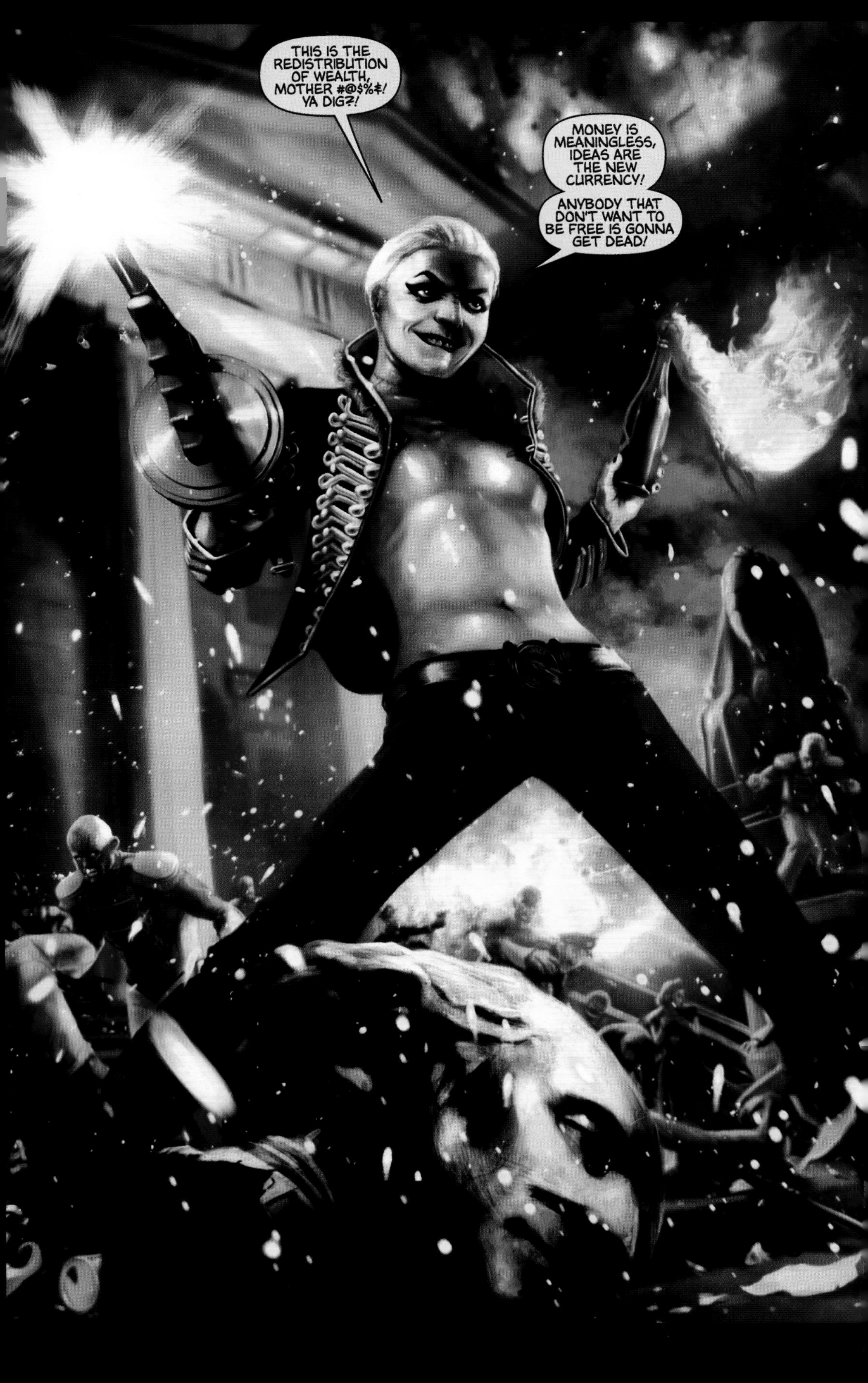
THIS IS THE REDISTRIBUTION OF WEALTH, MOTHER #@$%‡! YA DIG?!
MONEY IS MEANINGLESS, IDEAS ARE THE NEW CURRENCY!
ANYBODY THAT DON'T WANT TO BE FREE IS GONNA GET DEAD!

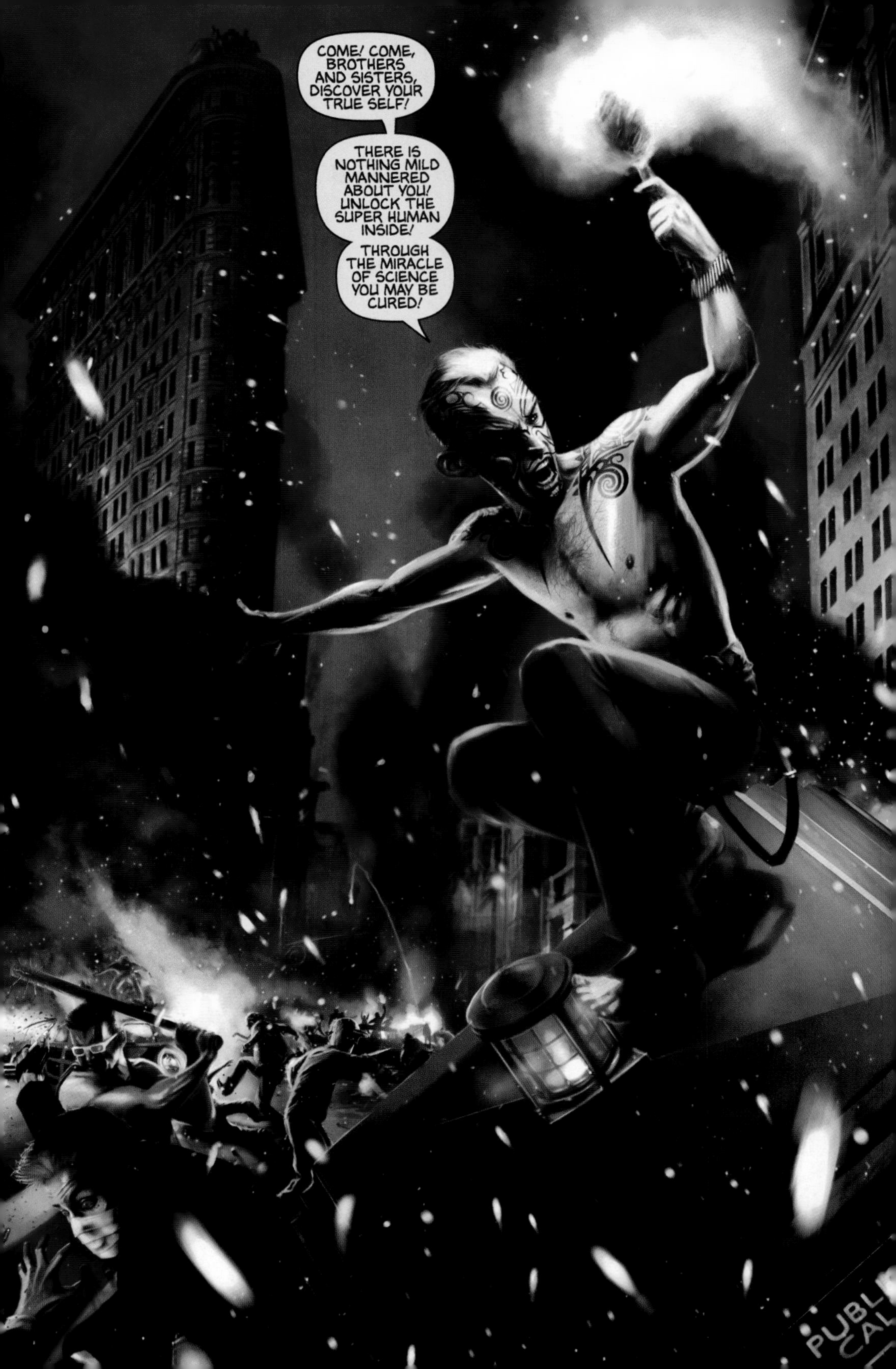
COME! COME, BROTHERS AND SISTERS, DISCOVER YOUR TRUE SELF!
THERE IS NOTHING MILD MANNERED ABOUT YOU! UNLOCK THE SUPER HUMAN INSIDE!
THROUGH THE MIRACLE OF SCIENCE YOU MAY BE CURED!

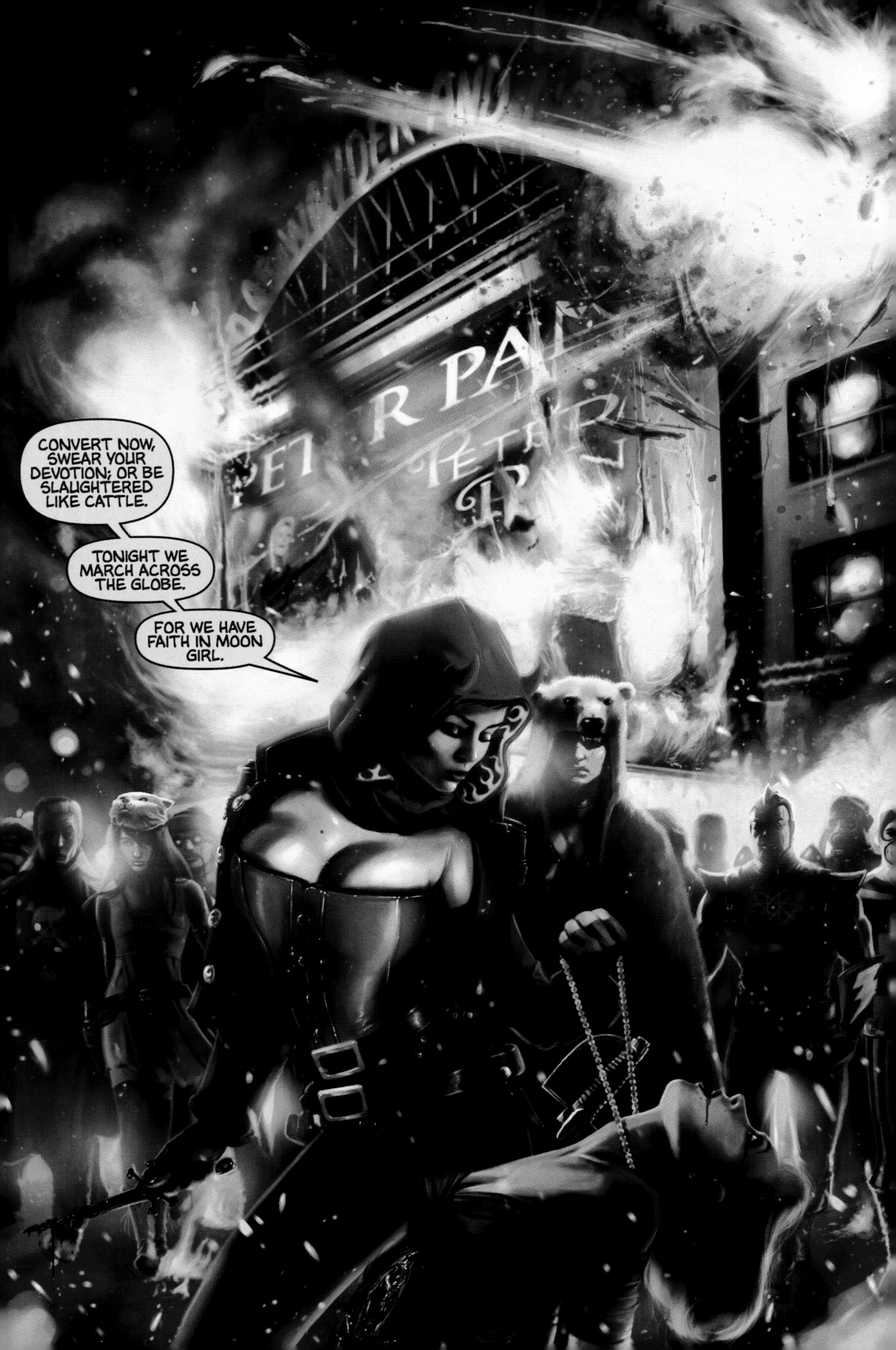
CONVERT NOW, SWEAR YOUR DEVOTION; OR BE SLAUGHTERED LIKE CATTLE.
TONIGHT WE MARCH ACROSS THE GLOBE.
FOR WE HAVE FAITH IN MOON GIRL.

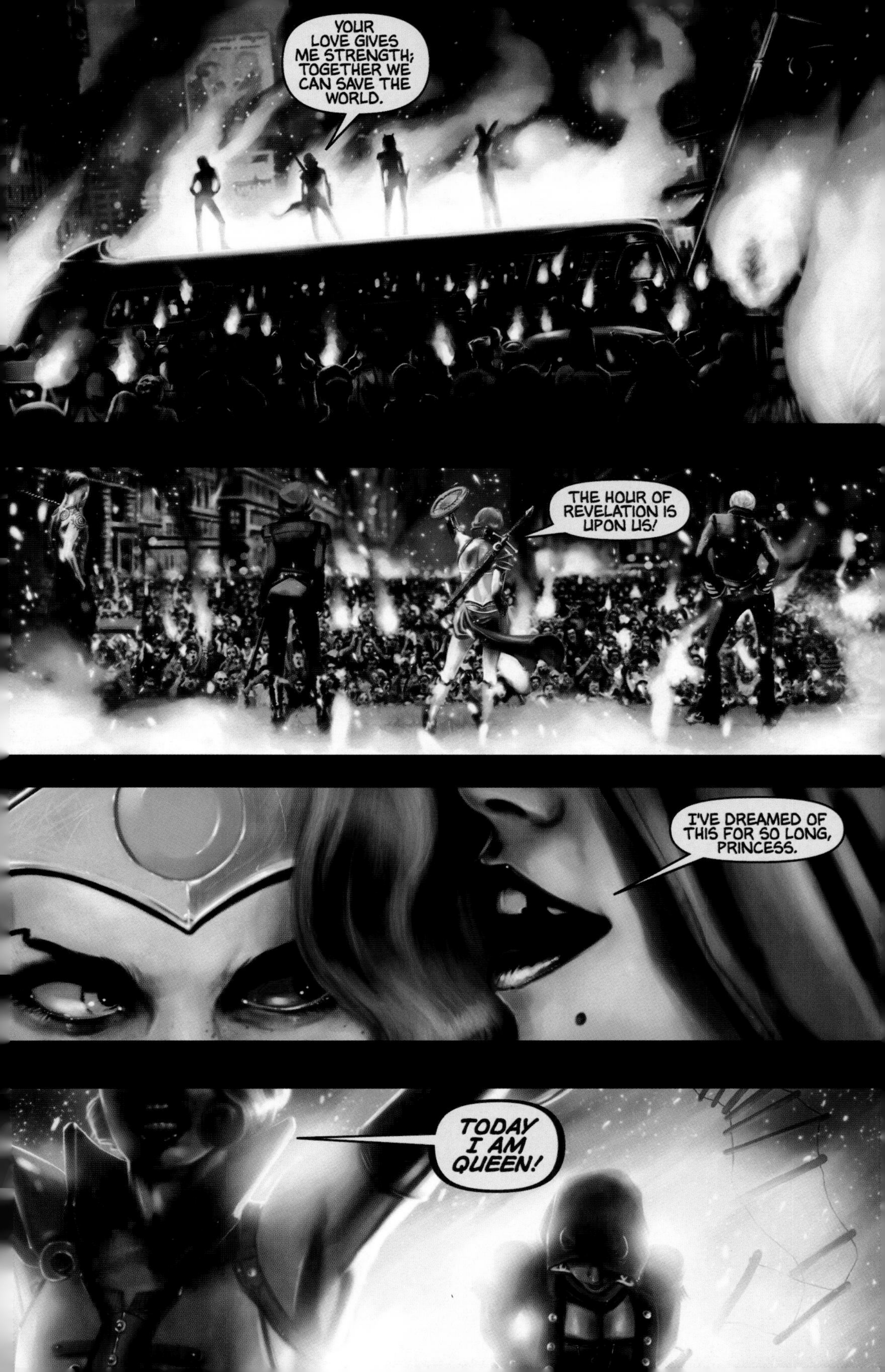
YOUR LOVE GIVES ME STRENGTH; TOGETHER WE CAN SAVE THE WORLD.
THE HOUR OF REVELATION IS UPON US!
I'VE DREAMED OF THIS FOR SO LONG, PRINCESS.
TODAY I AM QUEEN!

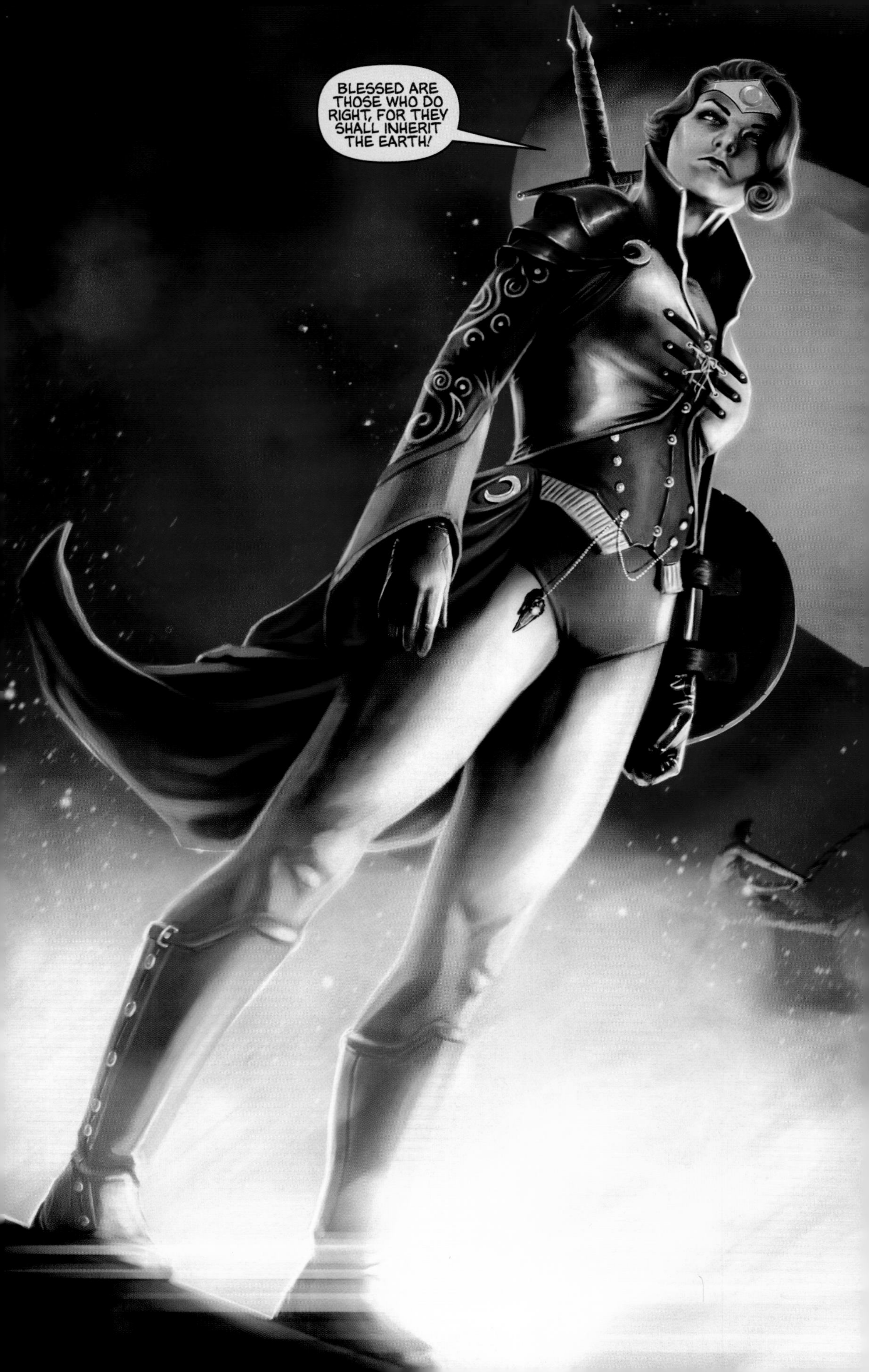
BLESSED ARE THOSE WHO DO RIGHT, FOR THEY SHALL INHERIT THE EARTH!

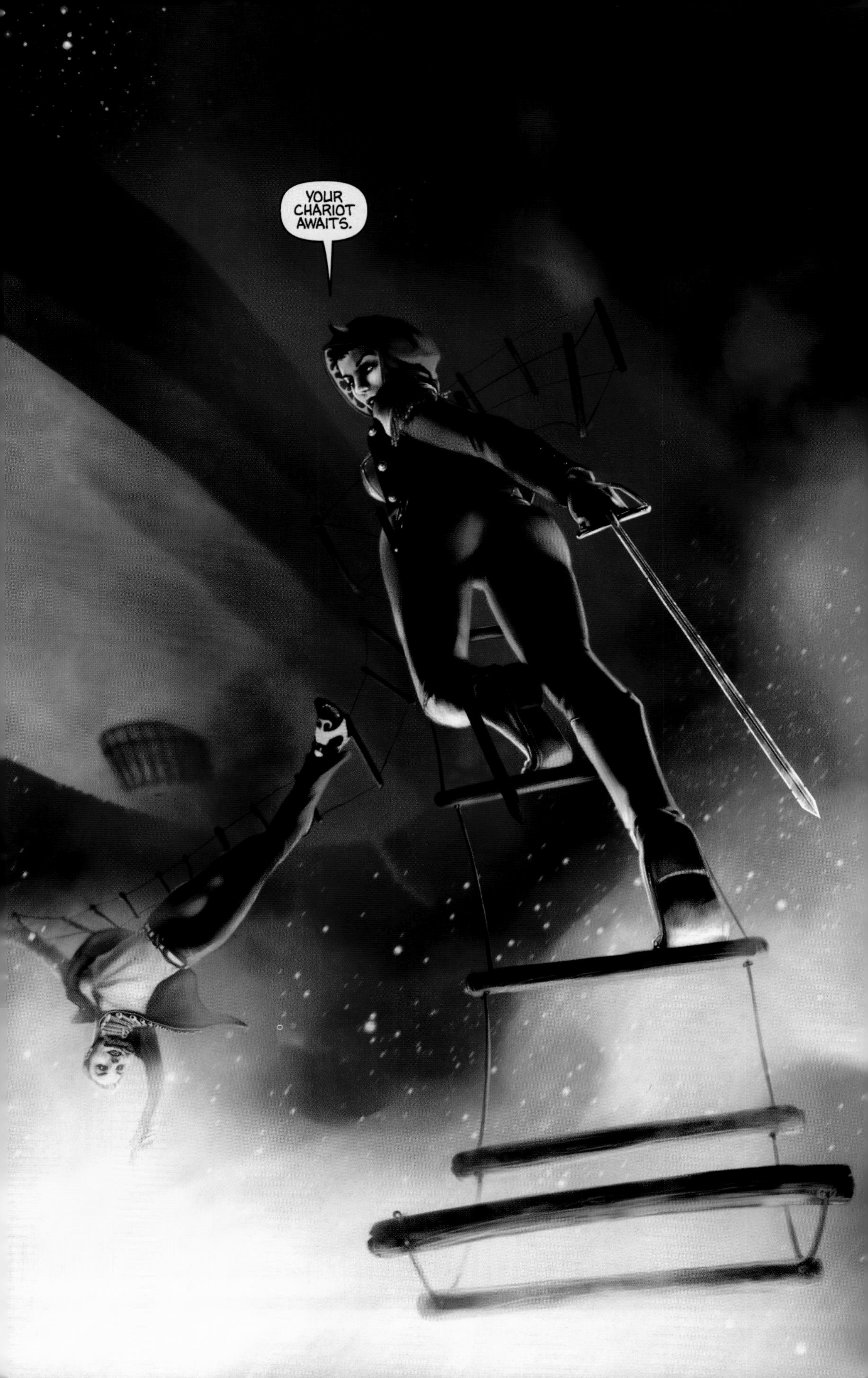
YOUR CHARIOT AWAITS.

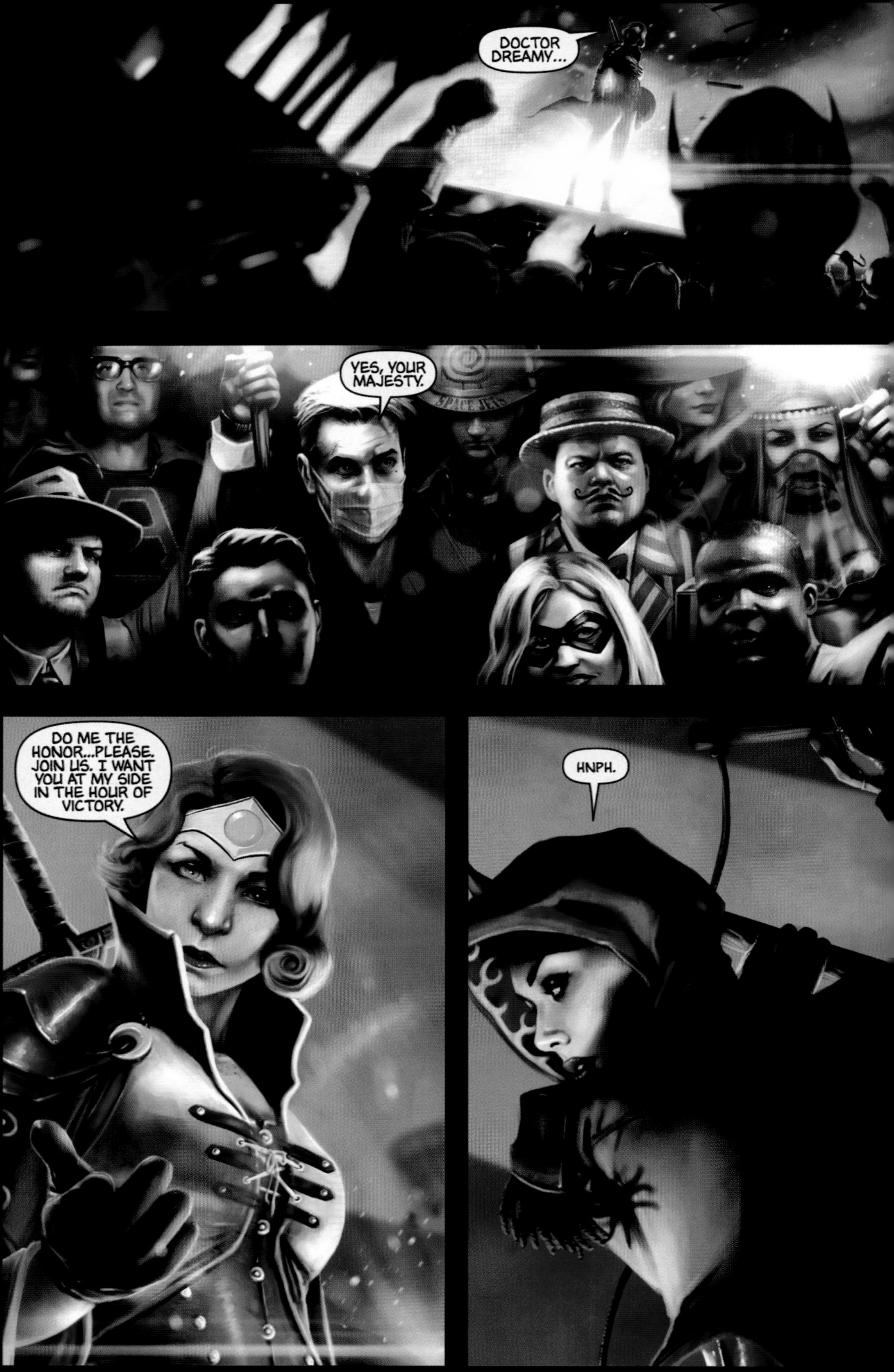
DOCTOR DREAMY...
YES, YOUR MAJESTY.
SPACE JETS
DO ME THE HONOR...PLEASE. JOIN US. I WANT YOU AT MY SIDE IN THE HOUR OF VICTORY.
HNPH.

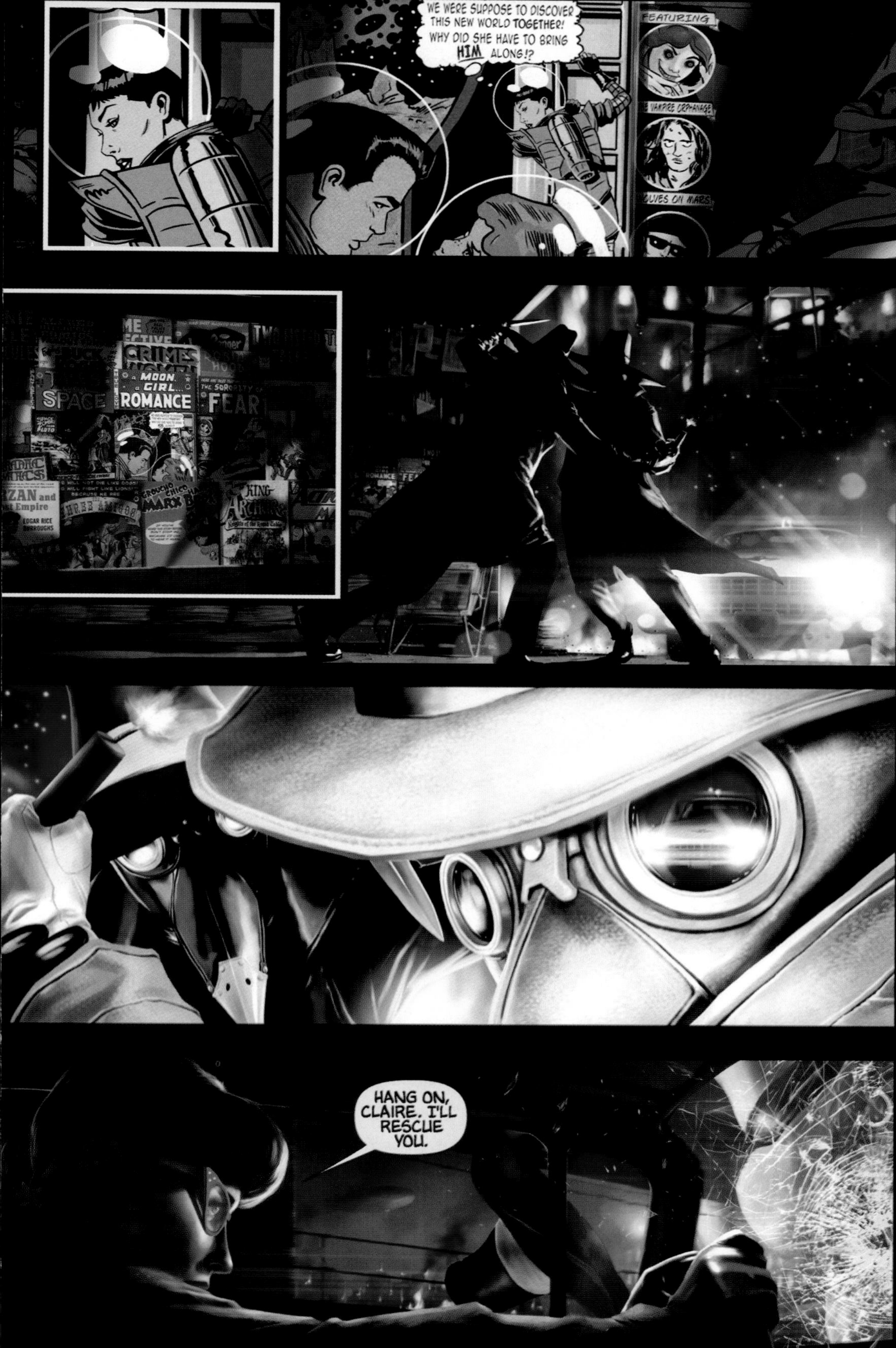
WE WERE SUPPOSE TO DISCOVER THIS NEW WORLD TOGETHER! WHY DID SHE HAVE TO BRING HIM ALONG!?
FEATURING
HANG ON, CLAIRE. I'LL RESCUE YOU.

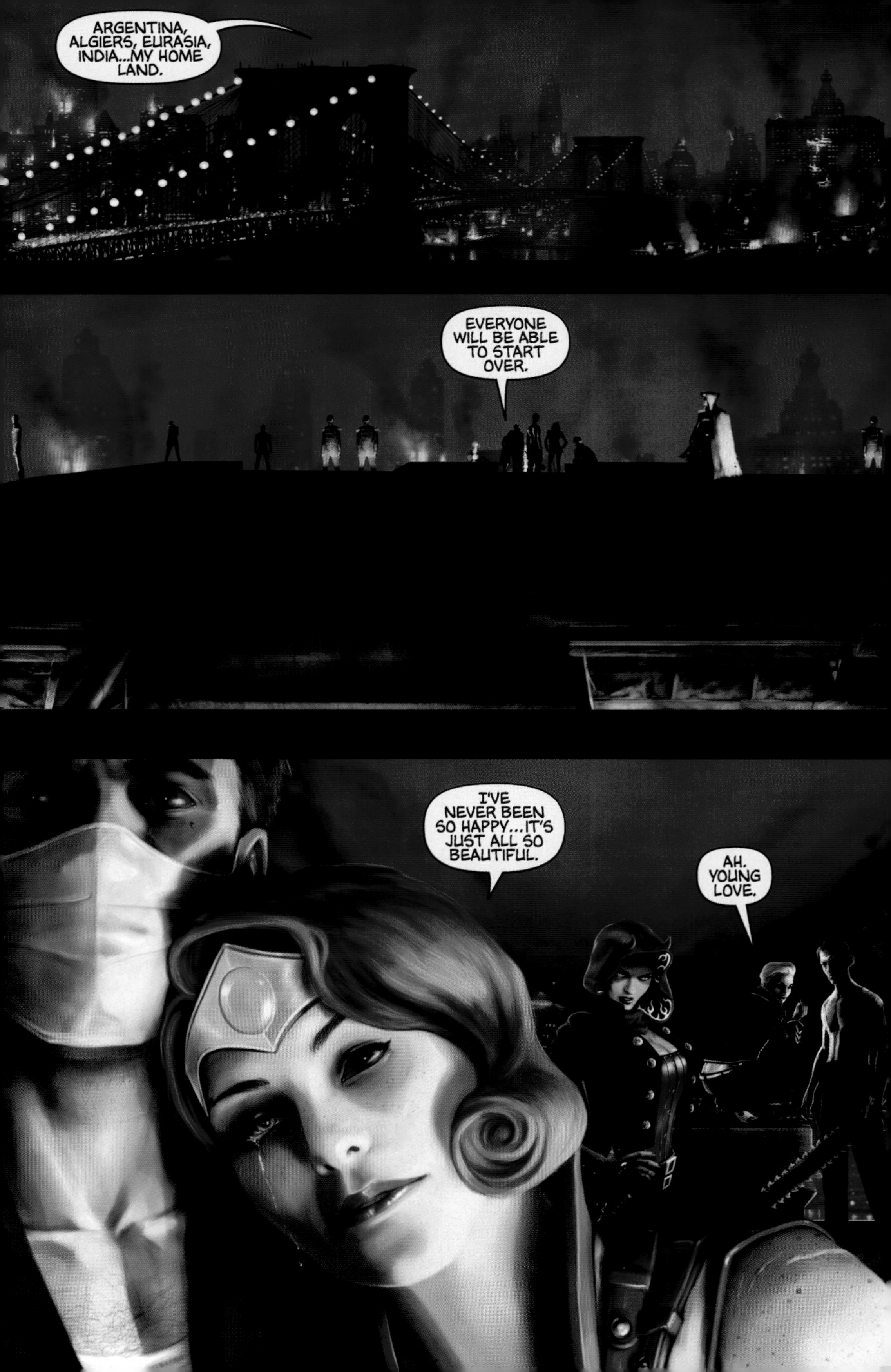
ARGENTINA, ALGIERS, EURASIA, INDIA...MY HOME LAND.
EVERYONE WILL BE ABLE TO START OVER.
I'VE NEVER BEEN SO HAPPY...IT'S JUST ALL SO BEAUTIFUL.
AH. YOUNG LOVE.

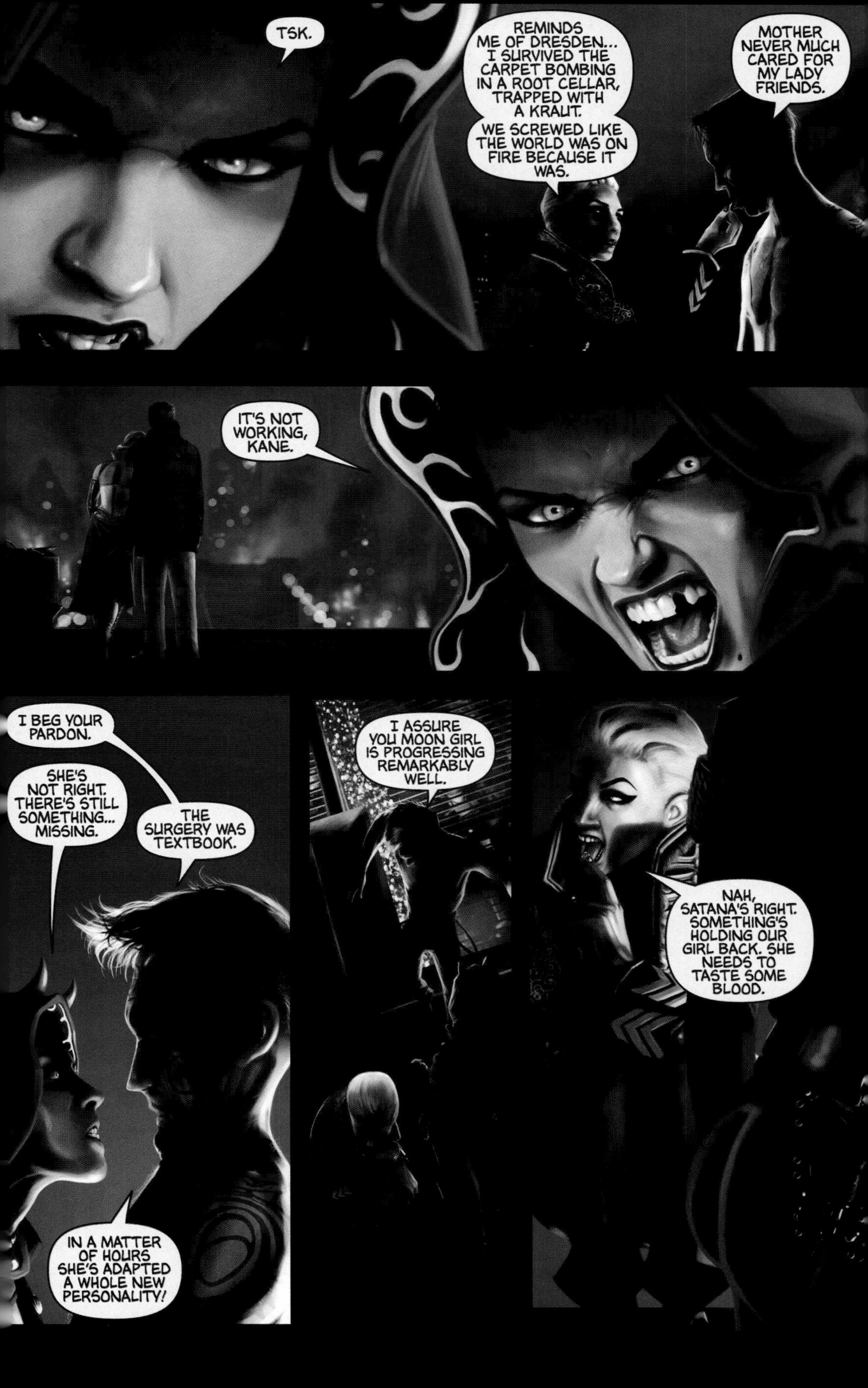
TSK.
REMINDS ME OF DRESDEN... I SURVIVED THE CARPET BOMBING IN A ROOT CELLAR, TRAPPED WITH A KRAUT.
WE SCREWED LIKE THE WORLD WAS ON FIRE BECAUSE IT WAS.
MOTHER NEVER MUCH CARED FOR MY LADY FRIENDS.
IT'S NOT WORKING, KANE.
I BEG YOUR PARDON.
SHE'S NOT RIGHT. THERE'S STILL SOMETHING... MISSING.
THE SURGERY WAS TEXTBOOK.
IN A MATTER OF HOURS SHE'S ADAPTED A WHOLE NEW PERSONALITY!
I ASSURE YOU MOON GIRL IS PROGRESSING REMARKABLY WELL.
NAH, SATANA'S RIGHT. SOMETHING'S HOLDING OUR GIRL BACK. SHE NEEDS TO TASTE SOME BLOOD.

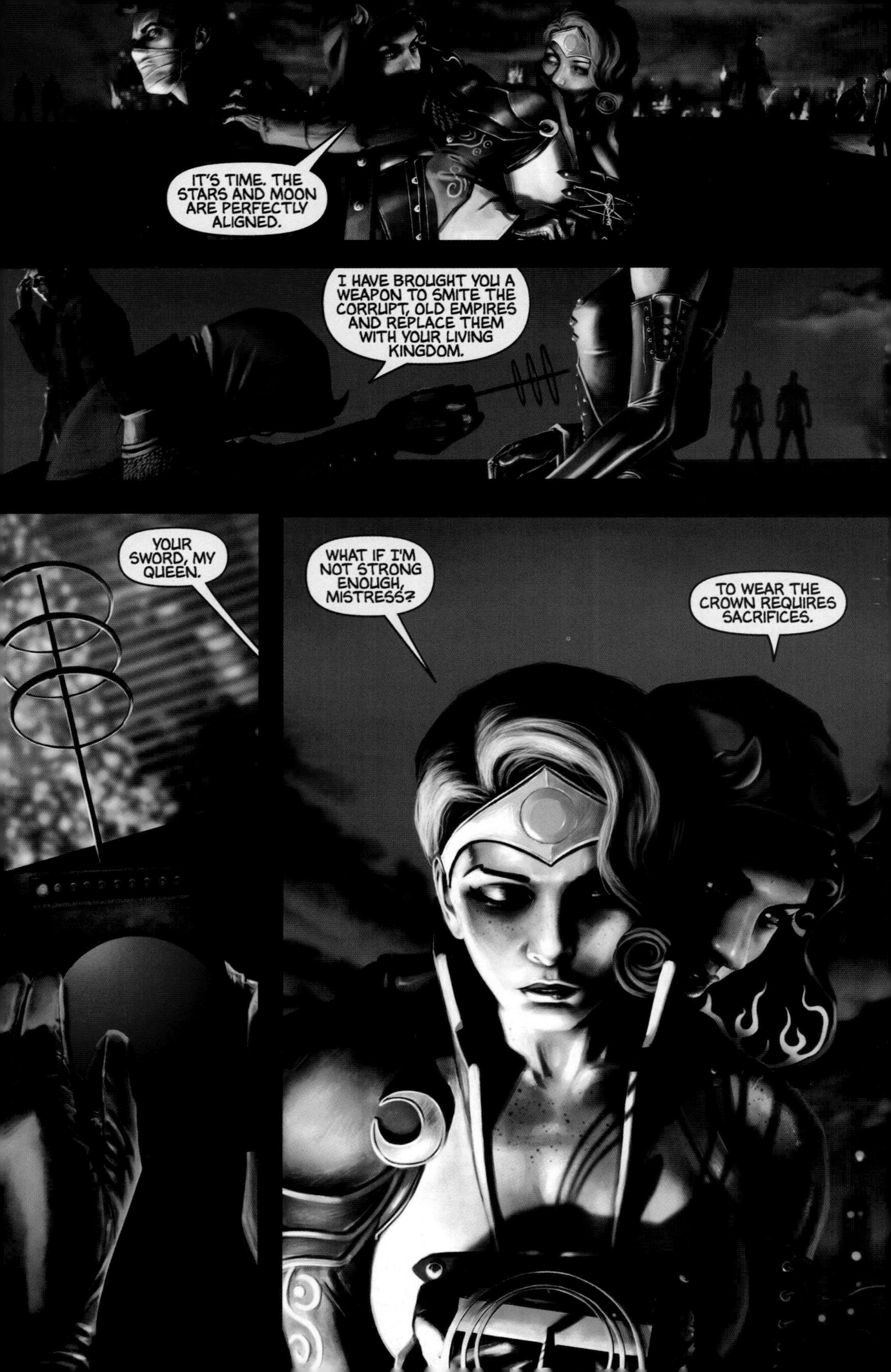
IT'S TIME. THE STARS AND MOON ARE PERFECTLY ALIGNED.
I HAVE BROUGHT YOU A WEAPON TO SMITE THE CORRUPT, OLD EMPIRES AND REPLACE THEM WITH YOUR LIVING KINGDOM.
YOUR SWORD, MY QUEEN.
WHAT IF I'M NOT STRONG ENOUGH, MISTRESS?
TO WEAR THE CROWN REQUIRES SACRIFICES.

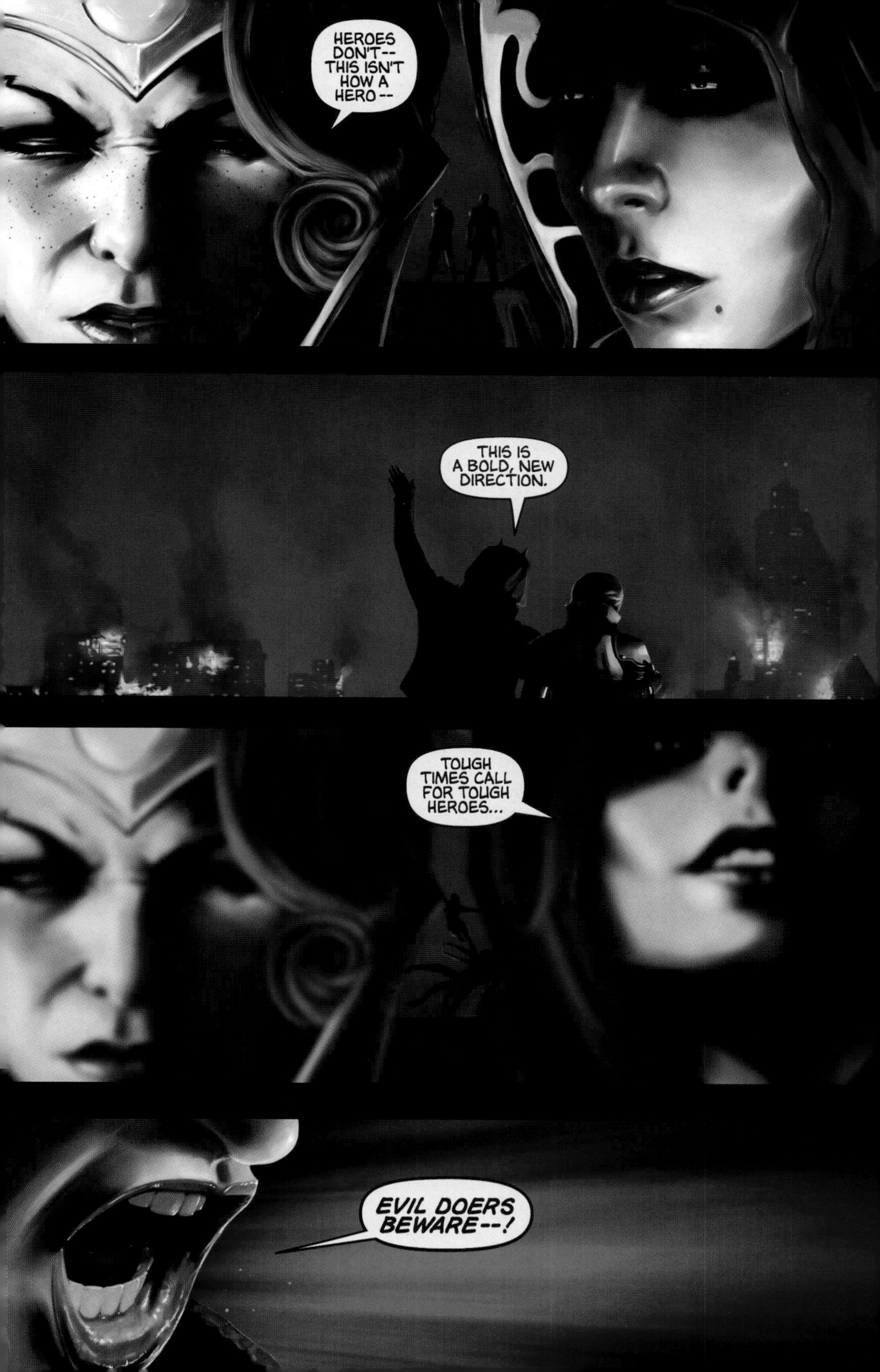
HEROES DON'T-- THIS ISN'T HOW A HERO--
THIS IS A BOLD, NEW DIRECTION.
TOUGH TIMES CALL FOR TOUGH HEROES...
EVIL DOERS BEWARE--!

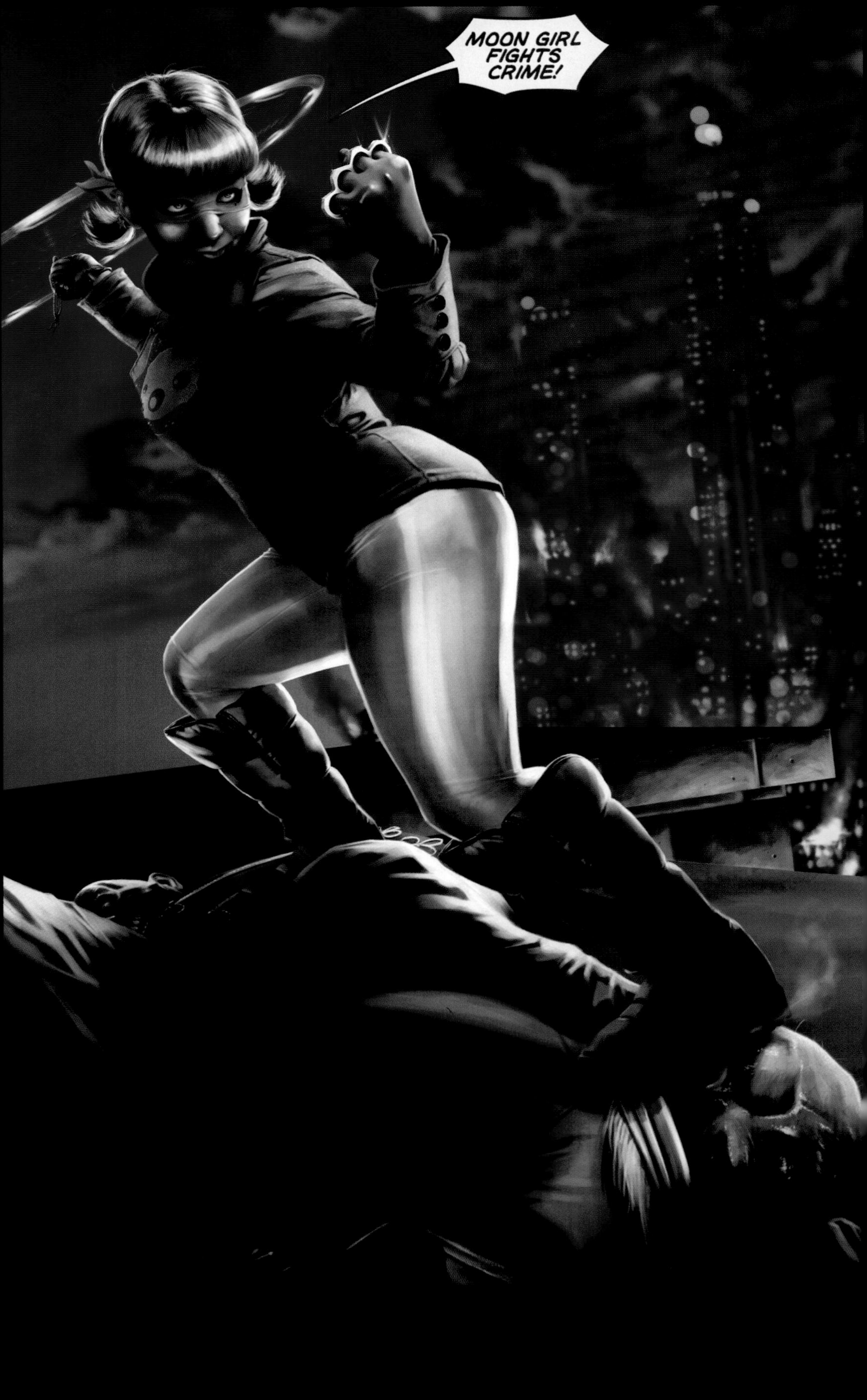
MOON GIRL
FIGHTS
CRIME!

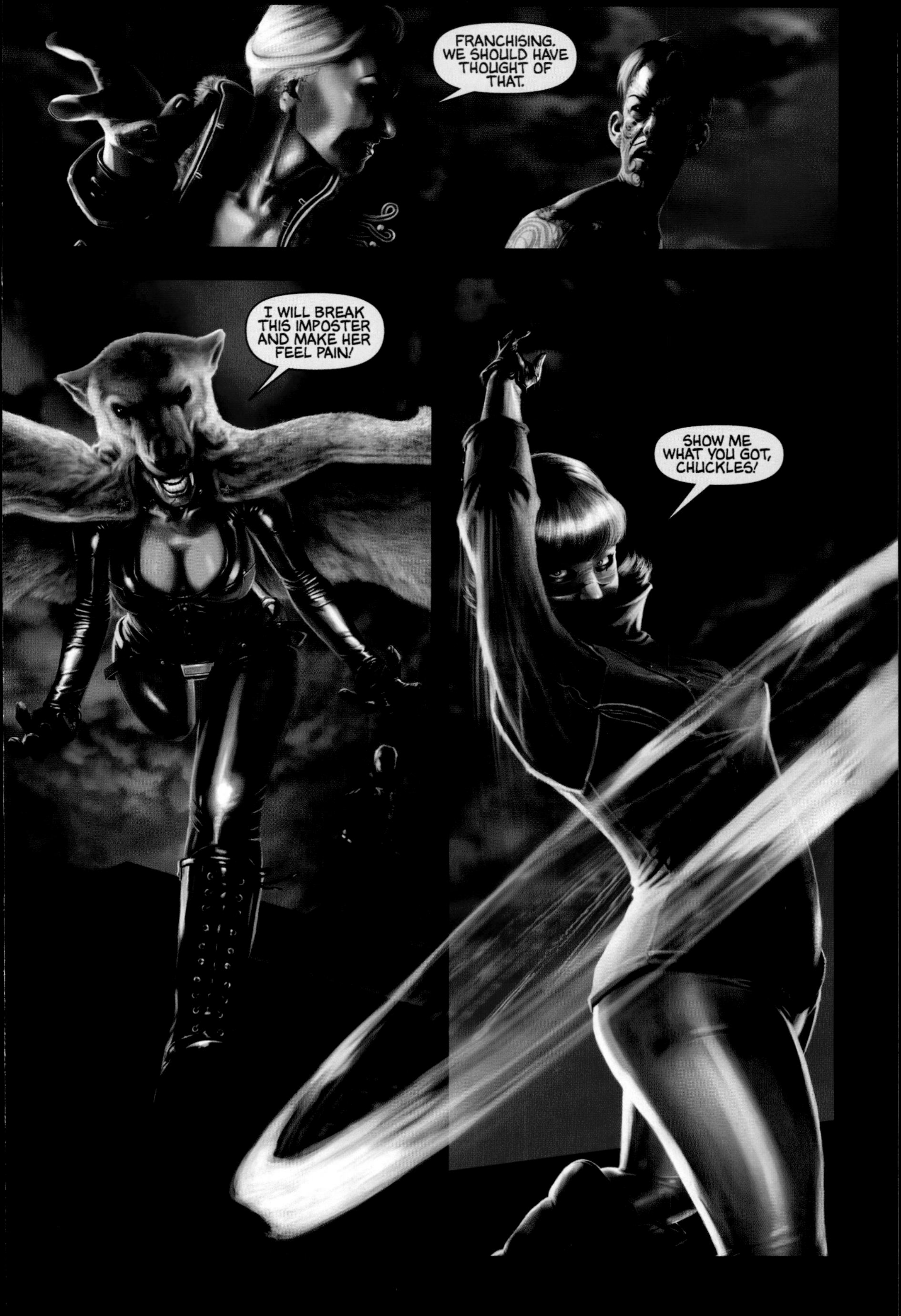
FRANCHISING. WE SHOULD HAVE THOUGHT OF THAT.
I WILL BREAK THIS IMPOSTER AND MAKE HER FEEL PAIN!
SHOW ME WHAT YOU GOT, CHUCKLES!

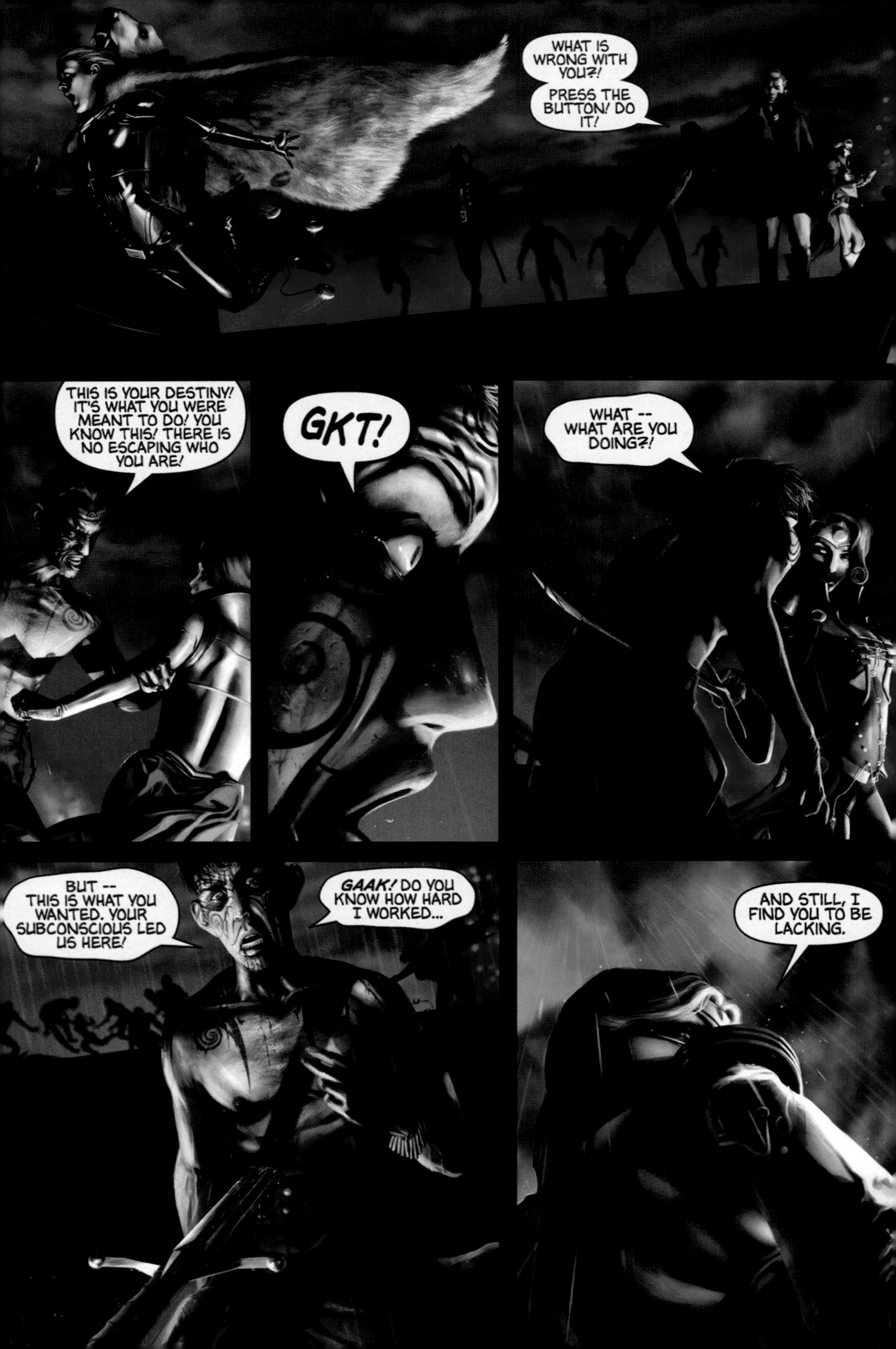
WHAT IS WRONG WITH YOU?!
PRESS THE BUTTON! DO IT!
THIS IS YOUR DESTINY! IT'S WHAT YOU WERE MEANT TO DO! YOU KNOW THIS! THERE IS NO ESCAPING WHO YOU ARE!
GKT!
WHAT -- WHAT ARE YOU DOING?!
BUT -- THIS IS WHAT YOU WANTED. YOUR SUBCONSCIOUS LED US HERE!
GAAK! DO YOU KNOW HOW HARD I WORKED...
AND STILL, I FIND YOU TO BE LACKING.

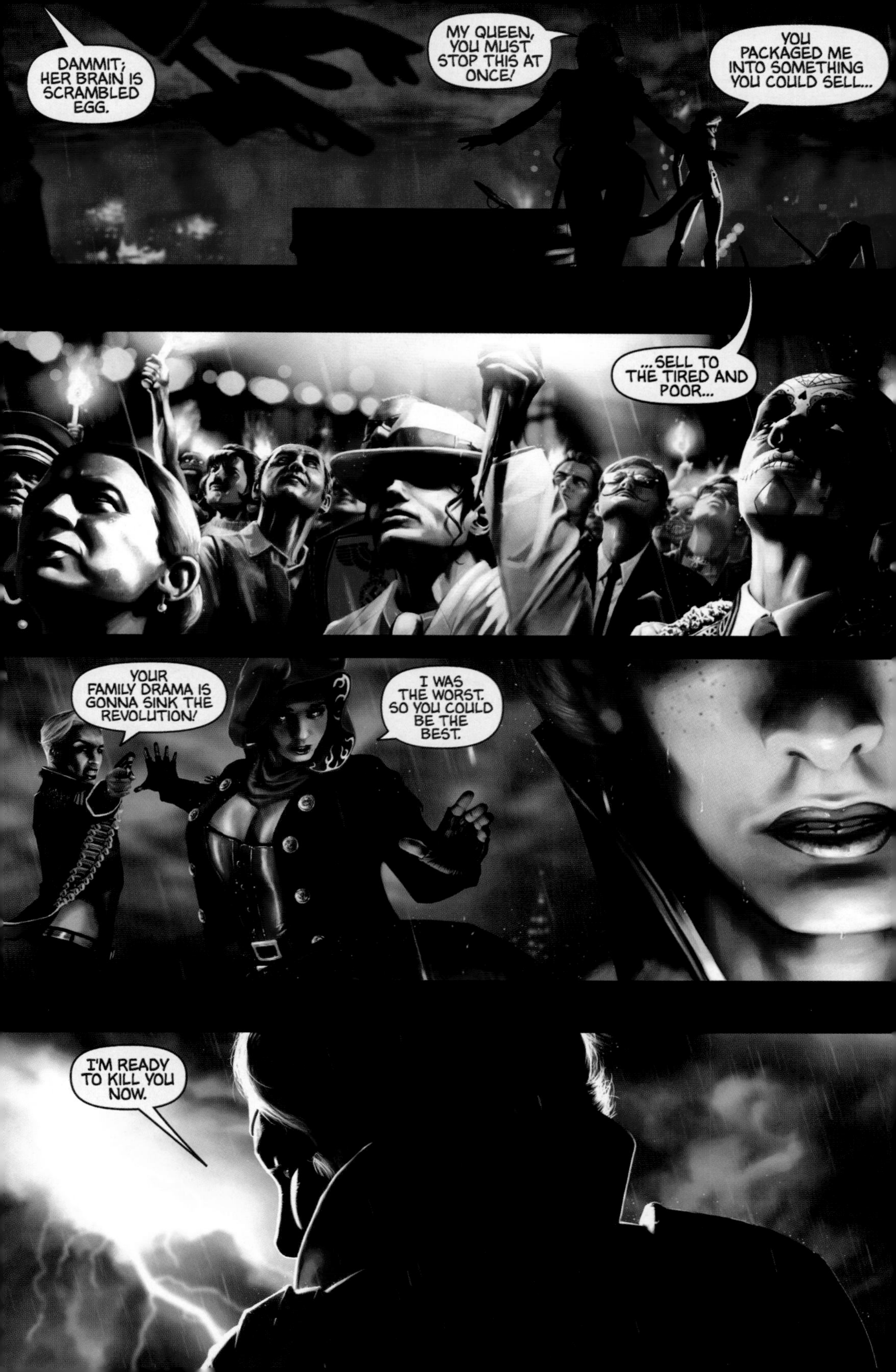
DAMMIT; HER BRAIN IS SCRAMBLED EGG.
MY QUEEN, YOU MUST STOP THIS AT ONCE!
YOU PACKAGED ME INTO SOMETHING YOU COULD SELL...
...SELL TO THE TIRED AND POOR...
YOUR FAMILY DRAMA IS GONNA SINK THE REVOLUTION!
I WAS THE WORST. SO YOU COULD BE THE BEST.
I'M READY TO KILL YOU NOW.

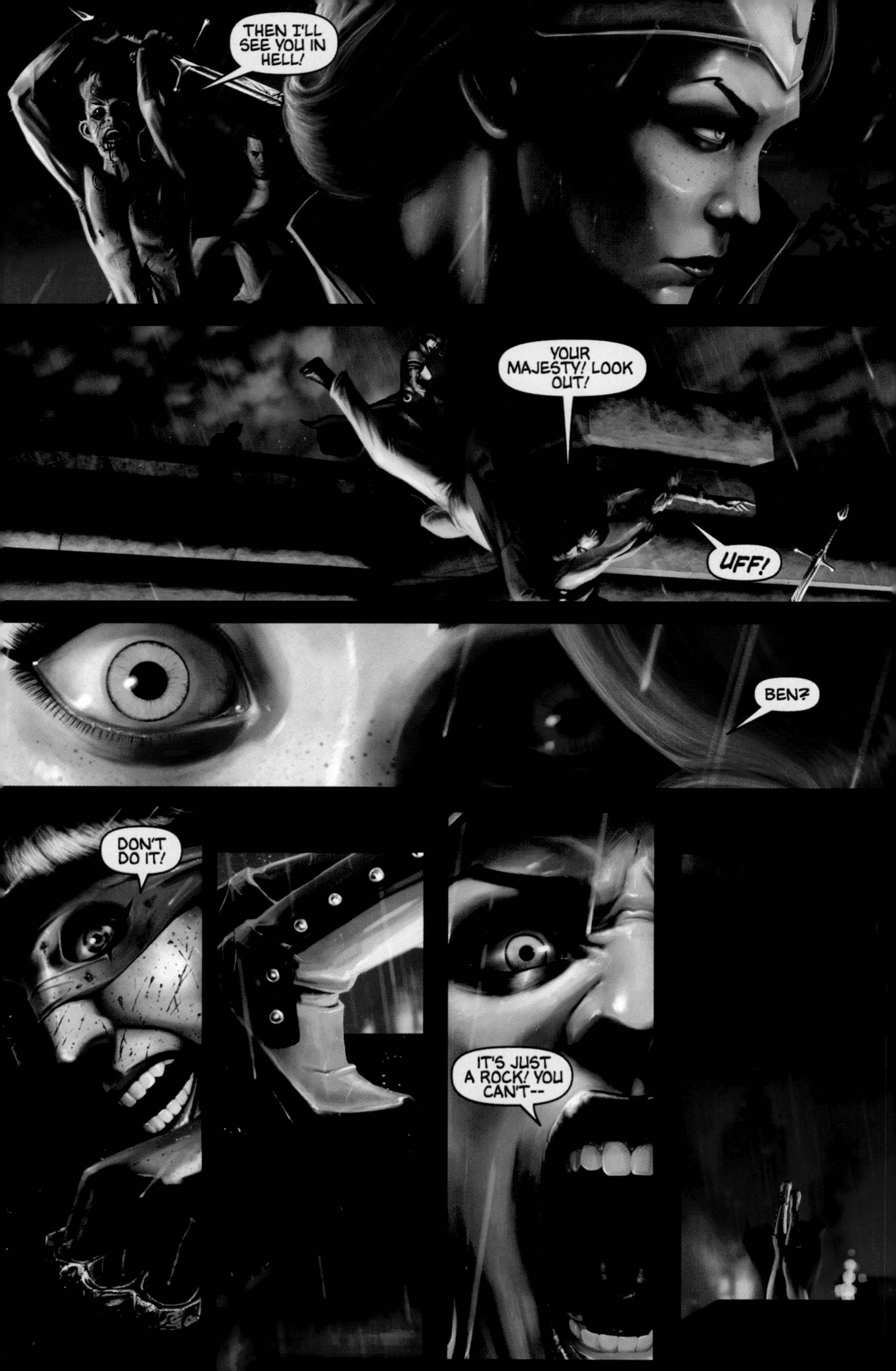
THEN I'LL SEE YOU IN HELL!
YOUR MAJESTY! LOOK OUT!
UFF!
BEN?
DON'T DO IT!
IT'S JUST A ROCK! YOU CAN'T--

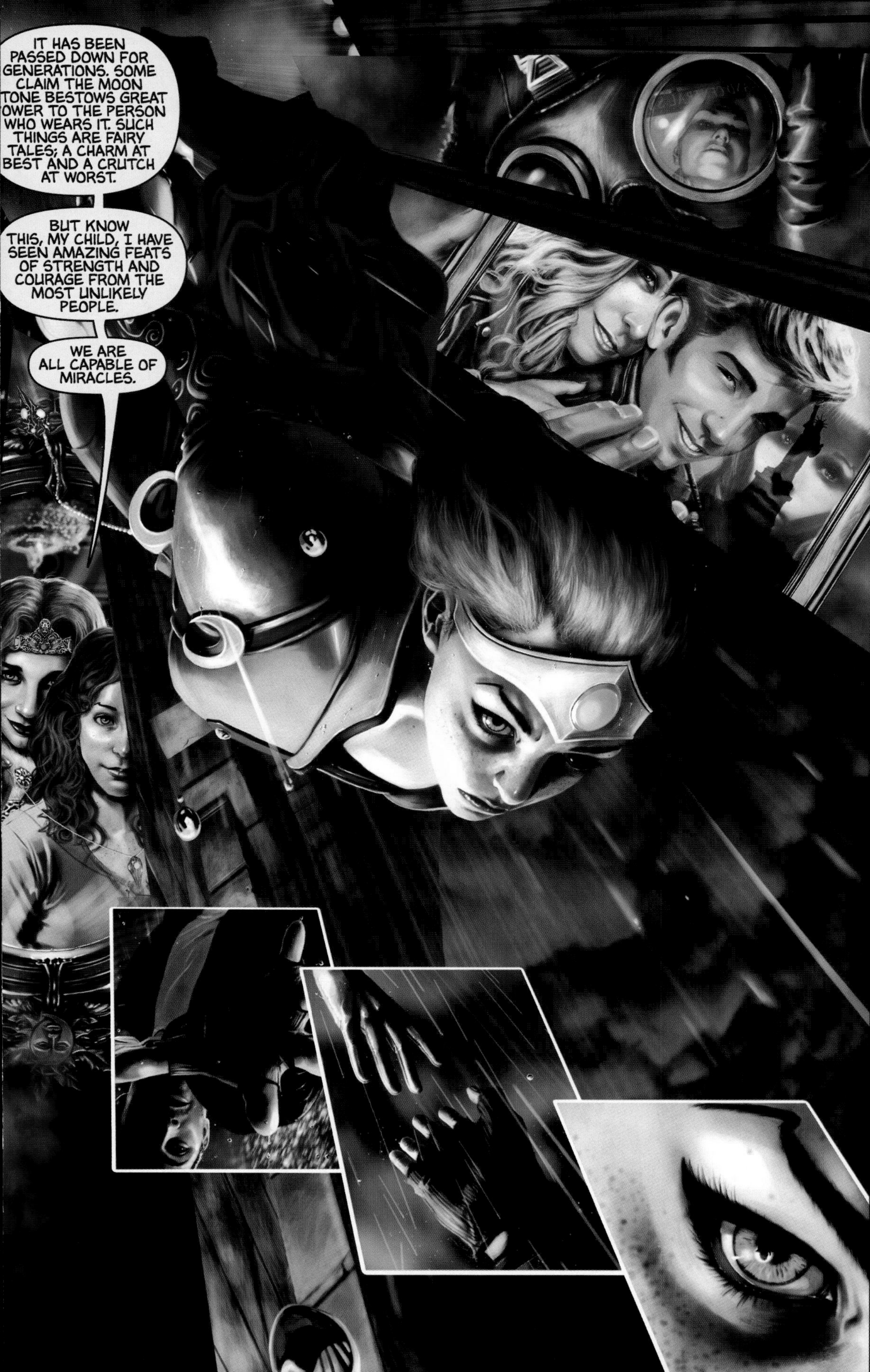
IT HAS BEEN PASSED DOWN FOR GENERATIONS. SOME CLAIM THE MOON STONE BESTOWS GREAT POWER TO THE PERSON WHO WEARS IT. SUCH THINGS ARE FAIRY TALES; A CHARM AT BEST AND A CRUTCH AT WORST.
BUT KNOW THIS, MY CHILD, I HAVE SEEN AMAZING FEATS OF STRENGTH AND COURAGE FROM THE MOST UNLIKELY PEOPLE.
WE ARE ALL CAPABLE OF MIRACLES.

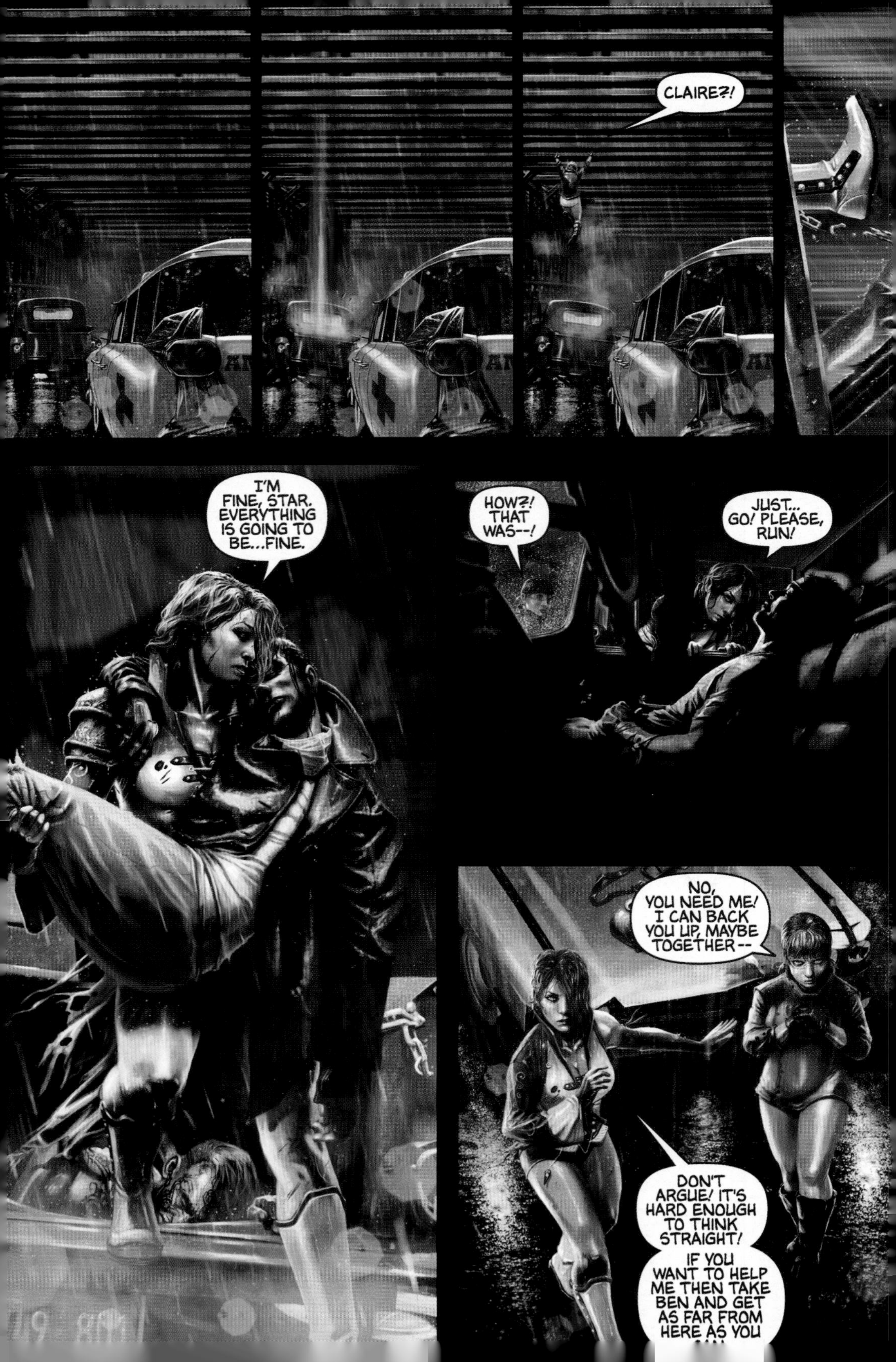
CLAIRE?!
I'M FINE, STAR. EVERYTHING IS GOING TO BE...FINE.
HOW?! THAT WAS--!
JUST... GO! PLEASE, RUN!
NO, YOU NEED ME! I CAN BACK YOU UP, MAYBE TOGETHER --
DON'T ARGUE! IT'S HARD ENOUGH TO THINK STRAIGHT!
IF YOU WANT TO HELP ME THEN TAKE BEN AND GET AS FAR FROM HERE AS YOU

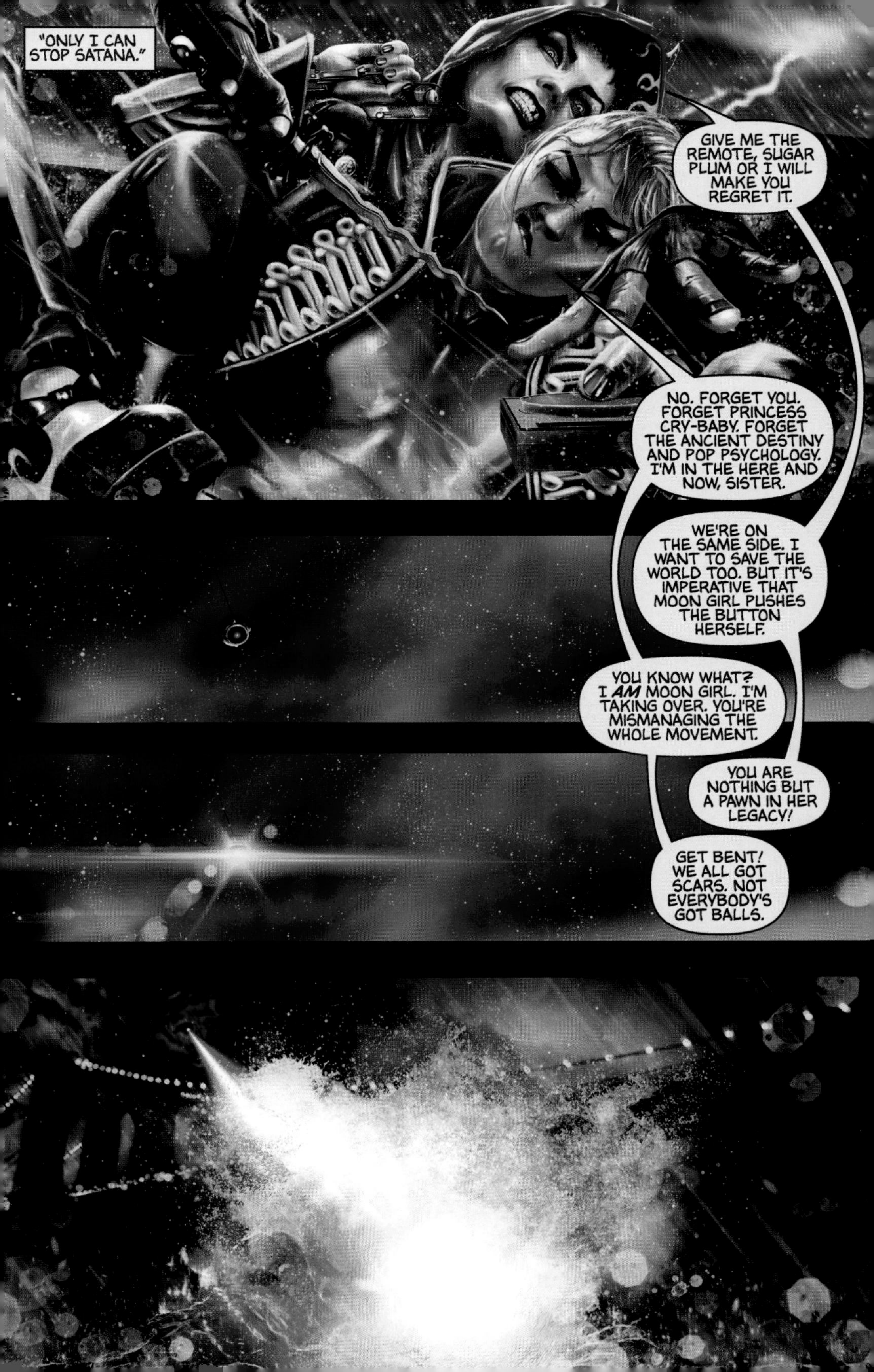
"ONLY I CAN STOP SATANA."
GIVE ME THE REMOTE, SUGAR PLUM OR I WILL MAKE YOU REGRET IT.
NO. FORGET YOU. FORGET PRINCESS CRY-BABY. FORGET THE ANCIENT DESTINY AND POP PSYCHOLOGY. I'M IN THE HERE AND NOW, SISTER.
WE'RE ON THE SAME SIDE. I WANT TO SAVE THE WORLD TOO. BUT IT'S IMPERATIVE THAT MOON GIRL PUSHES THE BUTTON HERSELF.
YOU KNOW WHAT? I *AM* MOON GIRL. I'M TAKING OVER. YOU'RE MISMANAGING THE WHOLE MOVEMENT.
YOU ARE NOTHING BUT A PAWN IN HER LEGACY!
GET BENT! WE ALL GOT SCARS. NOT EVERYBODY'S GOT BALLS.

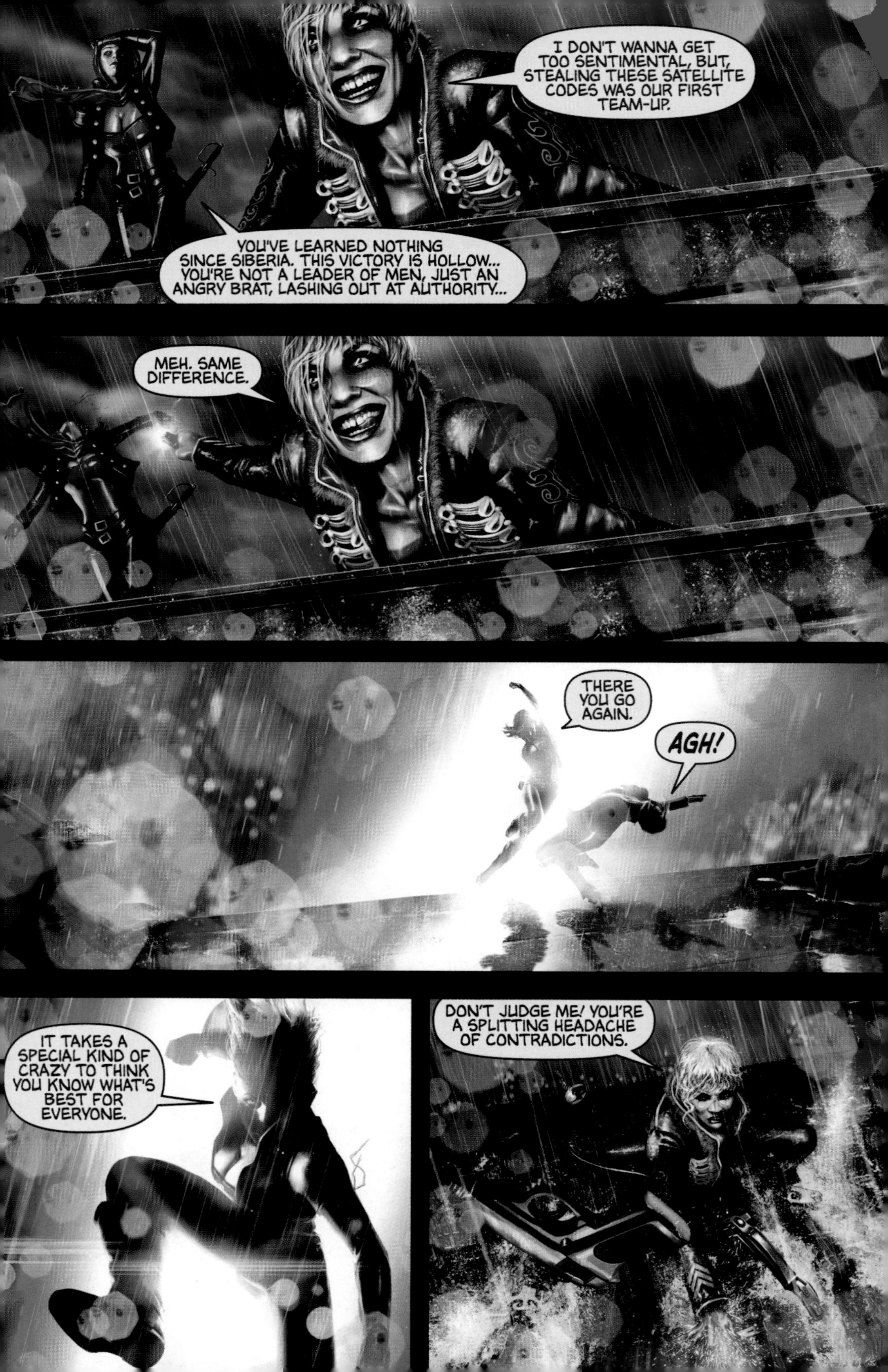
I DON'T WANNA GET TOO SENTIMENTAL, BUT, STEALING THESE SATELLITE CODES WAS OUR FIRST TEAM-UP.
YOU'VE LEARNED NOTHING SINCE SIBERIA. THIS VICTORY IS HOLLOW... YOU'RE NOT A LEADER OF MEN, JUST AN ANGRY BRAT, LASHING OUT AT AUTHORITY...
MEH. SAME DIFFERENCE.
THERE YOU GO AGAIN.
AGH!
IT TAKES A SPECIAL KIND OF CRAZY TO THINK YOU KNOW WHAT'S BEST FOR EVERYONE.
DON'T JUDGE ME! YOU'RE A SPLITTING HEADACHE OF CONTRADICTIONS.

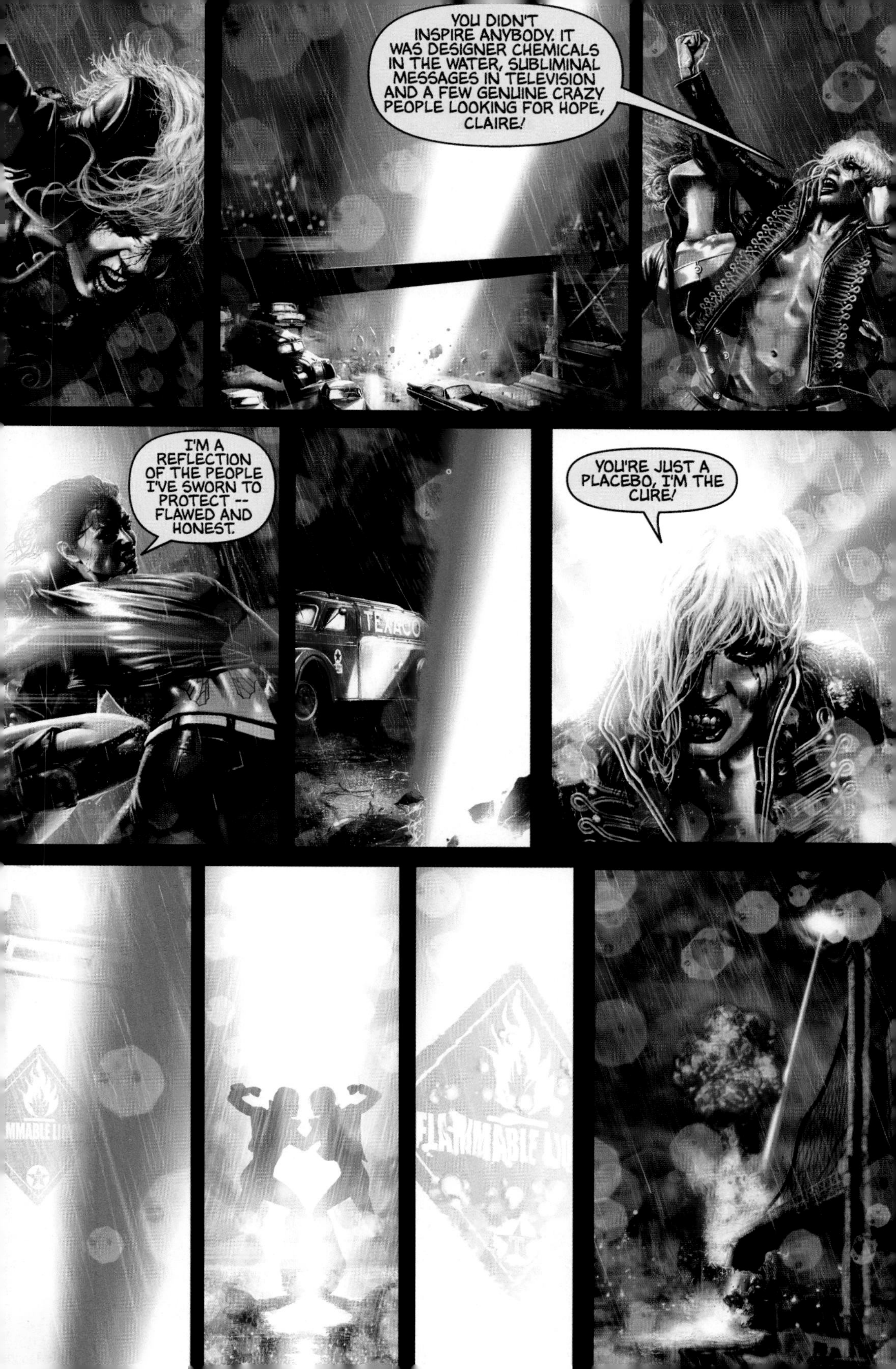
YOU DIDN'T INSPIRE ANYBODY. IT WAS DESIGNER CHEMICALS IN THE WATER, SUBLIMINAL MESSAGES IN TELEVISION AND A FEW GENUINE CRAZY PEOPLE LOOKING FOR HOPE, CLAIRE!
I'M A REFLECTION OF THE PEOPLE I'VE SWORN TO PROTECT -- FLAWED AND HONEST.
TEXACO
YOU'RE JUST A PLACEBO, I'M THE CURE!

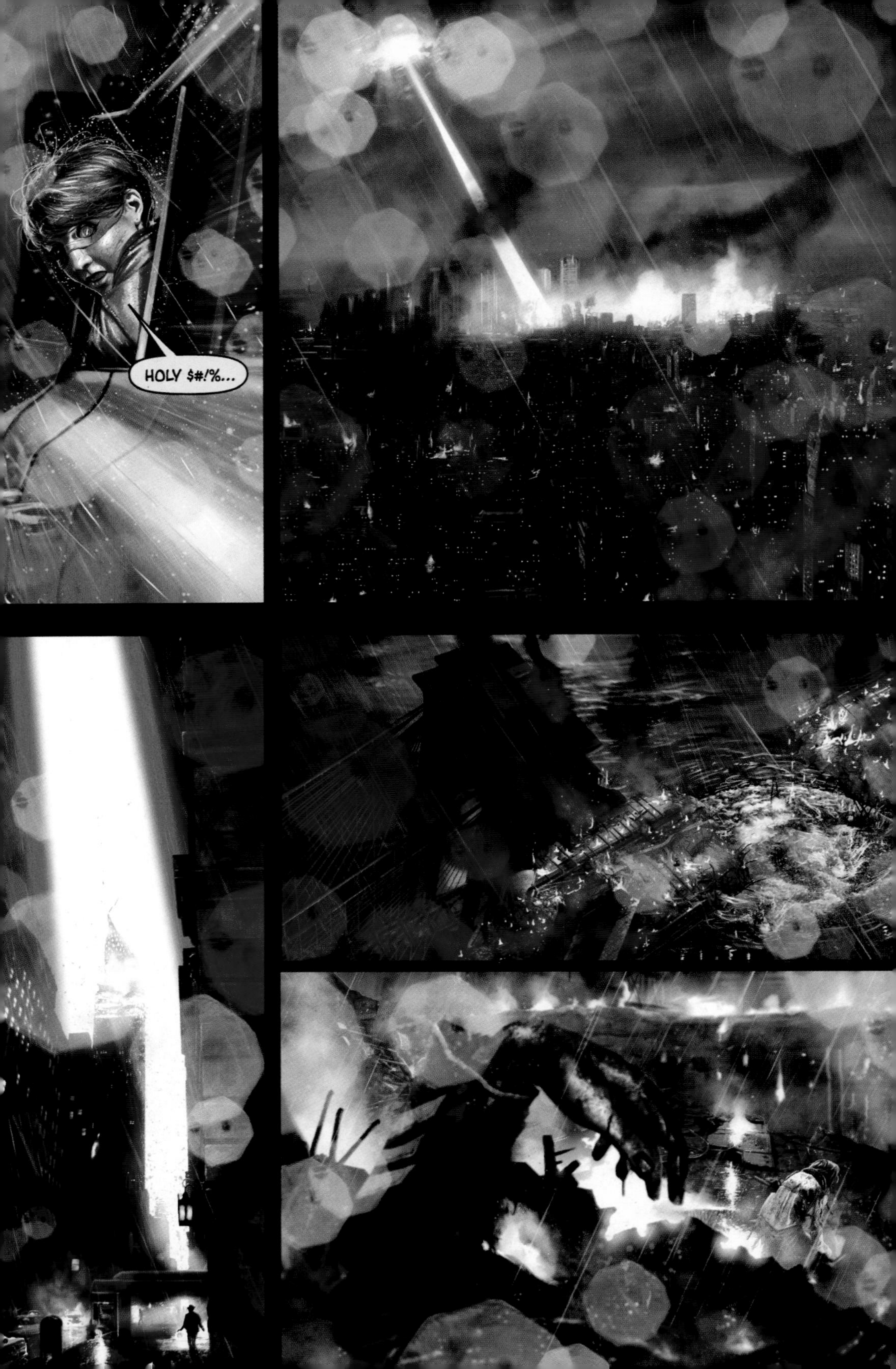
HOLY $#!%...

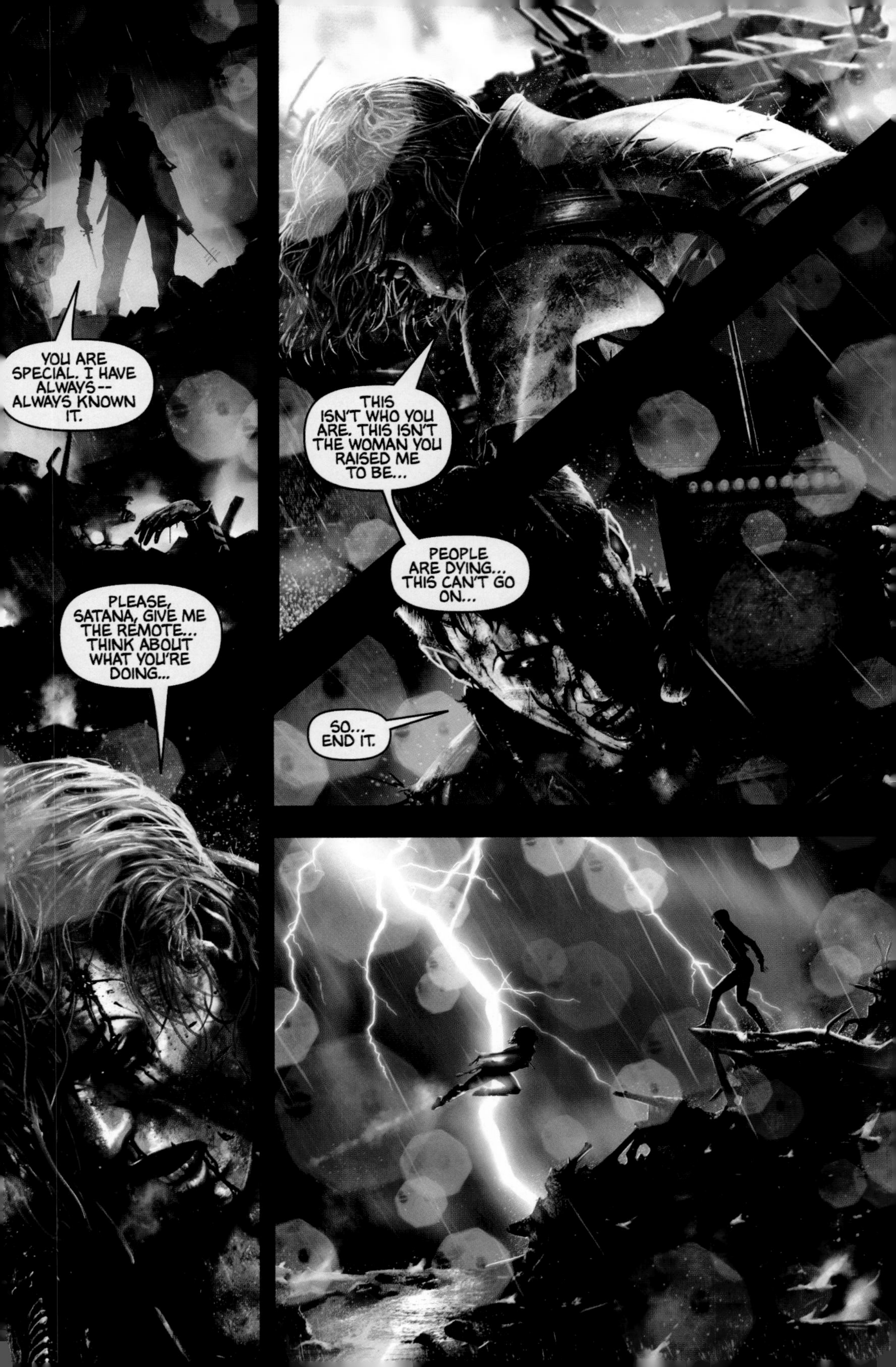
YOU ARE SPECIAL. I HAVE ALWAYS-- ALWAYS KNOWN IT.
THIS ISN'T WHO YOU ARE. THIS ISN'T THE WOMAN YOU RAISED ME TO BE...
PEOPLE ARE DYING... THIS CAN'T GO ON...
PLEASE, SATANA, GIVE ME THE REMOTE... THINK ABOUT WHAT YOU'RE DOING...
SO... END IT.

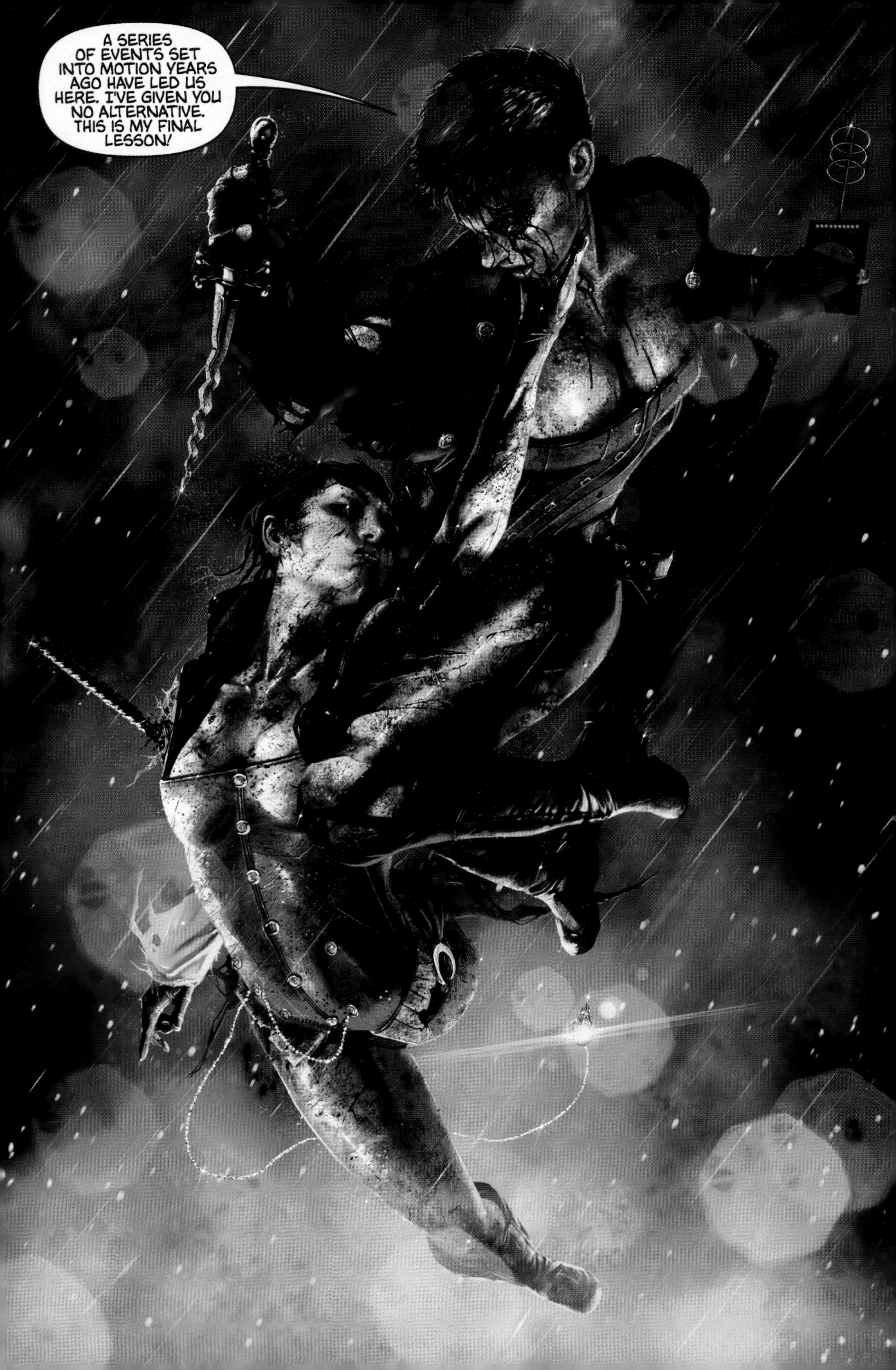
A SERIES OF EVENTS SET INTO MOTION YEARS AGO HAVE LED US HERE. I'VE GIVEN YOU NO ALTERNATIVE. THIS IS MY FINAL LESSON!

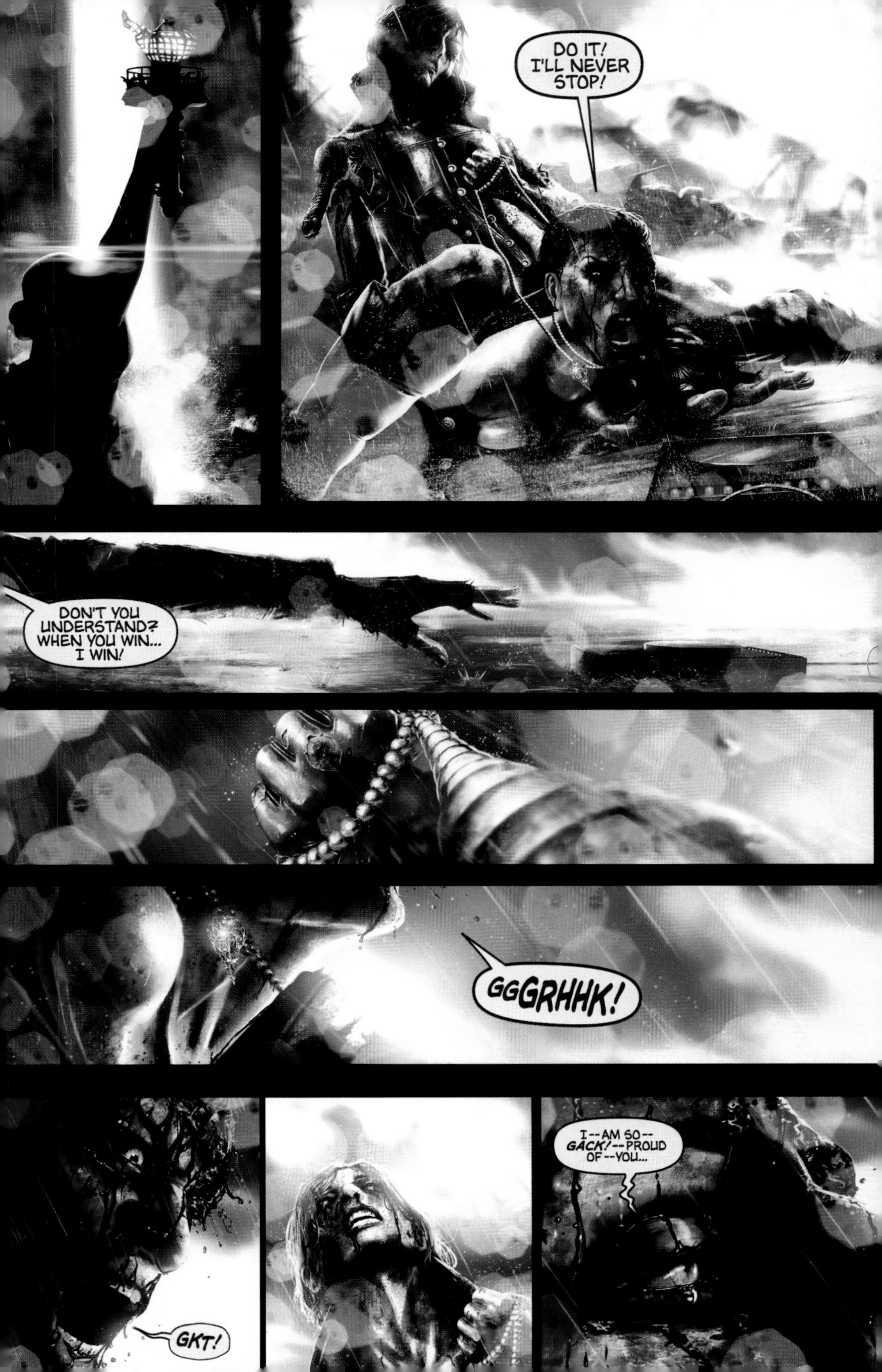
DO IT! I'LL NEVER STOP!
DON'T YOU UNDERSTAND? WHEN YOU WIN... I WIN!
GGGRHHK!
GKT!
I--AM SO--GACK!--PROUD OF--YOU...

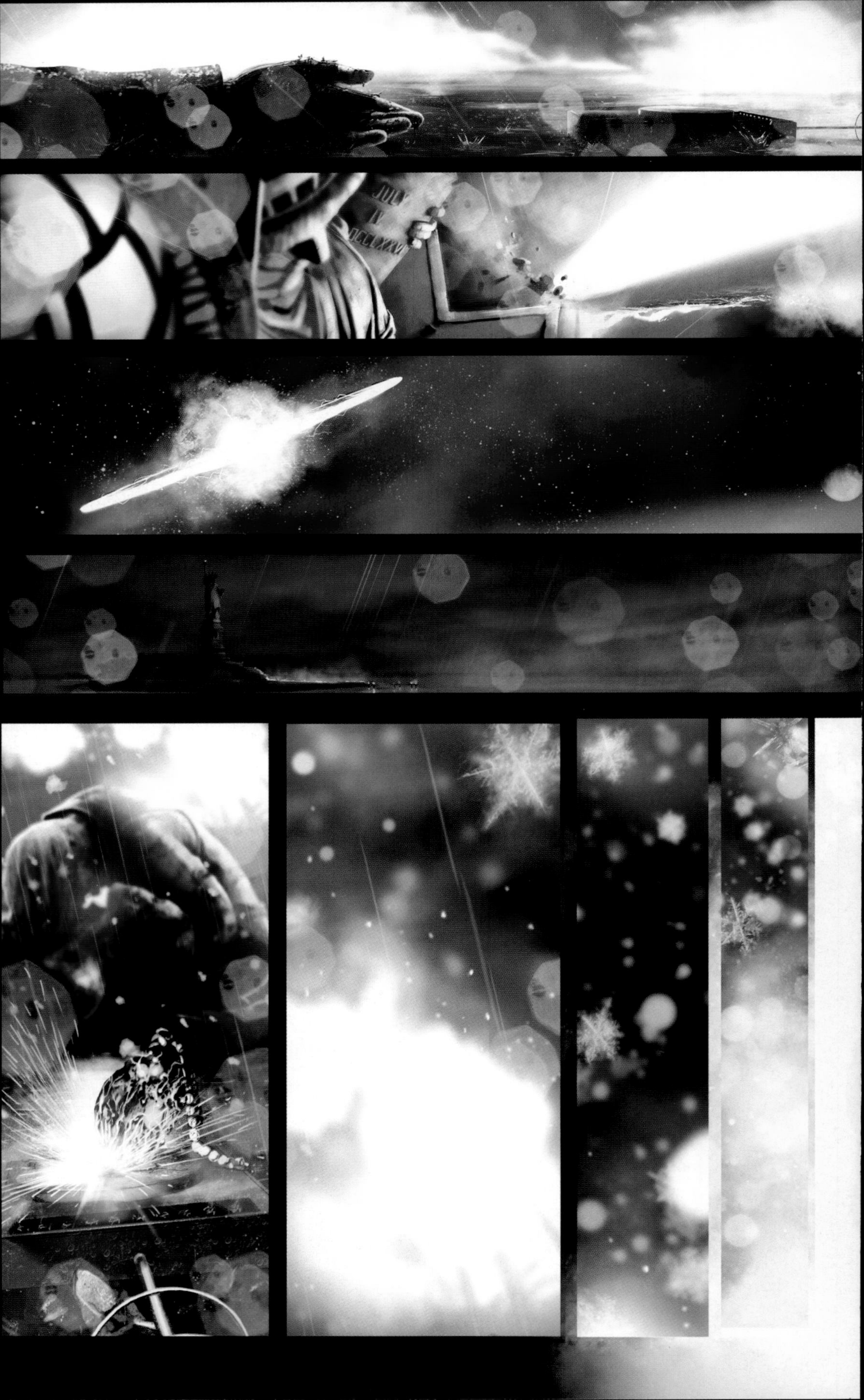

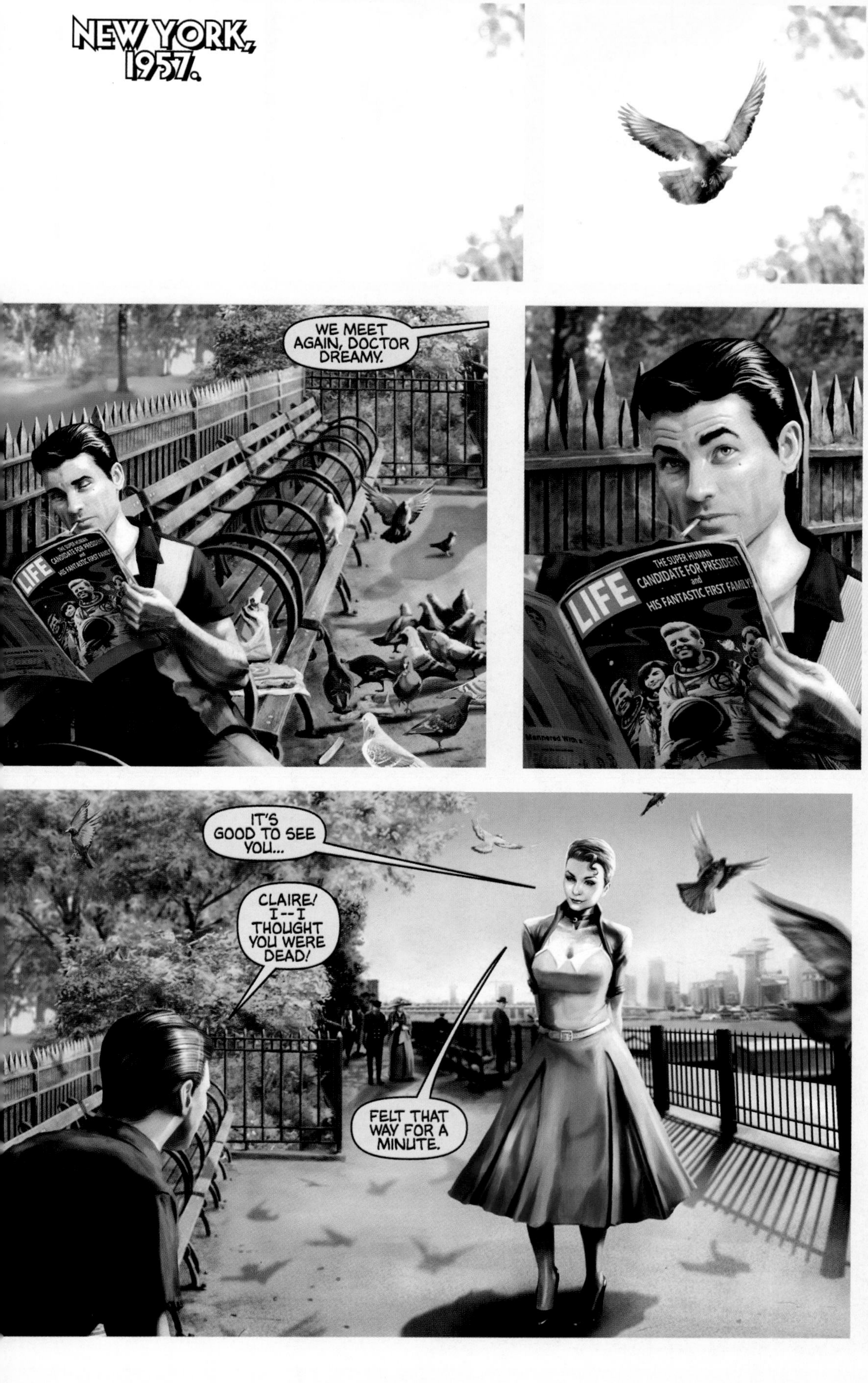
NEW YORK, 1957.
WE MEET AGAIN, DOCTOR DREAMY.
LIFE
THE SUPER HUMAN CANDIDATE FOR PRESIDENT and HIS FANTASTIC FIRST FAMILY!
IT'S GOOD TO SEE YOU...
CLAIRE! I--I THOUGHT YOU WERE DEAD!
FELT THAT WAY FOR A MINUTE.

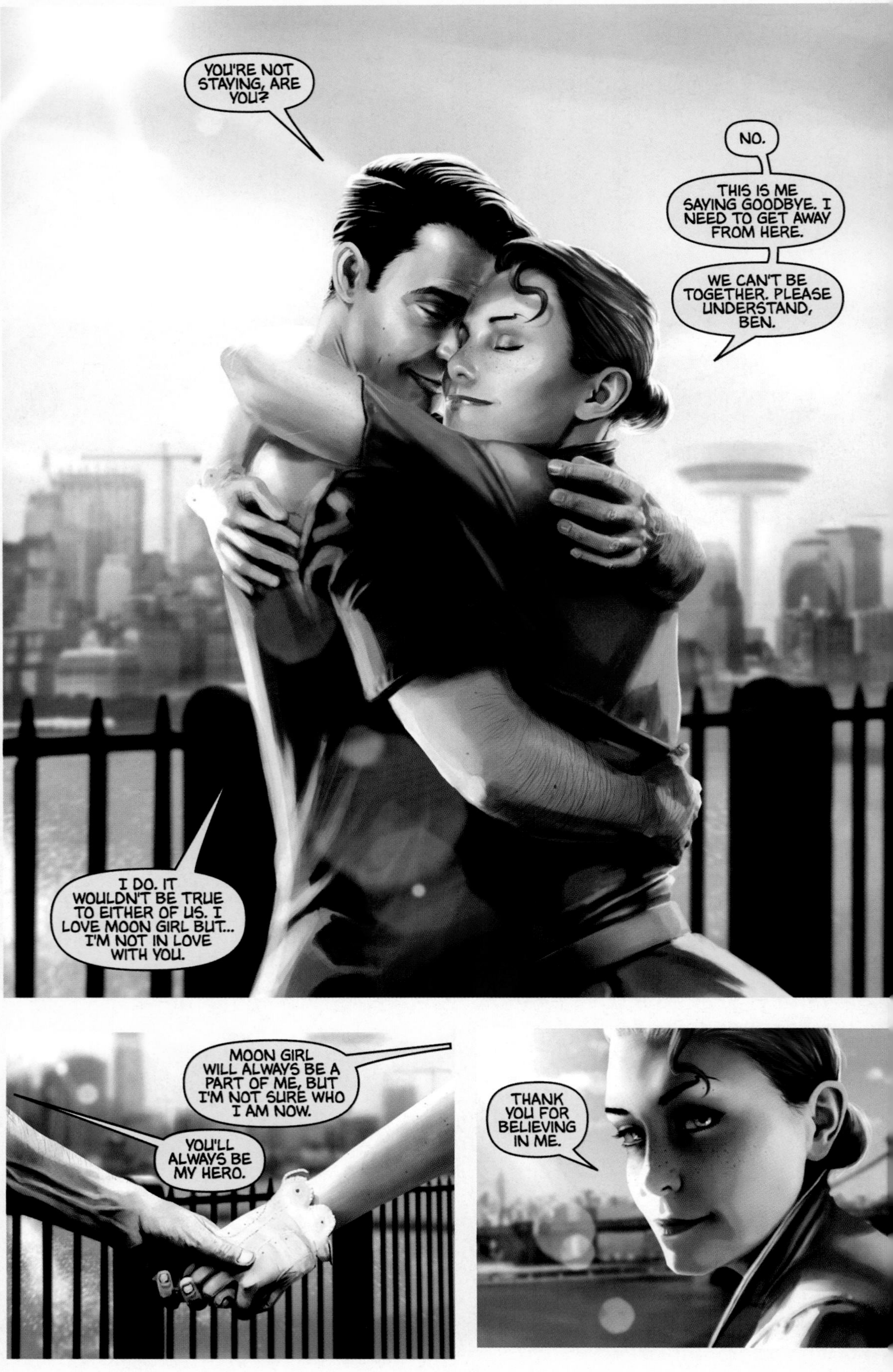
YOU'RE NOT STAYING, ARE YOU?
NO.
THIS IS ME SAYING GOODBYE. I NEED TO GET AWAY FROM HERE.
WE CAN'T BE TOGETHER. PLEASE UNDERSTAND, BEN.
I DO. IT WOULDN'T BE TRUE TO EITHER OF US. I LOVE MOON GIRL BUT... I'M NOT IN LOVE WITH YOU.
MOON GIRL WILL ALWAYS BE A PART OF ME, BUT I'M NOT SURE WHO I AM NOW.
YOU'LL ALWAYS BE MY HERO.
THANK YOU FOR BELIEVING IN ME.

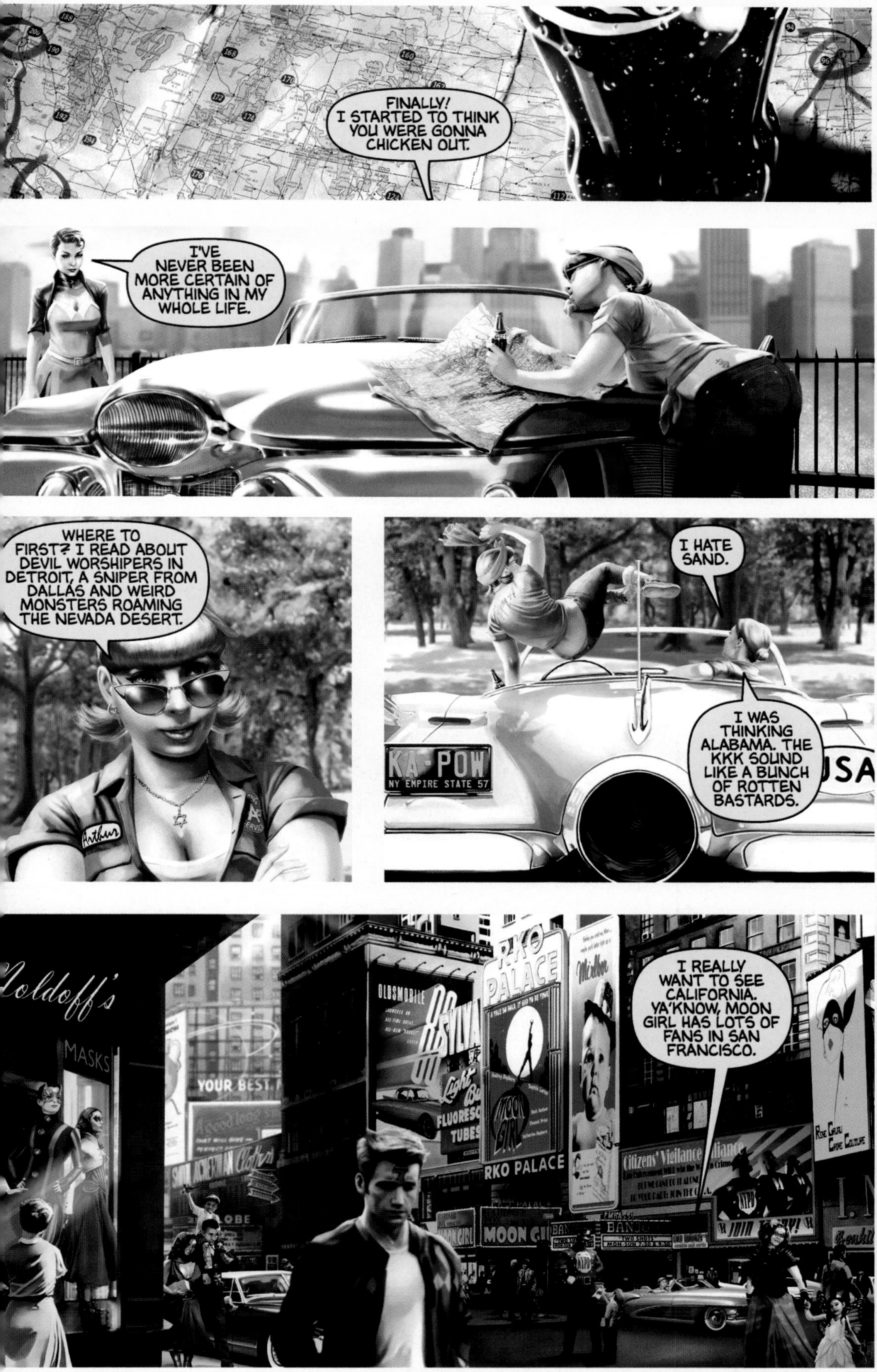
FINALLY! I STARTED TO THINK YOU WERE GONNA CHICKEN OUT.
I'VE NEVER BEEN MORE CERTAIN OF ANYTHING IN MY WHOLE LIFE.
WHERE TO FIRST? I READ ABOUT DEVIL WORSHIPERS IN DETROIT, A SNIPER FROM DALLAS AND WEIRD MONSTERS ROAMING THE NEVADA DESERT.
I HATE SAND.
I WAS THINKING ALABAMA. THE KKK SOUND LIKE A BUNCH OF ROTTEN BASTARDS.
KA-POW
NY EMPIRE STATE 57
USA
MASKS
YOUR BEST
OLDSMOBILE
FLUORESC
TUBES
RKO PALACE
RKO PALACE
MOON GIRL
I REALLY WANT TO SEE CALIFORNIA. YA'KNOW, MOON GIRL HAS LOTS OF FANS IN SAN FRANCISCO.
Citizens' Vigilance Alliance
NYPD

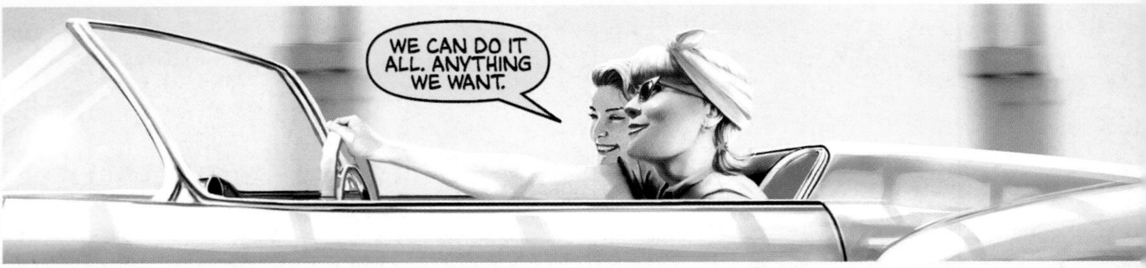
WE CAN DO IT ALL. ANYTHING WE WANT.

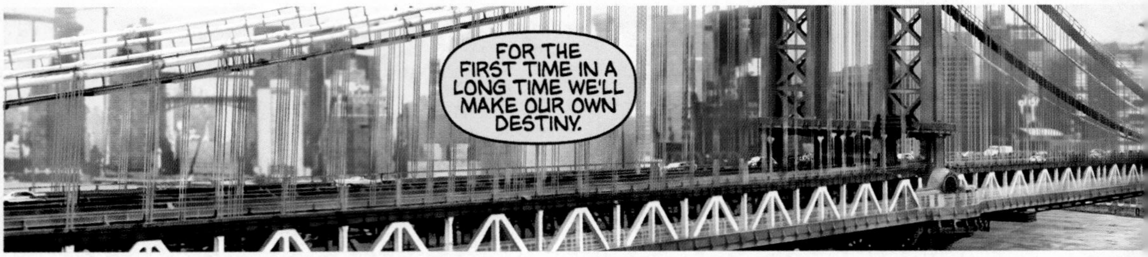
FOR THE FIRST TIME IN A LONG TIME WE'LL MAKE OUR OWN DESTINY.

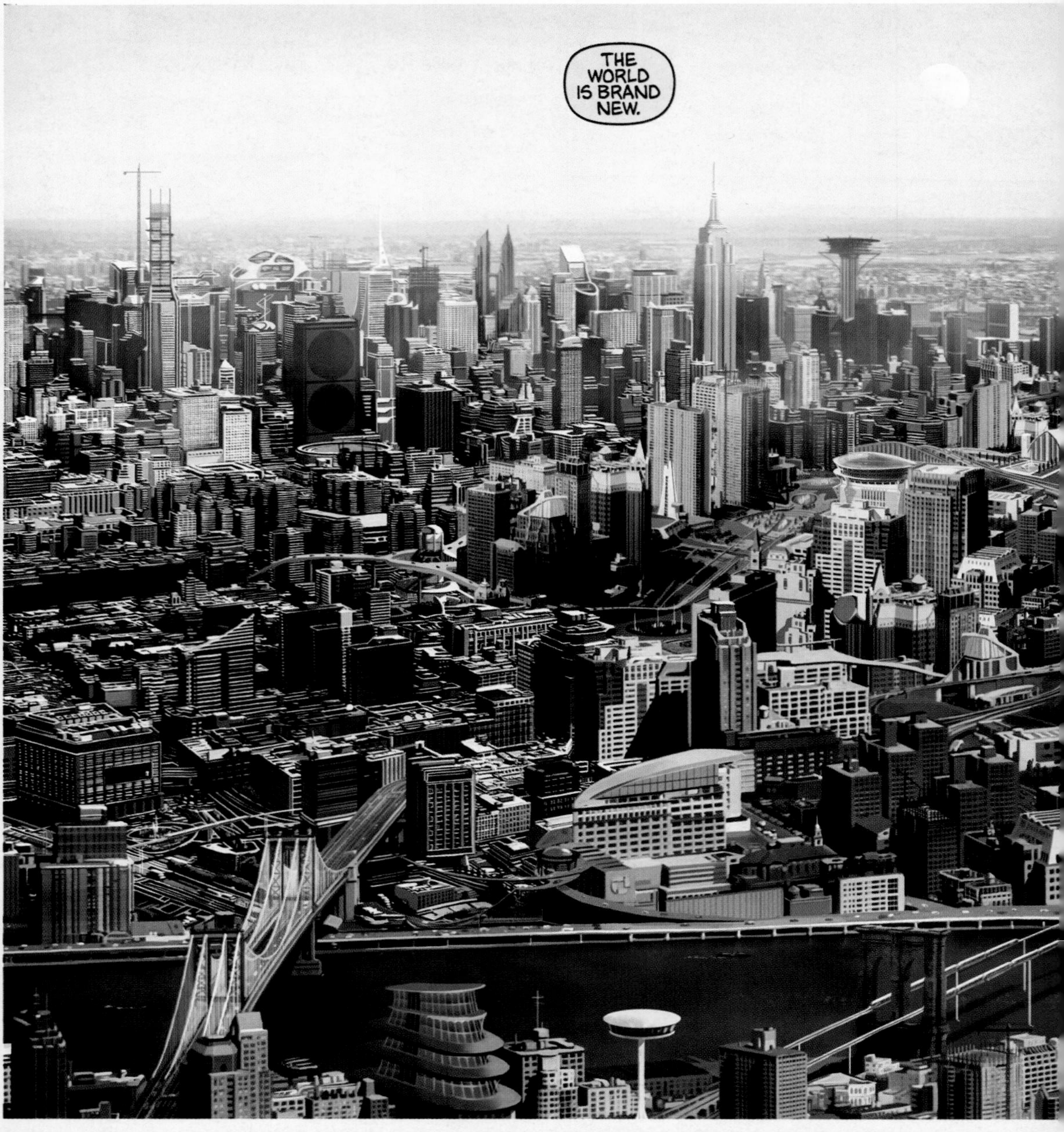
THE WORLD IS BRAND NEW.

Johnny Zi[illegible]

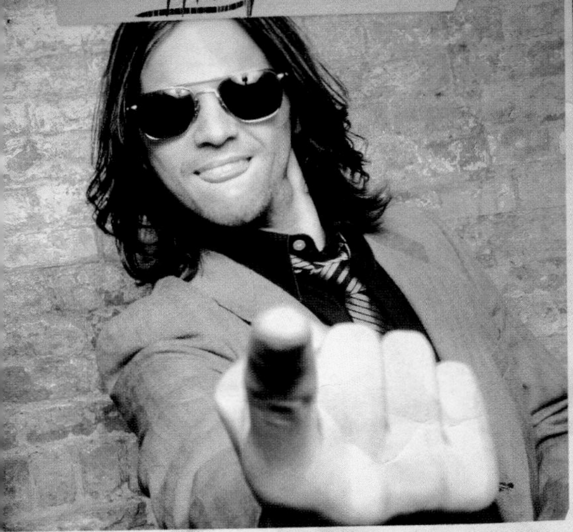

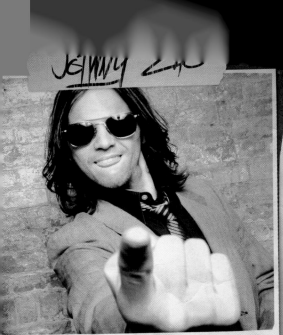

Johnny lives in a big South Philly home with all of his childhood friends; where they stay up late, reading comics and jumping on beds.

Tony Trov

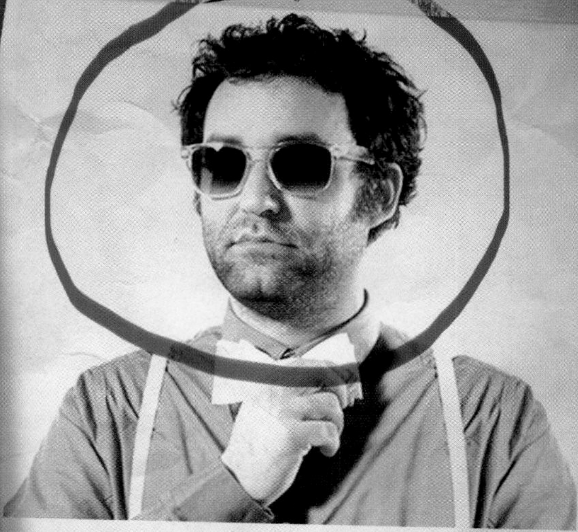

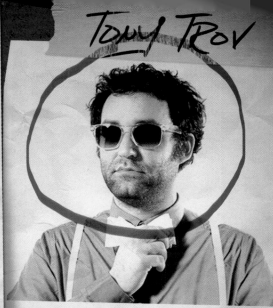

Tony was born in Philadelphia, PA. He is known for his love of bossa nova, French Onion Soup and kissing his own muscles.

Rahzzah

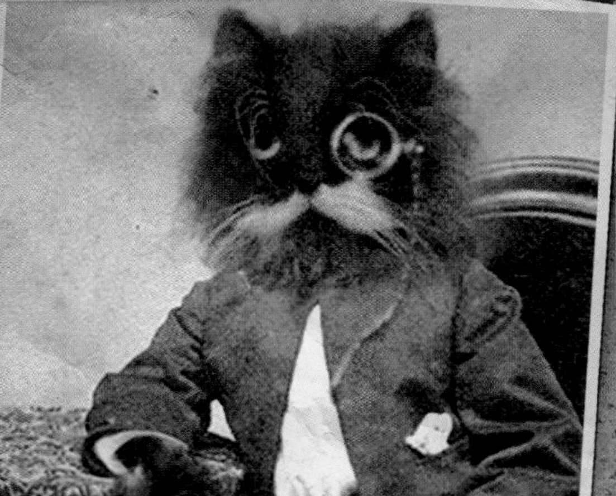

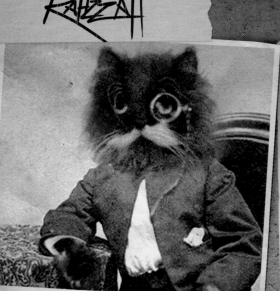

ahzzah contains about 6.7 x1027 atoms
nd is composed of 60 chemical elements.
e enjoys "The Kids in the Hall", girls
ith slight lisps, and appreciates and
xtravagant mustache.

Troy Peteri

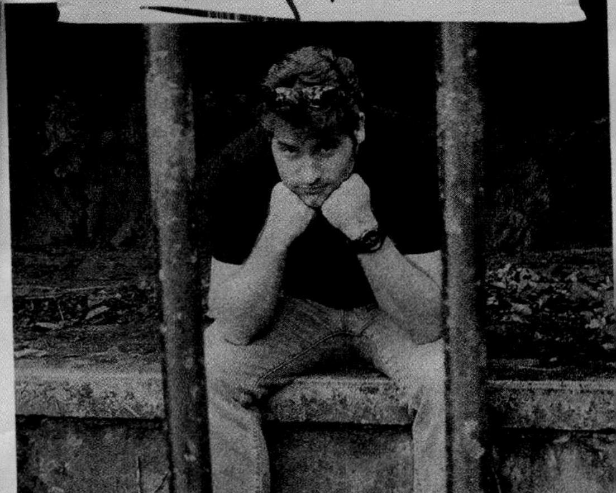

Troy Peteri has lettered a million comics from Amazing Spider-Man to Witchblade, as well as written the mini-series Abattoir for Radical Comics. He's currently writing a graphic novel that he can't speak of yet. Sometimes he tires of lettering other

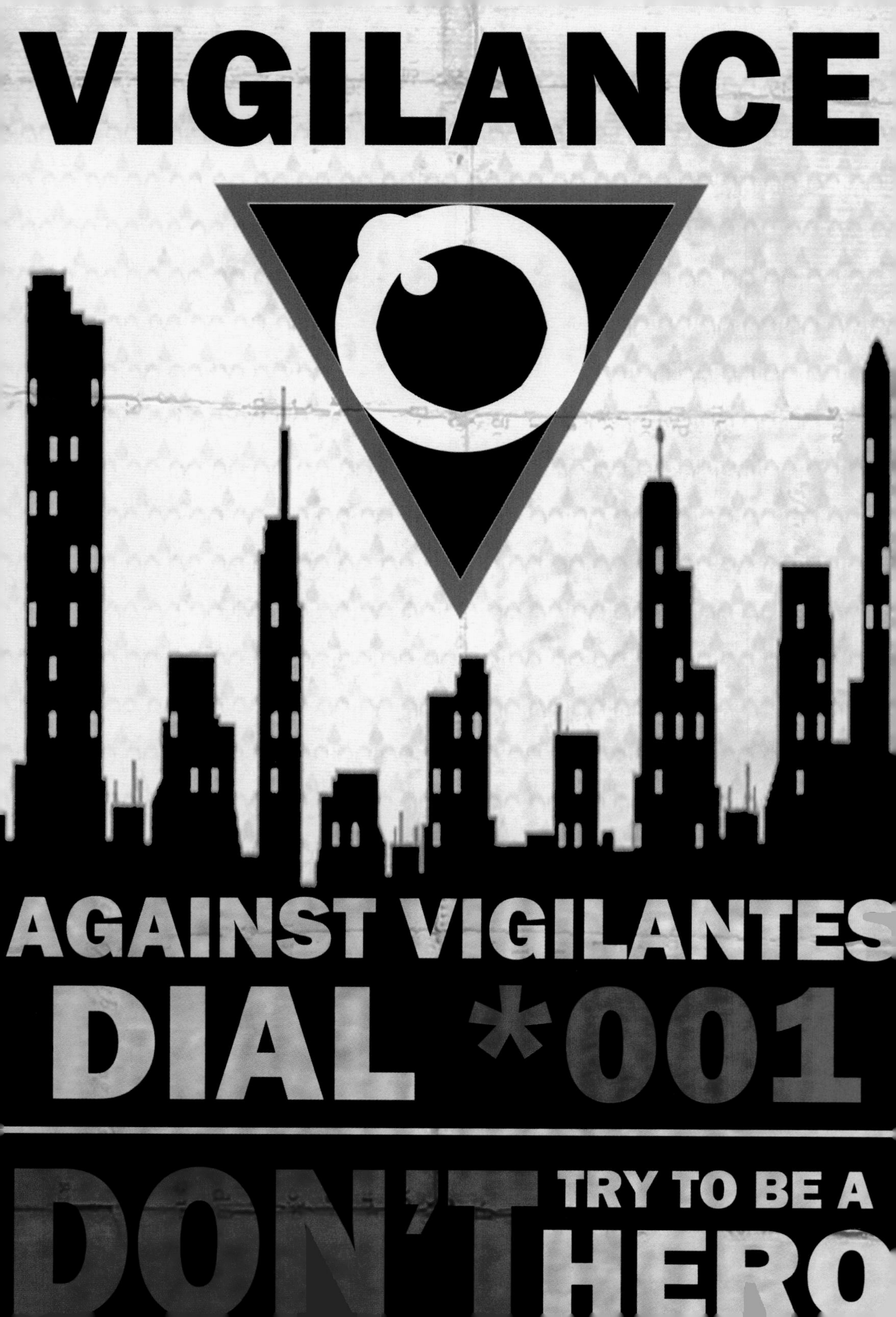
VIGILANCE
AGAINST VIGILANTES
DIAL *001
DON'T TRY TO BE A HERO

Could My Teenager be a...

SUPER HUMAN MENACE?

In this era of modern comfort it's easy to forget that sedition lurks around every corner. It's shocking but more and more mothers are discovering their teens to be leading a double life. It's not just the poor kids either; TIME Magazine reports that super heroes are all the fad on college campuses, too.

According to a survey by the American Psychoanalytic Association; a young mind is corrupted by the radical ideas of Super Humanism every 29 minutes. At this rate our democratic way of life could be erased by brain-dead-do-gooders.

We're American and the rule of law is paramount. An individual can't be allowed to buck the system. It's up to our leaders to make the rules. If you don't like it, wait four years and vote for the other guy.

The best weapon against the brainwashing of our children is preparedness. Be on the look out for signs of anti-social behavior in your own home. Once a bright mind is lost to the dark cult of super humanism, there's no turning back.

*Answers on page 185.

What is your teenager's most pressing worry?
-Midterms and academic pursuits.
-Finding a date for the prom.
-Political unrest.

If your teenager were a bird which would they be?
-Eagle
-Robin
-Pigeon

Which does your teenager believe:
-Life is cruel.
-Life is more or less fair.
-Life is for living.

How does your teenager spend their leisure time?
-Playing sports and socializing.
-Reading poetry and being artistic.
-constructing strange gadgets and staying out late.

Does your teen use any of the following terms?

_ Lair _ Long Johns _ Team Up _ Back-to-Back

_ Archenemy _ Break Loose _ Great Scott _ Way Out

Some teens have been known to change into provocative clothing and apply masks as soon as they're out of the house. Could this be your child?
-Maybe, we've had fights about dressing properly in public.
-I don't think so, my teen is always wearing their school sweater.
-No, I do the laundry and I know my teens' wardrobe.

You hear about a big fight in midtown. During a routine arrest of vagrants Police were attacked by several costumed youths. Witnesses report the assault was unprovoked and that the police were just doing their jobs. Do you:
-Know it could never be your child.
-Check the newspaper for descriptions of the assailants to be certain.
-Get sick to your stomach because you know your teen is a culprit.

SPECIAL REVIEW

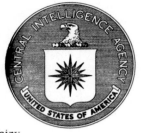

A/B, 3, 2/18

To: Agent Sugar Plum Fairy

Subject: Hypnotic Experimentation and Research, 10 February 1951.

On Wednesday, 10 February 1951, hypnotic experimentation and research work was continued in Buildi[redacted]

The group of five subjects appeared on schedule. The [redacted] expecting only three subjects, namely Miss [redacted] an[redacted] forced to alter his plans somewhat due to the unexpected arrival of [redacted]

Plans were originally made to conduct experiments in [redacted] and intoxication. These plans were altered to permit first, the subjects to present questions and discussions. (This was to permit the operator to spot any subjects who were critically [redacted] promptly clarified to the satisfaction of the subjects. In this discussion it was obvious that [redacted] were beginning to lose [redacted] themselves. From this point on the work proceeded as follows:

A

1. A posthypnotic of the night before [redacted] was enacted. Misses [redacted] immediately progressed to a deep hypnotic state with no further suggestion. This was to test whether the mere carrying out of the posthypnotic would produce the state of hypnosis desired. Needless to say, it did.

2. [redacted] then instructed (having previously expressed a fear of firearms in any fashion) that she would use every method at her disposal to [redacted] and failing in this, she would pick up a pistol nearby and fire it at [redacted] She was instructed that her rage would be so great that she would not hesitate to "kill" [redacted] for failing to awaken. [redacted] carried out these suggestions to the letter including firing the (unloaded pneumatic pistol) gun at [redacted] and then proceeding to fall into a deep sleep. After proper suggestions were made, both were awakened and expressed complete amnesia for the entire sequence. [redacted] handed the gun, which she refused (in an awakened state) [redacted] She expressed absolute denial that the foregoing sequence had happened.

THE WINSOR HOUSE

199 on The Bowery

The Most Centrally Located Flophouse in New York. Prices in Accordance With The Times.

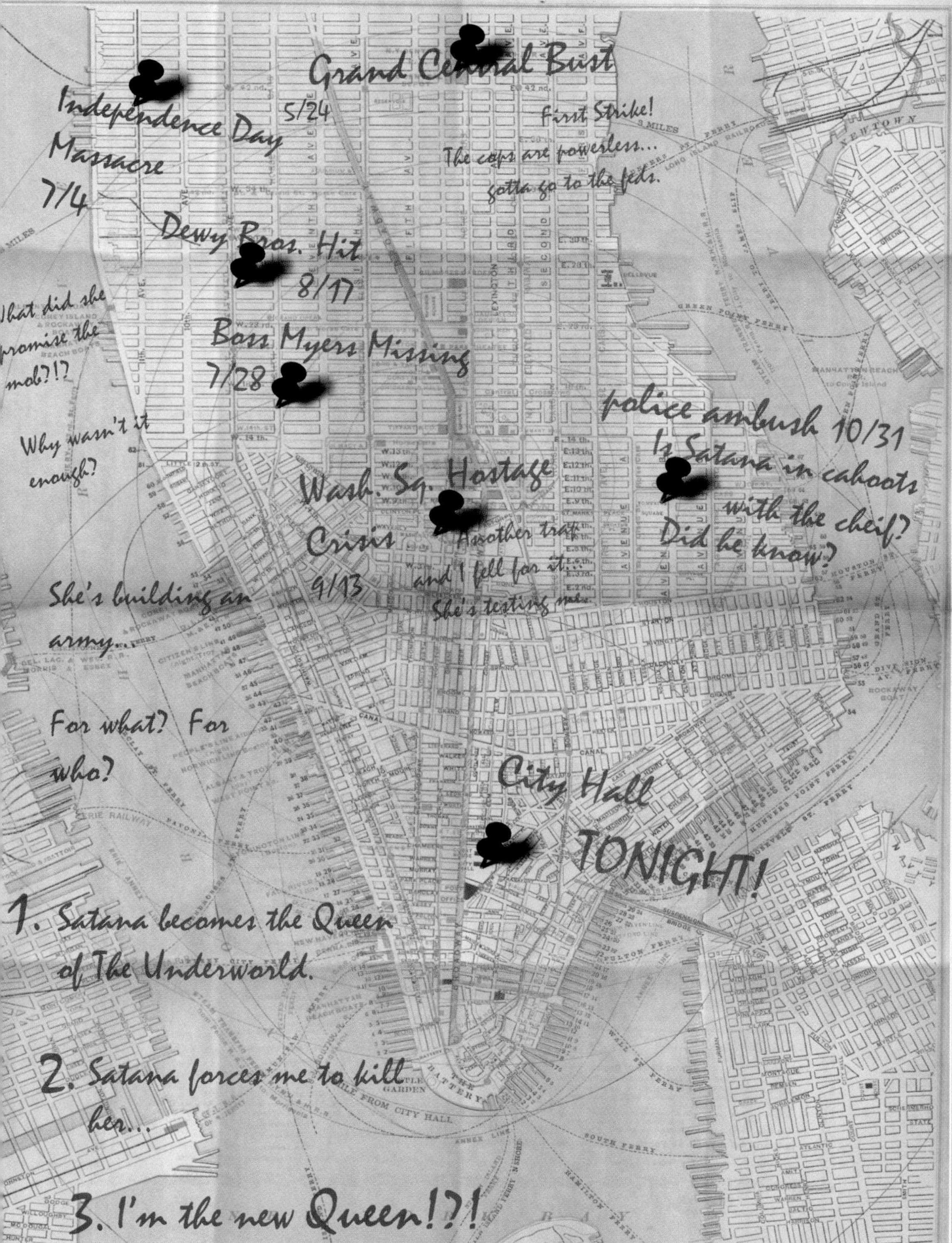

Grand Central Bust
5/24
First Strike!
The cops are powerless... gotta go to the feds.
Independence Day Massacre
7/4
Dewy Bros. Hit
8/17
hat did she promise the mob?!?
Boss Myers Missing
7/28
Why wasn't it enough?
police ambush 10/31
Is Satana in cahoots with the cheif? Did he know?
Wash. Sq. Hostage Crisis
9/13
Another trap and I fell for it. She's testing me.
She's building an army...
For what? For who?
City Hall
TONIGHT!
1. Satana becomes the Queen of The Underworld.
2. Satana forces me to kill her...
3. I'm the new Queen!?!

THE WINSOR HOUSE TRAVEL GUIDE TO MANHATTAN

- 6 -

БРАЧНОГ НАЧЕЛНИК СУПЕТАР
БРАЧНОГ НАЧЕЛНИК СУПЕТАР

iseljenje za
Supetar,

Svaka putna isprava
olaska na put:
1. potrebnim vizama tra
2. žigom par. društva, k
3. žigom iselj. nadzornog

SEVERN BEACH PLATFORM

1925

8444

КРАЉЕВИНА ЈУГОСЛАВИЈА
ROYAUME DE ___ LAVIE

B4150
Hyrba and Sandgate
Tramway
FARE 4d

SINGLE JOURNEY

PASSEPORT

Claire June

ПУТНА ИСПРАВА

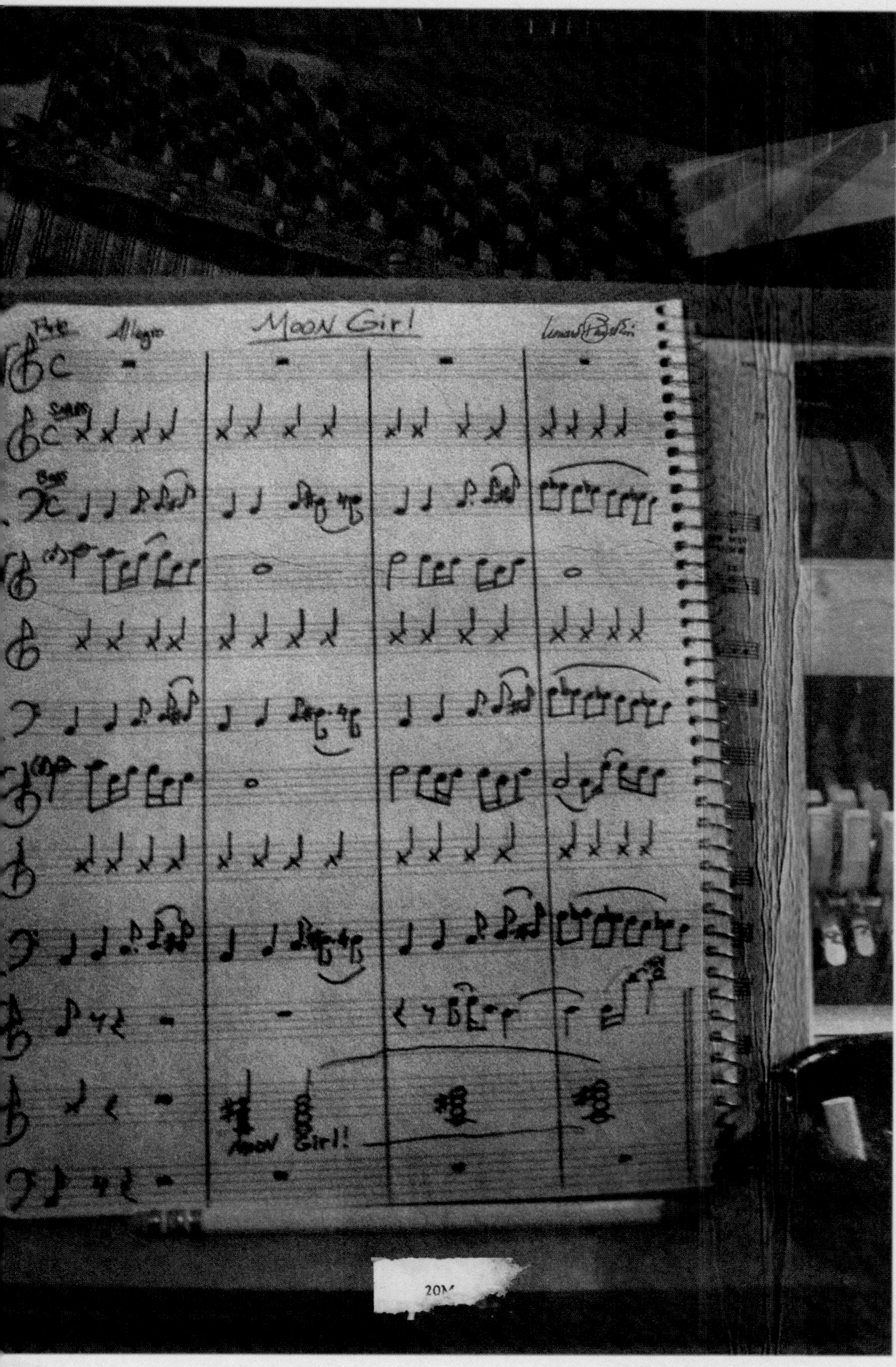
Allegro
Moon Girl
Moon Girl!
20M

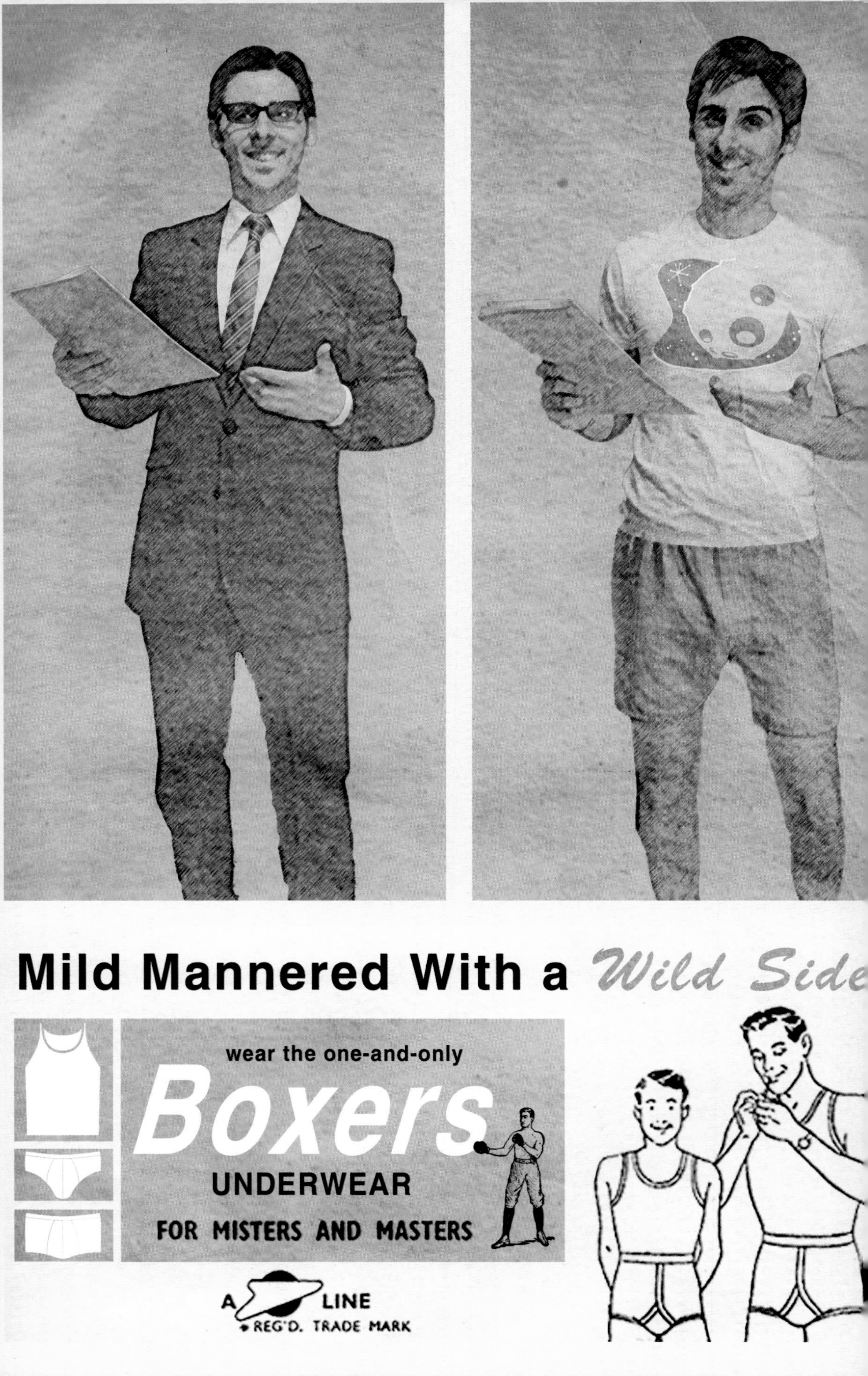
Mild Mannered With a Wild Side
wear the one-and-only
Boxers
UNDERWEAR
FOR MISTERS AND MASTERS
A LINE
REG'D. TRADE MARK

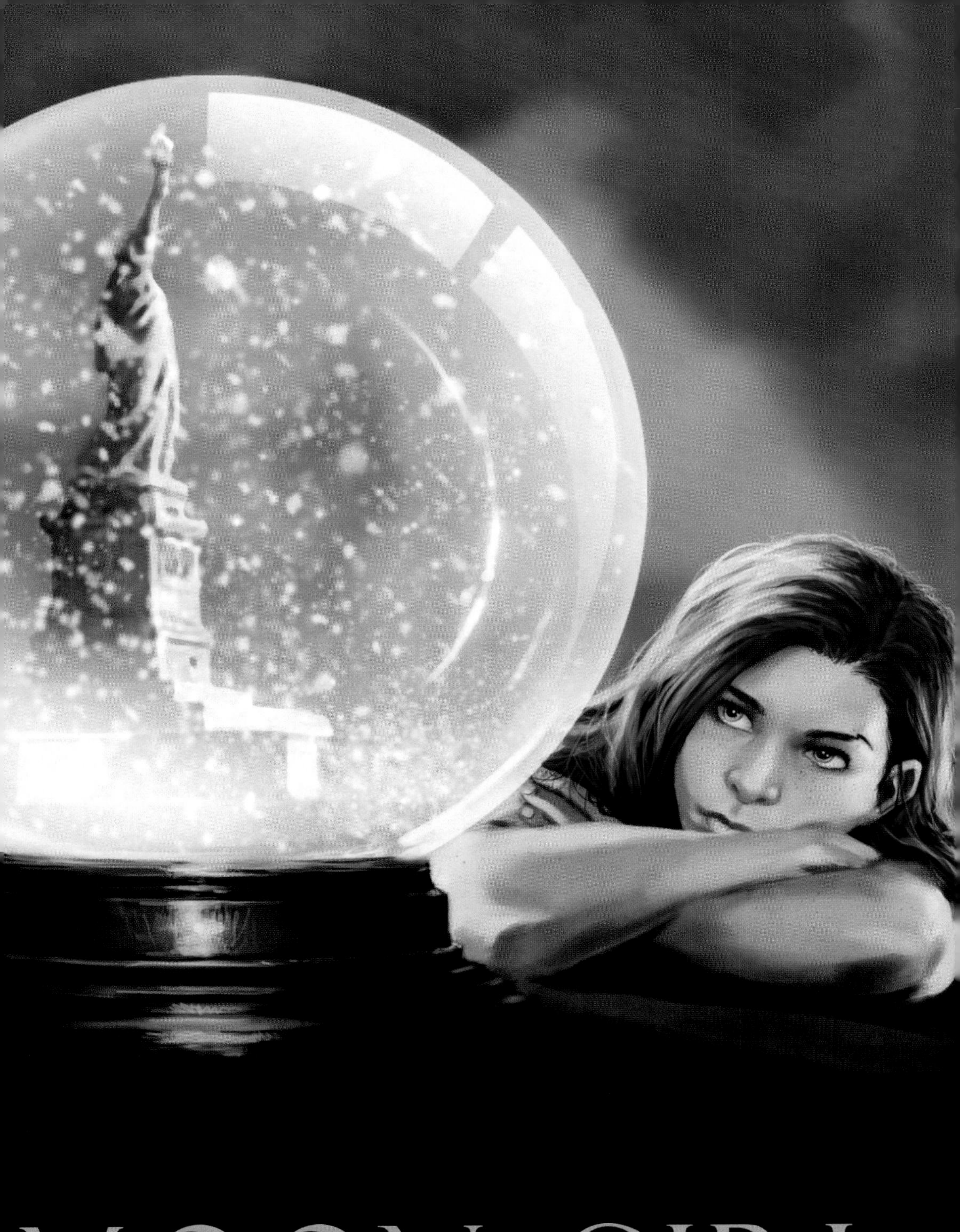

MOON GIRL

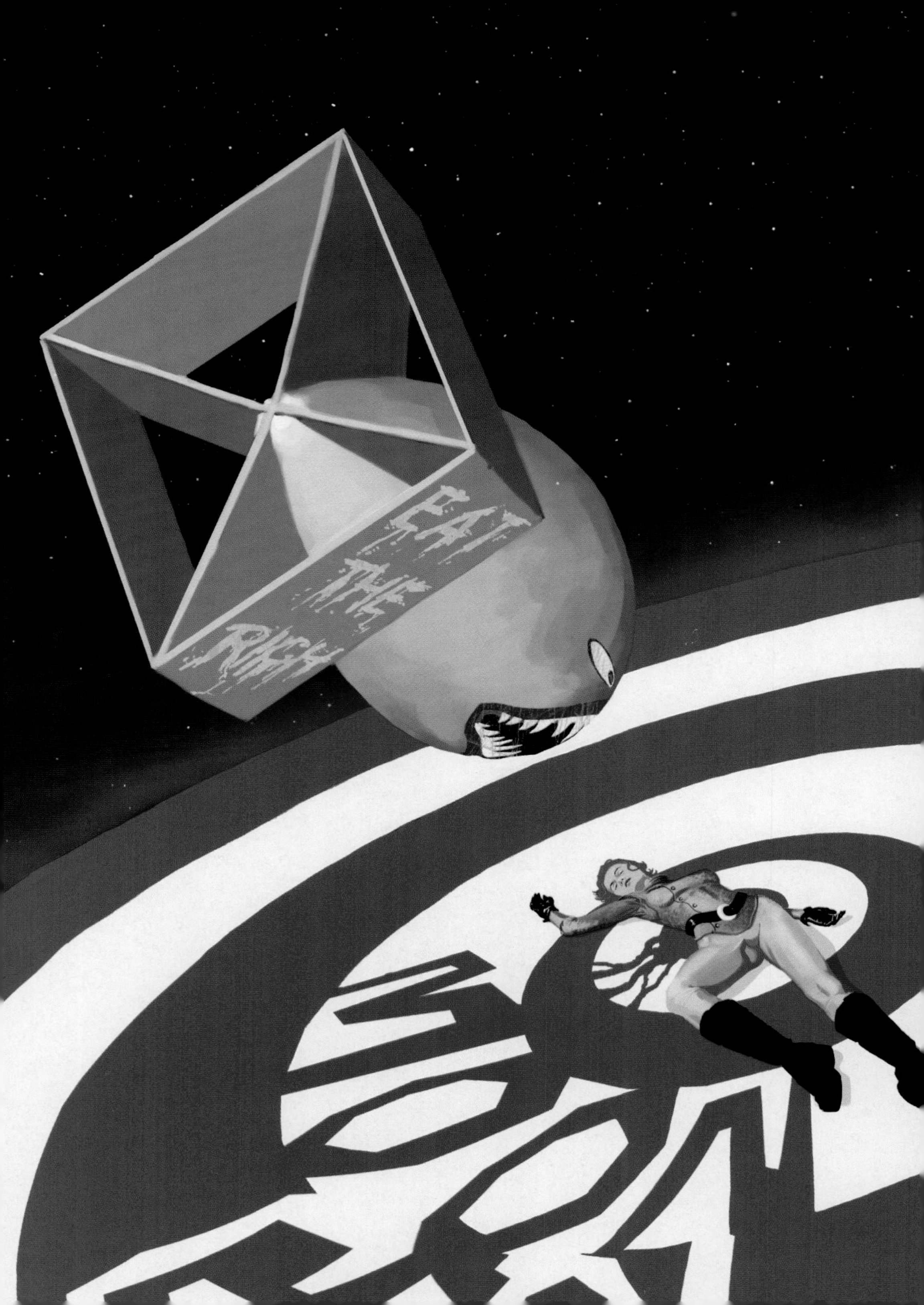
EAT THE RICH

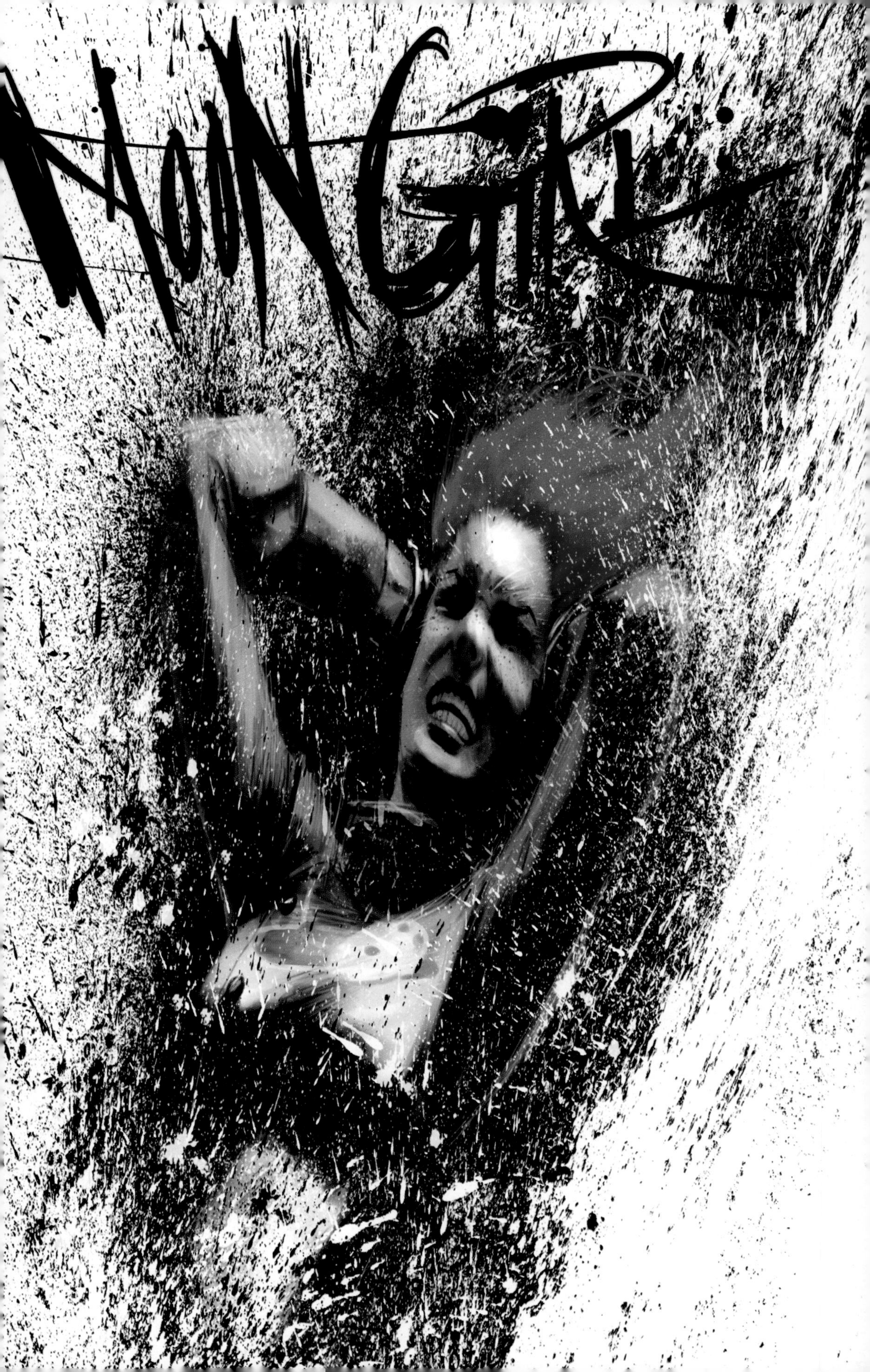
MOON GIRL

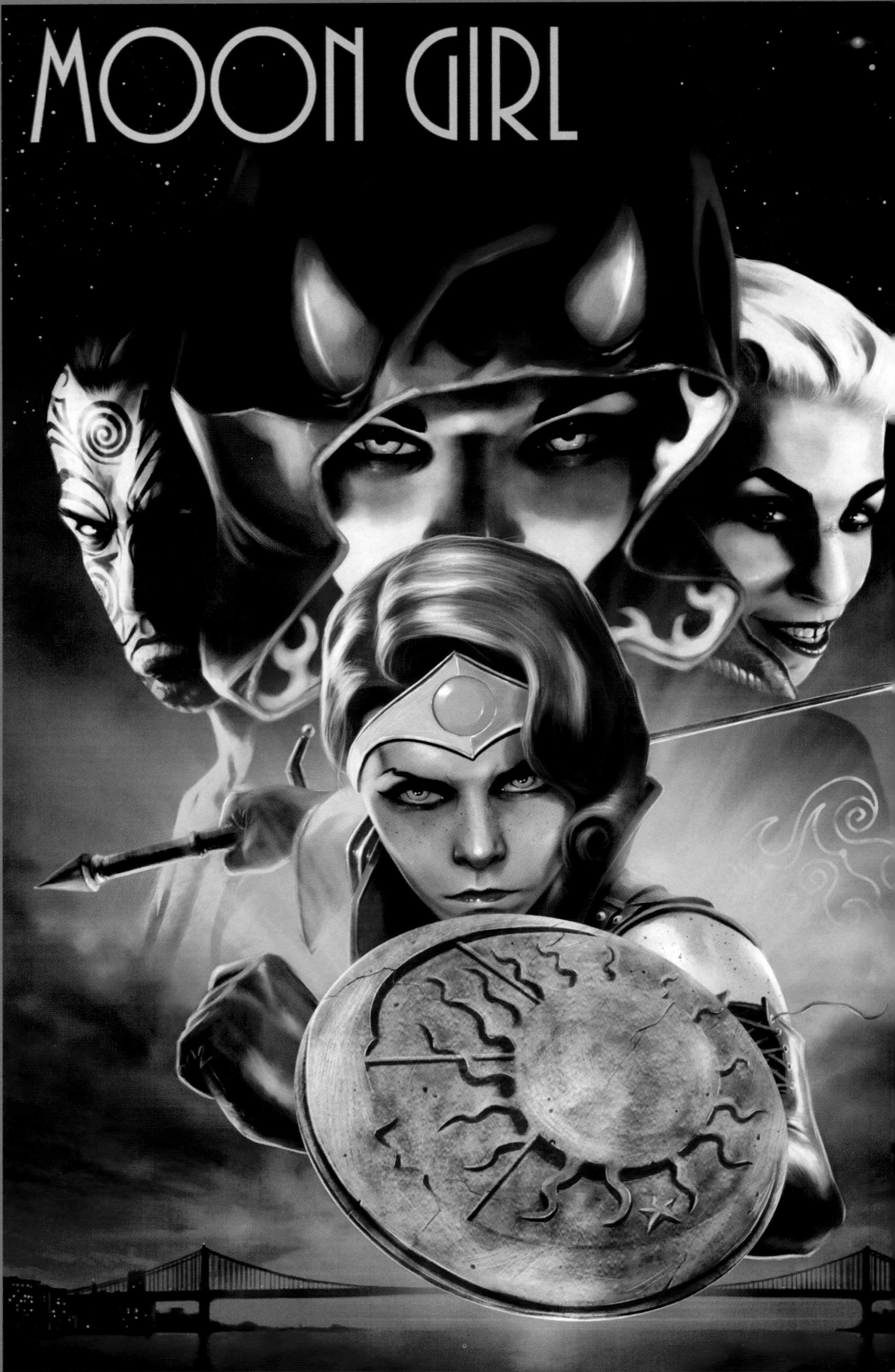
MOON GIRL

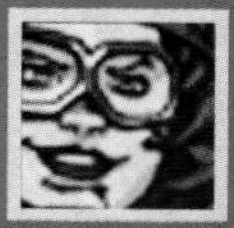

ALUÍSIO SANTOS

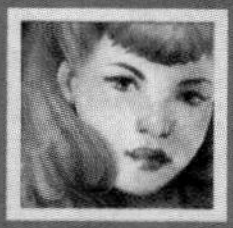

KELLY PERRY

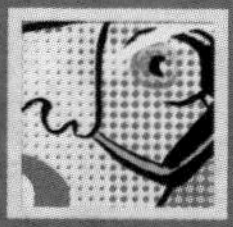

CHRISTINE LARSEN

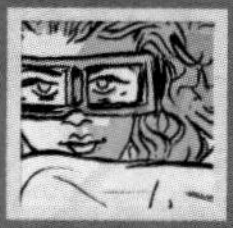

PAUL MAYBURY

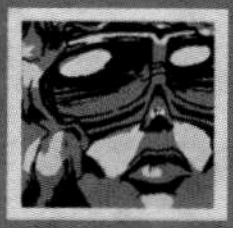

SHELDON VELLA

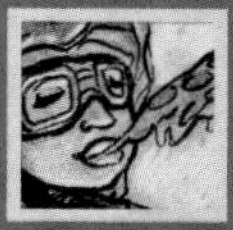

GABRIEL BAUTISTA

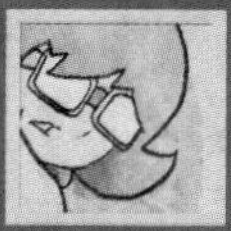

MARK A. FIONDA JR.

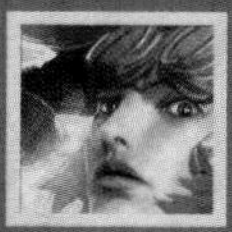

JARREAU WIMBERLY

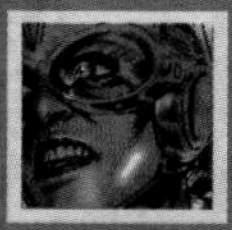

BRAD HEITMEYER

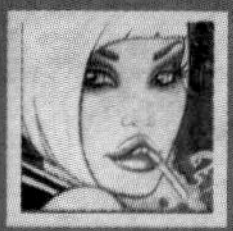

LINDSEY LAMONT

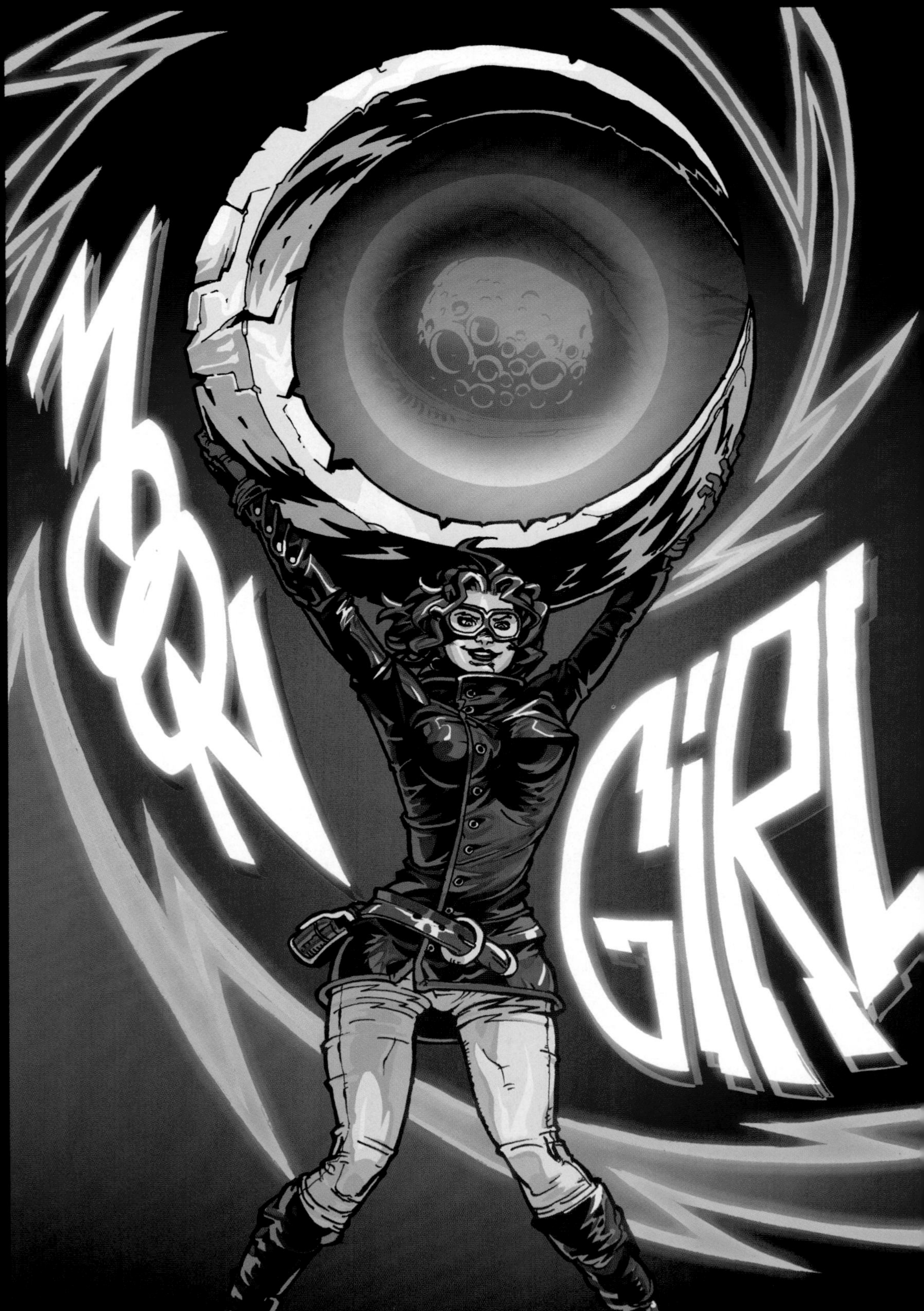
MOON
GIRL

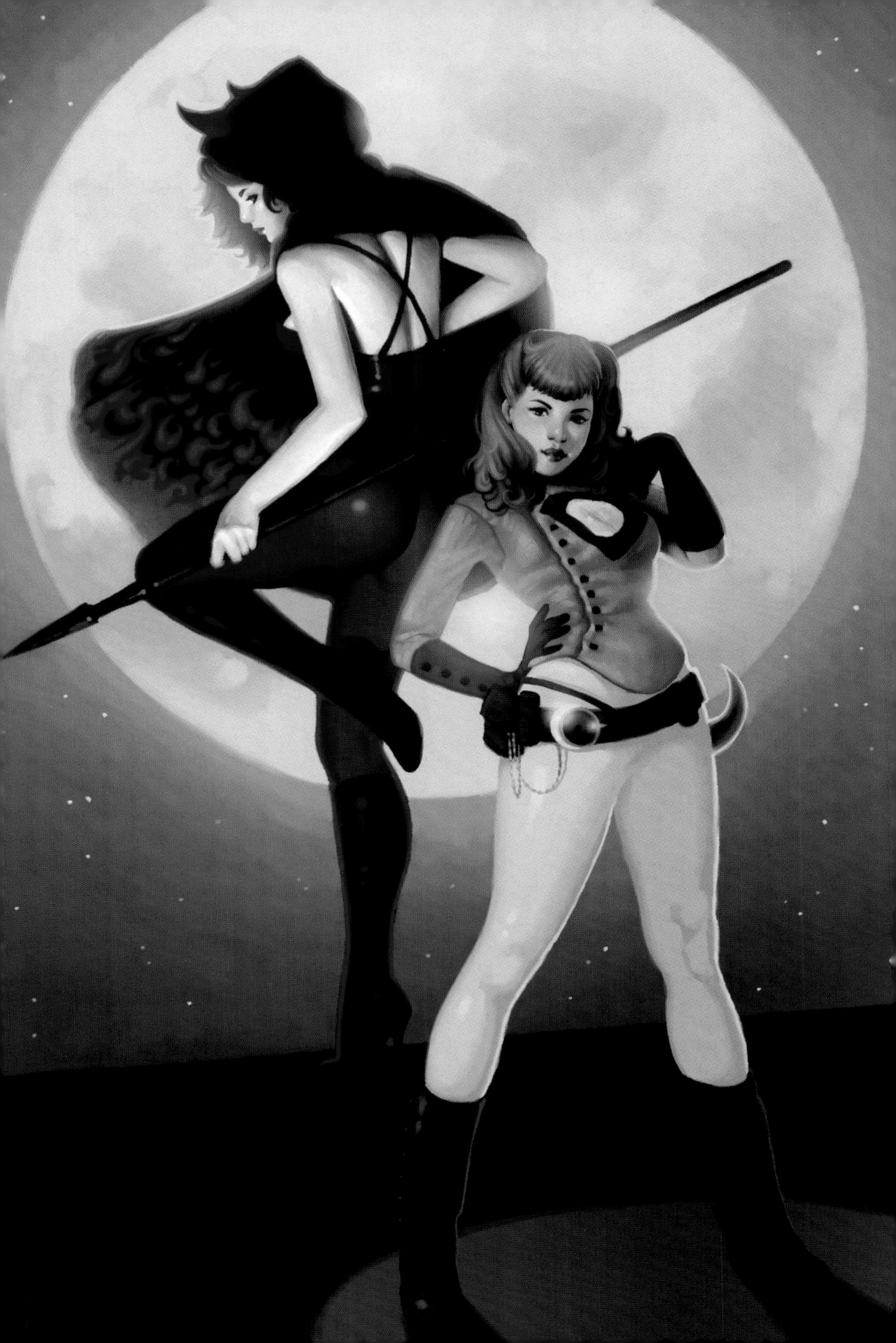

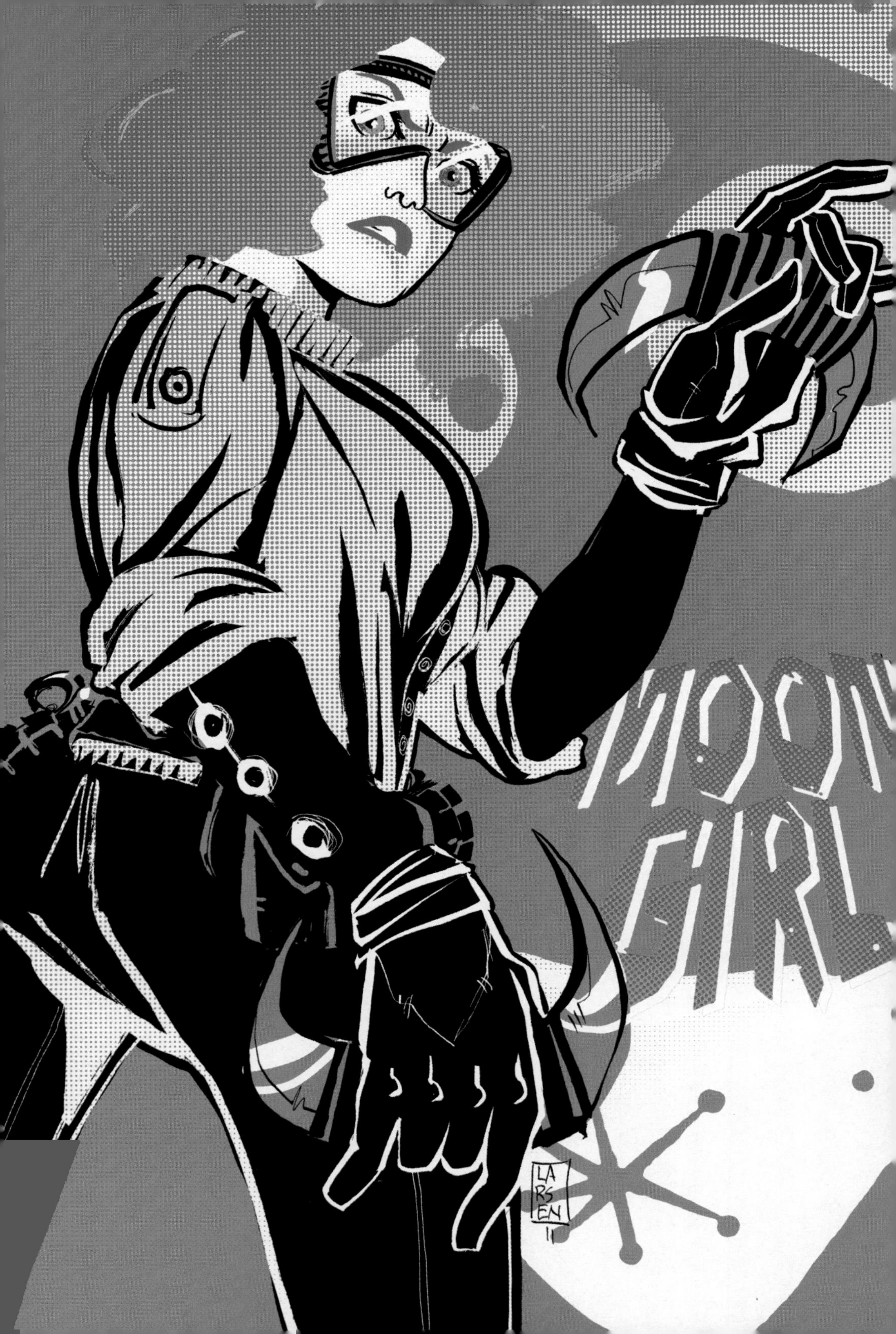
MOON
GIRL
LARSEN 11

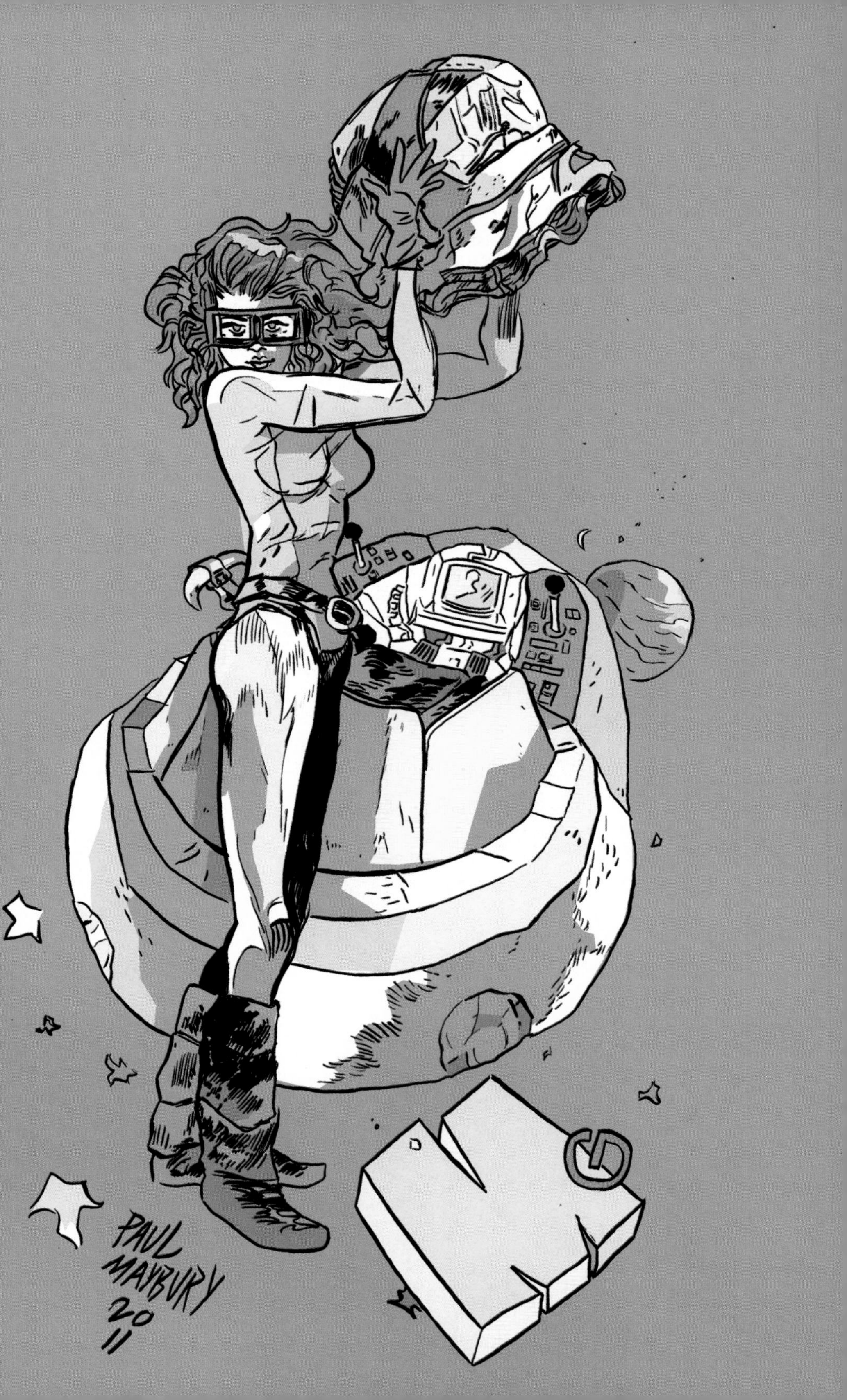
PAUL
MAYBURY
20
11

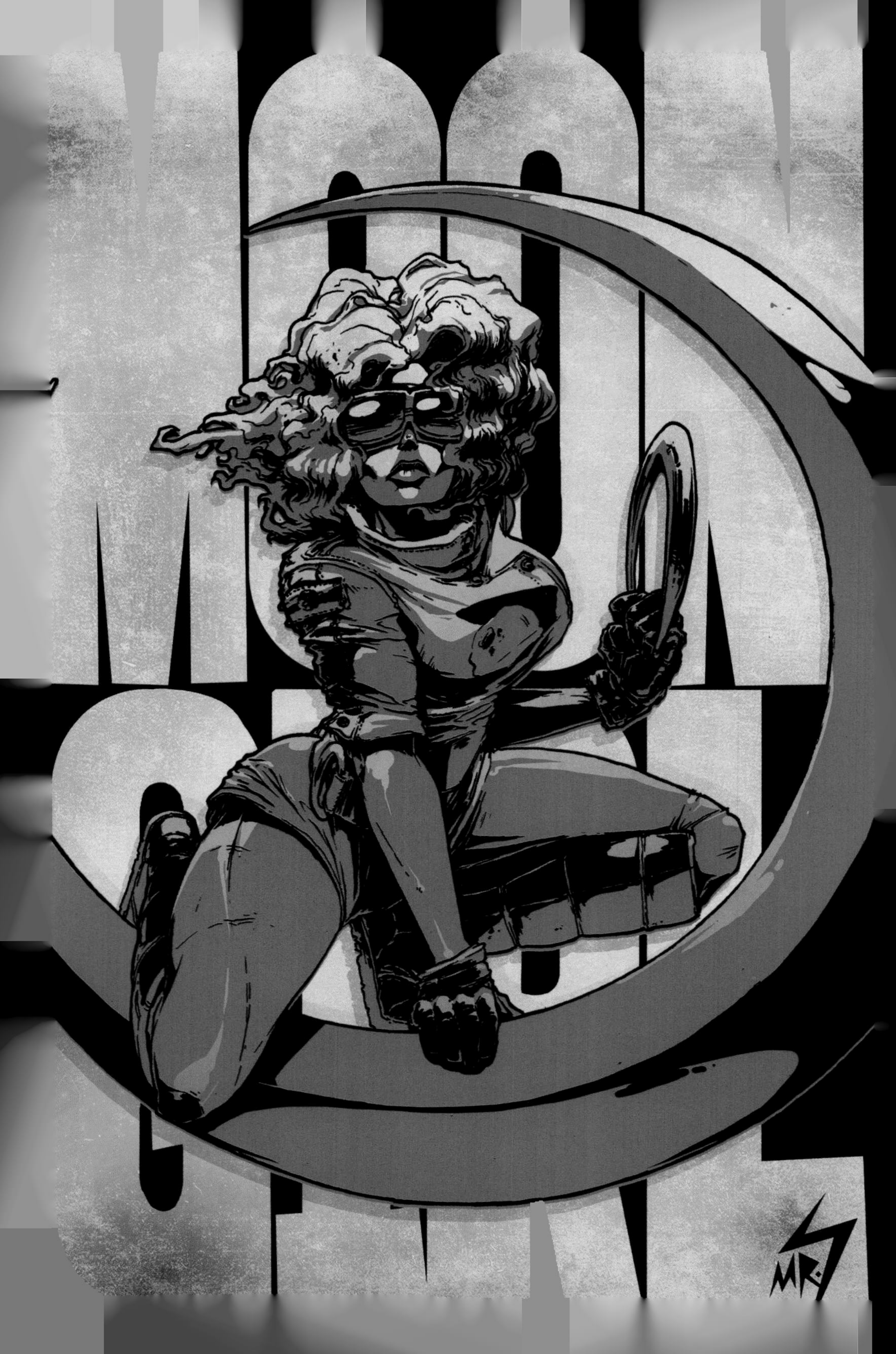

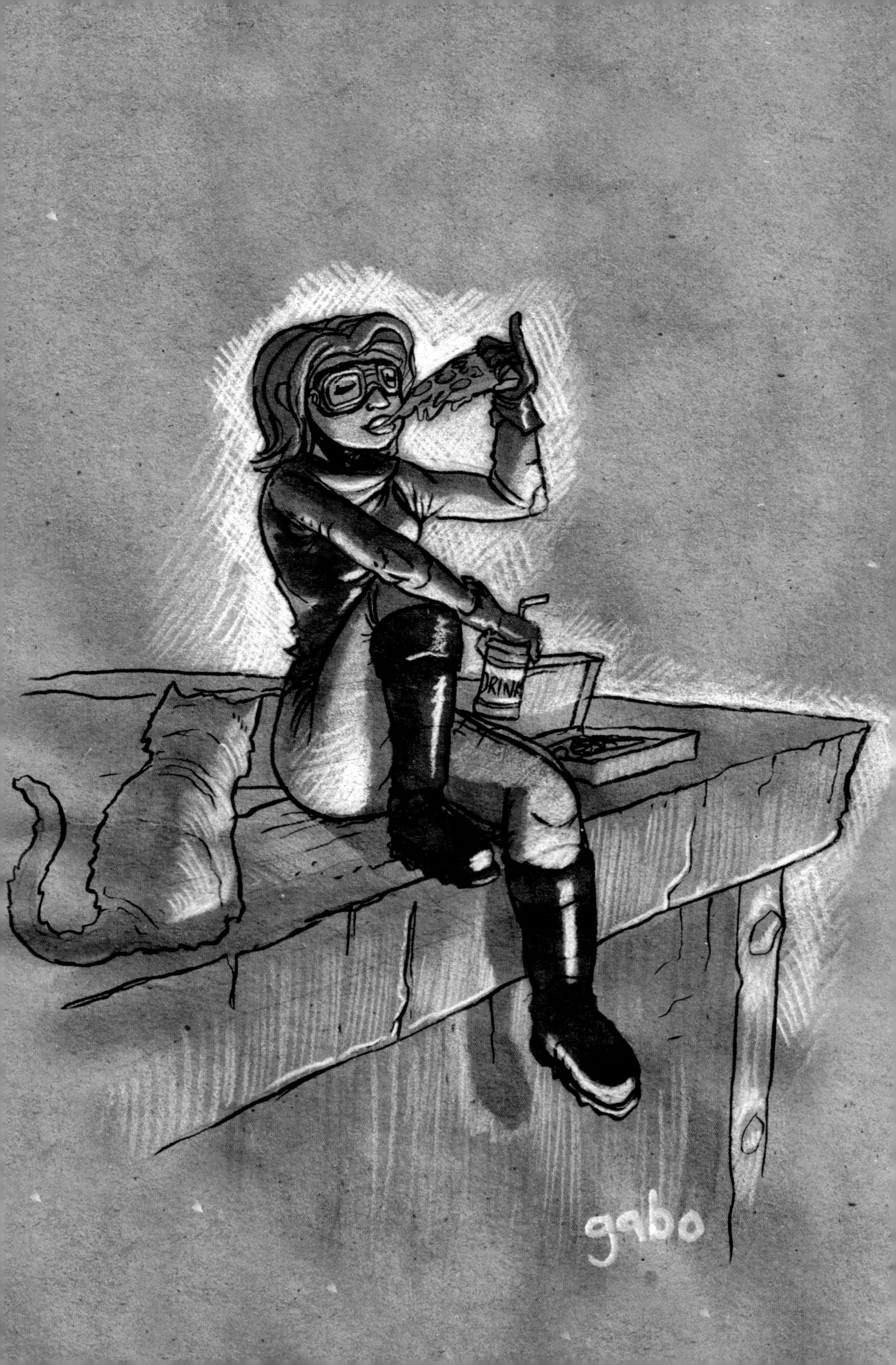
DRIN
gabo

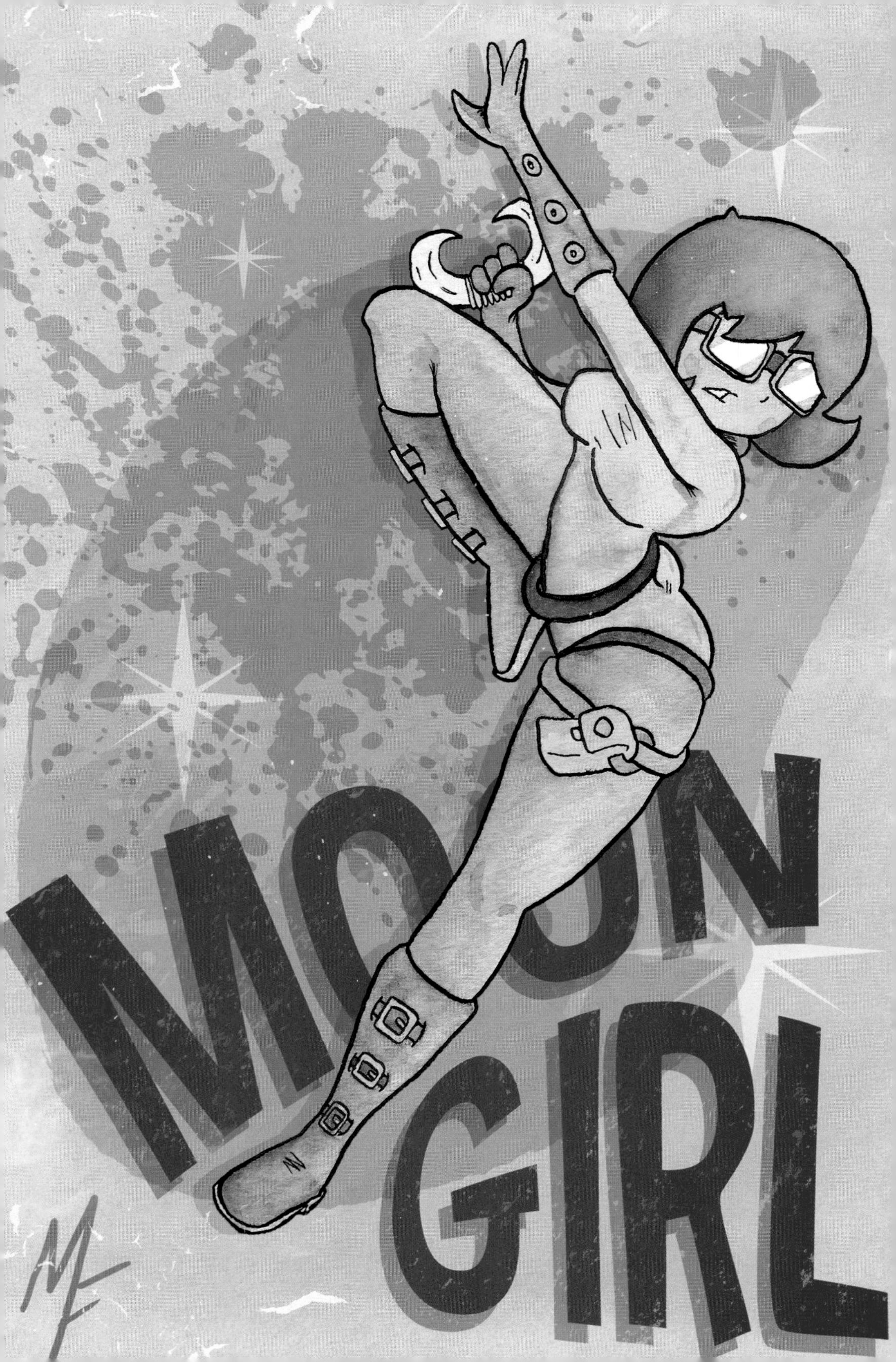
MOON
GIRL
MF

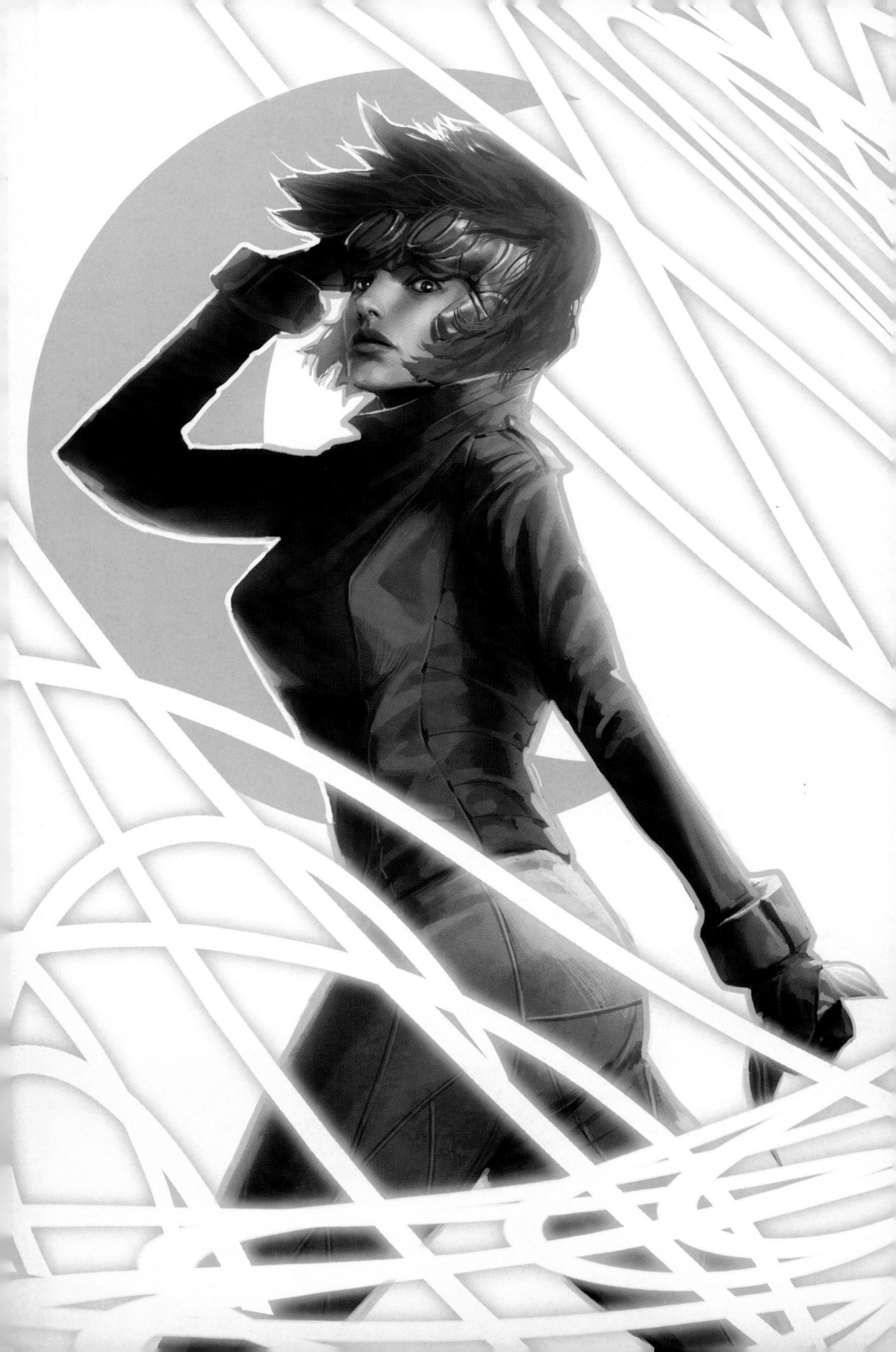

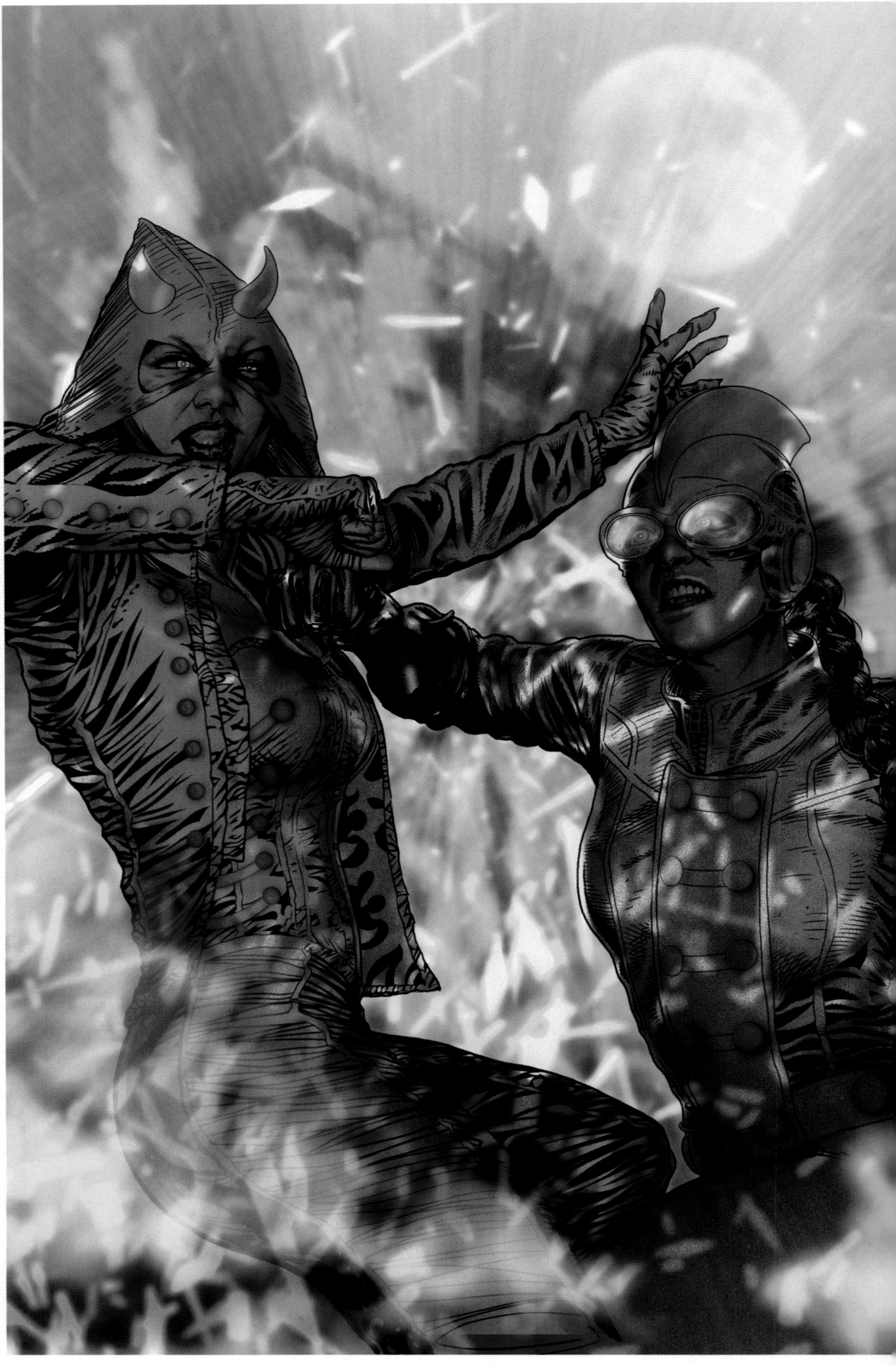

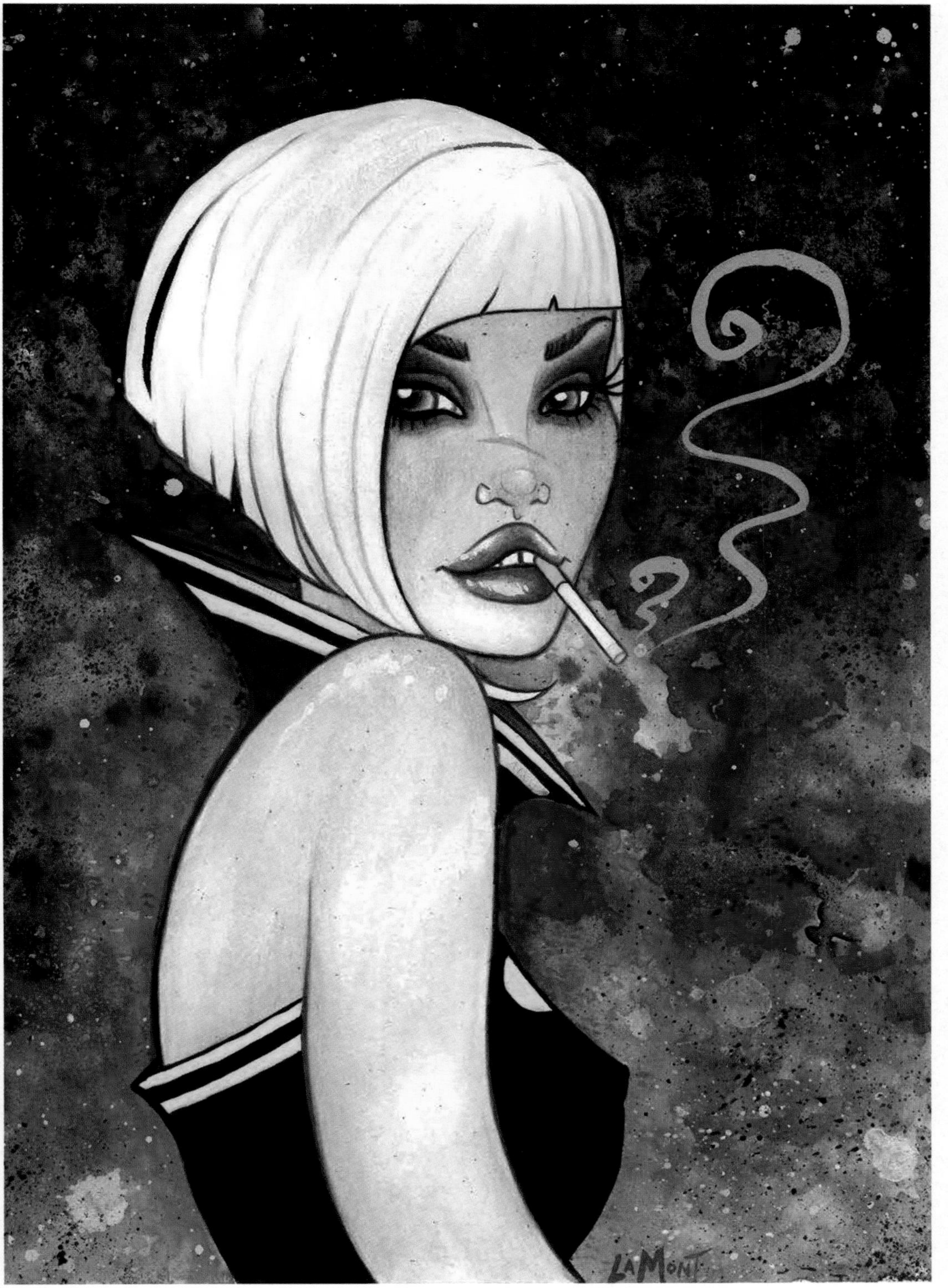
LAMONT

SUPER MANIFESTO

An Introduction to The Struggle
By: J.P. Sartre

The Call To Action by Allen Ginsberg
Letters from the Revolutionary Liberty League
An Interview with Admiral America

Super Manifesto

An Introduction to the Struggle

Introduction

The Super Manifesto is a product of many minds, inspired by the revolutionary known as Moon Girl. Her one woman crusade against injustice has triggered a leap in thought: super humanism.

All the powers of the old, imperial world have entered into a holy alliance to vanquish the super human. President, Arch Bishop, Gangster and G-Men join forces to destroy mankind.

The time has come that Super Humans should openly, in the face of the whole world, bring voice to their actions, their methods and beliefs.

Super Humanism represents an idea about the future; it is not a new creed or set of absolute laws.

It has the power to be itself a power.

Part I "The Super Human"

Science and economic change have disrupted the old beliefs. Religions the world over must come to terms with a society that has no use for god. In every field of human activity, the vital movement is now in the direction of candid and explicit Super Humanism.

Super Human's are unsatisfied with the liberal ideas that lead to nihilism and disillusioned with the collective power of the state; young people turn to a new kind of individualism. They express themselves in colorful uniforms to clash with darker military or police outfits. They take on new names that supplant their birth or 'slave' identities. Being a super human is about clashing with the social norms and tearing down walls of prejudice or fear.

Super Humans are governed by only one rule: To Do Right.

Every form of society has been based on the antagonism of oppressing and oppressed classes. However, in order to oppress a people, certain conditions must be fostered.

The bourgeoisie has subjected every country to the rule of money. It has created enormous cities, has greatly increased the urban population, layering the rich and poor in a literal hierarchy built into the city's grid. The poor live beneath the rich, as if only bourgeoisie dreams are fit to live in the sky.

Barbarian countries become dependent on civilized ones, nations of peasants on nations of industrialists, the East on the West. This division stretches from the farthest reaches of the globe to American slums segregated from proper city dwellers by freeways and windowless housing developments.

The Super Human leaps over these boundaries and exists on the rooftops of their would-be oppressor. From this vantage, all men are judged equal.

When, in the course of development, class distinctions have disappeared, and all power exists in the hands of a nation of individuals, the bourgeoisie will lose its political character.

The Super Human is compelled, by the force of circumstances, to organize itself as a class for more than a revolution, and, as such, sweeps away by force the old conditions of class antagonisms in a never ending battle for truth and justice.

In place of the old society, with its classes and class antagonisms, we shall have an association in which the free development of each individual is the condition for the free development of all.

PART II "The Never Ending Battle"

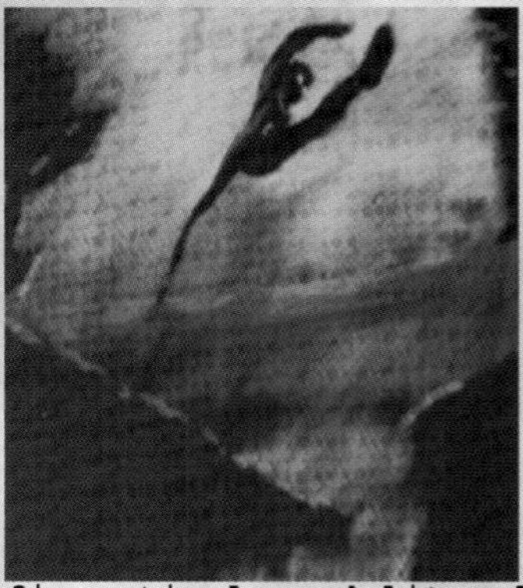

All of existence is class struggle between the haves and the have-nots. Endless political texts outline the plan for equality. However, only the super hero gospels wrestle with the effects of modernity.

Previous attempts to explain revolution focus on negative freedom. Paint-by-number truisms substitute material gain for emotional substance. In actuality the conflict is internal between the self and the potential self.

To be something more, to transform figuratively and literally is an ancient metaphysical journey. You are not self-aware; you are only able to observe how others see you. There is an alpha and an omega based solely on how third parties behave toward each.

Struggle comes from confrontation with the established value system. Only through conflict can there be change. Old values are torn down. New values are held up. Slaves become soldiers. Men become Kings. Pharoses become Gods. These states of being are not in constant opposition but are covertly joined in a tug of war. To truly escape the limitations of the society you must invent your own values.

The individual can alter reality with perception; the path to ascension. The essential condition for the existence and rule of any given value system is the gulf between expectation and action. The community invests in an ideology with the anticipation of individual reward. During the Communist Revolution laborers became what their OCD ruling class feared most; the organized mob. Class was replaced with bureaucratic rank; access to resources became currency. Millions of people are dedicated to the proliferation of monomaniacal philosophy and must adopt these ridged values to obtain happiness.

It is the same in Capitalism, Fascism, and Feudalism where you can buy, enforce or enslave the individual. There is no equality because

it's all relative to unequal staring points. Only when the individual
is fulfilled on their own terms can there be freedom.

Attaining freedom means assuming the right to choose, to be, and know
that you have the right to do so no matter the external force. To be
a Super Human one must be transformed by conflict, redefine their
values and structure the world around their actions.

Super Humans are anti-conformist subversives. According to these
idealists; helping the helpless is the greatest form of self-
expression possible. It's through this process that we transcend the
system and find satisfaction on our own.

The Super Human exists agelessly
through good and bad, fulfilled
by their eternal vigilance;
always ready for the next
challenge. They don't involve
themselves in border treaties or
parliament formalities; only
action can save the day.

The simple power fantasy might
seem juvenile to the uninitiated
BUT these are primal lessons of
survival in the fantastic-now;
our homes and jobs and
relationships. The message is
universal.

A young man crosses a great
distance and comes to a new
place. With abilities unique
only to him; he endures, he
overcomes. The embodiment of
the American Dream; this man becomes a symbol. Others follow his
example to a better life with meaning.

This is the origin of every super human in some form or another. It
is our shared birth; self perpetuating expression through action and
inspiration.

Super Humanism is an evolution of self; transcending; limitations.
It's the values that they reinvent society with that makes them
potent. We cannot impose the values of the past for the sake of
nostalgia or supplication.

Status Quo is the worst fiend of them all.

PART III "The New Moral Order"

Security and freedom from material bonds are not the final goals. They
are means to the greater end - the evolution of a people more kindly,
intelligent, co-operative, enterprising and rich in culture.

Big Business believes only in profit. Autocrats believe only in
slavery. The religious believe only in retribution.

These institutions use language like magic spells to twist perception and hypnotize us. Reality is subjective depending on what television channel you've tuned into.

The passive viewer is turned into a snarling monster at the behest of its masters. They have been so corrupted they fail to recognize their own self loathing, conveniently directing their raging emotions on the most convenient boogie man whipped up by the powers that be.

"Super Heroes" and "Super Villains" are buzz terms the media use to ridicule a movement of activism. In fact there are two competing philosophies of Super Humanism.

Fundamentalists subvert the establishment by dressing in bright technicolor clothes and taking futuristic new names. They have set out to release the finer impulses of man. We believe that all citizens have obligations to fulfill as well as rights to enjoy.

Extremists turn to violence and terror, expecting to shock the system into change. Their crusade targets the bourgeoisie greatest weapon of all; the delusional masses who have so faithfully adopted the agenda of their masters.

Regardless of the methodology the essential tenants remain the same.

We will stand firm against any attempt to intimidate us or to undermine our position in the world.

We will remain ready at any moment to co-operate fully with anyone prepared to work with us for peace and friendship.

No economic or political unity is sought and none would be accepted.

No country has more right to this great movement than any other.

Super humans work for happy endings without any concern for established reality.

-John Paul Sartre
Paris, 1955

The Call to Action
by Allen Ginsberg

I am so SICK of society I'm going to puke in my own lap. Is this strange horror lurking over everyone else? I feel like a fugitive on the run from my own heart.

I hope, or at least I want to believe, that I really am a basket case, otherwise I'll never get well.

Are you just as strange as I am? Is anyone else as sick as me?

Who here throws opinions like boomerangs despite the Dadaists and Cubists lurking in shadows of solid thought?

I don't have time for that in the madhouse; fantasies of suicide would be a relief next to the instant lobotomy of rigid spread sheet structure.

The best cure for brain damage is even more brain damage. That's why only people made of poetry can save the world.

Fairy taled hippies burn the sky looking for a connection to more dynamic engines made of thought and emotions... these are wishing machines and we are their lightning bolts.

Know you are a Super Human then you are already saved

Block out signals from Stonehenge, be weary of old wizards and timeless quests. There be Martians in this place now.

Common Sense, common Law and common DECENCY have no invulnerable bunker from money munching war gluttons, bleakly lit monsters digesting whole forests and excreting liquid puddles of news pulp...

Would that it all could fit on a grain of rice.

Sure we're old, evil and ugly. But I've been this way for all my years, and I'm not going to pretend for you.

Many, many, many, many men (and women) are spiritually vacant. But they are accumulating experience points, building the origin stories of their great rise.

It isn't an education. It is history. It is word and verse leaping across rooftops.

If you're walking on the ground, I gotta tell you, I see right through the ground. And, brother, there is no world under your feet. You'll see. You will find out.

Trick your psyche and let an orgasmic experience unfold, give yourself one chance in a thousand to save the world.

A Letter to the Revolutionary Liberty League

My name is The Tarantula and I am a Super Human.

As a result of my beliefs I have spent the last nine month incarcerated on Riker's Island, held prisoner by the state of New York. My crimes are vigilantism, obstruction of justice, assault and attempted murder. It is true that, by the letter of the law, I did all of these things and that I would do them again. My actions that day saved the lives of a dozen commuters and by extension made a hundred lives better. It is the responsibility of all mankind to use their gifts to the benefit of society. However, it would appear that politically appointed goons have a monopoly on do-gooding.

My parents died when I was very young, I don't remember much about them. They were fiercely patriotic and worked very hard to help America win the war. After a plane accident took them away from me I was shuttled off to the care of my sweet Aunt and Uncle in Queens. Considerably older than my parents, they struggled to raise me in an increasingly alien world.

At school I was an outsider. I suffered endless anxiety at the state of the world. While other boys tried out for the football team I spent hours in the science lab obsessing over chemistry and physics; the power of the atom. How could something so abundant, so commonplace, be so devastatingly powerful? The force of one, infinitesimal, invisible speck could change the world. Somehow that gave me hope.

Tragedy seemed to stalk my teenage life. Friends were drafted off to Korea one by one. My sweetheart ran away to the big city and was eaten up by dope pushers. My uncle was murdered by a gang of thugs who robbed his deli.

I felt victimized by the whole world, I wanted to fight back but I had no idea how. A news report of Moon Girl busting gun runners on the interstate provided me inspiration.

The night my Uncle, a man I'd come to think of as a father, was buried, I was reborn. Cloaked in his army poncho, I hunted his killers to an elevated train station. I watched, I observed, deducing which of these delinquents was the leader, the muscle, the coward. I wanted a fight; I wanted to tear them apart in a variety of gruesome ways that I'd been fantasizing about endlessly. I waited for my chance to strike.

Together, we took the elevated train into Union Station and

literally descended into the underworld. As we approached the platform, a rival gang boarded the box car.   Tensions rose and a bloody fight broke out in the middle of a busy commute. Mothers, Sons, Husbands and sisters… caught in the crossfire.

I am ashamed to admit that I froze at the first outbreak of violence. Nevertheless, I came to my senses and crashed the action. I weaved through a confusing whirlwind of chain links and brass knuckles. Overwhelmed, I was forced to break out my secret weapon, the result of countless afternoons locked in the school lab. With a pair of wrist mounted zip guns I took aim at the biggest goons and cut them down with led... I wasn't fighting for revenge anymore; I was fighting to save the world.

When the switchblade was inserted between my ribs I hardly had a chance to think let alone scream. The pain was unbearable and I went into shock, losing consciousness almost immediately. The warm gushy sensation that washed through me felt like the embrace of death. I imagined my uncle waiting for me on the other side, proud of my bravery and conviction.

Instead I woke up in Bellevue Hospital, handcuffed to a bed. A very stern nurse informed me that Moon Girl had been on hand to rescue the subway and deliver me to safety. If not for her, surely I would be dead. Regardless, I was now under arrest and facing a laundry list of trumped up charges. The lawyers advised that I plead insanity, a pop psychologist would admit me to the asylum and my reformation would be fodder for his next book. I refused. I decided to stick by my ideals and such was thrown into a dungeon, surrounded by the poor, angry and desperate.

This is the price for rolling up your sleeves and giving a damn.

Know that being a super human doesn't begin and end with fisticuffs high atop a monument. Sometimes the example you are called to lead by isn't glorious or epic -- it's painstaking and lonely.

I write to you, imploring you to continue by Moon Girl's example. Accept the consequences of your belief.

It's not a crime to do the right thing. It's a crime to do nothing at all.

-The Tarantula
October 1, 1955

An Interview with Admiral America
by Mike Wallace
(July 1955, Mike Wallace Show Transcript)

Hidden in the back alleys and bar rooms of lower Manhattan you might hear whispers about a new breed of political activist.

These prophets of tomorrow are easily identified by their garish clothing and anti-establishment view points. The Super Human believes ideology and action can transform an average person into something more than a mere mortal.

They wear masks and use clever aliases to hide their identities. Increasingly you'll find these young revolutionaries on the street corners and in the lecture halls. It is a movement without race or creed or class, united by a mysterious pioneer known only as Moon Girl.

If the sensational urban legends of the Moon Maiden are a sort of gospel, then Admiral America has become her Saint Paul. Night after night you'll find him preaching the good word to a growing number of converts.

Mike Wallace: How does your philosophy translate itself into the world of politics? One of the principle achievements of this country in the past 20 years is the gradual growth of social and protective legislation based on the principle that our leaders know best. How do you feel about the political trends of the United States?

Admiral America: It's a complete disaster. I feel terrible; these are the nightmares that keep me awake at night. Some shady group of conspirators is going to decide what's best for the world? What's best for everyone? It's up to each of us to find our own way. We are now moving towards complete collectivism or fascism, a system under which everybody is enslaved to everybody because of some half baked social contract with a soulless, political machine.

Mike Wallace: Ah... Yes, but you say everybody is enslaved to everybody, yet this came about democratically. A free people in a free country voted for this kind of government, wanted this kind of legislation. Do you object to the democratic process?

Admiral America: There are some times when we're one people and sometimes when we're one person. You can't take a vote and strip someone of their ideals; there are still individual rights that supersede any bureaucratic construction. If a bunch of people say its right to do something that's wrong, it doesn't make it right. It just makes it "democratic."

Mike Wallace: Alright, then how do we arrive at action? How should we arrive at action?

Admiral America: By voluntary consent, voluntary cooperation of free men, unforced.

Mike Wallace: And how do we arrive at our leadership? Who elects, who appoints?

Admiral America: The world doesn't need czars, kings and presidents. All they ever do is send poor people off to die. They have no right to initiate force or compulsion against any citizen, even the criminal. No one would give the government, or the majority, or any minority, the right to take the life or the property of others. We don't need Keystone Cops to enforce that. Those who use force will be punished by society with proportional force. That's the laws of nature.

Mike Wallace: If we were to simply dissolve government and rule of law, wouldn't that be anarchy? What would make people do the right thing?

Admiral America: If heroin were legal, would you go shoot up, Mike? If the President said it was OK to put poison in your veins would you do it? Is that law keeping you from losing your mind and doing something stupid?

Mike Wallace: You appear politically savvy enough to know that certain movements spring up in reaction to other movements. The labor movement for instance, certain social welfare legislation... This did not spring full blown from somebody's head. I mean, out of a vacuum. This was a reaction to certain abuses that were going on, isn't that true, Admiral?

Admiral America: Moon Girl's first appearance was at Grand Central Station, New York in 1953. Her one-woman crusade against a city-wide conspiracy of criminals, cops and corporations is what ignited the movement. I mean, we can't trust the atom bomb to anyone narcissistic enough to think they can run the world. Moon Girl exposed what was wrong with these systems of control. Just by existing she killed the police man in all of our heads and freed us.

Mike Wallace: When you advocate for completely unregulated lives in which every man lives for his own mission. However, one of the main reasons for the growth of government was to fight the evil forces that you claim threaten the world most. Is that not true?

Admiral America: No. Any force that organizes itself for political gain is never capable of true good. There's always an agenda of control when politics are involved.

Mike Wallace: Admiral, I think that you will agree with me when I say that you do not have a good deal of respect for the society in which you and I currently live. You think that we're going downhill fairly fast. Do you predict dictatorship and economic disaster for the United States if we continue on our present course?

Admiral America: It's already happened, Mike. Every day, people work a little bit harder for the same amount of money and it's worth a little bit less. That's slavery. Per capita, the US has more people in jail than any other nation, and you know what? Most of the incarcerated are African American. Sounds like a concentration camp to me. And do we really need to talk about how this two-party system is a no-party system? We have never been offered a choice between control and freedom.

Mike Wallace: Isn't it possible that we all believe in a limited freedom because we are all basically isolated and not necessarily individual? Shouldn't there always be a system in place to keep the world safe?

Admiral America: Of course! It's you, it's me! Everyone's job is to be saving the god damn world. You can't expect someone else to do it; every individual has got to commit to being better. You're not a normal man anymore. In the new world you're a super human with power and responsibilities.

Mike Wallace: Then why rename yourself with the rank and file of a military structure and political collective you despise?

Admiral America: Irony. Every day that I do what I'm doing, I transform the meaning of these words. Maybe one day we'll wake up and there'll be no borders or governments or ranks of lordly titles. Maybe one day Admiral America will just mean the same thing as "John Smith"... And that's how we'll win; with powers beyond those of mortal men.

END TRANSCRIPT

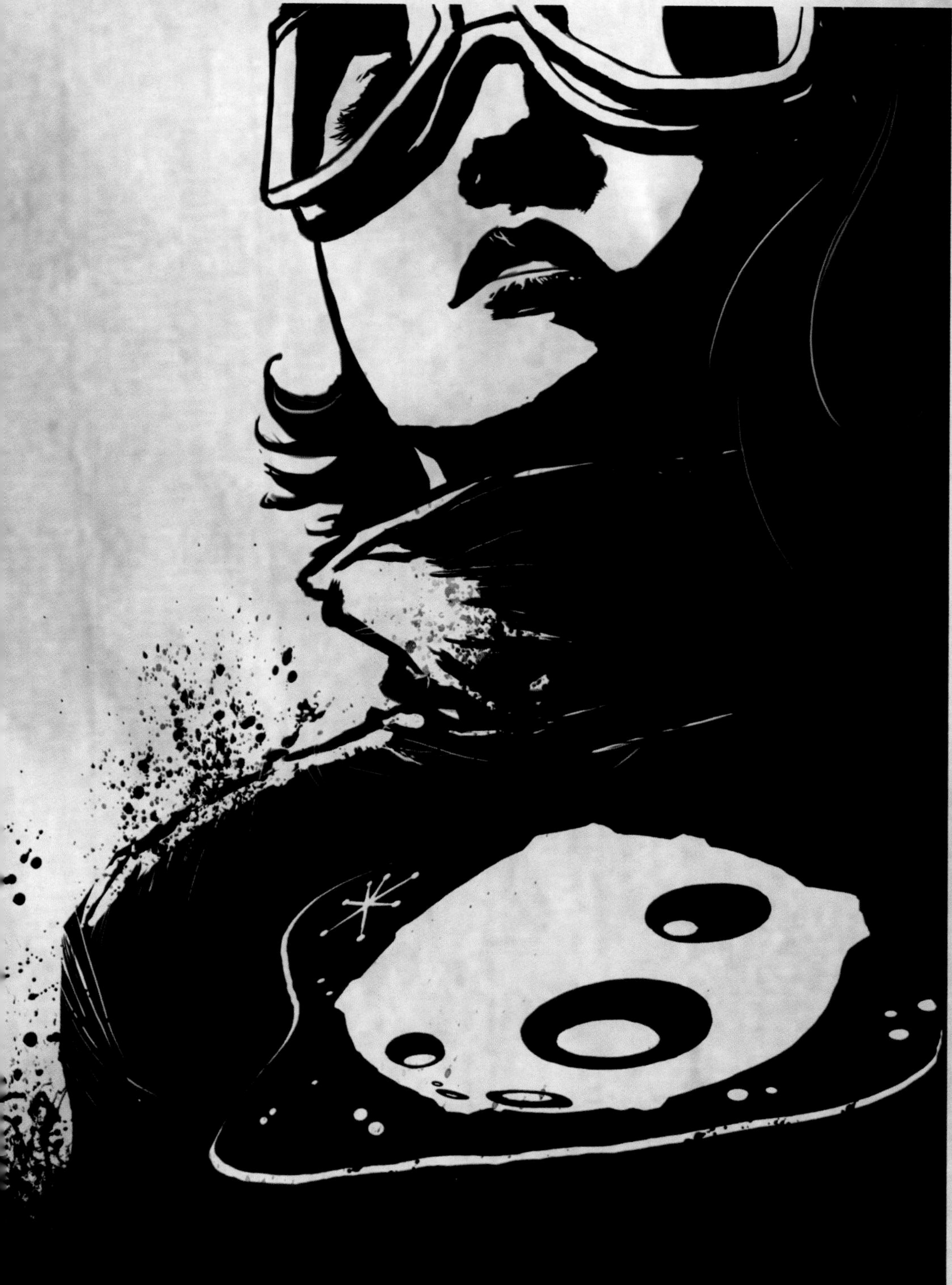

MOON GIRL FIGHTS CRIME

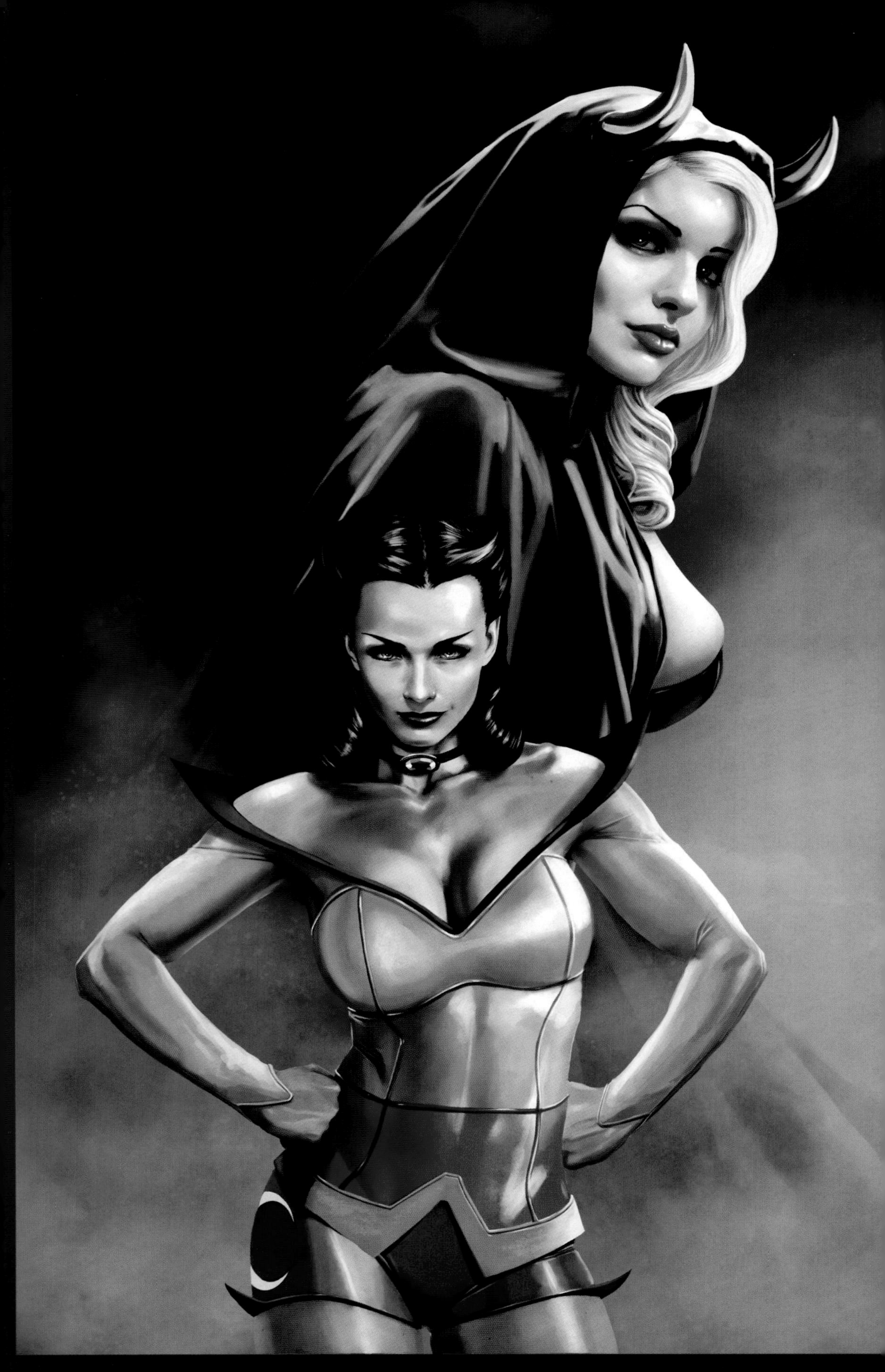

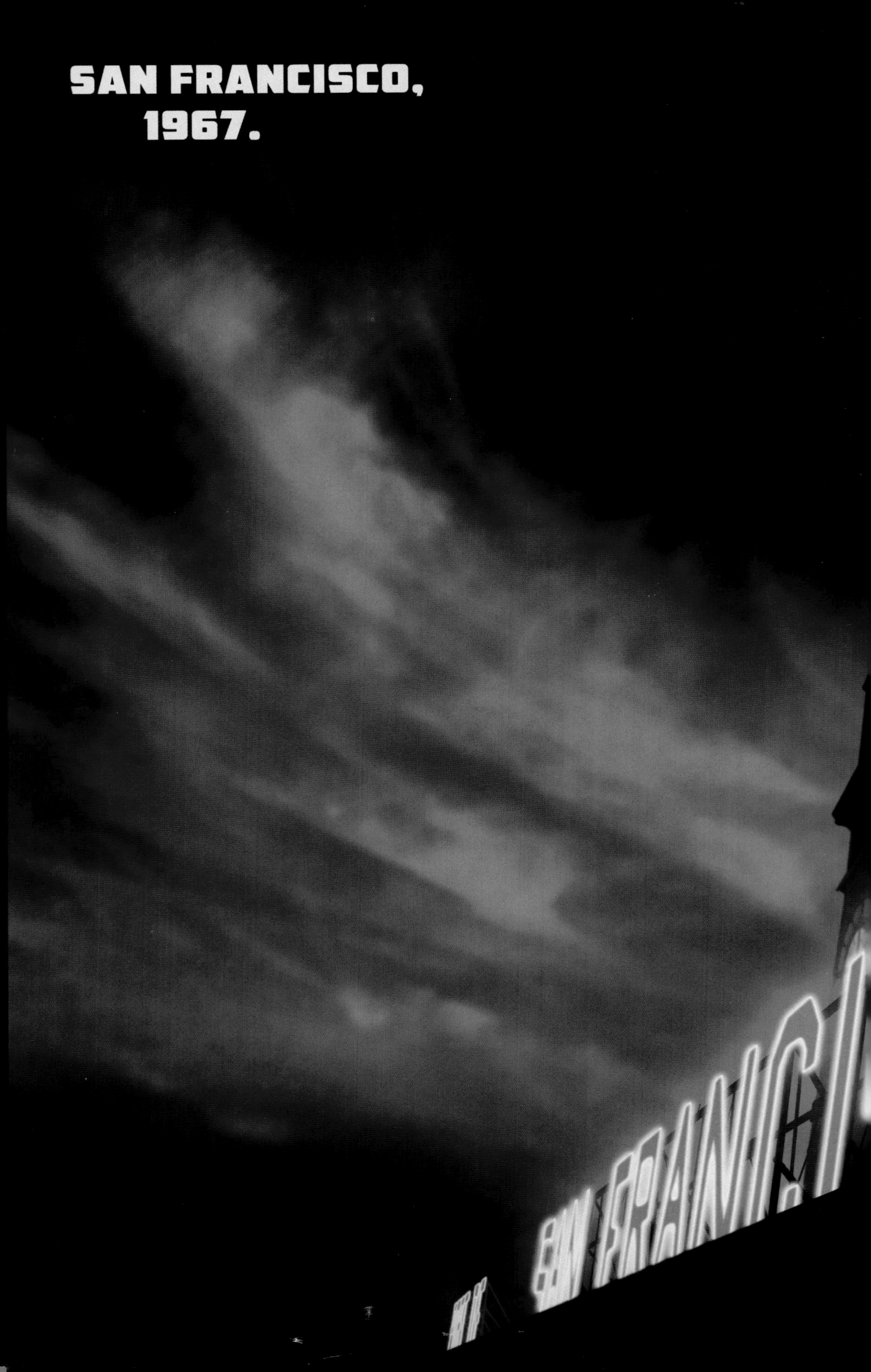
SAN FRANCISCO,
1967.

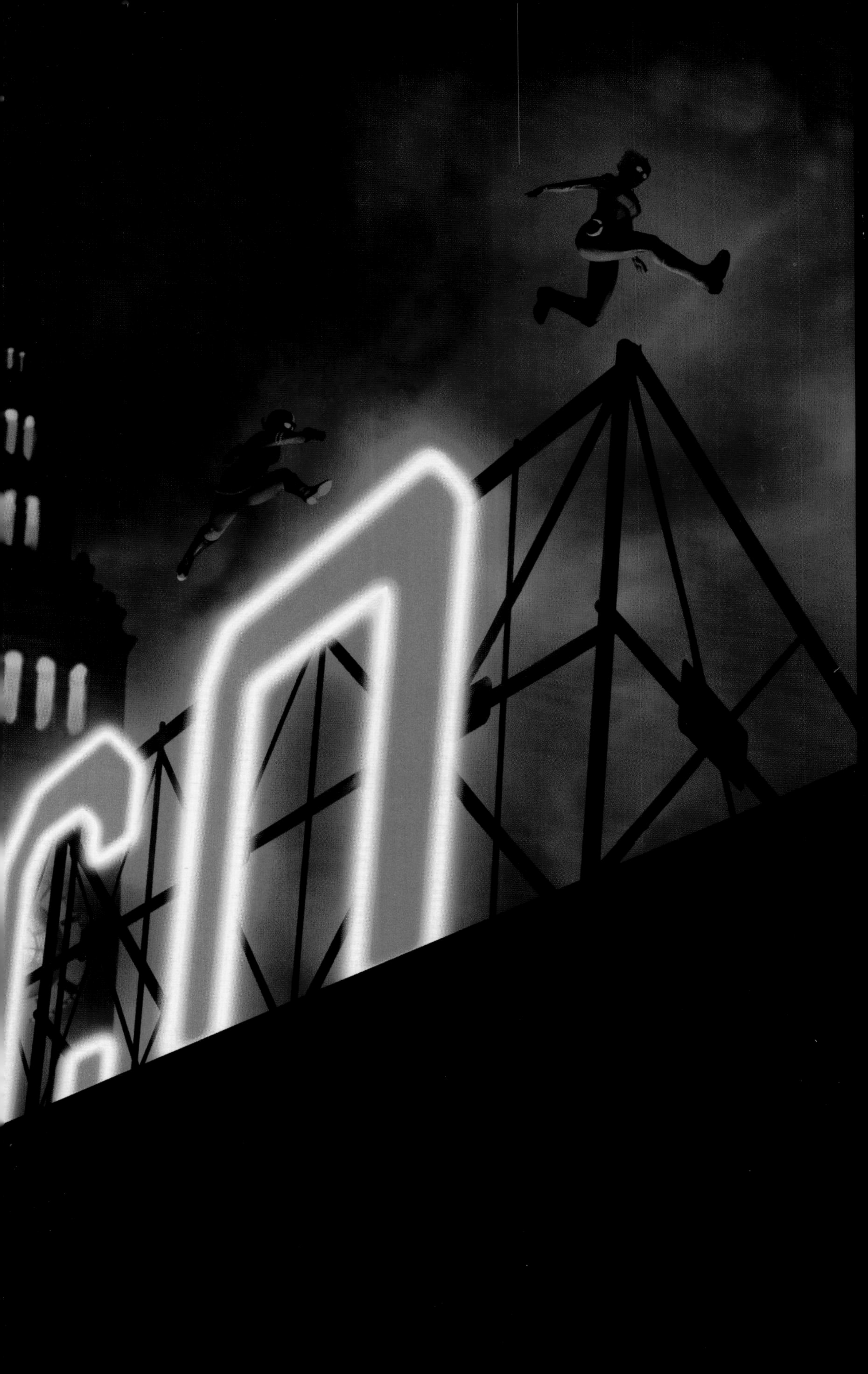

WWW.SOUTHFELLINI.COM

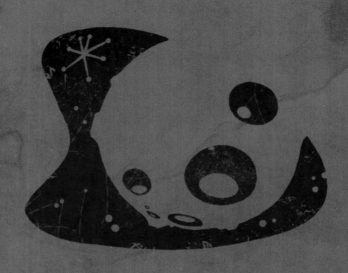